DARK SIDE OF THE TUNE:
POPULAR MUSIC AND VIOLENCE

Dark Side of the Tune:
Popular Music and Violence

BRUCE JOHNSON
University of Turku, Finland
Macquarie University, Australia
University of Glasgow, UK

MARTIN CLOONAN
University of Glasgow, UK

ASHGATE

Published by
Ashgate Publishing Limited
Wey Court East
Union Road
Farnham, Surrey
GU9 7PT England

Ashgate Publishing Company
110 Cherry Street
Suite 3-1
Burlington, VT 05401-3818
USA

www.ashgate.com

British Library Cataloguing in Publication Data
Johnson, Bruce, 1943–
    Dark side of the tune : popular music and violence. –
    (Ashgate popular and folk music series)
    1. Music and violence 2. Popular music – Social aspects
    I. Title II. Cloonan, Martin
    781.6'4

Library of Congress Cataloging-in-Publication Data
Johnson, Bruce, 1943–
    Dark side of the tune : popular music and violence / Bruce Johnson and
Martin Cloonan.
        p. cm.—(Ashgate popular and folk music series)
    Includes bibliographical references.
    ISBN 978-0-7546-5872-6 (alk. paper)
    1. Music and violence. 2. Popular music—Social aspects. I. Cloonan, Martin. II. Title.

    ML3916.J64 2009
    781.64—dc22

                                                                        2008017011

ISBN 9780754658726 (hbk)
ISBN 9781409400493 (pbk)
ISBN 9780754699606 (ebk)

Reprinted 2012, 2013

Printed and bound in Great Britain by
the MPG Books Group, UK

Contents

General Editor's Preface

The upheaval that occurred in musicology during the last two decades of the twentieth century has created a new urgency for the study of popular music alongside the development of new critical and theoretical models. A relativistic outlook has replaced the universal perspective of modernism (the international ambitions of the 12-note style); the grand narrative of the evolution and dissolution of tonality has been challenged, and emphasis has shifted to cultural context, reception and subject position. Together, these have conspired to eat away at the status of canonical composers and categories of high and low in music. A need has arisen, also, to recognize and address the emergence of crossovers, mixed and new genres, to engage in debates concerning the vexed problem of what constitutes authenticity in music and to offer a critique of musical practice as the product of free, individual expression.

Popular musicology is now a vital and exciting area of scholarship, and the *Ashgate Popular and Folk Music Series* presents some of the best research in the field. Authors are concerned with locating musical practices, values and meanings in cultural context, and may draw upon methodologies and theories developed in cultural studies, semiotics, poststructuralism, psychology and sociology. The series focuses on popular musics of the twentieth and twenty-first centuries. It is designed to embrace the world's popular musics from Acid Jazz to Zydeco, whether high tech or low tech, commercial or non-commercial, contemporary or traditional.

Derek B. Scott
Professor of Critical Musicology
University of Leeds, UK

Notes and Acknowledgements

This research topic has been largely overlooked in academic studies for reasons we discuss. The debate over violence in popular music has therefore been dominated by the media and sensationalist literature based on or playing to the moral panic reflex. A significant proportion of our sources therefore consists of ephemeral publications such as newspapers and press releases (hard copy and online), often lacking a specific byline or syndicated through news agencies. In some cases it was not possible to provide full detail so the documentation is uneven. We have given all the details we have available. If any detail, such as byline, headline or page number, is missing, it is because it is not available. We have taken care not to base our arguments on any single source of doubtful reliability. Online sources fall into several categories. In general, an online press item carries all byline, title of article, title of newspaper/journal, and full date, where these are all available. Unless otherwise given, the date of the item is also the hit date. In an era of highly sophisticated search engines we have generally not included URLs, unless there is a serious dearth of other reference information for a particular item. While generally retaining a definite article for newspaper titles in the main text for reasons of grammar, we have omitted 'The' from footnotes and the bibliography. Some sources are referred to by acronym after the first citation; for example *Sydney Morning Herald* becomes *SMH*.

Apart from specific footnoted acknowledgements throughout the book, we would like to thank Kalle Aaltonen, Gary Burns, Giana Cassidy, Ian Collinson, Jonathan Isakson, Morten Ove Johnsen, Ville Kabrell, Laura Mitchell, Marcus Moberg, Jonas Ridberg, Mikael Sarelan, Joonas Varjonen. A special note of appreciation to Liz Guiffré (Department of Contemporary Music Studies, Macquarie University, Sydney), for general discussion and unstinting assistance in locating sources. We would also like to thank Sam and Shannon Johnson, both performers and avid music enthusiasts, and son and daughter respectively of Bruce Johnson, for their continuing discussion of the topic. Likewise, Anu Juva (a musician and film music scholar) and her children Johannes and Ida for their conversations on music, and their patience with the authors' absorption in this work. Martin would also like to thank Claire. In addition to other institutional bases mentioned below, thanks to the Department of English, Media and Performance Arts, University of New South Wales for providing a Visiting Research Fellowship to Bruce Johnson, October 2007– January 2008. Apart from individuals named above from the following institutions, informal conversations with staff and students at the University of Glasgow, University of Turku, Åbo Akademi, Trondheim University of Science and Technology, Macquarie University, Institute of Popular Music at University of Liverpool, have been so wide-ranging that we must assume that we have omitted some names that merited special mention. We can only apologize for the oversight.

About the Authors

Bruce Johnson is Docent and Visiting Professor, Cultural History, University of Turku (Finland); Adjunct Professor, Contemporary Music Studies, Macquarie University (Sydney, Australia); Honorary Professor, University of Glasgow (Scotland, UK).

Martin Cloonan is Convener of Postgraduate Studies, Department of Music, University of Glasgow (Scotland, UK).

List of Abbreviations

ACLU	American Civil Liberties Union
AIF	Australian Imperial Force
ASBO	Anti-Social Behaviour Order (UK)
ASCA	Amsterdam School for Cultural Analysis (University of Amsterdam)
ATM	Automatic Teller Machine
BBC	British Broadcasting Corporation (UK)
CBS	Columbia Broadcasting System (US)
CCCS	Centre for Contemporary Cultural Studies (University of Birmingham)
CRESSON	Centre de recherché sur l'espace sonore et l'environment urbain
dB	Decibels (measure of volume of sound)
DeFRA	Department for Environment, Food and Rural Affairs (UK)
Dir.	Director
DIY	Do It Yourself
DMX	US-based company providing engineered sensory environments for retailers
Ed.	Editor
EL	External Locus of Emotion (compare IL; see Schubert)
EPA	Environmental Protection Agency (US)
FBI	Federal Bureau of Investigation (US)
FDR	Franklin Delano Roosevelt (US President 1933–45)
G8	Group of Eight (international forum for the governments of Canada, France, Germany, Italy, Japan, Russia, UK, US)
Hz	Hertz (frequency in cycles per second)
IASPM	International Association for the Study of Popular Music
IL	Internal Locus of Emotion (compare EL; see Schubert)
IPM	Institute of Popular Music (University of Liverpool)
LGA	Local Government Association
LRAD(s)	Long Range Acoustic Device(s)
MASK	Mothers Against Slipknot (Music censorship lobby group)
MDC	Movement for Democratic Change (Zimbabwe)
MEL	Music in Everyday Life (research project)
mm	millimeter
MOBO	Music of Black Origin awards (UK)
MOR	Middle of the Road (category of pop music)
MORI	Now Ipsos MORI, a UK-based research company
MP	Member of Parliament

MTV	Music Television
NBC	National Broadcasting Company (US)
NCO	Non-Commissioned Officer
NME	New Musical Express (journal)
NPCBW	National Political Congress for Black Women (US)
NWA	Niggaz With Attitude
NY	New York
PMRC	Parents' Music Resource Centre (Music censorship lobby group)
PMS	Popular Music Studies
POW	Prisoner of War
PsyOp(s)	Psychological Operations
RAF	Royal Air Force
R'n'B	Rhythm and Blues
RTLM	Radio Télévision Libre des Mille Collines (Rwandan radio station, 1993–94)
RV	Radio Van
SEM	Strong Experiences of Emotion (research project)
S/M	Sado-masochism
SMH	Sydney Morning Herald (newspaper)
SMM	Stop Murder Music campaign (UK)
SS	Schutzstaffel (elite Nazi force in Hitler's Germany)
Trans.	Translator
UBA	Umweltbundesamt (the Federal German environmental agency)
UEFA	Union of European Football Associations
UNESCO	United Nations Educational, Scientific and Cultural Organization
Unpub. Diss.	Unpublished Dissertation
US(A)	United States (of America)
UK	United Kingdom
WFAE	World Forum for Acoustic Ecology
WHO	World Health Organization
WW2	World War Two
ZANU-PF	Zimbabwean African National Union – Patriotic Front (Zimbabwean political organization)

Advisory Note

Please be advised that because of the subject matter this book by necessity contains material of a violent nature that could disturb and cause offence to some readers.

Introduction

Musical Violence and Popular Music Studies

Bruce Johnson and Martin Cloonan

There is no document of civilisation that is not at the same time a document of barbarism.[1]

The epigraph articulates the radical ambiguity which informs this study. We may include popular music among the 'documents of civilisation', and our present interest lies in its association with barbarism, both potential and actual. We could, and occasionally do, go further and dispense with the word 'popular', but in general we retain the term, partly because we are writing against a predominant pattern in popular music studies in particular. That pattern is characterized by a pervasive and often tacit assumption that popular music is inevitably personally and socially therapeutic. One of the reasons for this assumption is that academic case studies are generally written from 'inside' the category, from the position of fans of, or at least sympathizers with, the genre under discussion. From that narrative position, the emphasis is most often on the importance of music, and particularly popular music, in the emancipative construction of individual space (identity) and collective space (community).

The positive function of music which dominates popular music studies is concreted unquestioningly in such descriptions as Shakespeare's 'the food of love' and, perhaps the best known declaration on the subject, William Congreve's opening line to his 1697 play *The Mourning Bride*: 'Music has charms to soothe a savage beast.'[2] History of course provides abundant confirmation of this positive role of music. One of the most notoriously brutal of the Newgate gaol keepers was Andrew Alexander, appointed during the reign of Henry VIII, yet a letter from prisoner Edward Underhill in 1553 shows another side. Alexander and his wife used to take supper with some of the prisoners; on his first evening in gaol, a fellow prisoner said to Underhill:

---

[1] Walter Benjamin, 'Theses on the Philosophy of History', *Illuminations*, trans. Harry Zohn. ed. Hannah Arendt (London, 1970), p. 258.

[2] William Shakespeare, *Twelfth Night, or, What You Will*, I, i, 1, in *William Shakespeare: The Complete Works*, ed. Alfred Harbage (Baltimore, 1969), p. 309; William Congreve, *The Mourning Bride,* in *The Complete Plays,* ed. Herbert Davis (Chicago and London, 1967), p. 326.

I will show you the nature and manner of them. They do both love music very well; wherefore, you with your lute, and I with you on my rebeck, will please them greatly. He loveth to be merry and drink wine, and she also. If you will bestow upon them, every dinner and supper, a quart of wine and some music, you shall be their white son, and have any favour they can show you.[3]

Music therapy is based on the recognition of the positive power of music in the treatment of a range of traumas, disabilities and neuro-physical disorders. It seems that music can indeed be a 'magic' that sets us free. Deborah Wearing's memoir, *Forever Today*, movingly documents her husband's virally-induced amnesia. It is only music, which he can still play and perform, that enables him to break out of his isolation.[4] Similarly, the Japanese Nobel literature laureate Kenzaburo Oe wrote of his son, Hikara, who was born with severe disabilities including autism, epilepsy, and restricted vision, but with an idiot savant responsiveness to sound and music. He has perfect pitch, and has gained a strong reputation as a composer. In *A Healing Family*, Oe wrote that his son's ability to express himself musically had demonstrated the healing power of this artform.[5]

These are a few of many cases constituting the historical arc of Congreve's observation, confirmed again in the twentieth-century comment, 'Music's an excellent thing, it reduces the beast in men'. This acquires a darker undertone, however, when we know that its author was Joseph Stalin.[6] Stalin loved music. He had an excellent singing voice, and according to one of his lieutenants, could have been a professional singer. At social gatherings he presided fondly over the gramophone and as a hands-on political boss he helped write the music for films produced by the State Film Board, including the lyrics of the songs for the influential and popular production *Shining Path*.[7] As the tide of war turned in Russia's favour at Stalingrad, Stalin decided to replace the 'Internationale' with a new national anthem. He organized a contest in haste, so that it would be ready for celebrations planned for 7 November 1943. Fifty-four composers arrived in Moscow to participate in round one, and in the meantime Stalin had appointed two lyricists. They were installed in the Kremlin to work on the words, and were continually in receipt of Stalin's advice on revisions.[8]

War perennially provides the most extreme manifestations of the connections between music, identity and violence, in such abundant numbers that any illustration is arbitrary. The most engaging examples involve the consolations offered by

---

[3]   Anthony Babington, *The English Bastille: A History of Newgate Gaol and Prison Conditions in Britain 1188-1902* (London, 1971), p. 42.

[4]   Deborah Wearing, *Forever Today: A Memoir of Love and Amnesia* (London, 2004).

[5]   Kenzaburo Oe, *A Healing Family,* trans. Stephen Snyder (Tokyo, 1996).

[6]   Simon Sebag Montefiore, *Stalin: The Court of the Red Tsar* (London, 2003), p. 85.

[7]   Ibid., pp. 85, 167–8.

[8]   Ibid., p. 469.

nostalgic sounds of home in wartime such as J.B. Priestley's phonomnetic recollections of the church bells in his pre-World War 1 village,[9] fortifying POW communities under threat as memorialized in the film *Paradise Road*, calming men amid the stress of battle,[10] or evoking community traditions:

> Sometimes, all the 150 girls of Lieutenant Gennady Klimenko's [Russian] signals regiment would gather for an evening to sing folk songs. Long before they finished, tears were coursing down the cheeks of men and women alike. [von Lehndorff, as a POW of the Russians] wrote 'It is when they sing that we realise most clearly that they come from another world. They form a community then, and include us as hearers in some immeasurable expanse.'[11]

Such anecdotes help to consolidate the positive value of music in identity formation in ways that can be moving and inspiring. But they are all one-dimensional perspectives on a deeply paradoxical phenomenon, as reflected in the disconcerting cluster of perverse contradictions reported in the *Times* newspaper of 27 April 1918 during the fighting around Villers-Bretonneux, when an Australian subaltern

> ... mounted the parapet with a tin whistle and played 'Australia will be there' to the great joy of the surrounding men, who cheered and laughed as they led the machine-guns. Declaring that he would attract the Huns in greater numbers and thus provide a better target, he proceeded to play 'Watch on the Rhine', whereupon annoyed enemy machine-gunners concentrated their fire on him.[12]

An account such as this modulates with a disturbing logic to another less-quoted description of music as 'measured malice', in 1823.[13] Stalin's musicality illustrates the easy continuum between its negative and positive poles, with framing lines of force that eddy around violence, murder and the ugly triumphalism of one of the most brutal regimes of the twentieth century. Although the dynamic is articulated with particular force in his case, it is by no means aberrant. We will explore the

---

[9]   Richard Holmes, *Tommy: The British Soldier on the Western Front 1914–1918* (London, 2005), p. 96; 'phonomnesis' is a sound 'that is imagined but not actually heard. ... examples include recalling to memory sounds linked to a situation', Jean-François Augoyard and Henry Torgue (eds.), *Sonic Experience: A Guide to Everyday Sounds*, trans. Andra McCartney and David Paquette (Montreal, 2005), p. 85.

[10]   Max Hastings, *Armageddon:The Battle for Germany 1944–45* (London, 2004), p. 426.

[11]   Ibid., p. 141.

[12]   Cited John F. Williams, *Anzacs, the Media and the Great War* (Sydney, 1999), p. 220.

[13]   Charles Lamb, 'A Chapter on Ears', in *The Essays of Elia and the Last Essays of Elia* (London, 1959), p. 57. 'Measured Malice', with its complex pun, was in fact the title originally submitted by the authors for this study.

wartime deployment of music in some detail, but central to our argument is that the power of popular music is always mercenary. That is, musical energies can be appropriated by mutually contesting power blocs, and simultaneously so, as the actual site of conflict. On 1 August 1945 when Britain's House of Commons gathered to elect a speaker, Winston Churchill was greeted by his own party with 'For He's a Jolly Good Fellow'. The Labour benches responded with 'The Red Flag', in what Roy Jenkins called 'Competitive community singing'.[14] The same phenomenon may be heard every week in vast football stadiums as massed *a capella* choirs sing against each other. That music is complicit in relations of power is a truism of popular music studies. Less often recognized is that musical transactions are therefore double-edged. Every time music is used to demarcate the territory of self or community, it is incipiently being used to invade, marginalize or obliterate that of other individuals or groups.

The purpose of this enquiry is to investigate the negative side of popular music, but as the examples listed above should make self-evident, this entails far more than just a study of music. To gain some understanding of the relationship between music and violence, in the senses elaborated below, we must go well beyond music aesthetics. Violence is connected with pain, and we therefore need some discussion of the physiology of hearing such as may be found in psycho-acoustics and bio-acoustics. The deployment of music in the service of power relations is also an entry into cultural studies and, for a fuller perspective, cultural history. This implicates in turn such fields as semiotics, ethnography and ethnology. To understand the negative imprint of music, it is also useful to refer to the positive, of which it is a kind of reflection, so that music therapy will also provide valuable insights. That last word – insights – is, of course a (dead) metaphor for 'understanding', part of the obdurate sediment of scopocentrism which particularly characterizes the English language in the post-Renaissance era in its attempts to verbalize forms of knowledge. A certain level of linguistic self-reflexivity must also be hovering over the discussion if we wish to deconstruct that trope which so often misleads music discourse, and engage with the phenomenology of hearing itself as hearing and not as a dim satellite of vision. Music is not just an aesthetic or moral terrain, nor just a form of knowledge supplementary to visual modes. It is sound, part of the larger soundscape that constitutes our world, and when it inflicts violence it does so not only by virtue of what it means, but what it then is: noise. Our investigation will therefore also draw upon soundscape studies, or the overlapping field with which they are beginning to coalesce, acoustic ecology.

In addition, the study will inevitably draw on aspects of cultural theory. Discussions of taste will resonate with the work of Bourdieu, for example, and given the centrality of relations of power in the investigation, Foucault's work will have relevance. We wish to emphasize, however, that this study is not an application of cultural theory to cultural practice, as signalled in such subtitles that begin 'Towards a Lacanian reading of ...'. This is fundamentally an empirical study,

---

[14]   Roy Jenkins, *Churchill* (London, 2001), p. 803.

and while it is informed by a knowledge of relevant cultural theorists, including those working on popular music, to a large extent the analysis will test the limits of current theoretical modelling of that field. The social practices are the reference point for cognate theories, not the reverse. Nor is this an enquiry into disciplinary taxonomies. It is pre-eminently an attempt to understand something about the experience and impact of music. Without disentangling the various approaches summarized above as discrete lines of enquiry, we will draw on all of them.

The field of study in which this is most centrally situated is of course popular music. The origins of the field of Popular Music Studies (PMS) can be traced back to the work of Theodor Adorno in the 1940s and the 1950s. Adorno located popular music as part of the cultural industries, the purpose of which he saw as helping capitalism to reproduce itself for consumers whose 'spare time serves only to reproduce their working capacity'.[15] Adorno's work did not prevent an increase in PMS, often as a reaction against his bleak prognosis. Insofar as PMS can be traced back to Adorno, we have a degree of resonance with his problematizing of popular music, though for rather different reasons. We feel that PMS's marginal status within the academy has led to a certain defensiveness amongst its proponents, inclining towards unreflectively celebratory accounts of the subject. While the industrial processes involved have not been immune from academic criticism,[16] in general Adorno's arguments have produced indignation. Our attention here will be upon the development of anglophone PMS, which may be divided into two approaches (which are not mutually exclusive). The first may be described as textual analysis, focusing on music *per se* and while the relationship between PMS and musicology has always been fraught, this approach has often drawn upon musicological traditions.[17] The second is contextual, drawing on broader traditions within sociology[18] and cultural studies,[19] including inquiries into the industrial processes that mediate the music and the market.[20]

---

[15] Theodor Adorno, 'On popular music,' in *On Record*, eds Simon Frith and Andrew Goodwin (London, 1990), p. 310.

[16] See for example Dave Harker, *One For The Money* (London, 1980).

[17] See Susan McClary and Richard Walser, 'Start making sense! Musicology wrestles with rock', in *On Record*, eds Simon Frith and Andrew Goodwin, pp. 277–93; Richard Middleton, *Studying Popular Music* (Milton Keynes, 1990); Richard Middleton, 'Popular music analysis and musicology: Bridging the gap', in *Reading Pop*, ed. Richard Middleton (Oxford, 2002), pp. 104–21; Allan Moore, *Rock: The Primary Text* (2nd edition) (Aldershot, 2001).

[18] See Simon Frith, *The Sociology of Rock* (London, 1978) and *Sound Effects* (London, 1983), and Roy Shuker *Understanding Popular Music*, 2nd edition (London, 2001).

[19] See Larry Grossberg, 'Reflections of a disappointed popular music scholar', in *Rock Over The Edge*, eds Roger Beebee, Denise Fulbrook and Ben Saunders (London, 2000), pp. 25–59.

[20] See Keith Negus, *Producing Pop* (London, 1992) and *Music Genres and Corporate Cultures* (London, 1999).

The influence of cultural studies has been particularly strengthened in the UK by the establishment of the Centre for Contemporary Cultural Studies (CCCS) at the University of Birmingham in 1963, which helped legitimate the study of popular culture within the UK Higher Education. Synchronicities between the foundation of CCCS and the era ushered in by Beatlemania strengthened the connections and largely defined the profile of PMS.[21] While some intellectuals had been interested in the rise of earlier UK stars such as Tommy Steele,[22] it was The Beatles who attracted interest from traditional musicologists within broadsheet newspapers,[23] specialist journals[24] and academia.[25] This pioneering work often invoked legitimizing criteria derived from the canon of western classical music. While this now has a somewhat dated and Eurocentric feel, it nonetheless paved the way for the academic study of popular music. This was assisted by the influential rise of particularly literate pop lyrics as exemplified in the work of Bob Dylan, and which found their way into English Department poetry courses. While there are obvious problems in detaching the lyrics from their musical accompaniment,[26] Dylan's work was still studied at a high level by lyric-based analysis.[27]

PMS, however, would increasingly be characterized by an approach which located musical texts within their socio-political context. Key exponents of this approach were Dave Laing whose work, according to Dai Griffiths, allowed for 'a study of pop music, politicized at its inception',[28] and Simon Frith whose pioneering *Sociology of Rock* (1978) and its updated version, *Sound Effects* (1983), became staple PMS texts. Other sociologically inclined scholars of popular music also produced key texts.[29] Paul Oliver developed the serious study of popular music through such projects as *The Story of the Blues* (1970). Other landmark, if uneven,

---

[21]   See Bruce Johnson, 'Jazz as Cultural Practice', in *The Cambridge Companion to Jazz*, eds Mervyn Cooke and David Horn (Cambridge, 2002), pp. 96–113.

[22]   See Colin MacInnes, *England, Half English* (London: 1966) and Trevor Philpott's 1957 essay 'The Bermondsey Miracle', reprinted in *The Faber Book of Pop*, eds Jon Savage and Hanif Kureshi (London, 1995) pp. 63–6.

[23]   Wilfred Mann, 'What songs The Beatles sang', *Times*, 27 December 1963.

[24]   Deryck Cooke, 'The Lennon-McCartney songs', *Listener*, 1 February 1968.

[25]   Wilfrid Mellers, *Twilight of The Gods* (London, 1973).

[26]   Martin Cloonan, 'What is popular music studies? Some observations', *British Journal of Music Education*, 22/1 (2005): 77–93.

[27]   See Betsy Bowden, *Performed Literature: Words and Music by Bob Dylan* (Bloomington, 1982), and Christopher Ricks, *Dylan's Visions of Sin* (London, 2004).

[28]   Dai Griffiths, 'The high analysis of low culture', *Music Analysis*, 18/3 (1999), p. 402; the Laing texts are Dave Laing, *The Sound of Our Time* (London, 1969), *Buddy Holly* (London, 1971), *One Chord Wonders* (Milton Keynes, 1985).

[29]   See John Street, *Rebel Rock* (Oxford, 1986); Keith Negus, *Popular Music in Theory* (Cambridge, 1996) and Shuker, *Understanding Popular Music*.

historical accounts began to appear.[30] The pop/rock divide which opened up from around the release of the Beatles' seminal *Sergeant Pepper* album (1967) saw the development of rock criticism as a serious journalistic endeavour, and arguments for the art-status of rock that justified its serious analysis. A generation of journalists such as Nick Kent (1994) and Charles Shaar Murray (1991), helped to establish a sense of a rock community[31] whose artform deserved to be taken seriously. In part this involved taking on musicology at its own game. To counter rock's dismissal as an inferior, technically simplistic form of music it was necessary to identify an organizing ideology which legitimated its study. The concept of authenticity was crucial here. If classical critics persisted in scorning rock's supposed musical simplicity, they were liable to the accusation of ignoring the authentic voice of youth. While now rather discredited as a discursive construct, 'authenticity' helped to vindicate the serious study of popular music. It also retains a certain cachet in a number of popular music genres, from folk to rap. 'Authenticity' has also left a residue in the celebratory academic accounts of popular music which elided its potentially deleterious effects.

Meanwhile 1981 proved to be a momentous year for the academic study of popular music, with the founding of the International Association for the Study of Popular Music (IASPM) and the journal *Popular Music*, both of which were to provide a community forum for the often lonely world of the popular music academic. The Institute of Popular Music (IPM) at the University of Liverpool was founded in 1988, and would become a key location for academic work in the field. As PMS gained aesthetic and academic respectability it moved away from its initial concentration on major stars[32] and the 'big picture',[33] towards the local dynamics of musicians and fans[34] and to the use of music in everyday life. Likewise, our concern is less with the big stars and the multinational corporations than with the uses to which music is put, most specifically with musical violence in everyday life.

---

[30]   See Nik Cohn, *WopBopaLooBopLopBamBoom* (St Albans, 1970); Charlie Gillett, *Sound of The City* (London, 1983); Tony Palmer, *All You Need Is Love* (London, 1976).

[31]   Simon Frith, '"The magic that can set you free": the ideology of folk and the myth of the rock community', *Popular Music* 1 (1981): 159–68; the Kent and Murray texts are Nick Kent, *The Dark Stuff* (London: Penguin, 1994); Charles Shaar Murray, *Shots from the Hip* (London: Penguin, 1991).

[32]   See Wilfrid Mellers, *Twilight of The Gods* and *A Darker Shade of Pale* (Oxford, 1985).

[33]   See Dave Laing, *The Sound of Our Time* (London, 1969) and Simon Frith, *The Sociology of Rock* and *Sound Effects*.

[34]   See Sara Cohen, *Rock Culture in Liverpool* (Oxford, 1991); Will Straw, 'Systems of articulation, logics of change: Scenes and communities in popular music', *Cultural Studies*, 5/3 (1999), pp. 361–75; John Street, *Politics and Popular Culture* (Cambridge, 1997).

PMS has developed as a field of study, 'not an academic discipline' in the words of IASPM.[35] The editors of the academic collection *Popular Music Studies*, declared that:

> The study of popular music is, at its best, a uniquely interdisciplinary area of research, drawing significant contributions from writers, within a number of academic fields including musicology, media and cultural studies, sociology, anthropology, ethnomusicology, folkloristics, psychology, social history and cultural geography.[36]

These flexible boundaries have led to warm controversies over the location and methodology of PMS in curricula, and its relative emphases on musicianship, vocationalism and cultural theory.[37] The point we wish to underscore here, however, is that PMS emerged carrying the burden of some academic scepticism if not outright hostility. As an outgrowth of cultural studies, PMS suffered by association with a (part) parent derided as Hoggart's line in cheap hats.[38] Although PMS is now well established within UK Higher Education institutions, such attacks have persisted. On 23 January 2004 the *Times Higher Education Supplement* discussed the proposed introduction of undergraduate tuition, asking whether fees could be justified for courses which appeared to be 'dumbing down',[39] with popular music being cited as an example. Such attacks are in a larger tradition of the derision of popular music itself,[40] but they have also included scepticism from journalistic friends of popular music who ask 'can you really learn how to rock like The Strokes by sitting in a lecture theatre?'[41] or whether, as someone who writes books on Bob Dylan, Christopher Ricks is really a suitable appointment as Oxford University's Professor of Poetry.[42]

Thus some 40 years since it began to emerge as a serious field of study, PMS is still the subject of scepticism. We believe that one effect of this has been that its scholars have been reluctant to what we have termed as 'do the dirty' on

---

[35]   IASPM website, www.iaspm.net/iaspm/unis.html, accessed 10 April 2007.

[36]   David Hesmondhalgh and Keith Negus, *Popular Music Studies* (London, 2002), p. 2.

[37]   Ibid., 83–7; see also Cloonan, 'What is Popular Music Studies?', p. 83.

[38]   David Ward, 'A nice line in cheap hats' (1998), www.publications.bham.ac.uk/birmingham_magazine/b_magazine1996-99/pg14_98.htm.

[39]   Tony Tysome, 'Do they deserve degrees?', *Times Higher Educational Supplement*, 23 January 2004, pp. 8–9.

[40]   Paul Johnson, 'The menace of Beatlism', *New Statesman*, 28 February 1964, pp. 326–7; Ronald Butt 'The grubby face of punk promotion', *Times*, 9 December 1976, p. 14.

[41]   Doug Johnstone, 'We don't need no education', *NME*, 29 March 2003, p. 61.

[42]   See *Observer*, 16 May 2004, p. 4; John Ezard, 'Bob Dylan fan wins Oxford poetry post', *Guardian*, 17 May 2004, p. 8.

popular music.[43] Our objective in this book is not so much to 'do the dirty' as to contribute to the growing maturity of PMS. Describing PMS as 'established, though relatively marginal', Hesmondhalgh and Negus see it as emerging as a reaction against its host disciplines.[44] This position is consistent with a pervasive defensiveness,[45] manifested for example in PMS scholars' tendency to over-quote the 'great thinkers' in order to deflect lowbrow associations.[46] It is therefore hardly surprising that popular music academics have concentrated on pop's positive side rather than its more negative aspects. Thus pop has been celebrated variously for its contribution to people's identity,[47] its challenging of censorship,[48] its empowerment of marginalized groups[49] and its contribution to national pride.[50] While seldom as schematic as *Rolling Stone's* assertion that rock and roll was 'the magic that can set you free',[51] academic studies have been generally characterized by celebratory accounts which have, at best, underplayed pop's problems. Even the most respected observers can invoke this rhetoric, as for example, Simon Frith's concluding observation in *The Sociology of Rock* that rock 'will remain fun and the source of ... power and joy'.[52] Similarly, John Street's declaration that the music can create a socialism 'built of sensations and images, inspired by pleasure and personal desires' and a way in which 'we deny the right of the greedy and powerful to some part of ourselves'.[53] We do not dispute such statements, but seek to balance them.

Simon Frith also recently noted that for popular music scholars, 'the belief that music is a good thing has meant the celebration of the public use of ghetto blasters, an unswerving critique of any form of censorship, and even, by and large, a positive spin on the impact of rock on local music around the world in the name of hybridity

---

[43] Martin Cloonan and Bruce Johnson, 'Killing me softly with his song: An initial investigation into the use of Popular Music as a tool of repression', *Popular Music*, 21/1 (2002), p. 28.

[44] Hesmondhlagh and Negus, *Popular Music Studies*, p. 4.

[45] Ibid., p. 1.

[46] Jeroen de Kloet, *Red Sonic Trajectories* (Amsterdam, 2004), p. 189.

[47] See Andy Bennett, *Cultures of Popular Music* (Buckingham, 2001); Stan Hawkins, *Settling The Pop Score: Pop Texts and Identity Politics* (Aldershot, 2002).

[48] Martin Cloonan, *Banned!* (Aldershot, 1996).

[49] See Mark S. Hamm and Jeff Ferrell (nd), 'Rap, cops, and crime: clarifying the "cop killer" controversy', accessed 8 February 2008.

[50] See Sean Campbell and Gerry Smyth, *Beautiful Day: Forty Years of Irish Rock* (Cork, 2005); Gerry Smyth, *Noisy Island: A Short History of Irish Popular Music* (Cork, 2005).

[51] Cited by Simon Frith, 'The magic that can set you free'.

[52] Frith, *The Sociology of Rock*, p. 209.

[53] Street, *Rebel Rock*, pp. 221 and 226.

and modernity'.[54] Gary Andsell has argued that this is replicated within music therapy where music is seen almost automatically as being therapeutic.[55] In a work commissioned for the Performing Right Society in the UK, while Sue Hallam wrote that her study 'confirms the proven benefits of music' and was a 'fresh examination of the countless ways in which music enriches humanity',[56] she does nonetheless also acknowledge a potential darker side. There is also a long tradition of critique, though these have more generally been based on the music industries rather than the music. From the left Dave Harker has written of the construction of false identities through music[57] and of recording industry duplicity.[58] Meanwhile the right has not been averse to citing the music industries as a source of many of the world's problems.[59] However, we are unaware of academic accounts from within PMS which, for example, are pro-censorship, or which suggest that pop has a deleterious effect on identity formation or that it is politically ineffectual or rebarbative.

In this context we see this study contributing to an increasing maturity in PMS through a more balanced analysis that recognizes its dialectic. David Hesmonhalgh has cautioned that sampling practices may have 'a darker side'.[60] The darkness is intensified in our documentation of the purposeful use of music as an instrument of power, but power that is morally and socially ambiguous. If it can be liberating, it can also be exploitatively manipulative, as in the case of Muzak and telephone hold music.[61] The field of psychology offers a rich field of enquiry into the influence of music, as in the work in the UK of Adrian North (on whom Hallam also draws), referred to in Chapter 8. Tia De Nora has investigated the use of music in retail as part of a broader investigation into the use of *Music in Everyday Life*, suggesting that music 'is used to structure in-store conduct'.[62] De Nora's work included empirical studies of UK high street stores, including some who used

---

[54]   Simon Frith, 'Why does music make people so cross?', *Nordic Journal of Music Therapy*, 13/1 (2004): 64–8, see p. 66.

[55]   Garry Andsell, 'Response to Simon Frith's Essay', *Nordic Journal of Music Therapy*, 13/1 (2004): 70–72, see p. 70.

[56]   Susan Hallam, *The Power of Music* (London, 2001), p. 1.

[57]   Dave Harker, *Fakesong* (Milton Keynes, 1985).

[58]   Dave Harker, 'The Wonderful World of IFPI: Music Industry Rhetoric, the Critics, and the Classical Marxist Critique', *Popular Music*, 16/1 (1997): 45–79.

[59]   See Johnson, 'The menace of Beatlism'; Butt 'The grubby face'; Dennis R. Martin, 'Rapping about cop killing', accessed 8 February 2008.

[60]   David Hesmondhalgh, 'Digital sampling and cultural inequality', *Social and Legal Studies*, 15/1 (2006), p. 55.

[61]   See Joseph Lanza, *Elevator Music: A Surreal History of Muzak, Easy Listening, and other Moodsong* (New York, 1994); Hallam, The Power of Music, p. 21.

[62]   Tia De Nora and Sophie Belcher, '"When you're trying something on you picture yourself in a place where they are playing this kind of music" – musically sponsored agency in the British clothing retail sector', *Sociological Review*, 48/1 (2000): 80–110, see p. 80.

Muzak's products.[63] In addition she concluded that customer reactions to the use of music in clothing shops did not have any emancipative effects for customers, but that 'this form of aesthetic reflexivity can be regarded as consisting of the very commodity fetishism critiqued by Marx, a situation wherein the creative and expressive faculties are harnessed to consumption rather than the "making" of material goods and social relations'.[64]

A major proposition in our study is that not only can we talk of music in everyday life, we can also talk of musical violence in everyday life. This which leads us back to PMS. We are very mindful of the indebtedness of PMS to the socially interventionist critical tradition in Cultural Studies.[65] Dai Griffith argues that popular music writing 'is best understood as a certain literature of the left during the late twentieth century'.[66] PMS has also been part of a counter-hegemonic struggle, the dominance of (white, western, male-dominated) classical musicology. However that struggle has to go beyond uncritical celebration of all popular music in a Fiskean romanticization of every form of consumerism. It is necessary to problematize popular music, returning PMS to its roots in cultural critique. The founders of IASPM were from radical backgrounds and were often attracted to popular music precisely because of its potential role in counter-hegemonic struggles. But popular music is itself the instrument of macro- and micro-hegemonies. We remain firmly committed to PMS (and to the principles of IASPM's founders), yet we feel the need to open a debate on the implications, for musicians, fans and PMS scholars, of the darker side of popular music.

Since drafting the foregoing, our continuing research has led to a number of tactical and structural adjustments. In the most general terms, that research has confirmed with an almost bludgeoning force the ubiquity of the connections between music and violence. As originally planned, some sections of this discussion would now be, in our opinion, so much a labouring of the obvious that we have abbreviated them to little more than a reference, a brief sample of cases, and some extrapolation. If we are, for example, arguing for a basic circumstantial connection between violence and gangsta rap or black metal, but without wishing to argue causality, very little documentation is needed. Similarly, a chapter length section on violence and music in film has been contracted to a few pages. These adjustments are not simply a pragmatic response to the volume of information available, they are tactical. We are concerned not to exoticize the link between music and violence. Norwegian black metal and Los Angeles gangsta rap can for most readers be comfortingly displaced from the local musicscape. The use of music to torment political detainees or prisoners in Iraq is disturbing, but consolingly distant. Our argument is that the connection is part of everyday life in every modern conurbation. The capacity of sound in general and music in particular to

---

[63] Ibid., p. 88.

[64] Ibid: p. 98.

[65] Jim McGuigan, *Rethinking Cultural Policy* (Buckingham, 2004).

[66] Griffith, 'The high analysis of low culture', p. 395.

generate social violence is, to purposefully appropriate a military phrase, a 'clear and present danger'. This is not a conservative moral panic argument, and indeed, we regard the 'usual suspects' in those arguments as the least cause of concern, since they are so clearly badged and generically quarantined. Most violent crime is not the work of the sinister looking stranger, but of someone close to us, someone we know, someone like 'us', someone 'ordinary'. The connections we establish between music and weaponry are not a sensationalist analogy. Sound is a potential weapon, and ubiquitously actualized as such in everyday life, especially in its diverse technologized forms. It is there that it calls for a re-examination of assumptions about rights to free expression, censorship, regulation and policies relating to cultural and physical welfare.

The following argument begins with what we regard as self-evident fact: that however else we may classify music, it is fundamentally a sonic phenomenon. Music is heard. In Chapter 1 we therefore enquire into the distinctive properties of sonority in the generation of affect, with a particular focus on the connections between sound, pain and violence. Chapter 2 traces the history of this relationship, increasingly focusing on that particular form of sound which may be referred to as music. We argue that the relationship between sonic and visual information economies has been a key to the often violent power relations out of which modernity emerged. Chapter 3 examines the transforming effect on these relations of the convergence of sound and technology through the nineteenth century, literally and metaphorically amplifying the role of sound in the negotiation of conflict, and, especially from the First World War, transforming the sonic imaginary. The enquiry then sets out a provisional taxonomy of the relationships between sound and violence, with the objective of teasing out the vexed question of causality. Clearly popular music accompanies violence (Chapter 4), incites violence (Chapter 5), and arouses violence (Chapter 6). But how far are these connections causally complicit in social conflict outside the 'musical habitus'? It is increasingly recognized that music can function as a form of state-sponsored violence, as in interrogations and torture in formal conflict situations (Chapter 7). Nonetheless, we argue in Chapter 8 that by far the most pervasive function of music in generating social violence appears to be in everyday life. This has the most profound implications for such issues as regulation, censorship, social policy and, we argue, for the field of popular music studies itself.

Chapter 1
Context: The Sound of Music

Bruce Johnson

Much is made in popular music studies of the decisive and differentiating role of mediations.[1] Yet almost nothing is made of the most fundamental set of differentiating mediations, without which there can be no cultural transaction at all: the sensorium. As a broad introductory simplification, it may be said that in traditional musicology, music is generally categorized as an 'artform', the bearer of aesthetics. In popular music studies, the emphasis is on music as a 'culture', the bearer of meanings. Initially we wish to situate music in terms of its sensory materiality: music as sound. To do so recognizes the material and biological foundations of culture, and joins with recent emerging research fields such as the anthropology of the senses. As long ago as 1749, Diderot observed that the 'state of our organs and of our senses has a great influence on our metaphysics and our ethics, and our most purely intellectual ideas, if I may express it thus, are very much dependent on the structure of our body'.[2] In 1891 pioneer radio wave researcher Heinrich Hertz, who, appropriately in this context, would give his name to the frequency in cycles per second of sound, spoke of the 'narrow borderland of the senses' between consciousness and the 'world of actual things'. He declared that for a 'proper understanding of ourselves and of the world it is of the highest importance that this borderland should be thoroughly explored'.[3] The connection was largely overlooked in twentieth-century cultural theory. Studies of gendered identity and power relations, for example, have been marked by 'a preference for encountering embodiment via social, representational, or symbolic analysis at the expense of biological data'.[4] Emerging work in such fields as the anthropology of the senses, however, is gradually repositioning physiology into the study of culture.[5]

---

[1]   See for example 'Can we get rid of the "popular" in popular music? A virtual symposium with contributions from the International Advisory Editors of *Popular Music*', *Popular Music* 24/1 (2005): 133–45.

[2]   From Diderot's 1749 'Letter on the Blind', cited in Alvin Kernan, *Samuel Johnson and the Impact of Print* (Princeton, 1989), p. 14.

[3]   Cited in David Bodanis, *Electric Universe: How Electricity Switched On the Modern World* (London, 2006), p. 98.

[4]   Elizabeth Wilson, 'Gut Feminism', *Differences: A Journal of Feminist Cultural Studies* 15/3 (2004), pp. 66–94, see p. 78.

[5]   See further Bruce Johnson, '"Quick and Dirty": Sonic Mediations and Affect', forthcoming in *Sonic Mediations: Body, Sound, Technology*, eds Carolyn Birdsall and

To locate music *a priori* in the sensorium in this way opens the door to the distinctive phenomenology and physiology of sounding and hearing. Before a musical experience can be analysed as either an aesthetic or cultural transaction, it must be, by this categorization, a sensory episode experienced primarily through the ear. Of course a rich repertoire of reception and interpretation is also deployed. Music is also a tactile phenomenon experienced through vibration. It is usually accompanied also by visual impressions which might be a supplementary mediation of the acoustic event, as in the sight of a band performing or the view from a car or from a sofa as one listens to radio or recordings. And there are also gustatory and olfactory sensations that form part of the totality, as in the obvious example of dining and drinking in a restaurant with live or piped music. The experience is also entangled with memory, emotion, dynamics of identity and taste, relations of power or conflict. But all this is activated by a sound entering the ear. It is the special properties of sound in itself which invest music with certain forms of power that ally it to noise in a way that is not the case with other non-acoustic expressive forms like painting.

We do not wish to enter into the debates about the superiority or otherwise of acoustic *vis-à-vis* scopic modalities.[6] Our point is simply to underscore differences between them. Sound is capable of certain effects which are not available to the other major sensory partner in our public social transactions, vision. 'Sound has always been a privileged tool to "create an effect", to astonish. ... Sound undeniably has an immediate emotional power that has been used by every culture'.[7] Of special relevance here is the distinctive power of sound to arouse and also to produce organic damage. Sound in and of itself can produce profound distress. Among the most powerful of sounds, and the most often deployed in social intercourse, is the human voice. It has power as an acoustic presence, prior to whatever the specific utterance might generate semiotically. In 1662, a condemned prisoner in Newgate reported that the condemned hold had 'neither bench, stool, nor stick for any person there. They lie like swine upon the ground, one upon another, howling and roaring – it was more terrible to me than death'.[8] This is an example of the sonic

---

Anthony Enns (Cambridge).

[6]   See for example Walter J. Ong, *Orality and Literacy: The Technologizing of the Word* (London and New York, 1982); and Marshall McLuhan, *The Gutenberg Galaxy: The Making of Typographic Man* (Toronto, 1962), both of whom incline towards a valorization of orality that a counter-argument found in Tim Ingold, *The Perception of the Environment* (London and New York, 2000), pp. 243–87, would declare to be unrigorously romantic. A succinct overview of the debate is to be found in Leigh Eric Schmidt, 'Hearing Loss', in Michael Bull and Les Back (eds), *The Auditory Culture Reader* (Oxford and New York, 2003), pp. 41–59.

[7]   Jean-François Augoyard and Henry Torgue (eds), *Sonic Experience: A Guide to Everyday Sounds,* trans. Andra McCartney and David Paquette (Montreal, 2005), p. 11.

[8]   Anthony Babington, *The English Bastille,* p. 56.

effect appropriately called 'perdition'.[9] The well known example of the anguished final sounds made by Hamlet in the First Folio version of the play exemplifies the enormous resonant power of this sonic effect.[10]

There is an enormous range of non-lexical vocal effects apart from perdition, and popular music scholars are likely to understand this better than lexicon-bound legal and literary studies. And the more the voice is inflected by musicality, by factors over and above verbal denotation, the more arresting it becomes. It has been found that six-month-old infants 'showed more attention to their mothers' singing episodes than to their speaking episodes'. They were 'hypnotized' by video of their mothers' singing, 'glued' to the image 'for extended periods. Mothers' speaking was not as engaging as their singing'.[11] The scatting of a jazz singer, the pentecostal shrieks of gospel music, James Brown and Little Richard, denote nothing, yet declare everything about emancipation, abandonment, ecstasy. A non-German speaker can feel the power of Hitler's speeches. The oratorical manipulation of rhythm, repetition, disruption, timbre and volume produces sonic effects that can transcend deficiencies in linguistic sophistication. Transcribed on the page, a Baptist sermon by, for example, the Reverend Leo Daniels looks mawkish, naïve and emotionally negligible. Heard, it can transfix even the most sophisticated audience of literature students.[12] A ghoulishly corporealized illustration of the 'presence' of the voice, its organic origins and its ubiquity, was the reported case of one Edmund Kemper, who killed his mother because of her nagging. He decapitated her, excised the larynx and stuffed it in the garbage disposal unit. But when he switched it on, it spewed the remains back at him: 'Even when she was dead, she was still bitching at me. I couldn't get her to shut up.'[13]

---

[9]   'Perdition' is a 'semantic effect that might also be called the "dereliction" or "loss". This effect is linked to a feeling of perdition, in the double sense of a soul in distress and the dissipation of a sound motif. The sound seems to be emitted for nothing, for everyone to hear but requiring no answer. It is a sound without destination, absurd in the etymological sense; its entire expression is simply a sign of powerlessness. Often characteristic of extreme suffering constituted principally of tears and moans, this effect accompanies life situations that are violent or painful', Augoyard and Torgue, *Sonic Effects*, p. 84.

[10]   See further Bruce Johnson, '*Hamlet*: voice, music, sound', *Popular Music* 24/2 (2005): 257–67.

[11]   Isabelle Peretz, 'Listen to the Brain: a Biological Perspective on Musical Emotions', in John A. Sloboda, and Patrik N. Juslin (eds), *Music and Emotion: Theory and Research* (Oxford, 2001), 105–34, see p. 114.

[12]   I base this on the regular use of the comparison between transcription and recorded oration by Daniels for my literature students over several decades, in connection with discussions of 'literariness' and to illustrate the power of such 'literary' pieces as the sermon in Faulkner's *The Sound and the Fury*. Hear, for example, *Rev Leo Daniels: 'The Real Thing'*, Jewel Records LPS 0087 (Louisiana, 1974).

[13]   Oliver Cyriax, *The Penguin Encyclopedia of Crime* (Harmondsworth, 1996), p. 295. There is something about the drive to destroy the nagging voice, as in the use of the

The grotesquerie of this report is a trope for the physically intrusive aspect of sound. Unlike vision, sound enters the body with extremely intensity, as experienced in even relatively everyday situations such as a voice whispering in your ear at a dinner party, which immediately sets up an intimate secondary level of social engagement. Human sound emerges directly from inside the body, while sight plays over the surface.[14] The voice *is* the body, irreducible site of our social being and proclamation of life. The dead may be touched, smelled, seen and tasted – but not heard (again, a point made throughout *Hamlet*). It is to the characteristic of silence that we attached the word 'deathly'. The voice is the living body projected directly into the social space, a kind of nakedness, one reason our culture is discomfited at public vocalization such as yelling and singing, and especially involuntary vocalization such as sobbing. Unlike the projection of the body through its visual aspect, vocal utterance enters the body of the receiver, and is the sound of the body of the emitter, the sound of breath over complex internal interactions between tissue, bone, muscle, nerves, mediating identity in ways that are physiologically related to the cortex very differently from the visual faculty.

Sound and the voice are also able to instantly modify the radius of their impact. By shouting, whispering, changing timbre and register, the human being can control and transform the perceived character of her/his identity to a degree, range and rapidity unavailable to any form of identity projection. It is our most versatile faculty for acceptable public negotiation. Of all our organs the larynx has the highest ratio of nerve to muscle fibre, making it capable of an immeasurable range of expressive nuances which can circumvent semantics. Standing alone, the written words, 'I am going home' cannot achieve a fraction of the expressive possibilities available to their spoken/sung form, which may range from irony to disgust, sadness, fear, regret, elation, disappointment, triumph. At the extremes of experience, words fail us, but sound does not. The scream, the howl, the sob and sigh, all are both unintelligible to verbal analysis, yet ultimate modes of expressiveness.

The springs of this expressiveness are not semantic, but somatic. What is it about sound that invests it with such unique power in social interaction? There is

---

'bride's scold'. In 2006 it was reported that a Japanese man confessed to killing his mother because she nagged him about getting a job. He then dismembered her, grilled the parts on a hotplate before throwing the remains into the garbage, and embedded the rest in cement (No byline, 'Japanese man cooks mother on hotplate', *Sydney Morning Herald* (hereinafter *SMH*) online, 26 April 2006).

[14]   Excepting in such cases as anatomies and pornography. It is noteworthy that the rise of the anatomy theatre coincided with the ascendancy of an epistemology that identified the known with the visible; the human being could not be known until its interior was made visible; see for example Jonathan Sawday, *The Body Emblasoned: Dissection and the human body in Renaissance Culture* (London and New York, 1995); Roy Porter, *Flesh in the Age of Reason: How the Enlightenment Transformed the Way We See Our Bodies and Souls* (London, 2003); Benjamin A. Rifkin and Michael J. Ackerman, *Human Anatomy (From the Renaissance to the Digital Age)* (New York, 2006).

a further deeply ambiguous characteristic which provides a springboard to some of the answers. Sound floods the space it enters. It is an obvious enough point, but its ramifications for the power of sound *qua* sound are complex and far-reaching. Within the conventionally understood sensorium, only smell has the same property, but with none of the finely articulated and directed possibilities of sound. It is a property with ambiguous potential. On the one hand, sound becomes a unifying envelope, immersing all those present in more or less the same expressive flood.[15] Hearing internalizes, and sound projects, a shared experience. It constructs and mobilizes collective identity. 'The sonic effect produces a common sense because it gathers together into unified and harmonious listening what other disciplinary knowledge divides.'[16]

On the other hand, relative to the specular, sound is inescapable because ubiquitous. The CRESSON group (Centre de recherché sur l'espace sonore et l'environment urbain) in Grenoble, identifies the 'ubiquity effect', a conscious searching for the source of a sound, and at least a disorienting momentary failure to find it. 'The uncertainty produced by a sound about its origin establishes a power relationship between an invisible emitter and the worried receptor. The ubiquity effect is an effect of power.'[17] The ubiquity effect generally produces discomfort, ranging from mild anxiety, a feeling of faintness, to 'the most uncontrollable panic'.[18] '[N]ot to know where a sound comes from is almost to believe in the manifestation of a superior force or a transcendental power: God, the State, Nature, the Father.'[19] Thus, while the semantic content of utterance may be pivotal in directing its energies on behalf of or in opposition to particular interests, in the first instance the inchoate power thus harnessed derives from the phenomenology and physiology of sonic effects.

There is evidence that auditory stimuli – and therefore music – bypass 'conscious awareness' in eliciting emotions, suggesting that in some cases 'affect precedes inference'.[20] Furthermore, affect is involuntary, inescapable and difficult to revoke.[21] Zajonc argues that the affective system does not process, for example, the lexical elements of a message, but something more primary. Even when the 'content of recorded utterances is nearly completely obliterated by means of

---

[15] I say 'more or less' in recognition of variations in individual hearing acuity, and physical positions affected by acoustic blocking.

[16] Augoyard and Torgue, *Sonic Effects*, p. 11.

[17] Ibid., p. 131.

[18] Ibid., p. 137.

[19] Ibid., p. 139.

[20] John A. Sloboda and Patrik N. Juslin, 'Psychological Perspectives on Music and Emotion' in John A. Sloboda and Patrik N. Juslin (eds) *Music and Emotion: Theory and Research*, (Oxford, 2001), pp. 23–44; see p. 85. A contrary position is reported by Peretz, 'Listen to the Brain', in Sloboda and Juslin, ibid.: 118.

[21] Robert B. Zajonc, *The Selected Works of R.B. Zajonc* (New Jersey, 2004), pp. 257, 258.

electronic masking, filtering or random splicing of the tape, subjects can still encode the emotions expressed in these utterances quite reliably'.[22] That is, 'musicality' and intonation, rather than verbal content, have priority in the formation of emotional responses to sonic stimuli. Zajonc's arguments have been experimentally reinforced in the work of neuroscientist Joseph LeDoux, who found that the first stage of arousal is an involuntary reaction to sounds.[23] There are at least two pathways between aural stimulus and response, of different orders of complexity. The first is purely physiological; the second involves cultural processing, and is supplemented by the hippocampus, a processor that contextualizes the stimulus with memory.[24] For present purposes, the work of Zajonc and LeDoux suggests a 'foundation/scaffolding' model of sonic (and therefore musical) affect. That is, that there is a primary reaction to a threatening stimulus. It is physiological and involuntary, and creates a matrix within which a secondary and cognitively mediated response draws on cultural memory to articulate the precise nature of that threat. The implication is that certain emotional responses to sound are so-to-speak hard-wired, constrained biologically, rather in the manner of a foundation to a building that won't determine what is constructed on it, but which limits what may be.[25] Sound is power, unharnessed. Specific physical characteristics of sound and its relationship to the audient can alter physiological states.

The point can be illustrated through the connection between sound localization, its source in relation to the listener, and pitch. The body employs several systems of sound localization. 'Interaural intensity difference' relies on the reduced level of intensity experienced in the ear farther from a laterally directed sound source, and is less effective for lower pitched sounds, because the long wavelengths – as long as 40 feet for the lowest musical notes[26] – are unaffected by the presence of the head. It is thus most effective in localizing high-pitched sounds with a wavelength shorter than the width of the head – above around 200 Hz. Apart from the organic damage that low register sound might produce (see below), the difficulty of identifying its source can induce profound disorientation and anxiety. A second system is phase difference 'or temporal shift of arrival between the two ears,[27] also known as 'interaural time difference'.[28] These systems are impeded if sound comes from above rather than laterally, producing the confusion often felt in trying to locate

---

[22]   Ibid., p. 253.

[23]   Joseph LeDoux, *The Emotional Brain* (London, 1999), pp. 162–5; see further 239.

[24]   Ibid., p. 168.

[25]   See further Johnson, 'Quick and Dirty'.

[26]   Glenn D. White and Gary J. Louie, *The Audio Dictionary*, Third Edition (Seattle and London, 2005), p. 446. It is a useful reference point to note that the range of human hearing is generally between 20 and 20,000 Hz, and the range of frequencies for human speech is between about 400 and 3,000 Hz (E. Bruce Goldstein, *Sensation and Perception*, 4th edition (Pacific Grove Calif.,1996), p. 377.

[27]   Augoyard and Torgue, *Sonic Effects*, p. 136.

[28]   Goldstein, *Sensation and Perception*, p. 358.

the position of high flying aircraft. The Junkers 'Stuka' aircraft carried one bomb of limited lethal potential, but its siren as the plane dropped near vertically was a major factor in demoralizing the enemy during the German blitzkrieg on Poland. More recently the captain of a cruise liner attacked by Somali pirates, repelled the attackers using a device developed for the US military. It directed down to them a 'high-pitched, piercing tone with a tight beam', capable of reaching up to 150 decibels.[29] While spectral discrimination through the pinna remains operative for overhead sounds,[30] at least part of this disorientation appears to be attributable to the direction of the sound source and the physiology of hearing. Sound coming from above, such as from an organ loft, a highly elevated pop music stadium stage, or an apartment above us, is therefore more likely to produce a sense of unequal power relations than sound coming from the same level as in the case of a band in the corner of a small pub, or from next door. It is worth considering how far power relations are affected by the physiological ramifications of the difference between an upright piano projecting its popular songs laterally in a low-ceiling bar, and the art music of a grand piano projected up and out into a high-ceiling concert hall.

Frequency is also implicated in the physiological relationship with sound. Apart from being more difficult to localize, low frequencies activate the body's potential as a set of resonating chambers, generating such pathologies as motion sickness, 'or vascular or articular diseases'.[31] Similar pathologies are associated with bass sounds in popular music.[32] An account of a condition referred to as pneumothorax was published in the medical journal *The Thorax* in 2004. It is believed to be characterized by air entering the space between the lungs and their surrounding membranes. Risk factors include, among other things, smoking and alcohol. The physiology underlying such an attack is believed to be the different responses of the two sets of tissue to sound, triggered by low-frequency sound at high volume. In one case, the source was a 1,000 watt bass-box fitted to the patient's car stereo. In another, a young man experienced an attack while standing next to a loudspeaker in a club, and a third while attending a heavy metal concert. Symptoms range from chest pain and breathlessness, to lung collapse and consequent life-threatening deprivation of oxygen to vital organs.[33]

Film music composers have long recognized the connection between the sense of hidden menace and low frequencies, as famously illustrated in the 'shark' theme for Spielberg's *Jaws*. The relationship between power and pitch has been a factor in the gendered voice. One of the effects of the microphone on popular music vocalization was to attract the charge of feminization to crooners whose

[29]   No byline, AAP Reuters, 'Cruise ship captain gave pirates a sound thrashing', *SMH*, 9 November 2005, p. 12.

[30]   Augoyard and Torgue, *Sonic Effects*, p. 136.

[31]   Augoyard and Torgue, *Sonic Effects*, p. 107.

[32]   On the relationship between urban architecture and the foregrounding of bass registers in contemporary popular music, see further Johnson, 'Quick and Dirty'.

[33]   *BBC News* on-line, 31 August 2004 'Loud music lung collapse warning'.

vocal projection came closer to conversational registers than had been possible in unamplified performance venues. For men, this generally meant a rise from the more traditional performance register to what became known as crooning (hence, effeminacy). The microphone enabled women to lower their register, the effects of which included a shift in gender politics as projected in early twentieth-century popular music.[34] Low voices are most often associated with masculine power. Objecting to the description of General Franco as a dictator, a supporter explained it could not have been so, 'because he had such a small, high-pitched voice'.[35] When Australian politician Kim Beazley led the Australian Labor Party from the late 1990s, he was never able to take them into government. In spite of being held in high affection, he was never perceived as a national leader, and focus groups invariably disclosed that a factor in this perception was his high voice.[36] Conversely, high register vocalization is so closely aligned with the politics of the feminine, that in the misogynist Third Reich, where women were required to remain 'in role', the Swedish film star and popular singer Zarah Leander, a basso contralto, resident in Germany until 1943, was immensely popular in locally made morale boosting movies, but was rejected as 'alien' by radio listeners.[37] In the history of vocal practices in film and television, it is difficult to imagine the gruff vs shrill vocal profile of (vaudeville-trained) George Burns and Gracie Allen, ever permitting the same sparring equality achieved in the partnerships of Spencer Tracey and Humphrey Bogart with the deep voiced Katherine Hepburn and Lauren Bacall respectively.[38] A recent development of the cosmetic surgery repertoire enables individuals to have a 'squeaky voice' surgically altered in order to enhance, for example, their confidence and power in the workplace.[39]

A major factor in the relationship between sound/music and somatic impact is of course volume. Vladimir Konečni's experiments on musical arousal found that listening to music at very high volume 'is both arousing and aversive'.[40] In 2006,

---

[34]   See further Bruce Johnson, *The Inaudible Music: Jazz, Gender and Australian Modernity* (Sydney, 2000), pp. 81–135.

[35]   G.B. Harrison, *Night Train to Granada – From Sydney's Bohemia to Franco's Spain: an offbeat memoir* (Annandale NSW, 2002), pp. 376–7.

[36]   Shaun Carney, 'Transparent Tactic', *SMH* online 29 September 2007.

[37]   Michael H. Kater, *Different Drummers: Jazz in the Culture of Nazi Germany* (New York and Oxford, 1992), p. 184.

[38]   See further Johnson, 'Quick and Dirty'.

[39]   Hugh Wilson, 'Cosmetic enhancement, so to speak', *SMH*, 21 July 2004, p. 11. See also Graham Philips, 'Voices from the deep', *Sunday Telegraph,* 28 July 2002, p. 32. Neils Nehring comments on the connection between low-register vocalizing and 'gravitas' in the work of singer Frank Discussion of the band The Feederz, in 'The Situationist International in American Hardcore Punk, 1982–2002', *Popular Music and Society* 29/5 (December 2006), 519–30, see p. 524.

[40]   Vladimir Konečni, 'Social Interaction and Musical Preference', in D. Deutsch (ed.), *The Psychology of Music* (New York, 1982) 497–516; see 507–8. My thanks to Laura

an Italian neuroscience research team led by Dr Michelangelo Iannone reported that music played at dance club volume also worsened the 'comedown' effect of the recreational drug ecstasy.[41] Sound pollution driven by excessive volume is a major social problem.

> Ear damage is caused by the combination of loudness, the length of time of exposure and the time of recovery. Ear damage is permanent and incurable. Ear damage caused by noisy work environments and by pop concerts, dance-halls, parties, and walkmans is a concern of the Dutch government.[42]

Not only the Dutch, as later we shall review the level of concern in various countries over the impact of high volume acoustic technologies. Music can also be implicated in the onset of epileptic seizures. Hans H. Reese observed the phenomenon called musicogenic epilepsy: 'the association between musical stimuli and an epileptic attack, ... epileptic seizures are precipitated only by specifically irritating music'.[43] These musical potentialities are related to hearing in general, and take no account of individual variations affecting acuity, but which may well play a role in defining responses to music and sound. The deterioration with age in the perception of high register sounds has enabled the development of the Mosquito Ultrasonic Youth Deterrent which emits a continuous flatline sound at a frequency that is intended to be heard only by people under 25. The sound is so irritating that it drives away potential youthful graffitists, thieves and vandals.[44]

The word 'irritating' pushes us across the uncertain border between somatic and cognitive disorder. 'Irritation' is both an organic and psychic term, and physiological disorientation exists in a clear if ill-defined connection with intellectual and emotional destabilization, the latter of which may incorporate profound ambivalence. Thus, a report of a fetish and S/M club in London, where a speaker projects from the boot of a car to which 'a stream of girls are strapped': 'A bass note fills the room and rocks the car. It's meant to be the magic frequency 33Hz, which will bring a girl to orgasm. The girls enjoy it, but none of them appear

Mitchell for referring me to and discussing this article with me.

[41]   BBC News online (http://www.bbc.co.uk/), 16 February 2006.

[42]   Hannah Bosma, 'Different Noises in Electroacoustic Music', *ASCA Conference Sonic Interventions: Pushing the Boundaries of Cultural Analysis*, Reader for Panel 2: *The Sonic in the 'Silent' Arts and Bring in the Noise*, Coordinator: Sylvia Mieszkowski (2005), pp.18–23, see p. 18.

[43]   Hans H. Reese, 'Relation of music to diseases of the brain', in E. Podolsky (ed.), *Music Therapy* (New York, 1954), pp. 43–54.

[44]   http://www.compoundsecurity.co.uk/ at 17 January 2008; see also Lucy Ward, '3,300 sales and still rising – ultrasonic answer to teenage gangs sets alarm bells ringing', *The Guardian*, 17 March 2007, p. 13.

[sic] to go all the way.'[45] Physical and emotional arousal mingled with trepidation and uncertainty in a theatrical setting – the force field here seems appropriate to the tensions of sado-masochism, yet also reflects the ambiguity of so much sonic experience, which moves back and forth across the borders of pain and pleasure in ways that a reductive romanticization of music elides. There is no absolute threshold between sonic pain and pleasure that can be defined simply in terms of sonic effect, organic impact, musical form or genre. This is partly because the threshold is ambiguous – sometimes we enjoy what takes us to, and beyond, the limits of organic tolerability – and because it is not the character of the music that makes the difference. Organic damage may well be produced by music that provides some form of aesthetic or political pleasure, while music intended to induce a sense of physical and mental well-being may well generate violent conflict. It will be our argument that any music, however sweet or innocuous, can be deployed to engender pain.

I conclude this section with reference to an attempt to measure the relationship between music and pain thresholds, which underlines the complexity of the relationship between music, pain and pleasure. The results of Laura Mitchell's study, completed in 2004, were first recorded in her doctoral dissertation *An Experimental Investigation of the Effects of Music Listening on Pain*.[46] The following draws out some of her findings relevant to this study. Mitchell wished to investigate 'audioanalgesia' – how music might affect pain perception. She began with an investigation of 'the effects of water temperature and gender on tolerance and intensity rating' involving 26 participants (12 male and 14 female).[47] A cold pressor trial involves immersion of the subject's hand in a standardized circulating cold water bath at a temperature based on previous methodological studies. The object in this case was to measure tolerance time under different acoustic stimuli; that is, as measured by a stopwatch, how long is the subject able to tolerate the cold water? This was supplemented by other measurements, including a range of standardized discomfort ratings as estimated by the subject.[48] This was followed

---

[45]   Nick Barham, *Dis/connected: Why our kids are turning their backs on everything we thought we knew* (London, 2005), p. 190.

[46]   Laura Mitchell, *An Experimental Investigation of the Effects of Music Listening on Pain* (Unpub. Doctoral Thesis, Department of Psychology, School of Life Sciences, Glasgow Caledonian University, 2004). I wish to thank Dr Mitchell for allowing me to read, cite and paraphrase extensively from her, at that time unpublished thesis, and also for her follow-up discussions both face-to-face and by email correspondence. She has also taken time to read my own discussion, below, and confirms that the summaries of her work and findings are accurate and my own extrapolations are warranted.

[47]   Laura A. Mitchell, Raymond A.R. MacDonald and Eric E. Brodie, 'Temperature and the Cold Pressor Test', *The Journal of Pain*, 5/4 (May 2004), pp. 233–8; see p. 234.

[48]   Laura A. Mitchell and Raymond A.R. MacDonald, 'An Experimental Investigation of the Effects of Preferred and Relaxing Music on Pain Perception, *Journal of Music Therapy*, 43/4 (2006), pp. 295–316; see pp. 301–2.

by an attempt to determine the kinds of music with the greatest anxiolytic effect. 'Anxiolytic' is technically defined as music capable of reducing anxiety, but in more general usage as music with 'perceived pain relieving qualities'.[49] The enquiry then proceeded in three stages.[50]

Stage One involved a comparison of the effects of 54 participants' favourite choice of music, to a white noise control and to a sample of New Age anxiolytic, in the relief of experimentally induced pain. With the exception of one male who brought folk music from his country of birth, the profile of the 'preferred' music – chosen by each participant to bring to the laboratory – was categorized by Mitchell as 'popular. They encompassed a range of popular styles including 'ballads, folk/ rock, techno/dance, hip-hop and punk. The key point is, however, that there are no commonalties in terms of structural features of the music chosen'.[51] Generally, preferred music proved most effective in distraction from and control of pain. By some measures, there was no difference between white noise and anxiolytic.[52] A further stage was a survey involving 318 chronic pain sufferers (198 females and 114 males), ranging from ages 24 to 90-years-old, seeking to find out how many felt that music listening played a role in their pain management, and to investigate their own perceptions of the benefits.[53] Participants reported that distraction and relaxation were the most frequently perceived benefits of music in maintaining a general quality of life and in the management of pain.

Among Mitchell's theoretical extrapolations, the following are most relevant to this stage in our own enquiry:

> In the two main experimental studies, preferred music was found to increase tolerance of pain significantly more effectively than a white noise control, anxiolytic music listening and a mental arithmetic task. ... The findings regarding reduction of pain were less clear, with only female participants reporting significantly lower pain intensity

---

[49] Ibid., p. 43. Three genres often used for relaxation were used: 'classical, ambient dance and specially designed 'new age' music. In particular: *Eine Kleine Nachtmusik* (from 'The most relaxing classical album in the world ever' vol. II), *Carnelian* (anxiolytic New Age) from 'An introduction to music to relax, inspire and uplift you', vol III); *Softwatch*, by Craig Guiller (ambient dance). Participants reported the New Age music to be most relaxing, even though the ambient dance was preferred by most participants (ibid., p. 69) *Carnelian* was then selected as the anxiolytic sample in the first of these, described below. 'A white noise listening condition was also selected as a control' (ibid., p. 64).

[50] Accounts of these three stages have since been published, making them more accessible. Accordingly, I have cited these published reports where possible. When I have wished to draw on aspects of Mitchell's work not covered in those publications, I have cited the unpublished dissertation as 'Unpub. Diss.'.

[51] Ibid., p. 309.

[52] Ibid., p. 307. The complete list of musical items is given on pp. 315–16.

[53] An account of this stage is published in Laura A. Mitchell, Raymond A.R. MacDonald, Christina Knussen and Michael G. Serpell, 'A survey investigation of the effects of music listening on chronic pain', in *Psychology of Music*, 35/1 (2007): 37–57.

on visual analogue scale while listening to preferred music [,] than both anxiolytic music and white noise, with anxiolytic music in turn resulting in a significantly lower rating than white noise. ... sensory pain was significantly reduced in both genders in the preferred music condition as opposed to white noise.[54]

The sense of control is central to many negative reactions to music. Our studies will reinforce Mitchell's point that much music associated with violence is not in any obvious way physically or aesthetically painful, but its imposition is a matter of power relations, from the noisy neighbour to interrogation in captivity. Much ... but not all. Our enquiries below suggest that in the apparently unlimited range of music we considered, one common factor is that imposed music will always tend to constitute a form of violence to a greater or lesser degree, and in any society. However, music of choice in a given situation is not necessarily analgesic or unambiguously therapeutic. A substantial category of cases emerging from our own research reinforces the point, in that the choice of music can endanger the chooser and those around him. This is exemplified in the case of police in New South Wales who reportedly respond to the beginning of a high speed pursuit by putting on 'pursuit tapes' in police cars, recordings of heavy metal 'and other high energy music', in order to raise their level of risk-taking in the chase.[55] This is topical, but neither new nor localized, as exemplified in the examples considered below of war-cries of antiquity, and US tank crews in Iraq piping heavy metal through the vehicle's intercom to increase their aggressiveness.

The results of Mitchell's preliminary survey also indicated that most participants (six out of ten) declared that they preferred the ambient dance music, but five out of ten found the anxiolytic selection most relaxing.[56] That means that at least one – and probably more – preferred dance music but was more relaxed by anxiolytic. As we have seen, later stages of testing suggested that by all the measurements being applied, preferred music was more effective in the tolerance of pain than anxiolytic (and white noise). This suggests something very interesting about music preferences in a context of seeking relaxation: that the music someone prefers in relation to pain relief is not necessarily anxiolytic. Various subgenres of metal have become notoriously associated with violence. As in the case above of the New South Wales police, and in cases documented below involving military personnel engaged on aggressive patrols, heavy metal is often deployed in situations requiring increased aggression. But it is relevant also to note that metal can achieve the objectives of supposedly anxiolytic music, as suggested by the results of a study conducted at the University of Warwick, reported in March 2007. It found that highly gifted students whose status as 'gifted outsiders' led to feelings of frustration and anger, 'turn to heavy metal as a way of

---

[54]   Mitchell, Unpub. Diss., p. 150.

[55]   Anon (former police officer), 'All Pumped Up', *SMH News Review*, 13–14 November 2004, p. 34.

[56]   Mitchell, Unpub. Diss., p. 69.

relieving that stress'.[57] This foreshadows an apparent paradox that we shall return to later: that music that supposedly arouses aggression, can also simultaneously diffuse it. Music experience is ambiguous, with, in Galileo's words on certain tones, the capacity 'at one and the same Time to kiss and bite'.[58]

It appears that preferred music overall may be analgesic, therapeutic – good for the subject's welfare. But this is not so in the case of music that raises levels of personal risk. Furthermore, while lowering perceptions of pain is analgesic, it is not necessarily healthy in the long term. Pain itself is frequently a signal of organic threat. As in the case of certain drugs (notably alcohol) and painkillers (as used by athletes during sports events), diminishing the perception of pain can lead to serious organic damage. Preferred music might therefore lead to damage in the organism. The most obvious case – again, documented later in this study – is voluntary prolonged exposure to loud music in clubs or through personal stereos. It seems that the following conclusions may be cautiously drawn from Mitchell's study, conclusions which were also emerging from our own research:

1. Music listening can have analgesic/therapeutic effects, but most particularly if it is music over which we have control: ie, our preferred music at that moment.
2. Music which, because of its formal character, is likely to be regarded as anxiolytic, is rarely the preferred music in the control of pain, even though it is effective in pain relief, and perhaps even more so in anxiety relief.
3. The patient's relationship with the music is more important than its formal characteristics in assessing the use of music as analgesic.
4. The relationship between taste and analgesic benefit is ambiguous. An individual's preferred music is by no means necessarily the most beneficial to her/his own physical welfare. Musically, we don't necessarily know what it good for us.

These data emphasize further that the connection between the cognitive and the physiological effects of music is erratic and the distinction unclear. In conducting this study we have been constantly sucked into liminal spaces, and one of them is implied in the mind/body binary. I am invoking the distinction here primarily for purposes of arranging an argument, but in practice, and especially in music experience, it is misleading. The binary has some persuasive power in visual epistemologies (and is arguably historically coeval with it in the West), partly because of the close physiological connection between the eye and the cortex. The body seems to intervene less in the connection between seeing and knowing than in the distinctive phenomenology and physiology of hearing, which is a messier business in which the organic and the cognitive, the physical and the aesthetic, are stickily

---

[57]   No byline, syndicated from *Telegraph* (London), 'Metalheads not meatheads but scholars', *SMH* online, 23 April 2007. See further below, p. 115.

[58]   Cited in Schmidt, 'Hearing Loss', p. 51.

entangled with each other. Apart from what we have abstracted on this subject from the work of Zajonc and Ledoux, in reporting on her own research, Mitchell cites a number of studies which make it difficult to disentangle chemistry from sensibility in sonic experience. Melzack and Wall's 'gate control theory' and the relationship between laughter and physiological as well as mental stimuli, undermine attempts to detach aesthetic and moral predispositions from corporeal processes.[59]

Yet at the same time, Mitchell's sources also suggest that a given piece of music is likely to generate mind and body responses which are in tension with each other, 'to physiologically arouse and mentally relax concurrently'.[60] Furthermore, what might be widely regarded as anxiolytic music (and Mozart was one example), can be a source of profound irritation if imposed on people, even irrespective of musical preferences that include Mozart. Hence the use of Frank Sinatra, Barry Manilow or classical music as a way of regulating who occupies public spaces, as discussed below. It suggests, further, that subcultural identities can be targeted as 'niche victims'. It further implies that arguments about universalist aesthetics are nonsense unless one accepts the corollary: that those who are unresponsive to what we think of as the universal appeal of art are afflicted with subhuman sensibilities associated with such factors as genetics, place, class, race, gender and of course taste. This is a dangerous equation, since it enables us to alterize certain repellant forms of human conduct, to lose sight of the 'heart of darkness' that can be called up in anyone.

The fundamental message emerging from this discussion is that we cannot point to any piece of music and say that it must generate violence, but nor can we say that it cannot under any circumstances. One-dimensional demonization of any kind of music is simply specious. But so is romanticization. Some sounds incorporated into music will, it appears, have a potential to cause physiological damage, yet the music may nonetheless be to an individual's taste. And preference, no matter how inexplicable or perverse, seems central to musical politics. If we impose our own preferred music on someone else in a way that is beyond their control, even thinking to share our pleasure, we are more likely to take them closer to the experience of pain. Consider, then, how much music is imposed upon us both privately and in public spaces. And consider also therefore the pervasive potential for pain, irritation, violence, no matter what the music.

Conclusion: A Comment on Key Terms

The foregoing is intended to break up the terrain of music discourse impacted by the force and weight of cumulative public and academic simplifications. Our central terms in this book are 'popular', 'music' and 'violence'. Without wishing

---

[59]   Mitchell and MacDonald, 'Experimental Investigation', p. 296; Mitchell, MacDonald and Brodie, 'A Comparison', p. 344.

[60]   Mitchell, MacDonald and Brodie, 'A Comparison', p. 345.

to make them too cumbersome for the journey, we will make some explanatory comments about the terms. Like the description of man as a 'featherless biped', there is always someone waiting with the equivalent of a plucked chicken to confound definitions. But we need to dilate briefly on the way we understand these key tools, even if we shall deploy them rather crudely at some points.

'Popular'

Surely the most contested of our three terms. A history of debates about 'popular' would take us a great way towards understanding its politics, but also take us a great way from our present purposes. The terrain referred to by the word is travelled publicly in the media with an almost enviable heedlessness of the barely concealed hazards. It is to a great extent because the term is so widely used that it commands attention. Something is meant by it, but no-one seems to be sure what it is. The caution with which it is approached by popular music scholars is most heterogeneously exemplified in a recent debate in the journal *Popular Music*.[61] A number of points emerge from that debate that will help us in this brief overview to illustrate the complexity of the term.

It is sufficiently clear in academic scholarship that notwithstanding the untroubled media categorizations, it is not always possible to identify what people mean by the term just by pointing at a text or image. Contemporary mass mediations enable all images (acoustic and visual) to be taken over by anyone within the mass media network, sampled, cut 'n' mixed, reconstructed, internationally circulated. There won't be much disagreement that, say, Nirvana is popular music, while a concert hall performance of *Carmina Burana* or Wagnerian opera is not. But what are we to make of the use of Orff's composition when used as soundtrack music for John Boormann's film *Excalibur*, to sell instant coffee, as promotional music for the Sydney 2000 Olympics, sampled in a duet between rappers Nas and Puff Daddy on 'Hate me now', or used at US basketball matches 'to rile up' the crowds?[62] Where do we situate Wagner's music if it is coming from a helicopter to the accompaniment of an attack on a Vietnamese village in the film *Apocalypse Now*? Or Beethoven's 'Für Elise' when it is selling MacDonalds?[63]

---

[61] *Popular Music*, 'Can we get rid of the "popular" in popular music?'. Any of the following provides a useful introduction to current issues in popular music studies: David Hesmondhalgh and Keith Negus, *Popular Music Studies* (London, 2002); Bruce Horner and Thomas Swiss (eds), *Key Terms in Popular Music and Culture* (Oxford and Malden Mass, 1999); Roy Shuker, *Key Concepts in Popular Music* (London and New York, 1998); Jason Toynbee, *Making Popular Music: Musicians, Creativity and Institutions* (London, 2000).

[62] Ken McLeod, '"We are the Champions": Masculinities, Sports and Popular Culture', *Popular Music and Society*, 29/5 (2006): 531–47; see p. 533.

[63] On the rap duet and on 'Für Elise' references, see further Mina Yang, 'Für Elise, circa 2000: postmodern Readings of Beethoven in Popular Contexts', *Popular Music and*

This at least we can be clear about: to understand and categorize any musical 'text' as popular music, we have to think also of context. That context includes mediations. The astonishing proliferation of information, images, signs, representations, has transformed our understanding of popular culture. Contemporary electronic media provide access to visual and acoustic images from every place and every time. This radical transformation of our environment is an invasion, and largely a replacement, of the culture in which the idea of 'the popular' was first formed. Some centuries ago, popular culture – an idea at that time closer to the culture of 'the people' – would have included dancing, sports, theatre, bear-baiting, maypole dancing, playing music and singing, games: all 'realtime/realspace' activities.[64] The 'people' could not have got their hands on the image of the Mona Lisa or the ceiling of the Sistine chapel to play around with. Mass mediations have broken down the literal and metaphorical boundaries which once enabled high and low culture to be kept apart. Mass media, from print to internet, have democratized access to cultural images and practices which had previously been the sign of superior taste and refinement. Popular culture thus acquired an association with mass mediated culture. It is often now argued that popular culture is defined in terms of mass mediations. I think this is a necessary but insufficient recognition. Context includes usage, forms and places of cultural practice. An exclusive emphasis on mediations leaves out continuing realtime/ realspace cultural practices which are the historical foundations of the culture of everyday life: sports, games, domestic and public music-making and a range of hobby activities from hiking to cooking.

This is not to seek a watertight definition of the 'popular', but to signal that we knowingly embark on a leaky vessel in dangerous waters. For the most part, however, we remain on the safe side of the Pillars of Hercules. Our usage of the term will refer to musical form and genre, but also the mediations through which the music is embodied and circulated. It will also take into account usage, in particular the deployment of music outside the domain of high art.

'Music/Musicality'

Societies that have a word for music thus agree in recognizing its distinctiveness; but they will not necessarily agree on the point at which sound becomes music. Similarly, societies may agree on the existence of 'singing' but not on the point at which it may be discriminated from speech. Furthermore, the distinction between what is deemed 'music' and 'not-music', or (painful) noise, is in fact so central to much of our study, that the word cannot be taken as a given. We therefore wish the term, as we use it, to be understood in the broader sense of musicality. That is, the incorporation in sound and speech of features which are regarded as

---

Society 29/1 (February2006): 1–15.

[64]   A useful introduction to the early history of popular culture is Peter Burke, *Popular Culture in Early Modern Europe* (London, 1978).

manifesting musicality: purposeful variations in pitch timbre, rhythm, tempo and, in groups, the organization and patterning of collective utterance. The point about this graduated distinction may be illustrated in the unfolding of a black Baptist sermon, which begins in speech, and ends in song, but without the transitional point being clear.

By this model, we may describe a war-cry, the shouting in unison of political demonstrators or sports spectators, as manifesting musicality; likewise, musicality is to be heard in bells, sirens, and even in the tuning of motor engines for affect rather than mechanical efficiency. On the other hand it may be denied to exist by its opponents in what is presented as music, as reflected perennially in the emergence of new popular music forms from jazz, through rock, to techno and rap. Musicality may be therefore mediated through instruments, the voice (both non-verbal vocalization and lyrics), and '*sons trouvés*'.

'Violence'

Violence is linked with pain, since each can be the outcome of the other. Violence causes pain, but enduring high levels of pain can lead to violence. Apart from the dual (and generally simultaneous) levels of cognitive and physical violence/pain, these two may lie at many points on a spectrum, running from a minor negative cognitive response to physical torture caused either by music or in tactical or even incidental association with it. For present purposes therefore, we are locating violence in any response that is neither unequivocal pleasure nor indifference, or which induces physical or symbolic violation. We have articulated this in a way that recognizes that 'pleasure' sometimes derives from or is in defiance of self-inflicted physical damage. Masochism is still pain, suicide is still violence. 'Violence' carries with it a resonance that is most likely to induce feelings of unqualified abhorrence, yet, however unpalatable the idea, violence clearly has some kind of positive association and function in all societies. Considering the ferocity of some of the Somme fighting in the First World War, military historian John Keegan concluded that, 'easy killing does seem to generate in human beings symptoms of pleasure'.[65]

Given the focus of this study, it is apposite to extend Keegan's observation to participants in popular music. Apart from those who use music to incite violence upon others, there is abundant testimony to the pleasure of experiencing violence on the part of those involved in music. When Varg Vikernes of the Norwegian black metal band Mayhem was arrested for church arson he claimed that prison conditions were too lenient and asked the police to use violence on him.[66] Moshpits provide gratifying opportunities for experiencing violence as both giver and receiver.

---

[65]   John Keegan, *The Face of Battle: A Study of Agincourt, Waterloo and the Somme* (London, 2004, first published London, 1976), p. 278.

[66]   Michael Moynihan and Didrik Søderlind, *Lords of Chaos: The Bloody Rise of the Satanic Metal Underground* (Los Angeles, 1998), p. 42.

A bank-worker declared, 'I like to mosh. I like the violence. I like the violation of the pit', 'I like the pain of a rough pit. I get off on it ... I like a little pain'. It is not an uncommon view among moshers, as in the comment by an advertising agency employee, 'I have a passion for keeping a little violence in my life'. Another who works in a design agency described as 'a great feeling' the pain in his body after it had been 'abused' in the pit which, recalling Keegan's comments, he described as a zone of 'combat'. Others spoke of being advocates of 'unnecessary violence' and losing fear of pain: 'it should be violent'. Neil Busch, from the band And You Will Know Us By The Trail of the Dead and also an anthropologist, recalled that he found it 'very therapeutic to be covered in sweat and to crash into people'.[67]

It might be urged that these are aberrant pathologies, but the function of violence as an authorized form of socialization seems to be ubiquitous in communities. In his *Travels*, John de Mandeville reported a society that practised a form of ritual cannibalism. Upon receiving advice from their priests regarding the treatment of the sick that the patient cannot be cured, they kill her or him 'and then they slice up the body into pieces and invite all his friends to come and eat from his dead body, and they summon as many pipers as they can, and thus eat with great rejoicing and great solemnity. And when they have consumed him they take the bones and bury him singing and making great celebration and melody'.[68] De Mandeville's travel narratives were almost certainly apocryphal, which makes them a comfortingly oblique way of approaching the fact that violence is frequently institutionalized by societies for therapeutic and cathartic purposes, as in capital punishment. The practice he describes has clear parallels with more familiar forms of institutionalized violation, as in (among other religions), the Christian ritual of communion, the eating of Christ's body (whether actual or trans-substantiated) as a redemptive ceremony, accompanied by music.

Just as every musical transaction is potentially both positive and negative, violence itself is an ambiguous presence in civilization. We may applaud music for 'setting us free', but for another, our freedom threatens to become invasion. We may deplore violence as the brutal exercise of unequal power relations, but, however unpalatable the idea, violence gives pleasure to somebody. It is a sense of the double edge of both these phenomena – music and violence – that informs our study.

---

[67]   Joe Ambrose, *Moshpit: The Violent World of Mosh Pit Culture* (London, New York, Sydney, 2001), pp. 9, 11, 160, 168–9, 163, 166, 76.

[68]   Cited Carlo Ginzburg, *The Cheese and the Worms: The Cosmos of a Sixteenth-Century Miller*, Trans. John and Anne Tedeschi (Baltimore, 1992), p. 46.

Chapter 2
Music and Violence in History

Bruce Johnson

From Antiquity

The connection between music and violence extends back to farthest antiquity, and that history itself throws up issues which have explanatory power in the analysis of the present. The objective of this chapter is to correct any impression that popular music and its political dynamics are an exclusively modern phenomenon. Furthermore, the history of this relationship is a way of modelling the social, political and technological emergence of modernity. Apart from providing historical depth to the discussion, this chapter will also serve to help precipitate a developing taxonomy of the variety of connections between popular music and violence.

The connection between music and violence is a powerful and transcultural source of mythic and historical narratives. It is the potentially destructive power of music that underpins Homer's account of Ulysses and the sirens whose song drew sailors to their death, and whose connection with danger would be commemorated in the name given to a sound alarm invented in the nineteenth century.[1] So too the story of the Lorelei whose voices provoked suicidal melancholy which drove men to drown themselves in the Rhine. In the Old Testament, when Joshua's army besieged Jericho:

> So the people shouted when the priests blew with the trumpets: and it came to pass, when the people heard the sound of the trumpet, and the people shouted with a great shout, that the wall fell down flat, so that the people went up into the city, every man straight before him, and they took the city.
>
> And they utterly destroyed all that was in the city, both man and woman, young and old, and ox, and sheep, and ass, with the edge of the sword.
>
> The Book of Joshua, chapter 6, verses 20–21.

The Finnish national epic *The Kalevala* is assembled from stories that go back to the first millennium. The first major encounter is between its dominant figure,

---

[1] On the invention of the siren, see Michelle Duncan, 'Hydromancy: Of Sirens, Songs, and Soma', *ASCA Conference Sonic Interventions: Pushing the Boundaries of Cultural Analysis*, Reader for Panel 2: *The Sonic in the 'Silent' Arts and Bring in the Noise*, Sylvia Mieszkowski, Coordinator (Amsterdam, 2005), pp. 59–64.

Väinämöinen, the first man on earth, and a young challenger to his power, Joukahainen. The contest is conducted by the two men singing at each other until Joukahainen, musically overwhelmed, sinks into a slimy swamp, but spared on the condition that he promise his sister Aino to Väinämöinen. In a later period, a Pied Piper took revenge on the townsfolk of Hamelin by luring their children into the earth with music, never to be seen again.

Plato and Cassiodorus believed that certain modes could induce mental disturbances, and the early Christian church believed that pagan residues in music could be exploited by the Devil to produce depravity, and that witches used music to carry out their evil work. These connections are rearticulated in the tradition of pacts with the Devil, in which musical prowess was exchanged for the soul, a narrative that surfaces again in a range of myths, from Tartini's 'Devil's trill' and Paganini's virtuosity, to blues musician Robert Johnson's transaction at the crossroads.[2] Jacques Chailley wrote of the power of certain rhythms and tempos to unleash primitive and destructive instincts, and Stravinsky's *Rite of Spring* notoriously produced riots at its first performance.[3] In the twentieth century, every emergent popular music, from jazz to rock to rap, was regarded as inciting immoral and anti-social conduct, a conviction reinforced by sexual freedom among 1920s jazz flappers, seat-slashing and other vandalism by young 1950s rock audiences, and drive-by shootings in late twentieth-century Los Angeles. The Stones' Altamont concert is still often taken as a confirmation of the dark side of 1960s youth music.

Perhaps the most ancient, durable, and explicit deployments of music in the service of violence is the war song, or the war cry. Greek galley oarsmen around 400 BC had a range of chants, including one for battle.[4] Plutarch reported that no sooner did Cato the Elder lead his men into attack with a war cry and a blast of trumpets, the enemy fled.[5] When King Richard I arrived in Sicily to join the crusades, his 'resounding trumpets and loud horns struck fear and dread into the souls of the citizens'.[6] The value ascribed to military musicians for signalling orders, marching, religious observances, heraldic occasions and building morale, is indicated by the frequency of their presence on military expeditions.

---

[2]   The case of Tartini's 'Devil's trill', supposedly inspired by a dream in which Tartini heard Satan performing one of the former's sonatas, is an effect that continues to be explored in music technology: see Augoyard, *Sonic Experience*, pp. 129–30.

[3]   See further Juliette Alvin, *Music Therapy* (London, 1975), pp. 13–14, 40, 69.

[4]   David Proctor, *Music of the Sea* (London, 1992), p. 6.

[5]   Cited by Peter Denney, 'Scythes, Swords and the Bitter-Sweet Melody of Merry England', in *Plebeian Prospects: Landscape, Liberty and Labouring-Class Culture in Britain, 1700-1830* (PhD thesis, University of York). Denney's thesis itself includes a stimulating and deeply researched account of acoustically mediated class conflict. My thanks to Peter for making this available to me, and for extensive discussions of his work.

[6]   Proctor, *Music of the Sea*, p. 9.

Notwithstanding the financial and logistical constraints on the meticulously planned invasion of France which led to his victory at Agincourt in 1415, Henry V included 18 musicians in his own retinue, each occupying the same expeditionary space and receiving the same pay of 12 pence per day, as a fighting man-at-arms.[7] Ships of the Spanish Armada in 1588 carried trumpeters, drummers and fife players whose battle orders were to play incessantly to enliven their own men and frighten the enemy,[8] and as Nelson's fleet prepared to engage the enemy off Trafalgar in 1805, and in the bloody heat of the battle, naval bands on board played songs such as 'Rule Britannia', 'Britons Strike Home' and 'The Downfall of Paris'.[9] Tit for tat: as Napoleon's troops deployed before the Battle of Waterloo, their enthusiasm was aroused by the regimental bands playing marches of the revolution, mingled with the drums of the infantry and the cavalry bugles with, according to one participant, 'grandiose effect'.[10] Music itself could become the site of military contestation, as in the battle between seventeenth-century trade rivals, the Dutch navy and the Portuguese-held fortress at Macao: 'The ships drew off at sunset, but celebrated the expected victory by blowing trumpets and beating drums all night. Not to be outdone by this bravado, Lopo Sarmento de Carvalho ordered similar martial rejoicings to be made on the city's bulwarks.'[11]

In the twentieth century this form of state-based conflict would be repeated in such events as four decades of a 'sound war', in which North and South Korea exchanged 'anthems and invective across their common border through loudspeakers.[12] The effectiveness of sound and music in such violent contests had considerable historical as well as mythic authority. Preparing to cross the Rhone as he began his invasion of Italy in 218 BC, Hannibal's army was confronted by Gallic warriors who 'came surging to the river bank, howling and singing as their custom was, shaking their shields above their heads and brandishing their spears'.[13] Hannibal easily defeated these singing warriors, but he was less successful 16 years later at the battle of Zama that ended his campaign. According to Livy, music was a significant presence in this defeat:

> There were ... factors which seem trivial to recall, but proved of great importance at the time of action. The Roman war-cry was louder and more terrifying because it was in

---

[7] Juliet Barker, *Agincourt: The King, The Campaign The Battle* (London, 2005), p. 138.

[8] Proctor, *Music of the Sea*, p. 14.

[9] Tom Pocock (ed.), *Trafalgar: An Eyewitness History* (London, 2005) pp. 67, 81.

[10] Alessandro Barbero, *The Battle: A History of the Battle of Waterloo*, trans. John Cullen (London, 2005), pp. 86–7.

[11] Proctor, *Music of the Sea*, p. 33.

[12] 'Ended. A propaganda war' in the Milestones section of *Time Magazine*, June 28, 2004: 17.

[13] Livy, *The War With Hannibal*, trans. Aubrey de Selincourt (Harmondsworth, 1965), p. 67.

unison, whereas the cries from the Carthaginian side were discordant, coming as they did from a mixed assortment of peoples with a variety of mother tongues.[14]

The emphasis on the efficacy of concord foregrounds the idea of musicality in the war chant, and anticipates also an exhortation attributed by the historian Jordanes to Attila in 451 AD, urging his army to 'Despise this union of discordant men', as he prepared for a decisive battle with Roman and Visigoth forces under the leadership of Aetius and Theodoric on the Catalaunian Plains.[15]

From the ancient world through to the twentieth century, the historical record resonates with this connection between the organized collective sound and voice, and military prowess. In 1319, in a skirmish between English and a heavily outnumbered Scots force near Milton some 12 miles north of York, the Scots set fire to a large quantity of hay to confuse the enemy. 'As the smoke cleared, the English saw the Scots drawn up in a single schiltron which advanced towards them with a shout so terrifying that they lost all faith in divine protection and took to their heels.'[16] Nearly 500 years later at the crossing of the Berenzina river during the demoralized French retreat from Moscow in 1812 (a devastating attrition later to receive its own musical commemoration by Tchaikovsky), the attacking Swiss sang 'the old mountain lied "Unser Leben Gleicht der Reise"'.[17] In spite of changes in the acoustics of modern warfare, considered below, the unmediated massed voice of the enemy continued to have a powerful effect on morale well into the twentieth century. On the Eastern front during the Second World War, German General von Mellenthin recalled the terrifying effect of a Russian infantry charge, even on a well-armoured German position: 'A Russian infantry attack is an awe-inspiring spectacle; the long grey waves come pounding on, uttering fierce cries, and the defending troops require nerves of steel.' In a footnote he noted that the night before an attack the Russians were often supplied with vodka, and 'we could hear them roaring like devils'.[18]

Later in this study we will be discussing the importance of music in individual and collective disintegration, especially with the emergence of technologized acoustics and acoustic technologies. It is worth spending a moment, therefore, to remind ourselves again of this converse power of music in relation to violent conflict. Fighting morale and solidarity have always been fortified by musicality. Notwithstanding the bitter political and religious divisions within Ireland in the early years of the twentieth century, it was reported that both Catholic and Protestant

---

[14]   Ibid., pp. 661–2.

[15]   Cited in John Man, *Attila the Hun: A Barbarian King and the Fall of Rome* (London, 2005), p. 281.

[16]   Ronald McNair Scott, *Robert the Bruce: King of Scots* (New York, 1989, first published 1982), p. 193.

[17]   Adam Zamoyski, *1812: Napoleon's Fatal March on Moscow* (London, 2004), p. 473.

[18]   Cited in Keegan, *The Face of Battle*, p. 288.

Irish were united when 'the pipes of the Royal Irish howled out Brian Boru' during the assault on Guillemont in September 1916, and when a northern-raised battalion of Irish Rifles met a southern battalion on the march with its band playing the old rebel air 'She's The Most Distressful Country', there were cheers of approval.[19] As a volunteer wondering why he had enlisted in Kitchener's New Army in 1915, J.B. Priestley felt no military enthusiasm until becoming part of a cohesive acoustic community: 'All four battalions had a band; and all along the route we were waved at and cheered, not foolishly either, for an infantry brigade marching in full equipment with its bands booming and clashing is an impressive spectacle.'[20]

The resources devoted by armed forces to musicality throughout recorded history is clear enough testimony to the recognition of its value in mobilizing aggressive *esprit*, including in the heat of battle itself. The British *Infantry Training 1914* manual stipulated that when an assault was commenced, the commander 'will order the charge to be sounded, the call will be taken up by all buglers, and all neighbouring units will join in the charge as quickly as possible. During the delivery of the assault the men will cheer, bugles be sounded, and pipes played'.[21] The bugle, of course, was a logistical necessity for communicating orders, but their prescribed continuance, the cheering and the pipes are a recognition also of a crucial morale factor.

If the pagan, the Satanic and the secular drew on music to unite their allies and confound their enemies, so too did God, in a recurring motif of the Christian era, as in Benvenuto Cellini's 'Capitolo' poem as he reflects on his life to that point:

> I heard a trumpet with a sound like doom;
> With all revealed, I told them what it meant,
> My rashness forced on me by darkest gloom.[22]

---

[19]   Richard Holmes, *Tommy: The British Soldier on the Western Front 1914–1918* (London, 2005), pp. 154, 156.

[20]   Ibid., p. 160. In a less scopocentric culture, he might have thought to say, 'We sounded like soldiers', and referred to 'an impressive sound'. The profound importance of singing, as a military morale-builder, as a distraction and release (obscene, ironic or disrespectful songs), as a way of generating bellicosity, as a form of consolation (religious songs) is summarized in the account of various soldiers' songs, ibid., pp. 498–505, 535, 602–3. Among many other compilations of such songs, there is a useful guide to those sung by the Australian Imperial Force (AIF) in Chapter 4 and endnotes of Graham Seal, *Inventing Anzac: The Digger and National Mythology* (St Lucia Qld, 2004). Although tangential to this study, there is an intriguing investigation to be made of what appears to be the decline of troop singing between the First and Second World Wars, and its connection with more technologized forms of troop deployment and entertainment.

[21]   Cited in Holmes, *Tommy*, pp. 381–2.

[22]   Benvenuto Cellini, *Autobiography*, trans. George Bull (Harmondsworth, 1979), p. 236; written 1558–66; this edition copyright 1956.

It is the trumpets of God that will signal the last judgement, consigning the damned to the agonies of eternal damnation. Likewise in this world, one of the perennial functions of music-making has been to proclaim state-sanctioned punishment. Music traditionally accompanied public displays of justice, as in trumpets on the journey to the pillory and chants and the tolling of bells for the condemned and excommunicated.[23]

Equally, citizens' attempts to retaliate against the state have perennially been mediated at a site at which music and violence are complicit. Convicts under colonial Australian authority possessed a repertoire of songs that politicized their alleged criminality. Deported Irish rebels could proclaim their intransigence through the singing of nationalist songs, and in doing so ran the risk of even more extreme forms of punishment than was characteristically meted out for theft or absconding. The official punishment logs usually record up to 50 lashes for pilfering or dereliction, but for an intractable Irish prisoner William Riley, the chillingly impassive record reads '100 lashes for singing a song' – more than enough to flay a man to the bone.[24] The lash continues to be one of the measures taken to enforce such censorship, as in modern Iran where, in 2005, rock musicians placed themselves at risk of corporal punishment. Although some western pop records are now tolerated, acts such as Madonna and Abba are banned because of the 'Islamic ban on the female singing voice'. Bands who violate such rulings, by playing for example in private homes or underground car parks, risk punishment by lashing.[25]

Sound, and music in particular, has also been ritually deployed in confrontations within, and between various sections of, a community. Inter-racial tensions on the nineteenth-century Australian goldfields led to frequent incidents of violence and brutality. During the scalpings of Chinese at the Lambing Flats diggings in 1861, the politics of the encounter were proudly proclaimed as a band played 'Rule Britannia'.[26] In rural England the skimmington was a public spectacle 'often performed to chastise and humiliate community members whose marital behaviour

---

[23]   See for examples Anthony Babington, *The English Bastille*, pp. 27, 34, 62; Alain Boureau, 'Franciscan Piety and Voracity: Uses and Stratagems in the Hagiographic Pamphlet' in *The Culture of Print: power and the uses of print in early modern Europe*, ed. Roger Chartier, trans. Lydia G. Cochrane (Cambridge, 1989), pp. 15–58; see p. 29.

[24]   Convict Discipline: passim, see further Robert Hughes, *The Fatal Shore: A History of the transportation of Convicts to Australia 1987–1868* (London, 1987), p. 480. Floggings were themselves accompanied by ritual drumming, see *Convict Australia: Pardon and Punishment*, at 17 January 2008.

[25]   Robert Tait, 'Almost impossible to play rock in this hard place', *SMH*, 29 August 2005, p. 15. The subject of music censorship is a massive research field on its own account. See, for example, Martin Cloonan and Reebee Garofalo, *Policing Pop* (Philadelphia, 2005); Index on Censorship (ed), *Smashed Hits: Index on Censorship* 6 (1998); see also the Freemuse website: www.freemuse.org.

[26]   John Pilger, *Heroes* (London, 1986/9), p. 11.

was irregular, especially men who were "beaten" by their wives'. In 1636 one was organized by a civic-minded Samuel Moggs in Brislington, Somerset, who 'went to considerable expense to hire a professional drummer, and one from Bristol at that'.[27] A number of patterns begin to emerge from this transcultural and panhistorical miscellany of case studies in the complicity of music and violence. One is that that complicity may manifest itself in any violent encounter, whether nation against nation, tribe against tribe, state against citizenry and vice versa, or even the ostracism or punishment of a single individual. Sound in general and music in particular are a major site over which conflict is negotiated. We will be arguing that the struggle over who has the right to make public noise, and in particular music, is a way of tracing the history of the emerging modern age and defining its often violent tensions.

The Politicization of Sound: The State and the Citizen

In the sixteenth century we begin to find reports of hostility to the intrusiveness of travelling minstrelsy in the streets of one of Europe's most rapidly developing cities, London, and in particular, complaints about repetitiveness: 'the too speedy return of one manner of tune, doth too much annoy'.[28] About four centuries after these first signs of irritation at Tudor ghetto blasters, in 2005 a London poll reported complaints by shop assistants at having to listen to the same songs on piped rotation in the stores, with Kylie Minogue and Britney Spears among the most irritating.[29] Frequently, unwilling auditors to public music go well beyond complaint. In 1962, one Colin Chisam from Berwick-on-Tweed, fired shots at three youths passing his house for playing their transistor too loudly; they invaded his house and one of the intruders was killed in the scuffle.[30] The forced entry is a trope of one of the most significant threads in the development of modernity: increasingly intrusive sound. These historically separated episodes exemplify the progressive politicization of sound and silence that mediated notions of citizenship and criminality (authorized and unauthorized identity formations), and they punctuate a larger narrative about the acoustic order through which we can map the shift from the relatively static notion of social structures in the Middle Ages (based on status) to the emergence of the more dynamic model of class of the late- and post-Renaissance.[31] The role

---

[27] Arthur F. Marotti and Michael D. Bristol (eds), *Print, Manuscript and Performance: The changing relations of the media in early modern England* (Columbus, 2000), pp. 293, 294.

[28] H.E. Wooldridge, *Old English Popular Music* (New York: 1961), p. 58.

[29] *SMH*, 23 September 2005, p. 20, and news.com.au, 23 September 2005.

[30] Oliver Cyriax, *The Penguin Encyclopedia of Crime* (Harmondsworth, 1996), p. 541.

[31] On this transition, see for example Gary Day, *Class* (London and New York, 2001).

of the changing status of aurality and music in defining the politics of the early modern era, the emergence of modern conceptions of community (including the state), and the notion of the self, can be reviewed in areas including theatrical and literary practice, law and penology, and the development of the distinction between low and high music forms that underpins the now problematic opposition between art music and popular music.[32] Critical moments in these developments in musical terms are disclosed in forms of sonic violence.

The intensification of the politics of acoustics can be traced in the changing relationship between sound, music and silence in the negotiations of the state with its citizenry, and the way in which ownership of the identity of 'the state' changes in response to the shifting dynamics and conceptions of 'class'. The full development of this argument is for another place,[33] but aspects of it are relevant here as a framework for an understanding of the deeper politics of music and violence in the contemporary world. The history of the right to make noise or impose silence, and the right to describe sound as lexically intelligible, speech as acceptable, and noise as music, provide the cultural and historical context to an appreciation of the interplay between music and violence in the modern era. A particular site at which the balance of acoustic power is implicated in the class confrontations out of which modernity emerged is that of the law and punishment. An account of the English prison system was published by reformer John Howard in 1777, and included a number of proposals for improving the institution: 'Solitude and silence are favourable to reflection, and may possibly lead to repentance.'[34] Until the late eighteenth century, English prisons had been sites of extreme volubility. Newgate was described in 1719 as 'a Tower of Babel where all are speakers and no hearers'.[35] Howard's reflections herald a new phase in the philosophy of state incarceration, with silence becoming the signifier and the driver of civil obedience, and deference to the rule of law.

The campaign of prison reformer Elizabeth Fry is instructive in this connection. When she visited Newgate Prison in 1813, she reported being shocked by the conditions, including 'the filth, the closeness of the rooms, the ferocious manners and expressions of the women towards each other .... And *her ears were offended by the most terrible imprecations*'. She later spoke of 'the dreadful proceedings that went forward on the female side of the prison; the begging, *swearing*, fighting, gaming, *singing*, dancing, dressing up in men's clothes – the scenes too bad to

---

[32]   Exemplifying such arguments, see Bruce Johnson, 'Voice, Power and Modernity' in Joy Damousi and Desley Deacon (eds), *Talking and Listening in the Age of Modernity* (Canberra, 2007), pp. 114–22; Bruce Johnson, 'Sites of Sound' in *Sound Effects* (forthcoming).

[33]   See for example Bruce Johnson, 'Divided Loyalties: Literary Responses to the Rise of Oral Authority in the Modern Era', *Textus*, 19 (Spring 2006), pp. 285–304.

[34]   Babington, *The English Bastille*, p. 109.

[35]   Peter Linebaugh, *The London Hanged: Crime and civil society in the eighteenth century.* Second edition (London and New York, 2006; first edition 2003), p. 28.

be described'. In April 1817 Fry formed The Association for the Improvement of Female Prisoners in Newgate, which passed rules of conduct calling for the women to be engaged in approved employment, and that there should be no '*begging, swearing*, gaming, card-playing, *quarrelling or immoral conversation*', and that at 9 a.m. and 6 p.m. they should be gathered together to listen to readings from the Bible.[36] These led to changes, described by a male visitor:

> On my approach no loud or dissonant sounds or angry voices indicated that I was about to enter a place, which ... had long had for one of its titles that of 'Hell above ground'. The courtyard into which I was admitted, instead of being peopled with beings scarcely human, blaspheming, fighting, tearing each others' hair, or gaming with a filthy pack of cards for the filthy clothes they wore, ... presented a scene where stillness and propriety reigned ... a lady from the Society of Friends ... was reading aloud to about sixteen women prisoners who were engaged in needle-work. ... They all rose on my entrance, curtsied respectfully and then at a signal resumed their seats and employments.[37]

Silence thus became the sign of deferential decorum. The Prison Act of 1865 enforced the 'separate system' throughout Britain, whereby prisoners shall be

> ... prevented from holding any communications with each other, either by every prisoner being kept in a separate cell by day and by night except when he is at chapel or taking exercise, or by every prisoner being confined by night in his cell and being subject to such superintendence during the day as will prevent his communicating with any other prisoner.[38]

The silent system continued in some prisons well into the twentieth century, and also extended over the same period to the industrial workplace, as in the case of the strike led by Thomas I. Kidd, secretary of the Amalgamated Woodworkers' International Union, against the lumber company in Oshkosh owned by George M. Paine. Once inside the factory to commence work, the employees were locked in and 'no unnecessary talking was allowed'.[39] The strike itself testifies to the decline of such overt acoustic oppression, but while it may not have been *de jure* acceptable later in the twentieth century, there continue to be *de facto* ways of imposing versions of the silent system in the workplace, as emerged during the 'events' of 1968 in France, where factory conditions were often 'medieval by British or American standards'. In the Citroen factory: 'Men of different

---

[36]   The quotations relating to Fry are from Babington, pp. 153, 155, 156; my italics.

[37]   Ibid., p. 157.

[38]   Ibid., p. 222.

[39]   Irving Stone, *Clarence Darrow for the Defense* (New York, 9th printing of the authorized abridgement, 1961; first published by Doubleday, 1941), p. 52.

nationality – Algerians, Yugoslavians, Spaniards – are often placed side by side on the production line to cut out talking.'[40]

The control of sound and the imposition of literal and metaphorical silence has remained one of the primary manifestations of state and corporate power (generally in convergence) since the eighteenth century. The primary instrument of state control has been legislation. The British Riot Act of 1715 forbade the unlawful, riotous and tumultuous assembly of 12 or more persons, and if such an assembly failed to disperse within an hour of a magistrate's reading of the Act, 'they were guilty of a felony without benefit of clergy'.[41] The effect of such measures in 'silencing' restive underclasses was illustrated in 1717 when weavers assembled to protest the threat presented to their livelihood by the importation by the East India Company of cheap fabrics. The 'Riot Act was read by Magistrate Lade, and two weavers were arrested. In his report, Lade made reference to the Vox Populi, or the Rumour of the Mob'.[42]

Sound, Music and the Urban Mob

The reference to the voice of the mob takes us closer to the class-based ideologies underpinning the politicization of sound. The prison system provided a site at which the politics of sound and silence could be enforced most explicitly, but this was a brutal reflection of, rather than deviation from, developments of the meaning of sound which increasingly pervaded the general cultural record. The emergence of silent prayer from the late medieval period is connected with the later valorization of silence as the condition of secular learning.[43] So too in the literary record, including even the concept of literature itself,[44] as well as in specific literary works, as in the violation of music aesthetics that proclaim 'something rotten in the state' in *Hamlet*. When Ophelia enters singing (and in one version, accompanying herself on the lute), the fact of a woman of station singing in public at all, and the moral and aesthetic derangement of what she sang, would have been the clearest indication to an Elizabethan audience of the violence about to erupt in a state presided over by such a court.[45]

---

[40]   Patrick Seale and Maureen McConville, *French Revolution 1968* (Harmondsworth, 1968), p. 155.

[41]   Linebaugh, *The London Hanged*, p. 17.

[42]   Ibid., p. 20.

[43]   See further Paul Saenger, 'Silent reading: its impact on late medieval script and society', *Viator: Medieval and Renaissance Studies* 13 (1982): 367–414; Paul Saenger, 'Books of Hours and the Reading Habits of the Later Middle Ages' in Chartier, *The Culture of Print*, pp. 141–73.

[44]   See further Johnson, 'Divided Loyalties'.

[45]   See further Johnson, '*Hamlet*', pp. 261–3.

But it was the industrial city that became the most significant centre for the acoustic confrontations of modernity. From the late eighteenth century there was a growing tendency to associate public sound and street music with the perceived breakdown of order signalled in the emergence of the urban crowd or mob, so often described in terms of the noise it made. The class dimensions of the politicization of sound and music are also implicated with the changing relationship between public and private space, which is turn parallels the increasing sacralization from the eighteenth century of private over public property.[46] Perhaps the most succinct graphic presentation of all these tensions is William Hogarth's 1741 etching, 'The Enraged Musician'. From his solid domestic enclosure protected by a barred fence, a string player looks into the street, blocking his ears against the inescapable acoustic disorder of a crying infant, bellowing pedlar, a tinker grinding a blade, a child with a rattle, and various musicians. Noise came to be associated with the intrusiveness, in increasingly densely populated cities, of the lower and unruly classes, while silence denoted refinement. A neat exemplification of the shift in the class politics of sound is to be found in two separate historical moments. Erasmus' essay 'On the Body', advised against immoderate public laughter, but described it primarily as a visible phenomenon, a distortion of the face. This recalls the sixteenth century advice against gentlemen playing the trumpet, because it distorts the features beyond recognition.[47] In neither case is sound the centre of attention. This is in the sixteenth century. Two centuries later, Lord Chesterfield in his 1774 *Letters to His Son* advised against: 'Frequent and loud laughter ... it is the manner in which the mob express their silly joy at silly things. In my mind there is nothing so illiberal, and so ill-bred, as audible laughter.'[48] He opposes the noisiness of laughter to refinement, true wit, reflection, reason. By the time we come to Chesterfield, the complaint against laughter is based on the fact that it is a noise, confirming the emergence of spontaneous aural modalities as the site of ill-breeding and class antagonism. This valency is connected with the appearance of the purpose-built concert hall reflecting the evolution of an art music that cannot be contaminated by the vulgar everyday noises of social life, and the development of the idea of 'taste', which becomes a significant lever in conflicts over musical practices.

Between Renaissance humanist Erasmus and gentleman of sensibility and taste Chesterfield, we see an evolving model of the politics of sound, constructed on issues of social privilege and subordination, and the often violent confrontation

---

[46] See especially Linebaugh, *The London Hanged*. On the sonic aspects of increasing appropriations of public space, particularly rural, see Peter Denney, 'Scythes, Swords and the Bitter-Sweet Melody of Merry England'.

[47] John Buxton, *Elizabethan Taste* (New York, 1964), p. 8.

[48] The examples of Erasmus and Chesterfield are cited, although for other purposes, in Anca Parvulescu, 'The Sound of Laughter', *ASCA Conference Sonic Interventions: Pushing the Boundaries of Cultural Analysis*, Reader for Panel 2: *The Sonic in the 'Silent' Arts and Bring in the Noise*, Sylvia Mieszkowski, Co-ordinator (2005), pp. 117–19; see p. 118.

between literacy and orality. It has been argued both explicitly and implicitly through, for example, ethnomusicology, that sound is the most ancient, widespread and durable way of defining the territory through which human beings project their individual and collective identity.[49] Among the categories of sound deployed for these purposes, the voice, with its capacities for the most finely discriminated sonic semiotics, has been prominent. In western Europe, the authority of the oral was challenged by the advent of print and the spread of literacy from the late fifteenth century. The new technology achieved two things. First, it enabled the widespread dissemination of information in standardized form far beyond the radius of the human voice. As Tom Paine would later observe, comparing print to speech, the former enables a man 'to be everywhere and at the same instant'.[50] Scholars all over Europe could read the same things, and equally important, view the same images and diagrams. The other outcome was to create a new marker of class: those who could read and those who could not. As London commerce, with its peripatetic pedlars and their street cries demonstrated, everyone could shout, but not everyone could write.[51]

While we think of sixteenth-century England as being a richly literary culture, in fact by 1558 only one in five men and one in 20 women could even write their names.[52] The written text defined a new site of literal and cultural capital. Thus, coinciding with the rise of capitalism, to be able to read and write became a new interface of class confrontation. Wheale opens his study of literacy in fifteenth- and sixteenth-century England by noting that when Christopher Marlowe presents the seven deadly sins in *Doctor Faustus*, the plebeian Envy has developed a new resentment not apparent in his mediaeval predecessors: 'I cannot read, and therefore wish all books were burnt.'[53] This of course is not to make the absurd suggestion that people gradually stopped talking to each other, and the period was oratorically abundant, in theatre, pulpit and education. But there was a progressive decline in oral and aural sophistication as the dominant position gradually assumed by print in the information economy changed the status of sound in general and of the voice in particular.

These changes over several centuries constitute an instructive study in the complex operations of hegemony in and through intellectual and material culture. While the story of the printed text in England begins in the late fifteenth century, like all technologies there is a considerable 'take up' time before its impact has changed the norms of a society. Alvin Kernan dates the arrival of the 'generally accepted view that what is printed is true, or at least truer than any other type of

---

[49]   See for example R. Murray Schafer, *The Tuning of the World* (Toronto, 1977).

[50]   Cited in Schmidt, 'Hearing Loss', p. 53.

[51]   See further Bruce Smith, *The Acoustic World of Early Modern England* (Chicago and London, 1999), pp. 52–71.

[52]   Nigel Wheale, *Writing and Society: Literacy, print and politics in Britain 1590–1660* (London and New York, 1999), p. 41.

[53]   Ibid., p. 1.

record' to some time in the eighteenth century, relating it to the pervasiveness of print in the form of posters, bills, receipts, newspapers – part of the fabric of everyday life.[54] This raises the question: 'Whose everyday life?' Samuel Johnson's works, including his *Dictionary*, may be taken as confirming the triumph of print as a form of cultural authorization, the creation of the community of the 'common reader'.[55] But of course literacy in the mid-eighteenth century was by no means universal. If the idea of the common reader defined and validated membership of the community, clearly very large numbers of the population did not enjoy such authorization. If Johnson contributed crucially to the idea of a community defined through its readerly competencies, his *Dictionary* also created a zone of exclusion. He may be said to have created the English proletariat by creating the 'proletariat' in English. The word had appeared in the 1660s, but the lexicographic authority of Johnson's *Dictionary* formally located the category at the lowest level of society: 'mean, wretched, vile or vulgar'.[56]

This was one of many ways that the community of the British nation was imagined into existence during the eighteenth century, including through a new flag and anthem.[57] For purposes of this discussion, I want to foreground the connection between literacy and privileged membership of that community, or, more specifically, what it implies about exclusion and sound; the parallel importance of musical literacy will emerge in Chapter 8. Johnson's work contributed to the definition of this community as a linguistic entity with agreed protocols of literacy. The lexicon embraced by his *Dictionary* was thereby given stability and permanence. It became stationed in the landscape of the imagination as a form of British property. I use the word 'stationed' pointedly, for its associations also with print and something fixed in space (like property), as opposed to the 'mob', a word associated with both noise and rootlessness.[58] All that mattered culturally in the idea of the British nation was to be accommodated in and validated by the community of its common readers. Thus, the playwright for that richly oral and sonic forum, the Elizabethan stage, was progressively recuperated as the supreme 'man of letters' from the late seventeenth century – Shakespeare as the pinnacle of English literature.[59]

It is notable, then, that Johnson excluded from the lexicon of written English the diction of the underclasses as 'unworthy of preservation'.[60] The ability to

---

[54] Alvin Kernan, *Samuel Johnson and the Impact of Print* (Princeton, 1989), p. 49.

[55] Ibid., p. 240.

[56] See the discussion by Peter Linebaugh, *The London Hanged,* pp. 121–2.

[57] Ibid., p. 117.

[58] The two words, 'stationery' and 'stationary' converge in the fact that printers could not conduct their business as street pedlars, but required fixed 'stations' of business. The word 'mob' is cognate with 'mobile', being on the move and, as such, a threat to fixed property.

[59] See further, Johnson, 'Divided Loyalties'.

[60] Linebaugh, *The London Hanged*, p. 429.

read was already long acknowledged as a privilege in law through the tradition of 'benefit of clergy'.[61] Johnson's exclusions from his lexicography enlarged the community deprived of such benefits. His refusal to admit the diction of the labouring classes from the approved lexicon of Englishness was part of their progressive criminalization, that went back to the longstanding refusal of the courts to recognize the 'canting' language of the poor.[62] It also stiffened the disenfranchisement of non-literate cultures (both within and beyond 'the nation'). The spoken language – the cant – of the illiterate proletariat was increasingly regarded as in itself evidence of criminality.[63] Seen in terms of the historical confrontations between literate and sonic information circuits, this represents a further stage in the politicization of noise. Deprived of an 'authorized' (that is, written), language, the proletariat must choose between deferential silence and disruptive and seditious noise. The pathologies that defined the disenfranchised brought into being by the capitalist order included not just supposed illiteracy, but their immersion in the alternative communication circuit: sound. They make noise, and in doing so manifest themselves as a threat to a hegemonic textuality. The ruling orders maintain their power through print; the subordinated are identified in networks of orality. I am suggesting that the struggle over the right to make noise is a very useful way of tracing the history of relations of power since the medieval period. The rise of the mob, the urban crowd, the embryonic working class or the proletariat, those who were oppressed under capitalism, is figured as the rise of noise: that is, sound anathematized as being unintelligible or unmusical.

Whether defined in terms of class, or some other model of altereity, the rabble confronted the superior orders as noise, and indeed, any public sound they made was therefore unlikely to be classified as meaningful, as in speech or music, but *ipso facto*, as chaotic noise. Shakespeare had invoked these connections, including speech and music, in the Induction to Part Two of *Henry the Fourth*, where Rumour describes himself as 'a pipe … of so easy and plain a stop / That the blunt monster with uncounted heads, / The still discordant wav'ring multitude, / can play upon it'.[64] Hearing voices adjacent to where a number of Irish had been imprisoned awaiting trial for London's Radcliffe Highway murders of 1811, the magistrates enquiring into the cause were told 'Oh! It is nothing but those horrid Irish, who can never be

---

[61]   The 'benefit of clergy' originally exempted clerks in holy orders from the jurisdiction of criminal courts, and subject only to ecclesiastical authority. The privileges it bestowed included possible exemption from the death penalty in favour of less severe penalties, and were gradually extended to anyone who could demonstrate apparent literacy by reading a passage from the 51st Psalm, though many were canny enough to learn the passage and feign literacy. See further, Babington, *The English Bastille*, pp. 28–9.

[62]   Linebaugh, *The London Hanged*, pp. 71–2.

[63]   See for example ibid., p. 72.

[64]   William Shakespeare, *The Second Part of King Henry The Fourth*, 'Induction', lines 15–20, in *William Shakespeare: The Complete Works*, ed. Alfred Harbage (Baltimore, 1969), p. 707.

quiet'.[65] Just over a century and a half later, accounts of the 1968 uprising in Paris were pervaded by insubordinate volubility. One of the participants described the sense of emancipative resistance against the conservative authorities:

> Night was falling. Suddenly it came over us that we could speak at the tops of our voices, that we could sing or shout if we wanted to! By a vote, we had undone a year's work; some had even compromised their careers. And yet we experienced a sense of joy far sharper than that of receiving our degrees.[66]

Those who made noise were, in some sense or another, the inferior and insubordinate 'Other'.[67] John Picker documents the strength and cultural importance of the association between street music in Victorian London and swarthy foreigners, so that both were configured in terms of alien intrusion upon superior anglo-sensibilities.[68] That superiority might be defined along a range of axes which supplement economics and education. Mark M. Smith has traced the acoustic faultline between, for example, slaves and slave-owners as well as between north and south in early nineteenth-century America.[69] Unsurprisingly, gender politics are also implicated. As the politics of sound and silence shifted over centuries, they were also constantly being renegotiated back and forth across gender lines, as, during various liminal moments in cultural history, a new consensus had yet to emerge as to how silence was to be valued and, therefore, gendered. In nineteenth-century rural Ireland, the authority of orality remained robust through a male story-telling tradition, in which much was made of the connection between talkative wives and hen-keeping (hens make too much noise). 'Poultry-keeping, like talkativeness, was a sign that a woman was not under a man's control.'[70]

---

[65] Cyriax, *Encyclopaedia of Crime*, p. 626.

[66] Seale and McConville, *French Revolution 1968*, p. 113. See further pp. 84, 89.

[67] For a finely discriminated case study in this relationship, see Carlo Ginzburg, *The Cheese and the Worms*.

[68] John Picker, *Victorian Soundscapes* (Oxford, 2003), pp. 41–81. For a parallel study of a later period see Karen Bijsterveld, 'The Diabolical Symphony of the Mechanical Age: Technology and Symbolism of Sound in European and North American Noise Abatement Campaigns, 1900–1940', in Michael Bull and Les Back (eds), *The Auditory Culture Reader* (Oxford and New York, 2003), pp. 165–89.

[69] Mark M. Smith, 'Listening to the Heard Worlds of Antebellum America' in Michael Bull and Les Back (eds), *The Auditory Culture Reader* (Oxford and New York, 2003), pp. 137–63.

[70] Angela Bourke, *The Burning of Bridget Cleary: A True Story* (London, 1999), p. 45. On early modern gendering of sound, see Christina Luckyj, *In 'a moving rhetoricke': Gender and Silence in Early Modern England* (Manchester, 2002). As sounds came to be mediated technologically, and as technology became itself masculinized, so did loudness become increasingly associated with masculinity; see for example Hanna Bosma, 'Different Noises in Electroacoustic Music', *ASCA Conference Sonic Interventions: Pushing the*

Feminization was only one way in which the untrustworthiness of sound became inscribed in the language that produced the axioms 'Don't believe everything you hear' and 'Seeing is believing'. Authority is embodied in information and knowledge conceived in terms of a visual order: perspective, vision/visionary, envisage/envision, point of view, discover, disclose, observation, speculation, reflections, insights, second sight, revelation. It is a language in which a musical performance is likely to be called 'a reading', in which a sense of the 'picturesque' became a marker of sensibility in the eighteenth century as print itself consolidated its hegemony, in which we announce an idea with the words 'apparently' or 'it appears that', and we ask our interlocutor 'do you see what I mean?' and where a doctor about to probe and listen to the body begins by saying 'Let's take a look at you'. Conversely, a word such as 'hearsay' describes a form of hitherto respectable information which suddenly becomes suspect in the seventeenth century with the decline of oral custom and the consolidation of the written contract. The repertoire of words describing orally/aurally transmitted knowledge are now markers of (often feminized) unreliability: gossip, tittle-tattle, sounding off, chatter, whingeing, rumour, lip service, scolding, nagging, blab, babble, prattle – a network of the untrustworthy other: Chinese Whispers.

The primary focus of this book is, of course, music. It needs to be emphasized yet again that music is sound, and as such, it is the conflicting decisions as to whether a sound is music or noise that defines the lines of confrontation along which violence is incipient. The rise of the mob, the urban crowd, the embryonic working class or the proletariat, those who were oppressed under capitalism, is figured as the rise of noise, as in William Wordsworth's encounters with early nineteenth-century London.[71] At a distance, from Westminster Bridge and in the silence of the morning,

> Ne'er saw I, never felt, a calm so deep!
> The river glideth at his own sweet will:
> Dear God! the very houses seem asleep;
> And all that mighty heart is lying still![72]

In Book Seven of *The Prelude*, however, he is immersed in the crowded streets, and finds the city to be 'a monstrous ant hill', full of the 'Babel din, the endless stream

---

Boundaries of Cultural Analysis, Reader for Panel 2: The Sonic in the 'Silent' Arts and Bring in the Noise, Sylvia Mieszkowski, Co-ordinator, pp. 18–23.

[71]   See further Bruce Johnson, 'Unsound Insights', in Kimi Kärki, Rebecca Leydon and Henri Terho (eds) *Looking Back, Looking Ahead: Popular Music Studies 20 Years Later – Proceedings of the 11th Biannual Conference of the International Association for the Study of Popular Music, Turku, Finland* (Turku, 2002), pp. 704–12.

[72]   William Wordsworth, *Poetical Works*, ed. Thomas Hutchinson (London, Oxford, New York: Oxford University Press, 1969). All references to Wordsworth are from this edition.

of men'. As sound rises to challenge the aesthetics and order of an ocularcentric regime, urban music becomes situated as unruly noise, as opposed to 'art'. The city is full of an oppressive 'roar' (line 178), a 'deafening din' (line 155) which includes 'a minstrel band' (line 188), an 'English Ballad-singer' (line 180), 'some female vendor's scream, ... the shrillest of all London cries' (lines 182–3), all part of a 'thickening hubbub' (line 211). Singers do not make music, but are part of the 'uproar of the rabblement' (line 273). The city confronts Wordsworth with the rising tide of modern mass culture, the actuality of the contemporary 'common man'. And it is demonized as an acoustic culture, its music experienced as part of the noise, summarized in the 'anarchy and din, Barbarian and infernall', the 'screaming' of Bartholomew Fair, its hurdy-gurdies, fiddles, trumpets, timbrels, drums, all making up a 'Parliament of Monsters (lines 686–718). Wordsworth's putatively democratic respect for the voice of the 'common man' is tested beyond its limits in the urban soundscape, and his case suggests that an acoustic frame might significantly alter our picture of Romanticism. Wordsworth gives us a prefiguration of that moral panic at the collapse of received and authorized order which we think of as the conservative response to twentieth-century mass culture. And, as with that response, it can be largely configured as a confrontation with a resurgent acoustic order. Picker's study of Victorian soundscapes confirms the prevalence of this attitude on the part of the privileged urban classes.[73] Even writers who expressed sympathy with the underclasses were inclined to characterize them as sources of unseemly noise, as in the case of Elizabeth Gaskell's *Mary Barton*.[74]

Violence in one form or another is implicit or explicit in all the cases examined above. This discussion has foregrounded the role of sound in defining the shifting social dynamic of the early modern era. Among the sounds which people may make, music or musicality offers the opportunities for the most finely articulated projections of individual identity. However, in the period under review in this section, the range of such projection was limited to the idea embodied in the words 'within earshot'. The word may be taken as a metaphor both for the function of sound as a weapon, and for the limits of its radius of influence: the distance over which sonic power can be exercised. But all this is dramatically intersected by a new set of factors emerging from the late nineteenth century.

---

[73] Picker, *Victorian Soundscapes*.

[74] See further Johnson, 'Divided Loyalties', pp. 293–302.

Chapter 3
Technologized Sonority

Bruce Johnson

In this chapter we wish to explore the impact of modern sound and technologies on the connections between music and violence, reiterating the point made at the outset that we cannot form an adequate understanding of the connection between music and violence unless we recognize that, whatever else music might be, it is fundamentally part of a sonic field. As such, its own material, political and conceptual history as a social presence is inextricably connected with the history of sound. A decisive transition in that history – and therefore of music – is the modern technologization of sonority.

The overall usage of the term 'modern' is dependant on context. In the deepest historical perspective, the 'modern era' can refer to the post-medieval period as in Christina Luckyj's discussion cited above of 'early modern England', which begins in the sixteenth century. Douglas Bush commented that by 1660 the 'educated Englishman's mind and world ... were more than half modern', while Peter Burke's investigation of popular culture in early modern Europe begins with the eighteenth century. Much depends on whether the term refers to 'a form of life' or a 'period of history', a distinction made by John Jervis in his book *Exploring the Modern*, which confines itself to the twentieth century, as does Peter Conrad in his massive study of 'modern times'.[1] There is ample warrant, then, for the sense used in this chapter: 'modern' refers to cultural and material changes dating from the late nineteenth century.

The preceding overview has set up a particular historical logic regarding the potentialities in the politics of sound, which will help to prepare for an appreciation of the cultural impact of the connection between modern sound and technologies. That relationship may be approached in two ways: the increase in the sound of modern technology, and in the technological mediation of modern sound. Together they define the dramatic transformation of sound (including music) in the articulation of often violent power relations in the twentieth century and beyond.

---

[1] Christina Luckyj, *Moving rhetoricke*; Douglas Bush, *English Literature in the Early Seventeenth Century* (Oxford, 1945), p. 1; Peter Burke, *Popular Culture in Early Modern Europe* (London 1978); John Jervis, *Exploring the Modern* (Oxford, 1998) p. 1; Peter Conrad, *Modern Times, Modern Places: Life & Art in the 20th Century* (printed in Hong Kong: Thames and Hudson, 1998).

The Sound of Modern Technology

It is unnecessary to rehearse in detail the argument that one of the distinguishing features of that period is the exponential increase in the level of sound brought about by advances in technology since the industrial revolution.[2] One of the terms central to this study is violence, and its convergence with technology and sound in the twentieth century is nowhere more strikingly exemplified than in the changed auralization of armed conflict in the century's traumatic overture, the First World War. One point to be made as this investigation proceeds is that sonic violence is not confined to the special case of military action. Apart from throwing an arc across the earlier and later sections of this book, however, the First World War provides a bounded case study in any attempt to appreciate the transformation in the acoustics of the modern world. More than any other event, this war laid the foundations for the twentieth-century sonic imaginary and acoustic violence. It is therefore instructive to document that seminal moment.

War has always been a confluence of sound, music and violence, as cases already cited testify. The arrival of gunfire added to, but did not overwhelm the soundscape. The loudest sounds at the Battle of Waterloo were cannonades, described as deafening, but they did not drown out the sounds of men, animals and music. They were intermittent and distinguishable, closer than the sound of modern warfare to what Schafer called a 'Hi-Fi' soundscape.[3] Combatants could distinguish the rattling of musket volleys, the pinging and rattling of musket balls and shrapnel on swords, bayonets and armour. One soldier recalled the sound of fire from the British squares striking the enemy's cuirasses as 'the noise of a violent hailstorm beating on panes of glass'.[4] In addition to these noises of military technology, those present also recall organic noises: the men preparing for battle like 'the distant murmur of the waves of the sea', cheering, shouts, shrieks of anger and pain, commands, music including drums, pipers in the squares. There was also the noise of horses – neighing, galloping and screaming when wounded.[5] Acoustically, this was warfare on a human scale, and as in ancient times, troops could still inspire their comrades on the battlefield with music.

Accounts of the First World War still of course speak of death, dismemberment, disembowelment, but it is the sound of technologized violence that is the most pervasive in the traumatized accounts of its participants. Its new soundscape ranged from the rattle of the gas alarm, 'a terrible sound', to the noise inside and outside tanks under fire.[6] Above all, however, was the sound of guns and artillery.

---

[2]   See the work of R. Murray Schafer, *The Tuning of the World* (Toronto, 1977), esp. pp. 71–87.

[3]   Ibid., p. 43.

[4]   Allesandro Barbero, *The Battle: A History of the Battle of Waterloo*, p. 291.

[5]   Keegan, *The Face of Battle*, pp. 141–2.

[6]   Lyn Macdonald, *They Called it Passchendaele: The Story of the Third Battle of Ypres and of the men who fought in it* (London, first published 1978, this edition 1993), pp. 161, 163.

The first decisive use of a cannon is generally dated at 1453, when the forces of Sultan Mahomet II beseiged Constantinople to begin the 'first seige bombardment in history'. As it opened to the 'accompaniment of cymbals and drums' the massive siege cannon 'Mahometta' was fired. 'Since the creation of the world nothing like it had been heard.'[7] The identification of artillery with sound provided a bellicose trope for coming centuries. When Rome was besieged by the army of the Constable of Bourbon, Benvenuto Cellini was placed in charge of a battery of artillery, and described how he forgot his drawing, his studies, his music, in 'the music of the guns'. By the twentieth century this agreeable 'music' had become for a German infantryman a 'monstrous song'.[8] If we are looking for a single year in which the tune changed, 1916 suggests itself, with the opening of the Somme offensive on 1 July. Inaugurated by the most catastrophic casualties in British military history, it seems also to be the point at which the sound of technologized violence transformed the acoustic imagination.

The movie footage we have of that war suggests silence, omitting what participants often identified as its most horrific modality. Rowland Feilding, an officer with the First Coldstream Guards, wrote of going to see the 'Somme film' shown in a field. It was

> ... really a wonderful and most realistic production, but must of necessity be wanting in that the battle is fought in silence, and, moreover, that the most unpleasant part – the machine-gun and rifle fire – is entirely eliminated. Of the actual 'frightfulness' of war, all that one sees is the bursting shells; and perhaps it is as well. I have said that the battle is fought in silence; but no, on this occasion the roar of real battle was loudly audible in the distance.[9]

In 1915 a Second Lt. Edward Underhill had spoken of how impossible it was to describe the experience of the war to those who had not participated, giving priority to noise as the marker of that watershed: 'Nobody can realize what it is like unless they have heard shells rushing overhead.'[10] The sound of the conflict marked a new stage in the balance between man and technology. A German soldier recalled that the Somme barrage 'first made me aware of the overwhelming effects of the war of material. We had to adapt ourselves to an entirely new phase of the war'.[11] This 'new phase' was marked by the sheer mass of firepower. Rowland Feilding wrote of the opening barrage on 1 July:

---

[7] Erik Durschmied, *The Hinges of Battle: How Chance and Incompetence Have Changed the Face of History* (London), p. 49.

[8] Cellini, *Autobiography*, p. 76; Max Hastings, *Armageddon: The Battle for Germany 1944–45* (London, 2004), p. 215.

[9] Ibid., p. 47.

[10] Richard Holmes, *Tommy*, p. 529.

[11] Robert T. Foley and Helen McCartney, *The Somme: an eyewitness history* (London, 2006), p. 84.

Between 6.30 and 7.30 a.m. our bombardment was intensified. Major Watkins, a Coldstream officer, told me that on his corps frontage alone (about 3,600 yards), 42,000 shells were sent over by our artillery in sixty-five minutes, or nearly 650 shells per minute. I hear we have 360 guns on this sector, including 8-inch, 12-inch, and 15-inch howitzers.[12]

This massive weight of ordinance was accompanied by a hitherto unimaginable acoustic profile. Although dominated by heavy artillery, the likelihood of death was proclaimed in a heterogeneous sonic flood, each element insidiously promising its own form of injury, maiming and disintegration. The swish of the smaller shells overhead

> ... gave one the sensation of being under a swiftly rushing stream. The larger shells kept up a continuous shrieking overhead, falling on the enemy's trenches with the roar of a cataract, while every now and then a noise as of thunder sounded above all when our trench mortar shells fell amongst the German wire.

'It was rapid fire by every gun and noise was like hell let loose. As the shells passed over our heads the air hummed like a swarm of a hundred million hornets.'[13] There are descriptions of the rattling of shrapnel on the door of a dugout, the 'hissing and whistling devilishly' of shrapnel bullets, the thud of shrapnel hitting helmet. The 'appalling crash' of high explosive shells and the 'gigantic crash' of a shell followed by the clatter of splinters hitting trees and cottage walls.[14]

It was, however, the magnitude and remorselessness of this new regime of noise that had the most profound impact on mind and body. On the German side, 'The noise of the barrage was too monotonous and so prevented sleep for overtired people ... More than a week we had lived with the deafening noise of the battle'.[15] A participant in Third Ypres (Passchendaele) a year later recalled '... you don't really hear the explosions individually – you just see them going off like geysers shooting up into the air.[16] Of the opening of the German offensive in March 1918 an officer in the British front line wrote, 'Think of the loudest clap of thunder you have ever heard, then imagine what it would be like if it continued without stopping. That was the noise that woke us on Thursday, 21 March. I have never before or since heard anything like it'. Even deep in a dugout well behind the front, another officer 'awoke with a tremendous start, conscious of noise, incessant and almost musical, so intense that it seemed as if a hundred devils were hammering in my brain. Everything seemed to be vibrating – the ground, my dugout, my bed'.[17]

---

[12]   Ibid., p. 70.

[13]   Ibid., p. 72.

[14]   Ibid., pp. 79, 80, 81.

[15]   Ibid., pp. 68–9.

[16]   Macdonald, *Passchendaele*, p. 144.

[17]   Holmes, *Tommy*, p. 405.

What is emerging in these accounts is a deluge of noise that signals an almost animate malevolent technological presence, as in this description from August 1917: 'The chap who was with me was hit. A bullet hit him right in the shin-bone. It was the most extraordinary, terrible noise. The bullet screams if it hits a bone, it spins round and screams, twisting.'[18] There is a sense of sound actually reconstructing space with vicious, destructive autonomy, a prefiguration of the ubiquitous sonic torment to which so many, to a greater or lesser extent, would become subjected in later twentieth-century life. Describing the firing of a 15-inch howitzer, one officer wrote:

> I had to stand well behind and plug my ears. I was conscious not so much of the tremendous noise of the discharge ... as the sound made by the shell as it emerged from the muzzle and climbed into the sky. I felt as in a tube of sound. It was a sound made up of giant, unlubricated screwing as the shell spiralled away, of rushing wind as the air closed in like thunder behind it, of screaming and whining as fragments of copper driving band cut the air in its wake.[19]

Sound itself is the adversary, attacking both body and mind. The sounds were typically described as organically destructive: 'The noise was terrific, one's ear-drums felt as though they would burst, when, by chance, we passed close to a battery, firing rapid. We staggered like drunkards with the concussion.' Similarly, from a captain present at the Somme barrage: 'The noise was more nearly "ear-splitting" than anything I have known.'[20] The 'sonic effect' was part of an interconnected array of potentially lethal factors, as reported by John Keegan. Shell blast could 'create over-pressures or vacuums in the body's organs, rupturing the lungs and producing haemorrhages in the brain and spinal cord', with fatal effects.[21] As a phenomenon of variations of air pressure and wave motion, this effect is inextricably connected to the noise of shell blast: in that technological regime, you can't have the shell blast without the sound and you can't have the sound without the shell blast. Here is a case where a difference of degree – the level of air disturbance caused by First World War artillery as compared with Waterloo – produces a difference of kind, a form of lethality hitherto un-noted in war.

As discussed earlier, the distinction between organic and cognitive distress generated by sound is an uncertain one. Their sometimes inextricable complicity is manifested in a description from the German lines under the bombardment:

> In the course of the afternoon the firing increased to such a degree that single explosions were no longer audible. There was nothing but one terrific tornado of noise. ... From nine to ten the shelling was frantic. The earth rocked and the sky boiled like a gigantic

---

[18]   Macdonald, *Passchendaele*, p. 171.
[19]   Foley and McCartney, *The Somme*, pp. 63–4.
[20]   Ibid., pp. 71, 77.
[21]   Keegan, *The Face of Battle*, p. 264.

cauldron. … Innumerable shells came howling and hurtling over us. … Head and ears ached violently, and we could only make ourselves understood by shouting a word at a time. The power of logical thought and the force of gravity alike seemed to be suspended. One had the sense of something as inescapable and as unconditionally fated as a catastrophe of nature. An NCO of No. 3 Platoon went mad.[22]

The madness bred its own form of aural violence, in a grotesque 'feedback' loop, a trope which provides a purposeful prefiguration of the sonic logic of the later twentieth-century complicity of music with violence. The term 'perdition', as used above, might have been invented for the weeping of young men exposed for the first time to the sound of the barrage. 'They cried and one kept calling "mother" and who could blame him, such HELL makes weaklings of the strongest and no human nerves or body were ever built to stand such torture, noise, horror and mental pain.'[23] At Third Ypres in 1917, a patient in a hospital marquee which had a shell-shock ward, reported the effect of the continuing sound of the bombardments:

> The bombs were very near, and in the ward I was in some of the patients went berserk. They were very, very bad cases of shellshock, much worse than I was, and two of them in particular got up and ran amok in the ward with their hands over their heads, screaming and screaming and screaming. It was shocking as it was all in the dark, for they'd had to put the lights out because of the air raid, and they were charging around banging into things and this dreadful screaming going on all the time.[24]

The magnitude, the duration and the effects of these aural assaults seem to be both unprecedented in history, and a harbinger of one of the more extreme pathologies of modernity; that is, the capacity of technology to effect the violent subjugation of the human being by sound. The accounts of the noise of technology harnessed to impersonal and indiscriminate destruction convey the sense of being immersed so deeply in a sonic ocean, that human scale became infinitesimal. By sounding we assert our identity. Here, all identity is obliterated, human sonority made meaningless. The 'shrapnel and high explosives were falling so fast you could hardly hear yourself speak'. 'You couldn't speak, the gunfire was so terrific.' If a soldier fell into the mud: 'There was no good shouting for help because there was so much racket going on and shells bursting all around that no one would have heard you.'[25] The war was experienced and remembered as an acoustic phenomenon, and not surprisingly the truce of 11 November 1918 was most strikingly recalled as the end of noise, as in the words of a Captain Charles Douie, '… a soldier's abiding memory of the armistice was of silence free from gunfire, while the civilian's was one of enthusiastic noise'. Another soldier wrote: 'To me, the most remarkable

---

22   Foley and McCartney, *The Somme*, p. 84.

23   Holmes, *Tommy*, p. 66.

24   Macdonald, *Passchendaele*, pp. 158–59.

25   Ibid., pp. 141, 144, 143.

feature of that day and night was the uncanny silence that pervaded ... No rumbling of guns, no staccato of machine guns, nor did the roar of exploding dumps break into the night as it had so often done. The war was over.'[26]

But the sonic imagination was irrevocably transformed. Academic accounts of various forms of modernism privilege the visual, and rarely recognize this dimension of its expressiveness, a further reason for the emphasis here. The war had added the noise of technology to the expressive repertoire of the modern condition. In the lead-up to the Passchendaele offensive, a soldier reported that one of his colleagues had developed

> ... an irritating habit of imitating the noise of approaching shells, a bellicose parlour trick which he had perfected to a fine art. He was doing it now as they trudged towards the line – as if there weren't enough shells coming over and noise going on without Alf joining in. 'Why don't you shut it just for a change?' said Tom wearily. 'Whizz-z-z-z-z-z-z BANG!' replied Alf..[27]

That this demotic expressive tic is referred to as a 'bellicose parlour trick' discloses the degree of internalization of such noise into the everyday imaginary. And in a description of a captured artillery piece, we see a confluence of technologized sonority and the repertoire of artistic practices that characterized modernism. When the giant 280 mm gun captured by the Australians was placed on display at the Champs de Mars, it was described as 'sinister', a 'terrible engine', the camouflage hiding the metallic brightness and 'industrial nobility of the architecture of iron' is a 'baroque cloak' which contrasts with the 'polished steel and dazzling copper' of naval cannon in their turrets. 'Soiled with ochre and grey-green, this deformed construction seems coarse under its harlequin cloak and reveals none of its ingenuity, its power and its wiles.' And significantly, the account began by speaking of the ugliness of its 'cubist medley of colours with which its camouflagers have daubed it'.[28]

There is so much going on here about modernity and its relationship with Modernism. The word 'cubist' establishes the connection, together with notions of deformity (the colours, the word 'soiled', and the displacement of the gun from its naval turret – these were in fact naval guns adapted for land deployment), the sense of threat in both art and industry, deception/illusion, grossness and ugliness. We glimpse a common cause between modernist expressiveness and the material realities of modernity, both of them as threats to an old, stable, visible order in which we knew where we stood. The association emerges in Cocteau's description of a putatively jazz performance at the Casino de Paris in 1918 (lit by anti-aircraft searchlights), as having the impact of a tank.[29] The same convergence is to be

---

[26] Holmes, *Tommy*, pp. 613, 614.

[27] Macdonald, *Passchendaele*, p. 38.

[28] John F. Williams, *Anzacs, the Media and the Great War* (Sydney, 1999), p. 229.

[29] See Chris Goddard, *Jazz Away from Home* (New York and London, 1979), pp. 15–16.

found in literature, as the war transformed the poetic imagination, replacing earlier martial and civilian rhythms of walking and riding with the asymmetrical acoustics of sporadic disruptions of artillery, explosives and machine gun fire.[30] And inevitably, the new sonority of violence also contributed to the way music came to be imagined and deployed in the twentieth century.

The Technologization of Modern Sound

There are two mutually implicated aspects of the connection between music, violence and modernity. The first is the general establishment from the nineteenth century of a re-connection between sound as information, and class confrontation, and the second is the emergence of technologies which enabled this re-connection to become competitive with other information economies. This argument is foreshadowed in the discussion in Chapter 2 about the changing relationship between the political significances of sound and silence. At various points in that discussion I referred to a confrontation between an ocularcentric regime and a resurgent sonic order. If I now tease out that encounter, it will throw further light on the significance and impact of the contemporary politicization of sound and music, and provide some explanation of why that impact increased so dramatically from the late nineteenth century.

For as long as the range of music and speech was confined to earshot, it could not become competitive with the radius of circulation of the printed record as an information medium. Print not only came to monopolize the Western information economy, but it also sacralized particular conditions of its consumption, notably silence: the silence of the library, the class-room, the office and scriptorium. Print was able to internationalize silence as not only the ideal condition of learning and reflection, but as the marker of social refinement. It would require the technological enlargement of the range and reach of sound before it could resume sufficient authority to compete with print as an information circuit. The process was catalysed by the rapidly increasing urbanization of Europe in the nineteenth century. England led in this process, becoming the first nation to move from a predominantly rural to a predominantly urban demographic around the mid-nineteenth century.[31]

Dense conurbations, their commerce, business and bureaucracies, produce commensurately dense information flows that, finally, the scribal hand can no longer cope with. Modern information technology was generated by this proliferating traffic. The junction between modern sound technology and information may be dated from the 1830s with Morse telegraphy which, for the sake of speed, converted

---

[30]   See further Bruce Johnson 1999, 'From Gallipoli to Gundagai', in Richard Nile (ed.), *War and Other Catastrophes*, *Special Issue of Journal of Australian Studies*, 60 (1999), pp. 66–72.

[31]   See further Johnson, 'Sites of Sound'.

and transmitted information into permutations of a binary-based acoustic code: dot and dash. But it is the patent taken out on sound recordings by Edison in 1877 which marks the moment, unprecedented in human history, at which sound, and in particular music and the voice, could be stored and circulated without symbolic mediation (as in the musical score). Sound could be detached from its source and experienced beyond 'earshot'. Originally conceived as a stenographic device for offices increasingly overwhelmed with information-processing, the sound recording rapidly transformed the circulation of acoustic messages, dislodging the monopoly which print had enjoyed for several centuries. In so doing, it also threatened the power base of those who had controlled information through the production and circulation of print. The central trope of this book is music-as-weapon. Modern sound technologies produced effects analogous to modern military technologies: amplification produced greater range and greater impact.

The analogy was not lost on military planners, who quickly began to exploit the possibilities of sonic technologies, beyond simply passing orders up the line. As early as 1922, when the RAF was used to enforce the British presence in Mesopotamia, Squadron Leader A.T. Harris ('Bomber' Harris of WW2) described one technique: 'When a tribe started open revolt we gave warning to all its most important villages by loudspeaker from low-flying aircraft and by dropping messages, that air action would be taken after twenty-four hours.'[32] The loudspeaker would become a ubiquitous instrument of military strategy. In 1944 during engagements between enemy troops in Europe, propaganda loudspeakers were deployed by both sides during static periods. In 15th (Scottish) Division's sector late in September, a British officer broadcast a brutal running commentary to the German lines during an incoming Typhoon strike. This, he claimed, 'yielded a useful trickle of prisoners and deserters'. In January 1945, to cover the sound of tanks and guns being moved forward for a major assault on the German lines: 'Soviet propaganda loudspeakers blared music towards German lines night after night.'[33]

The sound recording became central in the resurgent aural information network. Unlike morse it directly rather than symbolically transmitted sounds, and unlike the telephone it was a technology for storage as well as dissemination. Without the means to record and store sound in some form, there would have been no growth in the musical repertoire of radio, no film soundtrack, no television, no personal stereo or internet music shareware. It was in its recorded form that sound and music began to emerge as a potential equivalent site of social power as print. In 1912 the popular and populist US attorney Clarence Darrow was accused of perjury and attempting to bribe a juror (and subsequently acquitted of both). Amid massive local and national publicity, an officer of the National Erectors' Association (aligned with the prosecution), was interviewed by a reporter for Hearst's *Examiner*. Among all the matters that could have been headlined it was a

---

[32] John Sweetman, *Bomber Crew: Taking On the Reich* (London: 2004), p. 6.

[33] Max Hastings, *Armageddon*, pp. 169, 277.

sentence referring to a sound recording of Darrow's conversations: 'I shall convict Darrow with my dictaphone.'[34] Suddenly an oral record assumed all the force of print in a court of law. What once would have been dismissed as 'hearsay' was now validated by sound technology. It was a legal weapon.

The role of sound in relations of power was globally expanded as an instrument of various forms of 'imperialist' violence. The earlier western art music that still dominates concert repertoires was intitially circulated only by the very limited migration of its practitioners, or by a score, the impact of which was limited by class factors such as education. Recorded music requires no symbolic mediation: anyone may hear it directly. The case of jazz is the paradigm. Within only months of its first recordings in 1917, jazz was being spoken of as far afield as Australia, and by the early 1920s was reportedly being played around the world, the most rapid diaspora of a new musical genre in history.[35] The sound recording thus made music potentially an instrument of global imperialism, particularly as the global industry was largely controlled by the US, through its Victor Talking Machine Company, and the Gramophone Company based in Hayes, Middlesex, but half-owned by the US.[36] Jazz was the first manifestation of this phenomenon (decades later, during the Cold War, it would be referred to as America's 'secret sonic weapon'),[37] and the frequent violence of its encounter with 'colonized' cultures (including inside the US, and defined by class as well as place), foreshadowed the twentieth-century dynamic of mass-mediated music. The 1920s was the great decade of the modern 'Aural Renaissance', and jazz is the exemplary musical case study, primarily through the boom in sound recording which culminated in the international 'gramophone fever' of 1929, by which time up to 50 per cent of North American and European households owned a record player, and record sales as far afield as Japan reached ten million.[38]

Jazz was also a leading player in the mass mediation of music through a slightly later development in sound technology, but which was coming into general public use over the same decade: that is, radio. Perhaps the most significant development presented by the new medium was that rather than one to one communication by wire – as in Morse – radio waves could be *broad*cast (that is, mass-mediated). In contrast to the printed press, it could also respond instantly to events, service the illiterate as well as the literate, and corporealize information because of the particular phenomenology of sound. Its acoustic flood carried and consolidated

---

[34]   Stone, *Clarence Darrow*, p. 197.

[35]   See further Bruce Johnson, *The Oxford Companion to Australian Jazz* (Melbourne, 1987), p. 3, and Bruce Johnson, 'The Jazz Diaspora', in Mervyn Cooke and David Horn (eds), *The Cambridge Companion to Jazz* (Cambridge, 2002), pp. 33–54, see p. 33.

[36]   Johnson, 'Jazz Diaspora', p. 37.

[37]   E. Taylor Atkins, 'Toward a Global History of Jazz', in E. Taylor Atkins (ed.), *Jazz Planet* (Jackson Miss., 2003), pp. xi–xxvii; see p. xvii.

[38]   See Pekka Gronow, *The Recording Industry: An Ethnomusicological Approach* (Tampere, 1996), pp. 61, 46.

the unifying values of communities and nations. This sonic information network immediately became competitive with print in terms of both mass distribution and validation of information. As Goebbels would declare in 1933: 'What the press was to the nineteenth century, radio will be to the twentieth.'[39] Its role in transforming US culture, which would become the dominant culture of western modernity, is eloquent. By 1931 in the US 50 per cent of urban families owned radios, and for the growing rural audience it was 'the first affordable and available direct communication'.[40] By 1940, radio news had overtaken the press as the primary source of information.[41] A survey of voters indicated that radio was their 'first source of political news'.[42]

Much of the power of the medium derived also from the capacity of sound to reproduce the immediate sense of being present at events in ways could be matched by no graphic form such as print, a score, or even a photograph. The sense that one was not present at a representation of an event, but at the event itself, made of radio an embodiment of reality. In the *March of Time* series, which began in 1931, mimics were used to create the impression of the voices of participants in reports, and the White House 'complained so strongly about the verisimilitude of the soundalike for FDR that he was dropped'.[43] Two events in particular dramatize the point. The famous 'live' report of the Hindenburg disaster in May 1937, consolidated the idea of radio as something like the authoritative account, even the source, of public events. Arguably it prepared public credulity for the impact of Orson Welles' *War of the Worlds* broadcast on 30 October 1938, and, more ominously, for the deployment of radio in various forms of propaganda throughout an approaching and non-fictional war.

The political significance of this proliferating medium by no means went unnoticed among the authorities. Echoing the association established between social disorder and sound of earlier centuries, Edwin E. Slosson commented in an article 'Voices in the Air' in the *New York Independent* April 1922: 'Broadcasting has turned the nation into a town meeting. But there is no chairman and no parliamentary law. This will bring about anarchy in the ether.'[44] This ethereal clutter grew notwithstanding Hoover's earlier guarantee that he would 'establish public right over the ether roads'.[45] Hoover went on to become one of the early beneficiaries of the way in which the new sonic information network would

---

[39] Cited in Horst J.B. Bergmeier and Rainer E. Lotz, *Hitler's Airwaves: The Inside Story of Nazi Radio Broadcasting and Propaganda Swing* (New Haven and London, 1997), p. 6.

[40] Sean Dennis Cashman, *America in the Twenties and Thirties: The Olympian Age of Franklin Delano Roosevelt* (New York and London, 1989), p. 320.

[41] Ibid., p. 334.

[42] Ibid., p. 336.

[43] Ibid., p. 322.

[44] Cited ibid., p. 312.

[45] Cited ibid., p. 318.

transform politics. In the US presidential campaign of 1928 which brought Hoover to the White House, Democrat candidate Al Smith was a 'vivacious' speaker in person, but

> ... could not be persuaded to stand still before a radio microphone and the effect of his voice, with its pronounced East Side accent, moving in and out of earshot, was grotesque and his words unintelligible to many in the South and West. By comparison, Hoover, who was a dull speaker, disciplined himself to talk directly into the microphone, have his shyness mistaken for modesty, and give a general impression of Midwestern sobriety.[46]

No politician of the era could afford to ignore the resurgence of sonority in the public circulation of information, and the major leaders during World War Two had shown a keen understanding of the new technologies well before the onset of hostilities. 'One of Roosevelt's first decisions in 1933 had been to appoint a committee to examine the role of government in regulating radio.'[47] During the 1930s, Roosevelt's regular broadcasts to the nation provided crucial comfort and reassurance through the parlous times of the Great Depression. Their title, 'Fireside Chats', shows an understanding of the power of the medium to lend friendly intimacy to impersonal public utterance.

Across the Atlantic, by 1931 another future wartime leader Winston Churchill 'was alive to the growing medium of wireless' and for several years had a 'running battle' with the chairman and director General of the BBC about their unwillingness 'to allow him to broadcast on India'.[48] Like Roosevelt, he understood the unprecedented power of the medium in times of national adversity. The first of his wartime Sunday evening broadcast speeches on 1 October 1939 was 'the forerunner of what from eight months later became the most famous series of sound broadcast declamations (for they were that rather than 'talks') in the history of the medium'. It was a 'great success', praised as 'inspiring' by Jock Colville, who as Prime Minister Chamberlain's private secretary and loyalist at the time was actually a Churchill sceptic, and praised as 'excellent' by Chamberlain himself.[49] During the war, as Prime Minister Churchill always saved his 'most resonant' speeches for Parliament and to the nation through the BBC.[50] The 1945 election which brought Churchill's surprise defeat was 'very much a battle of the sound broadcasts', with the possession of radios 'almost universal'.[51]

---

[46]   Ibid., p. 107.

[47]   Ibid., p. 325.

[48]   Roy Jenkins, *Churchill* (London, 2001), pp. 436, 437.

[49]   Ibid., p. 557.

[50]   Ibid., p. 662.

[51]   Ibid., p. 791. For further information on the role of radio in Churchill's post-war career, see ibid., 793, 805, 841.

But it was Hitler, in partnership with Josef Goebbels, who showed the most 'modern' appreciation of the emerging sonic information economy. It was his voice that first awakened Hitler to his own political destiny. He later wrote that as an education officer at a Reichswehr camp near Augsburg in 1919

> ... all at once I was offered the opportunity of speaking before a large audience; and the thing that I had always presumed from pure feeling without knowing it was now corroborated; I could speak ... in the course of my lectures I led many hundreds, indeed, thousands, back to their people and fatherland. I 'nationalised' the troops.[52]

What makes Hitler so 'modern' is not simply his oratorical power, but, along with Goebbels, the effectiveness with which he grafted this to possibilities for mass mediation. In the elections of 1932, through technologized mobility – the aircraft – his energetic 'Hitler over Germany' schedule enabled him to deliver speeches personally across Germany.[53] But it was sound technology that was crucial. Through sound-film and the distribution of over 50,000 recordings of his 'Appeal to the Nation' speech, Hitler flooded the country with that disturbingly electrified and electrifying voice.[54] Supplemented by rented *Lautsprecherwagons* – vans equipped with external loud speakers – to fill the streets with Nazi speeches and songs,[55] his voice became the basis of his connection with the German people, and would reach an estimated 20 million citizens as acoustic theatre through the new facility of *Volksempfänger*, the 'people's radio'. Warming up the radio audience for one of Hitler's early speeches as Chancellor in a February 1933 broadcast from a rally in the Sportpalast, Goebbels exploited the sense of actual presence that could be communicated by the medium, describing in detail the scene with hypnotically repeated references to the flags, the shouting and singing and 'the people, people, people – a mass of people'. To the crescendo of cheering and 'Heil' as Hitler arrived, he cried, 'You can hear it. The Führer has arrived![56] The arrival at the Sportpalast was thus also the 'arrival' of the Führer in the home of every German listening to the broadcast. The careful stage management of these

---

[52] Ian Kershaw, *Hitler*, Two Volumes (London, 2001; first published 1998), Vol. 1, p. 124.

[53] Ibid., pp. 363, 364, 369.

[54] Ibid., p. 369.

[55] There are several focused accounts of the importance of radio in the emergence of the Nazi party, though not all in English. Apart from Kershaw, my most immediate source for much of the information used here is Carolyn Birdsall, '"Affirmative resonances" in the City? Sound, Imagination and Urban Space in early 1930s Germany', in Sylvia Mieszkowski, Joy Smith, and Marijke and de Valck (eds), *Sonic Interventions in Race, Gender and Place* (Amsterdam and New York: Rodopi, 2007), pp. 57–86. My thanks to the author for permission to read and refer to a pre-publication draft, and for her generous sharing of information and sources in discussion.

[56] Kershaw, *Hitler*, p. 453; see also pp. 433, 440.

broadcasts explicitly politicized a paradox that crooners like Bing Crosby had stumbled upon: through the radio voice it was possible to reconcile the mass with the individual, to speak to everyone as though speaking directly to each.[57] There is a further link between twentieth-century US popular music and the Third Reich that is directly pertinent in this context. In spite of Goebbels' intense abhorrence of US jazz-related music, he recognized its power as a potential propaganda weapon, and established several carefully monitored Swing broadcasting bands, including Charlie and His Orchestra which presented US standards with new political lyrics and went out over the airwaves in conjunction with the programmes by William Joyce (Lord Haw-Haw).[58] No-one demonstrated more effectively than Hitler the re-uniting of voice, music and power through technology in the era of modernity.

In the way they impacted materially on the production, circulation and consumption of music, sound technologies enlarged the range of music as 'weapon' and through, for example, editing techniques, from splicing and remixing through to digitization, radically altered its relationship with its sources and destinations. These material changes redefined the ways in which sound and music could be deployed in confrontations over place, identity, class, territory, community. As we shall go on to document, the capacity of technologically amplified, mediated and circulated musics to participate in territorial, ideological and identity encounters, has been exponentially enlarged. This is not simply a matter of range and intensity, but also pervasiveness. In the (post)modern era the ubiquity of music is unprecedented in the West. Experimental monitoring has suggested that in any two hour period, forty-four per cent of activity involves the experience of music, though only two per cent of that is focused listening.[59] Even in a micro-scenario, the invasiveness of music can range from a barely audible and unintelligible music heard through an apartment wall, the fuzz of a Walkman listened to by a fellow bus passenger, or the ringtone of a mobile phone. Each of these opens up a broad range of axes along which the social impact of music may be examined. Apart from the usual approaches to music studies such as semiotics and aesthetics, the irritation caused by ringtones relates solely to the understanding of private and public space, and becomes a case study in acoustics as cultural history, more to do with acoustic ecology. The more intelligible the invasive sound, the more implicated in these other areas: semiotics, music affect, aesthetics, morality. Irritation caused by a song heard clearly though not at a painful volume, implicates private space with taste, opinion, belief. So: the person next door winds up the speaker. It is no longer a matter of someone else's 'private' sound intruding on my private space, but that the song might also be one that is morally and aesthetically objectionable. Sound technologies become sites of contemporary confrontation and violence,

---

[57]   See further, Johnson, *The Inaudible Music*, p. 101.

[58]   Bergmeier and Lotz, *Hitler's Airwaves*, esp. pp. 136–77.

[59]   John A. Sloboda and Susan A. O'Neill, 'Emotions in Everyday Listening to Music' in Sloboda and Juslin (eds) *Music and Emotion: Theory and Research*, pp. 415–29; see pp. 417–18, 420.

between private and public space: between car radios and ghetto blasters, versus corporate muzaks, piped anti-mall-lout music, and political appropriations of public acoustic/musical space, as employed by, for example, Blair (Britpop), Bush (country music) and Australian Prime Minister Howard, whose government used a Joe Cocker recording to sell its tax reform programme.

Thus far we have been setting out contextual scenarios for the association between popular music and violence: the distinctiveness of sonority in the human sensorium; the history of the music/violence nexus; the transforming impact on that nexus of the convergence of sound and technologies. We now move to more specific empirical studies of the links between music and violence in the contemporary world, working through a provisional taxonomy that proceeds from often merely adventitious connections, to increasingly intense forms of complicity in which the causal links between music and pain are both foregrounded and problematized.

Chapter 4

Music Accompanying Violence

Bruce Johnson and Martin Cloonan

In researching the linkages between music and violence, we have become extremely wary of assumptions of causality. At one end of a spectrum, media moral panic arguments frequently take it for granted that adjacency means causality. At the other end, often occupied by fans and popular music scholars, the connection is likely to be uncategorically denied. We have tried to avoid taking either position for granted. Many cases reviewed in this chapter have been presented as evidence for a direct causal relationship between music and violence, but at this point in our argument it seems that the most that can be initially assumed is that they have accompanied each other. The trajectory of the chapter works towards increasingly intense and provocative associations.

Music Representing Violence

Perhaps the most basic connection is to be found in musical narratives about violent people or violent acts. Violent imagery in pop music has become so commonplace that it would be gratuitous and patronizing to begin an inventory. However, it is worth briefly dilating on this category to exemplify the way in which the study of popular music can illuminate the larger history of modernity. A prominent subcategory of music about violence is the 'crime ballad', which appears to have proliferated suddenly from the early eighteenth century. Dick Turpin is a well known example of the posthumous 'merchandising' of a criminal through ballads such as 'Turpin's appeal to the judge'. In his own time, however, other criminals were at least equally if not more celebrated. The great criminal excarcerationist Jack Sheppard was commemorated in ballads and in John Gay's *The Beggar's Opera*, as was also one of his antagonists, the fence and underworld mastermind Jonathan Wild.

A full inventory would tediously restate the obvious, but there is a pattern to be observed here from which hypotheses may be drawn that throw light on modern relationships between violence and pop music, suggesting the potential value of a closer study of this category of violence in music, that would illuminate the larger history of capitalism. Over the eighteenth century, customary rights essential to the survival of a growing underclass came into increasing conflict with the fetishization of private as opposed to common property.[1] The expropriation of common rights by an emerging capitalist class in the interests of private profit through such measures as the enclosures in England and the highland clearances in Scotland also reverberated in cities with the growing industrialization of production and in the massive influx of displaced rural labourers and artisans.

Associated changes ranged from the introduction of new manufacturing technologies, to the criminalization of customary rights and perquisites. Central to this process was a legislative revolution in eighteenth-century England that pitted the 'ordinary' worker against the judicial system with unprecedented brutality. The dominant classes created the eighteenth-century criminal, by eroding his livelihood, by criminalizing custom and by multiplying crimes against property. Through the popular theatre of the criminal as visible prisoner, followed by a procession of humiliation through city streets, and finally as publicly executed victim of state power, the authorities sought to project a cautionary reminder of the wages of sin. But the proletariat audience inverted the meaning of the criminal celebrity into an inspirational reminder of the spectacular potential of their ordinariness, and one manifestation of this was the crime ballad. Far from being cowed by the theatres of state violence the underclasses saw them as metaphors of agency, and during London's Gordon Riots of June 1780 the mob burned Newgate prison to the ground. Beneath all the obvious differences, there are very instructive similarities between the social conditions that generated the Gordon riots and, for example, those of Woodstock '99, considered below. In both cases, a mob (albeit at very different levels of privilege), took revenge on what they saw to be those responsible for withholding entitlements they had been conditioned to expect. Its agenda is mediated through issues of perceived cultural and material deprivation and capitalist exploitation. And in both cases, music has been complicit in, though not precisely the 'cause' of, the public theatre of riot.

It is noteworthy, then, that in England, the crime ballad faded in the early nineteenth century, to resurface in frontier communities like Australia and the US, in bushranger and outlaw ballads respectively. We suggest that this marked the end of a particular phase of conflict in urban capitalism and its expression through state-sanctioned violence. With the gradual advent of the silent system, as surveyed in Chapter 2, judicial violence was hidden away. The last public Newgate hanging was in 1868. With invisibility and silence, the spectacle and the voice that provided the public theatre of criminality was abolished. The heroic celebrity criminal disappeared from London, and with it his capacity to mobilize the underclasses. In 1832 an article in *Fraser's Magazine* wrote about the underworld: 'Formerly the heroes of their party were fellows conspicuous and famed for daring acts of plunder, in which the whole body had a pride, and whome they all felt ambitious to imitate. ... All this kind of heroism has subsided.'[2]

---

[1]   Peter Linebaugh, *The London Hanged: Crime and civil society in the eighteenth century* (London and New York, 2006).

[2]   Fergus Linnane, *London's Underworld: Three Centuries of Vice and Crime* (London, 2004), p. 104.

The heroic celebrity criminals of the eighteenth century reappeared in nineteenth-century frontier spaces still undergoing the struggles between customary rights and new legal constraints characteristic of the earlier phase of capitalism exemplified in eighteenth-century London. In the American west the tensions between the open range cattlemen and the barbed wire fenced sheepmen, between the defeated south and the victorious north, between goldrush adventurers and new mining rights legislation, all created forms of criminal admired by the frontier underclasses. In Australia the conflicts between common property entitlements (land, wandering livestock) and new property legislation produced folk heroes among transported Irish and later itinerant underclasses, like the swagman in 'Waltzing Matilda', an iconic crime ballad. In the US the James Brothers' invocation of Jack Sheppard, and in Australia comparisons between Sheppard and Ned Kelly confirm the export of the celebrity criminal to earlier stages of capitalism.[3]

As economic destabilizations like inflation or the Great Depression again closed the gap between crime and the underclasses, the metropolitan and the rural criminal celebrity (like John Dillinger, and Bonny and Clyde) reappears. *The Beggar's Opera* reappears in 1928 in Weimar Germany, as Kurt Weill's *The Threepenny Opera*. Simultaneously the development of mass media circulated these narratives and stimulated public expectations of access to information, and the transgressive star emerges from the media industry itself. It is worth considering the connections between the decline of public executions in Europe from the nineteenth century, and the rise of media-constructed celebrity. In the modern cult of the celebrity transgressor and the transgressive celebrity, the ordinary person becomes a sacrifice to his own, and the public, desire for the extraordinary, even if that requires transgressiveness, and a kind of death.[4]

The scale of twentieth-century violence and the mass mediation of music have intensified interest in the musical representation of violence and pluralized its manifestations and functional possibilities. Recalling the earlier discussion about the new military technologies, we suggest that the increasingly mechanized character of armed conflict in the modern period has played a role in this process. Unsurprisingly, active service personnel showed a gallows-humour fascination with dismemberment through matérial, as in the Royal Flying Corps mess song:

> Take the pistons out of my kidneys,
> Take the con rods out of my brain.
> From the small of my back take the crankshaft,
> And assemble the engine again.[5]

---

[3] Linebaugh, *The London Hanged*, pp. 7–8.

[4] See further Johnson, 'Applause, Admiration and Envy: crime and the prehistory of stardom' (forthcoming).

[5] Alan Morris, *Bloody April* (London, 1967), p. 96.

This grim acceptance of the industrialization of war resurfaced in the Second World War in such examples as a Russian tank crew song which included the lines 'Our legs are torn off and our faces are on fire'.[6] In trench songs of the First World War, the dehumanizing burden and impact of military technology was ruefully contemplated in 'Living in the trenches':

> You should see my blinking pack,
> Rifle, sword and ammunition
> All in the Alert position.
> One smoke helmet, haversack,
> Fourteen bombs inside my pack.
>
> ...
>
> It's the seventeenth bloody shell we've had.
> Whizz-bangs, coal box, shrapnel soar
> And a blinking mine underneath the floor.[7]

Popular music's fascination with violence has increased. Lizzie Borden, who dismembered her parents with an axe, the ill-fated Tom Dooley, the 'Leader of the Pack' and Bonnie and Clyde were relatively unusual themes for mainstream popular music in their time (up to the 1960s), but subsequently such subjects have become a narrative genre in *oeuvres* including those of Bob Dylan (John Wesley Hardin, Hattie Jones, Emmett Till, Hollis Brown and 'Only a Pawn in their Game'), and Nick Cave (Murder Ballads). Jack the Ripper had to wait until 1974 to become the subject of a musical directed by Brian Rix at London's Ambassadors Theatre, while the gestation time for a Manson opera was only a little over two decades, written by John Moran in the 1990s. Sweeney Todd, the Fleet Street barber who supposedly murdered his customers and cooked them into pies, was staged in the nineteenth century, but turned into a musical by Steven Sondheim in 1979 and in 2008 became a film musical starring Johnny Depp. His 1990 off-Broadway musical cavalcade of US presidential assassins (*Assassins*) enjoyed much greater success when revived in 2004. The history of such music is an instructive supplement to the growing aestheticization of violence.

The rising profile both in size and complexity of musical narratives about violence has a parallel in the development of a repertoire of sonic anaphones for violence.[8] The question of how to musically reproduce rather than merely narrate violence has a lengthy tradition in the west. Monteverdi, who had personal experience of war, spoke of discovering appropriate music for the 'concitato' or agitated style, with rapid repeated notes, suitable for the expression of a man going

---

[6]   Hastings, *Armageddon*, p. 522.

[7]   Quoted Macdonald, *Passchendaele*, p. 158.

[8]   On Sonic Anaphones see Philip Tagg and Bob Clarida, *Ten Little Title Tunes* (New York, 2003), pp. 99–100.

into battle.[9] Hardly a composer has not at some time sought to represent violence in her or his work, from human violence (Prokofief's *Scythian Suite*, Britten's *War Requiem*) to natural violence, as in storms in Beethoven's *Pastoral Symphony* or Vaughan Williams' *Sinfonia Antarctica*. Conversely, some forms of warfare have been modelled in musical terms, such as the German night-fighters which, in 1943, developed a new attack approach on bombers, 'a disturbing new technique of upward-firing cannon (known as schräge musik: literally 'slanting music', but colloquially 'jazz')'.[10] The attempt to produce sonic anaphones for violence is now so common in pop as to require little more than remark in this context. A recent development of this moves disturbingly towards the 'reality television' formula, and raises questions that we will explore later. Playstations such as Kila Kela are music dedicated.[11] Def Jam Vendetta for example is a collaboration between record label and games publisher, and brings together 'underground gangs, hip hop and illegal fighting'. Players can draw music from actual performers into the game: Scarface, Public Enemy and Ghostface Killah, and you can play in the persona of one of the hip hop artists.[12]

This technology leads us to the association between music and moving image, the most prominent category of which is film music. We are particularly interested here in the intervention of modern technology in defining the links between music and violence. Film music so actively develops sonic anaphones for every imaginable form of violence (as for example in extradiegetic music in *Psycho* and *Jaws*, and diegetic music in the helicopter attack accompanied by Wagner in *Apocalypse Now*), that it hardly requires documentation. As in these three cases, the affective relationship between the music and the violence is relatively straightforward and mutually confirming. But shrewd deployment of both diegetic and extradiegetic music can add layers of meaning that nuance our understanding of power relationships. In *A Touch of Evil* (dir. Orson Welles, 1958) for example, violence is pervasive in the setting which is, appropriately, a border zone (US and Mexico), where moral agendas and agencies are ambiguously balanced. Through differentiated genres (most prominently jazz and rock), and media technology (radio, recordings and even the use of a player-piano), the music itself helps to align the various power blocs. The predominant flavour of the extradiegetic music defining 'home' is a progressive jazz score reminiscent of Henry Mancini's other work for the TV series *Peter Gunn*. The diegetic music, however, constitutes a mixture of styles disembodied by predominantly mechanized or technological delivery, which also emphasizes its status as 'the other' in the film's moral scheme. Prominent in this category of music is rock/r&b guitar work over brass riffing,

---

[9]   David Garrett, *Programme Notes* to Monteverdi's Books: Motets and Madrigals of Claudio Monteverdi (Sydney Philharmonia Choirs, April 30 and May 1, 2004), p. 20.

[10]   John Sweetman, *Bomber Crew: Taking On the Reich* (London, 2004), p. 151.

[11]   Nick Barham, *Dis/connected: Why our kids are turning their backs on everything we thought we knew* (London: 2005), p. 282.

[12]   Barham, *Dis/connected*, pp. 282, 287–8.

heard on juke boxes and radios, and evoking members of a leather-jacketed criminal subculture traversed by ambiguities of allegiance and even gender (as 'unnatural' as their music mediations). It is the music they play to victimize the heroine, by keeping her awake in her motel room, then drowning out the sound of her abduction. The fact that the diegetic music is primarily technologically mediated foreshadows the climax, in which the villain incriminates himself by relating his crime to someone whom he is about to kill, unwittingly transmitting the confession onto tape via a walkie talkie.

The point here is that film music has become a particularly useful vehicle for the problematization and differentiation of forms of violence and the moral *schemata* it occupies. While A *Touch of Evil* ingeniously balances sonic genres and media, nonetheless, in the 1950s there was nothing puzzling about the connection between, for example, rock and criminality. Film has since established more complex connections between music and violence, in particular by defamiliarizing the relationships between diegesis, and diegetic and extra-diegetic music, as in Stanley Kubrick's *Dr Strangelove* where comforting songs such as 'Try a Little Tenderness' and 'We'll Meet Again' exist in a disconcerting relationship with imagery of militarism and apocalypse. Similarly, in such films as *The Innocents*, *Clockwork Orange*, *Mean Streets*, *Silence of the Lambs*, *The Professional*, *Performance*, *Goodfellas*, *Reservoir Dogs* and *Blue Velvet*, the connection has become much more aesthetically ambiguous, morally confusing, and affectively ambiguous, as the music often seems strangely inappropriate to the horror or violence we are witnessing. Violence is inflicted to the accompaniment of bubble gum pop, and psychpoaths are lovers of art music.[13] These incongruities produce both a nervous perplexity on the part of the viewer, but also more individualized psychopathic profiles.[14] They imply that things are not what they seem, evoking the darkness under the genial and humane face of culture. There are implications here for the arguments about the banality of the music/violence connection, explored below. Link's overview of the power of what Chion calls anempathetic music, for example, points to an emerging formulaic connection between music and pain based on incongruity. The recent film *Be Cool* concludes with a Kylie Minogue-style video clip being filmed incorporating the image of a man apparently dancing, but in fact writhing because his clothes are on fire, suggesting something also about the re-emerging idea of violence as aesthetic, with its own self-justifying internal formal logic and beauty. The moral dubeities of this aesthetic, especially if draped also in the rhetoric of political protest, are particularly conspicuous in Madonna's egregious video 'American Life' which was withdrawn amidst controversy shortly after its release in 2003.[15]

---

[13]   On the latter, see further Mina Yang, 'Für Elise, circa 2000: Postmodern Readings of Beethoven in Popular Contexts', *Popular Music and Society*, 29/1 (2006): 1–15.

[14]   See further, Stan Link, 'Sympathy with the devil? Music of the psycho post-Psycho', *Screen*, 45/1 (2004): 1–20.

[15]   At the time of writing a concert version remains available on the DVD *Madonna: I'm Going to Tell You a Secret,* dir. Jonas Åkerlund, Warner Music Vision 7599 38681–2,

What all these examples so far have in common is that they remain in the realm of representation: violence as represented in music, theatre, and film. The overview suggests two hypotheses for further investigation.

1. That a fascination with and fashion for mainstream representations of violence has become more widespread in the west in the late twentieth century;
2. That over the same period our attitude towards violence has become increasingly confused and ambivalent – or, that the ambivalence that was suppressed by hegemonic public morality has now outed itself.

Music and Violence in Social Conduct

The foregoing review raises the question: as we now move from representations of violence in the media to violent practices in society, what is the correspondence between this cinematic version of psychopaths, and the musical tastes associated with violent temperaments or episodes? Does it appear actually to be the case that psychopaths themselves deliberately juxtapose anempathetic music and violence, or music which seems to be alien to the affect of violence. Do they carry around (or listen at home to) tapes of Bernard Herrmann's shower scene music from *Psycho*, or is this kind of music specific to cinematic stylization?

When music accompanies overtly violent and psychopathic social practice *what is it actually like*? What do psychopaths really listen to during their violent episodes, and how far might the connection be synergistic? Of course we have media alarms which report the discovery after the event of tapes and videos of the usual suspects (Marylin Manson is one of the first to be rounded up), in the bedrooms of the alleged killers (why always the bedroom rather than in the living room hi-fi cabinet? Further evidence of guilty 'loner' indulgence?). But evidence of the actual soundtrack to violent acts is much more slender. One example of which we have scarifying evidence is the use of music in Nazi concentration camps. It is impossible to do appropriately sensitive justice to this topic in the space available here, but its importance requires that it receives some remark, especially as it still shadows the musical conscience.[16] Music played a number of important roles

---

2006. For an incisive analysis of its politics see Martin Scherzinger and Stephen Smith, 'From blatant to latent protest (and back again): on the politics of theatrical spectacle in Madonna's "American Life"', *Popular Music* 26/2 (2007): 211–29.

[16] Since the end of the war, attempts to use music as part of the healing process have included a performance of Beethoven's Ninth Symphony in May 2000, with British conductor Simon Rattle and the Vienna Philharmonic Orchestra, in the grounds of the former Mauthausen concentration camp in Austria. To his detractors, Rattle declared that the alternative was silence, which was not an option (Martin Kettle, 'Ode to Mauthausen', *The Guardian*, 28 April 2000, part two, pp. 2–3). The BBC also staged a concert in Auschwitz

in all the camps. Guards could order prisoners to sing when marching or during punishments. In his account of life in Auschwitz, Primo Levi describes the music played to march prisoners to their work:

> The tunes are few, a dozen, the same ones every day, morning and evening: marches and popular songs dear to every German. The lie engraven on our minds and will be the last thing in Lager that we shall forget: they are the voice of the resolution of others to annihilate us first as men in order to kill us more slowly afterwards.... What more concrete proof of their victory.[17]

Music was thus a soundtrack to institutionalized psychopathic violence. Szymon Laks writes of his time in Birkenau that: 'music was simply one of the parts of camp life and that it stupefied the newcomer in the same way as did everything else he encountered in his first days in the camp and to which he gradually became "habituated"'.[18]

What kind of music? A dismayingly wide range, from popular and jazz-based music to choral and orchestral groups. The role of music in the Czech camp Terezin (in German, Theresienstadt) is a summation of the unspeakable and inhumane ironies of death camp pathologies. The camp functioned as a way station for Auschwitz, but was also the location for propaganda exercises, including the shooting of a film cruelly entitled *The Führer Donates a Town to the Jews*. Apart from sending to Auschwitz aged inmates who would spoil the appearance of youthful vigor, the camp was cleaned up, painted, and equipped with fake facilities. The camp featured music groups, including the Ghetto Swingers, Jewish fans of the Benny Goodman Swing style that was regarded with such opprobrium by the Nazi leaders. The Ghetto Swingers, however, performed regularly for the camp elite and for the SS itself. They featured in the film, along with a Jewish string quartet playing a classical repertoire, and an orchestra that specialized in Jewish repertoire who also regularly performed for the camp commandant. 'The "reward" for the participating principals was to be transported to Auschwitz', where the leader of the Swingers, Bedrich Weiss (aka Fricek) perished with all his family. Singer Kurt Gerron who had been appointed by the commandant Karl Rahm to run the Terezin cabaret, 'was marched to the gas chamber while being forced to sing the song that had made him famous, the "Canon Song" from *The Threepenny Opera*'.[19] Some who survived joined bands and orchestras in Auschwitz, which

---

in January 2005 to commemorate the sixtieth anniversary of the liberation of the camp, featuring the Russian violinist Maxim Vengerov.

[17]   Primo Levi, *Is This A Man* (London, 1979), p. 57.

[18]   Szymon Laks, *Music of Another World* (Evanston, 1989), p. 117.

[19]   The Nazis have no monopoly on this particular form of cruelty. In his account of the Pol Pot regime, John Pilger describes the fate of the 'much-loved Khmer singer' Sin Sisamouth: 'He had been forced to dig his own grave, and to sing the Khmer Rouge anthem, which is about blood and death. After that, he was beaten to death.' Johh Pilger, 'Year Zero

included an all-woman unit and a swing group called – how can one write this? – The Merry Five.[20]

Music was used to bolster German culture at the same time as it humiliated its victims. At the Belzac camp in Poland the orchestra was forced to play the popular German song 'Everything Passes, Everything Goes By' for arriving prisoners. Laks recalls that at Birkenau, 'the marches we played ... were gay, lively, joyous, and their role was to encourage work in the name of the camp slogan *Arbeit macht frei*'.[21] There were numerous examples of forced singing and music being used to torment prisoners.[22] A forest near that Struthof detention centre in France became known as the 'forest of songs' because of the screams of those tortured by the Nazis to the accompaniment of classical music over loudspeakers.[23] 'Music was used by the perpetrators to destroy their victims psychologically as well as physically.'[24] While some accounts have suggested that the music may also have helped prisoners resist, this is dismissed by Laks.[25] He also argues that at the heart of the use of music in the camps was a contradiction that music – 'that most sublime expression of the human spirit – also became entangled in the hellish enterprise of the extermination of millions of people and even took part in this extermination'.[26] Ultimately this was music '*in a distorting mirror*'.[27] Thus, like Cusick, cited below, he sees the association of music and violence as a grotesque aberration. As our study proceeds, we suggest precisely the opposite: the link is mundane and ubiquitous, part of the potential 'evil of banality', to reverse Arendt's formulation.

In the meantime, the foregoing review of music in the death camps, in which all moral and aesthetic logic is violated, should be borne in mind when assessing arguments about causal relationships between specific kinds of music and violence. The art-music preferences of concentration camp authorities have become a cliché of ironic *dis*association between musical taste and daily conduct. But what little media coverage we have of less state-bureaucratized and maverick psychopath

---

1979' in *Tell Me No Lies: Investigative Journalism and its Triumphs*, ed. John Pilger (Great Britain: Vintage, 2005), pp. 120–57; see pp. 156–7.

[20]   The two quotations are from Michael H. Kater, *Different Drummers*, pp. 179, 181. See pp. 177–201 for a general account of music and especially jazz in the camps.

[21]   Laks, *Music*, p. 17.

[22]   For example see Joseph Moreno, 'Orpheus in Hell: Music in the Holocaust' in Steven Brown and Ulrik Volgsten (ed.), *Music and Manipulation* (Oxford, 2006), pp. 264–86.

[23]   Rory Carroll, 'The Alsace vote for Le Pen was just a protest. Wasn't it?', *The Guardian*, 27 April 2002, p. 11.

[24]   Guido Fackler, '"This music is infernal": Music in Auschwitz', http://lastexpression. northwestern.edu/essays/Fackler2.pdf, accessed 8 February 2008.

[25]   Laks, *Music*, p. 119.

[26]   Ibid., p. 5.

[27]   Ibid., p. 7.

incidental music, is almost disappointingly untinged with the urbane cultural sophistication of Hannibal Lecter. Indeed, it would seem to play directly to the agenda of the anti-pop jeremiads of moral panic. So, for example, the night before Kimveer Gill rampaged through Dawson College, Montreal in September 2006, killing one student and wounding 19 others, he wrote on his blog that he was drinking whisky and listening to heavy metal.[28] In Australia in 1987, when one Gladys Dickinson asked her son to turn down the Dylan album *Desire* at 4 a.m., he trampled her to death to the accompaniment of the song 'One more Cup of Coffee for the road', then sprinkled instant coffee over the body.[29] In Snowtown near Adelaide in the 1990s, the most prolific serial murderers in the history of Australia, John Bunting and sidekick Robert Wagner, with other sometime accomplices, murdered and in many case also tortured with appalling ingenuity, mutilated, dismembered and de-fleshed twelve men and women. Many were tape-recorded during their ordeal, reciting confessions to paedophilia and homosexuality forced upon them by their tormenters. In the course of time the ritual came to include playing the CD album *Throwing Copper*, by the group Live, at full volume, with apparently a particular liking for track two, 'Selling the Drama'. The closest the lyrics come to what could be called acts of violence are actually about resistance to violation: 'hey, now we won't be raped, hey, now we won't be scarred like that'.[30]

Taxonomies: Music as the Muse of Modern Violence

What, then, may be discovered about the connections between music and acts, rather than representations, of violence. The order in which we deal with these represents an increasing intensification of the nexus between music and violence. At one end of a spectrum this connection can be apparently fortuitous – just a coincidence – at the other, the music and violence are in a form of collaboration. The most interesting section of this spectrum is the point at which the boundaries between a coincidental and a collaborative connection break down, because, as we shall see in a case study, this is the point at which the much debated question about 'causality' arises. That is: does violent music cause violent behaviour?

At the supposedly 'fortuitous' end of the spectrum, innumerable examples include violent aggression by and against musicians. The history of jazz and its forerunners is punctuated with episodes of violence. James Reese Europe's

---

[28]   Sheldon Chad and Maggie Farley, 'Montreal killer wanted to die in a hail of bullets', *SMH* online, 16 September 2006.

[29]   Cyriax, *Encyclopedia of Crime*, p. 232.

[30]   Susan Mitchell, *All Things Bright and Beautiful: Murder in the City of Light* (Sydney, 2004), pp. 129, 143, 146. See also Andrew McGarry, 'Live song soundtrack to Snowtown murders, court told', *Weekend Australian* 1–2 March 2003, pp. 6, 21. The version of the lyrics reported by McGarry corresponds more closely than Mitchell's to the online version at www.azlyrics.com/lyrics/live/sellingthedrama.html, as at 2 September 2007.

drummer set the hurdle high with a double whammy – musicians as murderer and victim – when he stabbed his leader to death while the band was on tour in 1919. The jazz chronicle is seasoned with every kind of violence from almost casual mayhem to assault with deadly weapons – beatings (Art Pepper, Vido Musso), armed robbery (Stan Getz), knife confrontations (Dizzy Gillespie and Cab Calloway). On the other end of the transactions, violence inflicted upon musicians includes, almost routinely in some *milieux*, police beatings (Robert Johnson, Red Rodney, Miles Davis), and murder. John Lennon's assassination stands in a long tradition. Trumpeter and contemporary of New Orleans jazz pioneer Bunk Johnson, Evan Thomas, was stabbed on a gig (1931), Robert Johnson was probably poisoned (1938), Chano Pozo was murdered (1948), King Curtis was stabbed outside his New York house in 1971, and Albert Ayler's body was found in New York's East River in 1970, possibly the victim of a gang slaying.[31] Among many other publications, the Freemuse website (www.freemuse.org) catalogues cases from other parts of the globe in which musicians are the target of forms of censorship that range from beatings to execution.

More recently, and especially since the advent of punk, violence has become Jacobean in its theatricality, a comparison we make not simply for illumination, but to caution against the assumption that this phenomenon and its milieu are entirely unprecedented markers of our times. From the late twentieth century it has become a performance accessory, and death a 'lifestyle', from Sid Vicious to Pete Doherty, and the band American Head Charge which succumbs to 'violent bursts of knife-wielding insanity'.[32] Violence is a genre staple in the Gangsta Rap milieu, whose victims include Randy 'Stretch' Walker (killed 1995), Tupac Shakur (killed 1996), Notorious B.I.G. aka Christopher Wallace (killed 1997), Freaky Tah aka Raymond Rogers (killed 1999), Big L aka Lamont Coleman (killed 1999), 50 Cent aka Curtis Jackson (wounded 2000), Jam Master Jay aka Jason Mizell (killed 2002), Suge Knight (wounded 2005), Fabolous aka John Jackson (wounded 2006), and Proof aka DeShaun Holton (killed 2006). At Lisa Maffia's (from So Solid Crew) launch for her debut single 'All Over' (for which she failed to appear), a group of men with a gun entered the club (Turnmills, near The Observer building), then emerged, shots were fired 'and a man killed as he drove away in his Audi TT, a car whose street popularity is due partly to its inclusion in UK garage videos

---

[31]   For the less familiar of these examples see: Europe: LP notes for *Steppin' On The Gas: Rags to Jazz 1913–1927* NW269 1977: 3; Pepper: Art Pepper and Laurie Pepper, *Straight Life: The Story of Art Pepper* (New York and London, 1979), p. 209; Musso: Carol Easton, *Straight Ahead: The Story of Stan Kenton* (New York, 1973), p. 104; Gillespie/ Calloway: Dizzy Gillespie with Al Fraser, *Dizzy: The Autobiography of Dizzy Gillespie* (London, 1980) pp. 128–32; Thomas: Tom Bethell, *George Lewis: A Jazzman from New Orleans* (Berkeley, Los Angeles, London, 1977) p. 89; Pozo: *The New Grove Dictionary of Jazz*, ed. Barry Kernfeld (London, 1988), vol 2, p. 330; Curtis: ibid., vol 1, p. 260; Ayler: ibid., pp. 46–7.

[32]   Alexis Petridis, 'On the edge', *Guardian* Arts, 16 February 2005, part two, p. 12.

and lyrics'.[33] In February 2001 outside Hot 97 Radio Station in Manhattan, as Li'l Kim (Kimberly Jones) and her entourage left after she and the band M.A.F.I.A. had been on-air guests, a shootout involving a rival hiphop group (about 31 shots were fired) left one man injured.[34]

The association with violence is one of the markers of cred or authenticity for African-American rap and hip hop performers. Police believed that when Texas Rapper Big Lurch aka Antron Singleton tortured and killed Tynisha Ysais, it was to 'boost his "gangsta rap" image'.[35] 50 Cent promoted his new publishing venture as devoted to books 'about life on the street and no one knows it better than us', a life of 'death, deceit, double-crosses, ultimate loyalty, and total betrayal'.[36] NWA (Niggaz With Attitude), promoted itself as 'the World's Most Dangerous Group'.[37] Weapons are a standard costume accessory, from 'a collapsible police baton' which Snoop Dogg tried to smuggle onto a commercial aircraft, to the gun he was booked for having in his car along with a large stash of marijuana.[38] In 2007, Grammy-nominated Busta Rhymes (aka Trevor Smith) was ordered to face four successive trials for assault and driving violations.[39] In an upsurge of alarm, joined by then Australian Prime Minister John Howard, over violence on YouTube, it is noted that many of the acts of abuse are accompanied by rap music.[40] The association between this form of music and violence is so endemic that it was reported that New York police have set up a special group to monitor the local hip hop business.[41]

---

[33]   Barham, *Dis/connected*, p. 57; see further Sandra Laville and Hugh Muir, 'So Solid Crew killer gets life sentence', *Guardian*, 29 October 2005, p. 13; Hugh Muir, 'Gun crime squad face questions over Megaman trials', *The Guardian*, 30 September, 2006, p. 11; Hugh Muir, 'So Solid Crew leader cleared of ordering street murder', *The Guardian*, 29 September, 2006, p. 5.

[34]   Gail Appleson, 'Rapper "lied over gun battle"', *The Guardian*, 2 March 2005, p. 17.

[35]   Paul Harris, 'Eight miles of murder', *Observer, World*, 16 April 2006, p. 26.

[36]   No byline; Reuters, 'Books hip-hop off the shelves', *SMH* online, 10 January 2007.

[37]   Edward G. Armstrong, 'Gangsta Misogyny: a Content Analysis of the Portrayals of Violence Against Women in Rap Music, 1987–1993', *Journal of Criminal Justice and Popular Culture*, 8/2 (2001): 96–126; see p. 98. See further NWA World, http://www.nwaworld.com/bio.shtml.

[38]   No byline, 'Rapper Snoop Dogg arrested in the US', *SMH* online, 28 October 2006; see further Jacqueline Maley, 'Snoop Doggy Dogg held by police after Heathrow brawl', *Guardian*, 28 April 2006, p. 7. Dogg's violent reputation led to his being refused entry to Australia, see http://news.bbc.co.uk/1/hi/entertainment/6594557.stm, no byline.

[39]   'Rapper to face four trials', *The [Melbourne] Age* online, 11 July 2007 (hereinafter, *Age*). See further on Busta Rhymes, 'Bodyguard of Busta Rhymes shot dead', *Guardian* 7 February 2006, p. 23.

[40]   Catherine Munro, 'Vandalism and violence', *SMH* online, 15 October 2006; Jano Gibson, 'PM blasts "sickening" gang videos', *SMH* online, 24 January 2006.

[41]   Gary Younge, 'US police put hip-hop under surveillance', *Guardian* online, 11 March 2004, http://arts.guardian.co.uk/news/story/0,,1166792,00.html.

There seems to be no particular pop genre that is not associated with violence of one kind or another.[42] However, apart from gangsta rap, violence is notoriously associated with various Metal genres, and most particularly in the case of Scandinavian Black Metal bands. In 1998 Jon Nödtveit from the Swedish band Dissection was convicted of being an accessory to the murder of an Algerian homosexual. He killed himself in 2006.[43] In 1992, an attempt was made to burn down the house of Christopher Jonsson near Stockholm. Jonsson was the 'frontman' of the Death Metal band Therion, and had been in an argument with Varg Vikernes of Mayhem, referred to above. A note signed 'The Count' was left on the door threatening to return. Shortly afterwards he received a letter from Norway from 'Count Grishnackh of Burzum' (implying the persona of Vikernes, who led the band Burzum under the Count's name) threatening a 'lesson in fear. We are really mentally deranged, our methods are death and torture, our victims will die slowly, they must die slowly'. The perpetrator of the attempted arson was Suuvi Mariotta Puurunen, whose diaries indicated an infatuation for The Count.[44] Mayhem was at the centre of a considerable amount of mayhem. Norwegian Bård Eithun was a follower of the band and played in the bands Stigma Diabolicum, Thorns and Emperor. In 1992 he killed a homosexual he encountered by chance outside a pub, leading him into the woods. 'I was just waiting to get out some aggression. ... It was meant to happen, and if it was this man or another man, that's not really important.'[45] In 2005 Gaahl, vocalist with Norwegian band Gorgoroth was convicted for beating up a man and threatening to drink his blood.[46] On 7 November 1995, an article in Norway's *Aftenposten* newspaper listed the current toll of church burnings as: 1992, 13 fires, nine solved; 1993, ten fires, five solved; 1994, 14 fires, seven solved. A police spokesman declared that in every case solved, Black Metal 'satanists' were involved.[47]

In Italy the Milan-based band Beasts of Satan and its circle achieved notoriety with a pattern of homicides allegedly related to satanism. Andrea Volpe was sentenced to 30 years jail for the murder of his former girlfriend, assisted by his

---

[42] Country music, for example, has been the subject of debate regarding its connections with suicide; see for example Steve Stack and Jim Gundlach, 'The effect of country music on suicide', *Social Forces* 71/1 (1992): 211–18, and a discussion that followed over several years, concluding with Steve Stack and Jim Gundlach, 'Country music and suicide: Individual, indirect and interaction effects. A reply to Snipes and Maguire', *Social Forces* 74/1 (1995): 331–5. Also relevant is Charles T. Wolfe and James E Akenson (eds), *Country Music Goes To War* (Lexington, 2005).

[43] Keith Kahn-Harris, *Extreme Metal: Music and Culture on the Edge* (Oxford, 2007), p. 46.

[44] Michael Moynihan and Didrik Søderlind, *Lords of Chaos: The Bloody Rise of the Satanic Metal Underground* (Los Angeles, 1998), p. 91.

[45] Ibid., p. 110.

[46] Kahn-Harris, *Extreme Metal*, p. 46.

[47] Moynihan and Søderlind, *Lords of Chaos*, p. 102.

current girlfriend and fellow band member Nicola Sapone. Volpe also led police to the grave of two former band members who had been maimed and buried alive as a sacrifice following a gig. Pietro Guerrieri received 16 years after confessing to a double murder, while other members were under suspicion of encouraging suicide. In the wake of these revelations, Milan police began reopening other cold cases.[48] Apart from the high-profile cases of Norwegian Black Metal and Beasts of Satan in Italy, there are similar if less spectacular connections in Germany, France, England, Russia, Poland and the US.[49]

There are also various forms of self-harm among musicians and fans, including suicide, from jazz altoist Sonny Criss 1977[50] to Kurt Cobain, and possibly Richie Edwards, of the Manic Street Preachers, who also exemplifies self-mutilation, carving the words '4 Real' in his arm.[51] Iggy Pop's inclination to self-abuse is notorious to make the subtitle of his most recent biography, *Open Up and Bleed*.[52] Pete Doherty created an inscription in his own blood for the cover of a special issue of the London magazine *Full Moon* on the self-destructiveness of fame.[53] Brian Yap Barry of One Minute Silence claimed to have gone onstage with 83 stitches from a self-inflicted knife wound which he had found a cathartic experience.[54] These are just an Anglo-US sample. Swedish Black metal band Apruptum reportedly inflicted self-torture during their recording sessions, and the vocalist with Norwegian band Mayhem, stage-name Dead, mutilated himself with a broken bottle on stage. He shotgunned himself to death in 1991.[55] The main cause of the statistically high early death rate (around twice the average) among pop musicians is, however, drug (including alcohol) abuse, according to a report of a study conducted by Mark Bellis of Liverpool's John Moores University, of over one thousand prominent pop stars over the last 50 years.[56]

The symbolic barrier between stage and auditorium provides no protection for audiences either. Notwithstanding the riots that broke out at the premiere performance of Stravinsky's *Rite of Spring* in 1913, it is popular music which carries the greatest audience risks. Victims include casualties waiting for pop stars

---

[48]   John Hooper, 'Beast of Satan band members jailed for killings', *Guardian* online, 23 February 2005; James Jam, 'Italian goth metal murder', *NME*, 12 March 2004, p. 25.

[49]   Moynihan and Søderlind, *Lords of Chaos*, pp. 241–88.

[50]   Kernfeld , *New Grove Dictionary of Jazz,* vol 1, p. 255.

[51]   Richard Jinman, 'Fans keep hopes alive for missing', *Guardian*, 1 January 2005, p. 7.

[52]   Paul Trynka, *Iggyi Pop: Open Up and Bleed* (London, 2007).

[53]   Patrick Barkham, 'Doherty expresses pain of fame in blood and Goethe', *Guardian*, 1 February 2005, p. 7.

[54]   Joe Ambrose, *Moshpit: The Violent World of Mosh Pit Culture* (London, 2001), p. 117.

[55]   Moynihan and Søderlind, *Lords of Chaos*, pp. 113, 53.

[56]   Bellinda Kontominas, 'Rock and Poll: Talking 'bout my degeneration', *SMH* online, 4 September 2007.

such as The Beatles in Australia in 1964;[57] the 11 reported killed in the rush for concert seats for The Who in Cincinatti 1979; ten killed in a crush caused by too few exit doors after a rock concert in Central Java province in 2006, reportedly only the latest of several such cases in Indonesia.[58] In the case of the nine killed during Pearl Jam's performance at Roskilde, Denmark in 2000, explanations included poor speakers making the crowd move closer, the rain which made it easier to slip, and U-shaped metal barriers which impeded attempts to get the crowd to back off. All of these were possible contributors, but basically, the problem seems to have been a crowd dynamic, and one factor that seems to have been dismissed was irresponsible behaviour by audience, band or security.[59] Dance parties, venues and festivals have attracted negative attention because of associations with drug deaths, most notoriously ecstasy, although frequently more dangerous amphetamines passed off as such.[60] Other alleged causes include excesses of enthusiasm at festivals (Leeds and the 1999 Woodstock commemoration – see further below) or concert venues (the Stones at Altamont Speedway), and over-zealous police at illegal raves.

Many of these appear to be related to the same Dionysiac dynamic of large crowds as produces casualties in sports arenas, and indeed there are significant crossovers between music and sports events, which invite a reconceptualization of the former as an explanatory model in cases of violence. Fledgling rapper Kevin Federline (K-Fed) arrived at the taping of a wrestling show in October 2006 to be faced by catcalls. He taunted the crowd and offered to rap, but wrestler John Cena responded with the rather provocative suggestion that K-Fed was less talented than Paris Hilton. Challenged to fight it out, Cena bodyslammed the rapper, leaving him 'writhing in agony'.[61] In 1991, rapper Heavy D (aka Dwight Myers) was involved with other musicians in organizing a celebrity basketball game in New York. When 5,000 fans showed up at the gymnasium venue which was designed to hold only 2,700, nine students were crushed to death in the ensuing stampede, and Heavy D took to court the insurance company whom he declared should have

---

[57]   Bruce Johnson, 'The Beatles in Australia', in Yrö Heinonen, Markus Heuger, Sheila Whiteley, Terhi, Nurmesjärvi and Jouni Koskimäki (eds) *Beatlestudies 3: Proceedings of the Beatles 2000 Conference*, (University of Jyväskylä, Department of Music, 2001), pp. 69–78.

[58]   No byline; Reuters, 'Ten killed in Java rock concert stampede', *SMH* online, 20 December 2006.

[59]   Ambrose, *Moshpit*, p. 159.

[60]   Shane Homan, *The Mayor's a Square: Live music and law and order in Sydney* (Newtown NSW, 2003), pp. 137–54; Harriet Alexander and David Braithwaite, 'Annabel drug alert as woman charged', *SMH* online 22 February 2007; 'Dozens of arrests, three overdoses at dance party', *SMH* online, 26 February, 2006; 'Eight in hospital after dance party', *SMH* online, 2 July 2006; Les Kennedy, 'Party girl's dance with death', *SMH* online, 11 August 2007.

[61]   'Federline attacked by wrestler', *SMH* online, 19 October 2006.

paid damages.[62] The linkages between dynamics of sports and stadium music events cover a spectrum from adjacency (as in the Three Tenors concerts held in conjunction with the World Cup tournaments in 1994 and 1998) to synergy, as in the use of anthemic music to arouse the crowds, sometimes in ways that overlap with militarism.[63]

New opportunities for audience violence were presented by the development of the mosh-pit out of the punk scene, and variations such as the wall of death, in which the outdoor crowd divides into two groups which then run at each other.[64] Although intended to be dispassionately statistical this review is beginning to sound like moral panic journalism. This is an apposite moment, therefore, to frame the account of mosh-pit violence with a general caveat: all participants we have spoken to agree with all nuanced accounts we have read, in emphasizing that the mosh-pit is normally a place of harmonized – if robust – interdependencies. This is most evidently so in small local club scenes, where participants know and look out for each other, with the same instinctive attentiveness as any high energy 'dancing' in a confined space, like jitterbugging or jiving. One of Berger's metal-musician informants declared it to be 'good clean violent fun' which he had never seen turn into 'fully-fledged riot'.[65] We shall return to this below, but for the moment, it is the violent aspect of this good clean fun that we wish to refer to.

In 1994 a 23-year-old male at a Motorhead gig in London and a 17-year-old female at a rock club in New York died of head injuries. Club venues now videotape the pit for evidence that the damage is not their responsibility.[66] The travelling Lollapalooza festival, developed from 1991 by ex-Jane's Addiction Perry Farrell, became associated with a proliferation into mainstream space of 'moshing, rioting and injury'.[67] In 1994 it produced two paraplegic cases, at Rhode Island and at a Sepultura/Pantera show in Maryland. In July 2000 at Rockingham North Carolina a triple bill (Metallica, Kid Rock and Korn), attended by 30,000 produced eleven hospitalizations (four with drug/alcohol problems, three with orthopaedic injuries, three with lacerations and one with a peptic ulcer). Thirty-five others who just passed out or were enervated were treated on site, as were 14 orthopaedic injuries, 12 respiratory problems, five victims of assault, and three seizures.[68] At a Rage Against The Machine show in Seattle in 1996, a

---

[62]   Associated Press, 'Rapper sues over fatal basketball stampede', *SMH* online, 31 October 2006.

[63]   See further Ken Mcleod, '"We are the Champions": Masculinities, Sports and Popular Culture', *Popular Music and Society*, 29/5 (2006): 531–47.

[64]   See examples at http://www.youtube.com/results?search_query=wall+of+death&search=Search.

[65]   Harris Berger, *Metal, Rock, and Jazz: Perception and the Phenomenology of Musical Experience* (Middletown CT, 1999), p. 71; see similarly Ambrose, *Moshpit*, p. 93.

[66]   Ambrose, *Moshpit*, p. 4.

[67]   Ibid., p. 43.

[68]   Ibid., pp. 91–2.

14-year-old boy suffered severe brain injury. In March 2000, at a Brixton Academy concert by Slipknot, 20 people were reportedly hospitalized with 'pit' injuries. In December of the same year at the Karisma DJ nightclub in England a 25-year-old man died of a brain haemorrhage induced by 'strenuous activity'.[69] Pit violence is so common that a free clinic in San Francisco's Haight Ashbury established a Rock Medicine programme 'devoted entirely to dealing with mosh injuries'.[70] Karaoke has also provoked its share of violence, including five hospitalized after a brawl in a Sydney karaoke bar, a South Korean billionaire leading a revenge attack after his son was hurt in a karaoke club fight, and the fatal shooting by a security guard who couldn't stand the singing of a karaoke performer in the Philippines, where it is reported such incidents are not uncommon, with performances of 'My Way' being particularly risky.[71]

Just how adventitious are all these connections? The logistics of the music event bring together the participants, but how far the violence of the event is actually caused or made more likely by the musical force-field, is debatable. In January 2004 a nurse died after falling at a beach party in Brighton featuring Fatboy Slim.[72] An unhappy accident, or was she a little distracted, a little careless, because of the music, or because of the total dynamic of the music event? Does the combination of a form of the romantic angst of the artist, a pop culture of theatrical excess, and the carnivalesque, encourage and/or attract public self-mutilation? A report on two teenage girls who tied themselves together and then jumped 17 floors to their deaths in front of their boyfriends, referred to their shared interests: 'They dressed the same – always black, lots of make-up – and they liked the same music, Marilyn Manson, goth rock, metal …' A note in one of their pockets declared that life is not worth living.[73] A provocatively similar case was a double suicide on the outskirts of Melbourne in April 2007 by two young fans of Emo, a genre characterized by a morbid and theatrical romanticism. The press canvassed other Emo fans, including 15-year-old Corey Warren, who has also been through episodes of self-mutilation, something critics say is a pronounced trend in the Emo culture.[74]

The phenomenon of self-harm among youthful music fans has attracted carefully conducted clinical attention, as opposed to the more reductive alarms beloved of the media. That is, they identify statistical tendencies, but problematized by other

---

[69] Ibid., pp. 125, 139, 208.

[70] Ibid., pp. 4, 90.

[71] 'Karaoke bar brawl: five taken to hospital', *SMH* online 14 April 2007; 'Korean tycoon indicted for karaoke brawl', *Age* online 5 June 2007; 'Man shot dead for bad singing in Philippine Karaoke bar', Yahoo news online, 31 May 2007; see also http://forum.vgcats. com/showthread.hp?t=18613.

[72] *Guardian* on-line, 17 July 2004.

[73] Jon Henley, 'Teenagers jump to death in front of boyfriends', *SMH*, 28 September 2005, p. 8.

[74] Neil McMahon, 'Bullying on teen's sad road to oblivion', *SMH* online, 28 April 2007.

variables. North and Hargreaves investigated the relationship between what they described as 'problem music' ('hard rock, hip hop/rap, & punk') and self-harm.[75] Their findings are 'consistent with the notion that there is an association between problem music and self-injurious thoughts/behaviours'. The usual caveat has to be entered however: '... this association is mediated by several other factors (particularly self-esteem) and does not appear to be causal'.[76] A study of self-harm among Goth fans published in the *British Medical Journal* comes to the same kind of measured conclusion:

> Identification by youth aged 19 as belonging to the Goth subculture was the best predictor of self-harm and suicide attempt. This effect was not attenuated by adjusting for identification with any other youth subculture. Self-harm could be a normative component of Goth subculture including emulation of subcultural icons or peers who self harm (modelling mechanisms). Alternatively, it could be explained by selection, with young people with a particular propensity to self-harm being attracted to the subculture. [77]

As in the case of North and Hargreaves, the statistical connection is unequivocal, but the causal connection is 'unclear'.[78] Apart from the questions that always hang on the size of the samples, popular music scholars and fans themselves would be likely to add other cautionary comments, particularly on the assumed homogeneity of the various musical categories and fan communities. But in a refreshing alternative to moral panic spokespersons, such studies do provide carefully framed and (literally) measured responses to the problem.

At the heart of that problem is the relationship between physiological and psychological effects of music and the totality of the musical event. Do certain kinds of music incite violence, or attract violent temperaments? It appeared so to the court hearing charges against a 38-year-old Australian Black Sabbath fan who was found guilty of committing sexual offences against a 13-year-old girl, inspired by hearing that Ozzy Osbourne had allegedly done so.[79] The 'like attracts like' suggestion has plausibility in the celebrated case of the Stones at Altamont: a band, (their 'Satanic Majesties' who 'Let it Bleed'), that had already gained a

---

[75]   Adrian C. North and David J. Hargreaves, 'Problem Music and Self-Harming', *Suicide and Life-Threatening Behaviour*, 36/5 (2006): 582–90, see p. 582. The reading list of this article gives some indication of the range of such studies.

[76]   Ibid., 'Problem Music', p. 589.

[77]   Robert Young, Helen Sweeting and Patrick West, 'Prevalence of deliberate self harm and attempted suicide within contemporary goth youth culture: longitudinal cohort study'. *British Medical Journal online* (bmj.com) 13 April 2006.

[78]   Ibid.

[79]   Leonie Lamont, 'Ozzy Osbourne fanatic's bid to rape girl', *SMH* online, 31 August 2006.

reputation for its association with violence, as is noted by Sheila Whiteley.[80] Her conclusion that the band's music spoke of society's conditions and that blame for the violence lay with the Hell's Angels and other countercultural hucksters is perhaps illustrative of a reluctance amongst popular music scholars to consider that the music *might* be culpable.[81]

Neither The Beach Boys nor The Beatles, on the other hand, had any conspicuous association with violence. The infamous Charles Manson was an aspiring folk/rock artist, and on his arrest for murder he listed his occupation as 'musician'.[82] For some months in 1968 he and members of his 'Family' took up uninvited residence in Beach Boy Dennis Wilson's house. During the occupation Wilson made some (unsuccessful) efforts to interest record producer Terry Melcher in Manson's music.[83] At various times Manson claimed to be working with the Beach Boys, composing, arranging and touring.[84] Finally Wilson had to vacate the house himself, and later received death threats from Manson.[85] On 5 August 1969, Manson visited the Esalen Institute where he played his guitar. Responses among those present ranged from dozing off to walking out. Three days later Manson sent members of his family on a killing spree.[86] Among the authorities Manson claimed for his beliefs and actions were the Bible, Hitler, and The Beatles.[87] Manson would declare that The Beatles ordered the murders and described at length the hidden meanings on their double 'White Album' of 1968 which directed his activities.[88] Chief among these was 'Helter Skelter', which became Manson's code word for the Armageddon he would trigger with the Tate murders.[89]

Like all leisure activities, the musical event engages specific kinds of (in)attentiveness and expectations. These can be exaggerated when mood-altering substance indulgence is present. The bank clerk who crowd surfs in the moshpit after a night on the piss or the nurse who falls off a wall at a concert, are not *caused* by the music, but are risks entered into as part of the total repertoire of the occasion. The more dominant the music in that occasion, the more significant

---

[80]   See Sheila Whiteley, *The Space Between The Notes* (London, 1992), pp. 82–102.

[81]   For a counter-position see Norma Coates, 'If anything, blame Woodstock. The Rolling Stones, Altamont, December 6, 1969', in Ian Inglis (ed.), *Performance and Popular Music* (Aldershot, 2006), pp. 58–69. She also notes the Stones' aura of violence (p. 61), but builds a very different argument from it. See further below.

[82]   Vincent Bugliosi, with Curt Gentry, *Helter Skelter: The Shocking Story of the Manson Murders* (London, 1992), pp. 287, 302, 254.

[83]   Ibid., pp. 211, 213, 339–40.

[84]   Ibid., pp. 174, 643.

[85]   Ibid., pp. 338–40, 286, 338; see other Manson/Beach Boys connections, pp. 117, 213, 235, 248.

[86]   Ibid., p. 374.

[87]   Ibid., pp. 317, 639–41.

[88]   Ibid., pp. 511, 300, 321–30.

[89]   Ibid., p. 376.

its role. In the words of a moshpit habitué: 'When you're psyched up about a band anyway, and you get the chance to see them live, you are really psyched up beforehand about going into the pit. ... People do things in the pit at these gigs that they'd never dream of doing in the real world.'[90]

Case Study: Woodstock 1999

Let us consider a case study in the ambiguity of this relationship between music and actual violence. In July 1999, a music festival commemorating the original Woodstock was held at Griffiss Air Force Base, in Rome, New York.[91] Although marketed as the first Woodstock commemoration over three days, an earlier one held in the Catskills in 1994 also ended in violence, raising questions about the general practicability of such commemorations so long after the original. Running from Friday 23 to Sunday 25 July 1999, it was attended by about 225,000 on the base's 1,300 acres. Two main highly elevated stages East and West, were at opposite ends of the site, two thirds of a mile or a mile apart by different estimates. For a further charge, at a separate stage for smaller bands an Action Lounge provided skateboard, roller blade or mountain bike facilities, though in order to compete with 'action' that developed outside, it also quickly organized various 'nude competitions'.[92] There were also a 280 acre camping ground, an airplane Rave Hangar also for showing movies, and two food courts. The triangular site was surrounded by two and a half miles of a 12-foot high 'Peace Wall' designed to keep out gate crashers. Security 'Peace Patrol' personnel wearing yellow T-shirts numbered 1,250.[93]

From the first night there were outbreaks of riotous conduct, such as pelting Alanis Morissette with shoes, overturning metal garbage cans to use as drums and throwing plastic bottles. Small fires lit by patrons were extinguished by officials, to the annoyance of those who started them. The arrival onstage of Korn on the first night was accompanied by increased frenzy in the moshpit and a sudden influx of injury and OD cases at the medical station, and which was also the place and

---

[90]   Ambrose 109–10.

[91]   Two of the sources for events described below are Stephen Vider, 'Rethinking Crowd Violence: Self-Categorization Theory and the Woodstock 1999 Riot', *Journal for the Theory of Social Behaviour*, 34/2 (2004), pp. 141–66, and David Moodie and Maureen Callahan with Mark Schone (reporting) and Michael Schreiber (photographs), 'Don't Drink The Brown Water', *Spin* 15/10 (1999), pp. 100–114. Our thanks to Liz Giuffré, of the Department of Contemporary Music Studies, Macquarie University, Sydney, for referring and making available a copy of the first, and to Tove Forssell of Åbo Akademi, Turku, for the second. Further relevant information may be found on-line, as for example at www.spin.com/features/magazine/2003/12/soap_opera_year_fred_durst_acts_up/.

[92]   Moodie et al., 'Brown Water', p. 102.

[93]   Vider, 'Crowd Violence', p. 144.

occasion of the first reported rapes.[94] By most accounts, however, a major turning point was during the Saturday afternoon performance to an 'already surly'[95] crowd by Limp Bizkit (Vider spells it 'Bizcuit'), who exhorted the crowd to 'break stuff' before launching into the song of the same name. Plywood was torn from barriers and used to surf across the crowd, and the Peace Wall was being demolished. In the mosh pit there were incidents of violence. During the set there were numerous sexual assaults, including a woman stripped and raped, who later told police she was afraid that if she called out she would be beaten up.[96] Following the Bizkit set, an announcement from the stage called for calm, and for medical teams to be allowed access. By now the medical tent near the stage was dealing with around 200 cases an hour, including broken ribs and a compressed spinal fracture.[97]

On Sunday morning, according to the subsequent recollections of security personnel, there were rumours that a riot might be imminent; there were also rumours (untrue) that kids had been killed in the mosh pit, and other rumours of grotesque injuries – such as a woman's pierced nipple being torn off.[98] On the Sunday night the venue was burnt to the ground by rioters, using, ironically, 'peace candles' handed out by a group called Pax, which were provided for use in a candlelight tribute to Jimi Hendrix.[99] The worst of the fires began during a performance by the Red Hot Chili Peppers. There had been rumours during the week of a special festival finale, but it ended with what was for many a disappointing video/light-show of Hendrix's 'Star-Spangled Banner'. In the course of the riot, food vendor tents were looted, ATM machines were smashed open, an overturned Mercedes was torched, and portable toilets, speaker stands and the main speaker tower were overturned. Some rioters set up their own 'music', forming a 'drummer's circle, banging on trash cans, chanting and dancing'.[100] At this stage many had left, but it was estimated that there were 155,000 still present, of whom some 200–500 participated in the riot, while thousands watched.[101] Seven were arrested during the riot, and another 32 later on the basis of video surveillance footage.[102] In all, two were dead, five rapes were reported,[103] 253 treated at local hospitals and officially between 4,000 and 4,500 at on-site medical stations, though unofficial estimates ran as high as 10,000.[104]

---

[94]   Moodie et al., 'Brown Water', p. 103.

[95]   Ambrose, *Moshpit*, p. 20.

[96]   Ambrose, *Moshpit*, pp. 20–21, Moodie et al., 'Brown Water', p. 106.

[97]   Ambrose, *Moshpit*, p. 20, Moodie et al., 'Brown Water', p. 106.

[98]   Vider, 'Crowd Violence', pp. 153–5.

[99]   Ambrose, *Moshpit*, p. 22, Moodie et al., 'Brown Water', p. 110.

[100]   Vider, 'Crowd Violence', p. 145.

[101]   Ibid., pp. 144–5; Moodie et al., 'Brown Water', talks of several thousand rioters, but how to distinguish between rioters and over-excited spectators?

[102]   Vider 'Crowd Violence, pp. 144–5; Moodie et al., 'Brown Water', gives a total of 44, p. 114.

[103]   *Village Voice* said eight rapes and sexual assaults; Ambrose, *Moshpit*, p. 16.

[104]   Moodie et al., 'Brown Water', p. 114.

Drugs and alcohol were arguably factors, since studies suggest a link with these and 'a predisposition to violence', the common factor being 'sensation-seeking'.[105] Beer, LSD, Ecstasy, PCP, heroin, mushrooms, ruphinol and nitrous oxide were circulating during the festival, resulting in 37 arrests before the riot, and a stream of bad trip/OD cases to the medical facility. No-one, however, made any study of the correlation on this occasion.[106] Apart from this lacuna raised by Vidler, several other aggravating factors call for remark. The record high summer temperatures, endured on an almost shadeless expanse of concrete tarmac where drinking water was not easily available, contributed to hundreds of cases of heat exhaustion and dehydration, and in one case the death of a veteran of Woodstock 1969 who had recently undergone heart surgery.[107] These circumstances in turn point to major deficiencies in the organization of the event.[108] There was inadequate plumbing for all purposes, including various vendors, ablutions and toilets. The Port-a-Sans were already overflowing by late on Friday. Some one hundred patrons who sought relief from the heat by jumping into a muddy puddle were actually frolicking in human waste, which, by Saturday, had overflowed into campsites. By Sunday shower facilities were either turned off or simply lost pressure.[109]

Nor was clean drinking water easily to hand. In that vast but enclosed space, profiteering was rife. On-site vendors were subcontracted by Ogden Corporation, part owners of Metropolitan Entertainment which in turn was co-owned by one of the festival promoters. Ogden sold water at a little over three dollars a bottle to the vendors, who then sold it to patrons at four dollars. The only free water taps were at 'vast distances from the stages'.[110] When Ogden ran out of water on Saturday, vendors with their own supplies wanted to sell bottles at two and three dollars each, a move also urged by medical staff. Ogden insisted the price remain at four dollars, threatening closure or fines.[111] So with other services and facilities. To sustain its on-site monopoly, Ogden forbade patrons from bringing in sandwiches or bottled water, in addition to other items like drugs or alcohol. Security guards on the gates conducted random searches, and allowed contraband in for a price.[112] The Peace Patrol security staff, drawn from a range of labour pools including the local unemployment office, were housed in such spartan conditions that, already understaffed, about a hundred had quit by Friday night. Many simply removed their badges and T-shirts and joined the party, and only 175 signed in for Saturday night

---

[105]   Vider, 'Crowd Violence', p. 145.

[106]   Vider, 'Crowd Violence', p. 145; Moodie et al., 'Brown Water', pp. 103, 104, 105, 106.

[107]   Moodie et al., 'Brown Water', p. 103.

[108]   The parallels with Altamont are notable, if we replace heat with cold as an aggravating factor. See Coates, 'If Anything', p. 66.

[109]   Moodie et al., 'Brown Water', pp. 102, 101, 104, 108.

[110]   Ibid., p. 102.

[111]   Ibid., p. 108.

[112]   Ibid., p. 102.

duty. At the height of the riots they felt they had little choice but to abandon their positions, leaving crowd control to incoming state troopers with pepper spray.[113]

Vider reviews a number of explanatory theories. Self-categorization theory would propose that the formation of social identity, proclaimed in the social categories implied in participants' comments about how 'we' felt and why 'we' acted, was a determining influence. But, as he asks, 'what category does this "we" represent? The concert-goers? The rioters only? The younger generation present?' Each of these is implied in some statements, and they are not mutually exclusive. Several commentators identified the riots as a reaction against filthy conditions by white, suburban middle class, predominantly male, youth, a profile that tends to be confirmed by photographs in *Spin*.[114] Is this what was in their minds when they said 'we'? Vider asks, 'Did this social self-categorization [however articulated] cause the riot or did it emerge as an effect?'[115] Most instructively, Vider discusses the importance of memory,[116] which he notes is especially powerful in a commemorative event like Woodstock 1999, as evinced in some significant accounts by those who attended:

The American Dream died in the 60's, but every new generation finds it amusing to unearth the poor mother for a renewed kick in the ribs.

Woodstock (the original) symbolized 'rebellion against the mainstream'. (But this raises another far-reaching question: what can you do when rebellion *is* the mainstream, fully commodified in acts such as Nirvana and Eminem? We pursue these issues below.)

Vider's study is admirably nuanced, though underplaying the pervasive squalor, and decribing the festival as running 'relatively smoothly' until the last night.[117] It is hard to reconcile this with the moshpit violence and sexual assaults of the previous days. Compared with other accounts, he tends to present the rioting as a discrete outburst rather than as a culminating act. Our interest is in the relationship between music and violence, and we shall focus on music as woven throughout the larger ambience. Prior to the worst rioting on the Sunday, that ambience was described by one of the promoters as that of 'a frat party'.[118] Glib, but a good start. The festival opened with the MC calling from the stage 'Show us your titties' and James Brown began the music with 'Sex Machine' and 'It's a Man's Man's Man's World'.[119] Some called the event 'Tittystock' in reference to its sexual and sexist flavour. During Jewel's set on Sunday evening audience members held up a sign

---

[113] Ibid., pp. 102, 104, 105, 112.

[114] Ambrose, *Moshpit*, p. 24.

[115] Vider, 'Crowd Violence', p. 146.

[116] Ibid., p. 161.

[117] Ibid., p. 144.

[118] Moodie et al., 'Brown Water', p. 108.

[119] Ibid., p. 101.

reading 'JEWEL: FUCK ME NOW'.[120] Public and group sex were rampant, but by no means always consensual. Apart from rape itself, in the moshpit women were groped and assaulted, in one case to the cry 'Rip her apart' from a male onlooker.[121] One male fan was reportedly heard to say that the pit was 'the closest thing to assault and battery you're going to get without getting arrested'.[122] Masculinist energies were certainly not dissipated by facilities like the Action Lounge, and manifested themselves in national as well as gendered tribalism. When Canadian act Tragically Hip elicited an impromptu *a capella* 'O Canada' from audience members decked out and painted with the maple-leaf flag, other sections of the crowd sang 'The Star Spangled Banner' and threw missiles at the Canadians.[123]

This brings us to music and stage conduct. All accounts suggest an association between transitions in the festival dynamic and music-making both on and off stage. According to the *Spin* account the first performer to explicitly incite violence was Jamiroquai's Jay Kay on Friday afternoon. Telling the crowd to throw shit, he found himself on the receiving end.[124] But if we are assigning responsibility, let us note that Alanis Morissette suffered an apparently unsolicited hail of shoes. While the arrival of Korn coincided with increased moshpit violence, there is no record of the band having explicitly incited it. However, at Friday night's performance, Offspring's Dexter Holland beat up an effigy of the Backstreet Boys with a baseball bat.[125] On the same day Lit's Jeremy Popoff set his guitar alight, and the next day Wyclef Jean tried to do the same thing in emulation of Jimi Henrix, but succeeded only in burning his hand.[126] In the minutes *before* Limp Bizkit took the stage on Saturday evening the crowd was already throwing missiles and demolishing plywood structures.[127] The order of events was not always reported thus. But these destructive energies were certainly not diminished when Fred Durst called out 'How many people have ever woke up in the morning and just decided you're going to break some shit?' as the lead into 'Break Stuff'. A little later he urged them to 'get all your negative energy out'. The crowd obliged with increased missile barrages and moshpit violence. He later exhorted fans to be careful of injuring each other, but also told them *not* to 'mellow out'.[128] First aid stations treated 'at least a dozen serious injuries; ten people with head trauma were removed by ambulance'. Insane Clown Posse staged a fight with a man in police uniform. On Sunday Ice Cube presented 'Fuck Tha Police'. Shortly thereafter security personnel suffering various forms of assault began to hide their Peace Patrol insignia, and later in the

---

[120]   Ibid., p. 110.

[121]   Ibid., pp. 104, 103, 105.

[122]   Ambrose, *Moshpit*, p. 20.

[123]   Moodie et al., 'Brown Water', p. 104.

[124]   Ibid., p. 101.

[125]   Ibid., p. 103.

[126]   Ibid., pp. 104, 105.

[127]   Ibid., p. 105.

[128]   Ibid., pp. 105–6.

evening state troopers would withdraw in the face of missiles. 'Follow us', called one fan, 'We're gonna go kill the cops with glow sticks'.[129] While acknowledging that, in Buford's words, 'A crowd creates the leaders who create the crowd', Vider notes that 'at the very least, their lyrics and behaviour reinforce social norms of destruction and rebellion'.[130]

With our focus on music, we want to explore some developments of Vider's enquiry. First, not all crowds, including music crowds, riot; nor are all rioting crowds music fans. The high profile provocations by performers mentioned above tend to obscure the fact that there were at least two dozen acts at the Festival (as listed in *Spin*), and in the great majority of cases no acts of incitement are recorded. Some of the on-stage imagery of violence, such as simulated fights and effigy-bashing, also suggests a strong element of the kind of game- and role-playing such as that found in forms of theatre never charged with generating social violence, from Punch and Judy to Commedia dell'Arte. The simple causal link from music to riot alleged by some media coverage, remains unclear. On the other hand the lack of balance between costs and services seems to have been particularly important. 'Burning stuff isn't the nicest thing to be doing, but it was justified', said one girl. 'They took advantage of us. ... I was forced into paying $50 for water that cost $1 in the supermarket.'[131] 'It wasn't Woodstock. It was Commercialstock', said one rioter.[132]

There is much in this comment, since it invokes the original youth music event as a reference point for dissatisfaction. The Woodstock thirtieth anniversary festival explicitly invoked that model, and invited members of a new generation to live out its *mythos*. Co-promoter and 'original Woodstock Guru' Michale Lang declared ingenuously that the objective was, as in the first Woodstock, 'to liberate them so they can live the way they want to do'.[133] The aura of the original Woodstock has been strongly interrogated, as in Norma Coates's robust essay on the 'mass-mediated fantasies divorced from the actual realities of events' that haloed the late 1960s counter-culture, which was 'rarely counter anything, especially that long-standing villain, capitalism'.[134] Few of those present at Woodstock '99 had been born at the time of the original, which thus existed only as a highly mediated event – music clips, photographs and most likely rose-tinted recollections of parents – that had romanticized the music and its emancipatory possibilities.

Given this, and the profound changes in the character, function, semiology, technology and industry context of pop over those 30 years, the original, as imagined, could never be recreated. A 19-year-old women noted the change: 'I'll tell you what, man, its a generation of ambivalence. ... Older people will never get

---

129   Moodie et al., 'Brown Water', pp. 110, 112.
130   Vider, 'Crowd Violence', pp. 154–5.
131   Moodie et al., 'Brown Water', p. 114.
132   Vider, 'Crowd Violence', p. 148.
133   Ambrose, *Moshpit*, p. 18.
134   Coates, 'If anything', p. 59.

it.' And from a male participant: 'Our generation ain't stupid. We're going to get our money's worth, *then* riot.'[135] Ambrose suggests that the Generation X-ers of Woodstock '99 were not as fortunate as the hippie audiences of the original. They live 'inside society, often living at home with parents and step-parents indifferent to their needs or behaviour'. There were no roads out, no communes, no Marrakesh Express.[136] Steve Berlin of Los Lobos (who performed at the riot) observed

> This is the first generation that's been branded their whole lives. They've been identified as a market opportunity since they drew their first breath. And when you take those people and tell them this is going to be culturally and historically important and it turns out to be another commercial, I'd probably get pretty pissed off too.[137]

The cynicism was reflected in a comment from Everlast:

> People are trying to blame bands for what the kids did and say what a reflection is is on this generation. All those people are nostalgic for something that happened 30 years ago. I don't think anything real came out of that first experience – it was just three days of sex and drugs and 'Oh the world is such a . great place!' then they went home, became yuppies, and fucked the whole country up.[138]

Perhaps the particular problem with pop music is that it so often explicitly proclaims the possibilities of transcending the political economy which largely produces it, and to which it must submit and limit itself. What can you do with a chocolate bar that doesn't give you a new life after all, especially if that promise was so obliquely inscribed as to be subliminal? Ah, but music. Apart from what we may suspect about its physiological effects, pop is implicitly and often explicitly about transcending this banal quotidian. Being so intensely a site of an emancipative imaginary, its failure to deliver brings to a point of angry focus the accumulated force of all those other promises that consumerism fails to deliver, especially if experienced as part of an array of the other disappointments that accompanied 'Commercialstock'.

If music was implicated in this riot, a great part of the reason seems to be that it was music billed in a way that required it to bear a semiotic and mythic burden far beyond its capabilities.[139] Arguably, this has generally become true of cultural commodities in the late twentieth century, when the combined imperatives of consumerism and advertising have invested commodities with promises well in excess of what they can deliver. It is not just music, but cars, jeans, computers, coffee – every commodity within the consumerist network – that promise not

---

135   Moodie et al., 'Brown Water', p. 114.
136   Ambrose, *Moshpit*, p. 24.
137   Ibid., p. 25.
138   Moodie et al., 'Brown Water', p. 108.
139   See similarly Coates, 'If Anything', pp. 62, 68.

simply basic use value, but transcendence of the utilitarian. This product, from tampon to taco, will give you freedom, identity, meaningfulness. And of course they cannot honour these promises. Apart from the absurd disparity between product and promise, to honour the promise, to provide satiety, would break the acquisition/consumption/production cycle, and destroy the basis of consumerism.

Popular music proclaims itself as a space in which aspirations to transcendence are mandated, and thus offers itself as the space where, and through which, those disappointed aspirations seem most appropriately to be theatricalized. Pop music spectacle focalizes consumerist disappointment. It is notable how much of this riot consisted of theatre and spectacle: the objects destroyed, the incantations, the conduct of the rioters and even their accounts of what they were doing. 'This is to show everybody that we're young and we don't care, just burn everything.'[140] Woodstock '99 was rather like – and in some ways was – a civil war. The music event creates an authorizing space for a range of particular personal and local agendas. Apart from Woodstock '99, moshing in general exemplifies the point, as in the description of a co-mosher who was 'getting really violent in the pit. He'd say that sometimes he got so angry that he wanted to kill people. He was hooked on crack and couldn't hold a job down. He'd punch guys in the pit. He'd bite people. I didn't like being in the pit with him'.[141] A female mosher complained about male 'tough guy' conduct in the pit, which she described as 'a great way to work out all the shit that's going on in your life'.[142]

In the case of the Woodstock '99 festival the moshpit was one of the sites of injury and sexual assault. It is useful to recall, then, the point made about the relative safety of small-scale local club moshpits, which normally seem to play the same cathartic rather than inflammatory role as other contact sports in contained spaces.[143] The relationship between an underground metal band and its local audience, is not the same as exists between a pop mainstream metal group and the regionally diversified audiences that arrive in their hundreds of thousands for a massive festival, as at Woodstock '99. Each aggregation constitutes a different kind of 'interpretive community'. The smaller local event is indeed a 'community', within its own familiar space with shared histories, agendas and understandings of itself. An event such as Woodstock '99 embodies a very different internal dynamic, with different relationships between all participants and a wider range of invisible agendas.

> The worst pits are ... connected with stadium nu-metal and rap-metal. A lot of these bands are the mainstream chart acts of the moment, attracting the largest possible numbers of extremely young fans. ... They're often of an age when they imagine themselves to be

[140] Vider, 'Crowd Violence', p. 146.

[141] Ambrose, *Moshpit*, pp. 107–8.

[142] Ibid., p. 170.

[143] See Berger, *Metal, Rock, and Jazz*, pp. 271–3.

tough guys, and they're at the receiving end of an intimidating amount of corporate propaganda which expects them to act up.[144]

This suggests that it is the size and audience profile that makes a large rock festival a likely site for violence. The history of the annual Leeds Festival certainly tends to reinforce the hypothesis. In 2002 the final night witnessed violence between around 500 fans and the police during which 71 mobile toilets were burned.[145] Forty arrests were made and damage was estimated at £250,000. Eight fans were later sentenced to community service and made to pay compensation of between £200 and £500.[146] The festival was then moved from Temple Newsham to Braham Park, but the new site was also the subject of violence in 2005 when a series of fires were started after the festival.[147] In 2006 concern about such incidents led to the formation of a campaign called Love Not Riots. Its aim to counter what it terms as 'a trend growing for last night riots at festivals' recognizes a generic tendency.[148] However, Norma Coates suggests that while rock festivals assemble a volatile audience, the problem presented by scale is transgeneric, citing the violence at the Newport Jazz Festivals which led to its cancellation in 1961.[149] We could add to these the cases of jazz festivals in the UK, notably Beaulieu in 1960, where personal injury and assaults on property – climbing and destroying media scaffolding, setting fire to cars – attitudes to the media and the post mortem moral outrage strikingly anticipated the pattern at Woodstock and Leeds. And we should note that 1960 seems to have been a critical year, reminding us of the importance of the moment as well as the event. Writing of that Beaulieu 1960, George McKay makes an observation that resonates very strongly with the dynamic of Woodstock '99, that two versions of national identity were in competition.[150] The focus on 'rock' in the discussion and condemnation of festival violence might be usefully shifted to 'festival'.

But there appears to be an intensification of violent potential in the case of late twentieth-century rock. In the larger picture, rock's offer of an escape from the banal and the ordinary, its promise of (positive or negative) transcendence, makes it a focal point for all the broken promises and disappointments of consumerism. Berger's ethnography suggested that 'a crucial context' of metal in particular is the 'frustrations of blue-collar life in a declining economy', especially as experienced

---

[144]   Ambrose, *Moshpit*, p. 93.

[145]   Martin Wainwright, 'Mob's antics may force festival move', *Guardian* 27 August 2002, p. 5.

[146]   'Leeds festival violence: eight sentenced', *NME* 1 March 2003, p. 4.

[147]   'Leeds looks to future after more scenes of violence', *NME* 10 September 2005, p. 10.

[148]   www.lovenotriots.com/about.php.

[149]   Coates, 'If Anything', p. 60.

[150]   George McKay, *Circular Breathing: The cultural politics of jazz in Britain* (Durham NC, 2005), pp. 75–7.

by males.[151] Joe Ambrose's experience of Slipknot gigs suggests that its fanbase is largely disenfranchized working class kids who are promised all, given nothing, and who never come up to the standards of success circulated in the lifestyle media. This view is shared by at least one member of the band who sees its success as 'payback time for middle America. "All of us were so used to having the middle finger thrown at us that when we finally threw it back, we did it with ten times the venom"'.[152] The gap between promise, engineered desire, expectation and delivery has widened between the two Woodstocks. In Ambrose's words, moshing is 'a placebo for the life none of us can have' or, to quote Berger, 'an arena in which the participants engage with emotions denied in daily life'.[153]

The desire for spectacular theatrical statement contributed to a very ambivalent attitude towards the media at the Woodstock '99 festival. On the one hand, as a symbol of the resented corporate exploitation, media apparatus came under attack. Apart from the destruction of speaker towers and other equipment already mentioned, MTV personnel were abused and attacked. Sheltering from assault on the Saturday night, they decided not to go ahead with plans to tape Limp Bizkit.[154] Some rioters also stood atop the overturned speaker towers 'in triumph'. This posture illustrates the ambiguity of the media presence: it was also a potential platform for self-display, and encouraged, both actively and unwittingly, sensationalist transgressive behaviour in its immediate vicinity. A local radio station 'put two naked women on top of its RV and used the loudspeaker to recruit willing females'.[155] Like all riot coverage from Watts to Paris, those actually in the affected space were often bewildered by media images, having had little or no exposure to them at the time. This was a huge space, two stages about a mile apart, and evidently with unsynchronized dynamics. Rage Against The Machine was at the festival only for a few hours, but in that time band member Tom Morello saw enough to suggest that the media coverage 'was grossly unfair and youth-bashing and tried to vilify an entire generation'.[156] Most bands and fans were apparently as well-behaved as is reasonable to expect at a pop festival, and many departed before the worst of the rioting. For these, the riots were indeed a media event.

And this was often so for the rioters themselves. One participant eagerly declared, 'I can't wait to watch this on TV and see what it looked like'.[157] In what is almost an afterthought, Vider spoke of an 'uncanny sense of performance' in the conduct of the rioters. We would bring that forward. One participant said: 'We knew we had to go back to dull, boring lives and wanted something to remember

---

[151] Berger, *Metal, Rock, and Jazz*, p. 283; see also p. 74.

[152] Ambrose, *Moshpit*, pp. 132, 133.

[153] Ambrose, *Moshpit*, pp. 79, 232; Berger *Metal, Rock, and Jazz*, p. 291.

[154] Moodie et al., 'Brown Water', pp. 102, 103, 105.

[155] Ibid., p. 104.

[156] Ambrose, *Moshpit*, p. 25.

[157] Vider, 'Crowd Violence', p. 162.

Woodstock by.' Another: 'I tried to start a riot twice today because I was bored.'[158] Bored, disappointed at the continuity of a boring life and with the boredom at what promised transcendental theatre. So we make our own liberating theatre.

> When things were really raging, we saw a couple of guys strip naked and start doing indigenous dances as if their whole life had led up to that moment. One guy climbed on top of a display speaker. He was giving a sermon like Christ – as if he was the chosen, with his hands up in the air, yelling, 'Praise me, I'm God'.[159]

Why were the rioters mostly male? Is it that it is they who are conditioned to theatrically demonstrate public mastery and control, and who are most aggrieved when they are falsely promised such transcendent public mastery? They were compelled to make noise. The impromptu percussion on upturned garbage bins that began on the first day became increasingly central as a focus of mob identity and solidarity. When the state troopers and a fire engine rolled in on Sunday at the peak of the rioting, they were attacked by the mob who were also in process of bringing down the fifty foot speaker tower at the East stage. 'Almost 200 formed a drumming circle, banging on overturned garbage cans with their hands, chunks of wood, a sledgehammer, an axe.'[160] As the troopers finally succeeded in forcing the rioters back towards the campsite, when they got to drum circles, 'resistance stiffened'.[161] Noise is one of the constituents of the mob, integral to its solidarity and to the understanding of its dynamic. The presence of music should be centralized in any study of mob activity.

One of the issues this discussion works its way towards is the vexed question of causality. This is much debated in the general issue of the relationship between representations and acts of violence. There are two categories which arise from this relationship: music which explicitly incites violence, and music which arouses violence. Both of these have been present in the samples reviewed in this chapter, yet the overlap between them is extremely erratic. They are separable constructs, because incitement is in the music, and arousal is in the listener, and it is instructive to the study of music affect to recognize this difference. In a way that the varieties of musical taste make obvious, music may incite, but fail to arouse a particular audience. It may also not seek to arouse violence, yet become complicit in it. Thus, two further categories of the connection between music and violence are foreshadowed.

---

[158]   Ibid., p. 149.
[159]   Moodie et al., 'Brown Water', p. 14.
[160]   Moodie et al., 'Brown Water', p. 112.
[161]   Ibid., p. 114.

Chapter 5
Music and Incitement to Violence

Bruce Johnson and Martin Cloonan

The *Compact Oxford English Dictionary* defines the verb 'incite' as to 'urge or persuade to act in a violent or unlawful way'. In our discussion the emphasis is on the term 'violent', and while much of the violence takes us into the realm of the 'unlawful', this is not always the case. Incitement may be explicit encouragement, or latent in the peer-group validation of violence as a social option, an example of how one may behave, and in this sense the cases cited below can be supplemented by reference back to some of those referred to in the previous chapter. We distinguish 'incitement' from other connections between music and violence, such as 'causing', 'generating' or 'arousing' by virtue of the fact that incitement is in the music, while the others are in its audience. We recognize that the distinction is not absolute, as in the example of a band that destroys its equipment while performing. We also recognize, and discuss below, that some forms of vilification are 'symbolic violence', so that incitement is itself a form of violence. That having been said, we find the distinction we have made a useful way of erring on the side of caution in the matter of causality. We have therefore restricted our examples of 'incitement' to its explicit presence or apparent endorsement, with appropriate qualifications. This also involves a rather literalist interpretation of the term that emphasizes lyrics rather than music, and we take this up in the following chapter.

One further caveat, which will resonate through the chapters that follow. When we speak of incitement being 'in a piece of music', we do not necessarily imply that the music overall is therefore to be regarded as inciting violence, any more than the exhortation to violence by a character in a play implies that the play seeks to incite violence. The authors are in some disagreement on this matter, but both accept that it is not axiomatic that the narrative voice of a lyric expresses the overall thrust of the song containing the lyric. To circumvent our differences of emphasis on this, we have confined our examples of incitement to statements which are not part of a dialogue within the song, and which are not in some obvious way contested by any other aspect of the music. Whatever their ontological status, the words 'Smack your bitch up', or 'Kill the Jews', belong to the category of incitement. We refer to them as 'being in the song' in the sense that they are not anywhere else in the musical event. We make that distinction as part of the larger distinction between incitement and arousal, and we shall return to it in the next chapter.

Incitement: State-based

Incitement to violence in popular music continues an ancient tradition which is state-sanctioned rather than unlawful, as in the war cries discussed in Chapter 1. And what could be more fully authorized than a national anthem? The second verse of the UK national anthem includes a prayer that God will 'scatter her enemies and make them fall'. The more graphic sanguinity of France's 'Marseillaise' is sustained by the refrain

> To arms, citizens,
> From your battalions
> Let us march, let us march,
> May tainted blood water our fields.

Stalin's interventions in the composing of a new national anthem, referred to in the Introduction, included the addition of a rousing verse about the destruction of the Fascist forces.[1]

In times of conflict various forms of nationalism brutalize musical expressions of patriotic and political causes. During the 'troubles' in Northern Ireland from the late 1960s, each side used song to vilify the other, as in the Loyalist 'I Was Born Under a Union Jack' (to the tune of 'Wandering Star' from the 1969 film *Paint Your Wagon*), which spoke of killing Taigs (Roman Catholics).[2] Nationalist songs over recent decades have reflected the violent pornification of forms of popular culture, incorporating vilification and detailed exhortations that would certainly attract condemnation from its own advocates if found in pop music. The wars in the former Yugoslavia produced hate songs in the style and tenor of Gangsta Rap, as in the Croatian band CLF's 'Hrvatska Mora Biti Slobodna', with its reference to 'home boys'. and lines addressed to Slobodan Milosevic like 'suck my dick' and 'fuck you!'[3] In 2005 *NME* reported a spate of 'terror pop'.[4] It included Egypt's Sha'ban Abed al-Rahim, whose single 'I Hate Israel' claimed that the US itself destroyed the twin towers on 9/11. In Russia, 22-year-old Nato, a 'suicide bomber singer', used al-Jazeera, Nasdaq and al-Qaeda imagery in videos, and had his 'terror concert' in Moscow cancelled because it was scheduled so soon after the Beslan massacre.[5] In Zimbabwe a song attacking Tony Blair referred to a local latrine whose inventor shares the PM's name. The lyric includes "The Blair I know

---

[1]   Montefiore, *Stalin*, p. 469.

[2]   David Wilson, 'Ulster loyalism and country music, 1969–85', in Wolfe and Akenson, *Country Music Goes To War*, pp. 192–208, see pp. 198–199.

[3]   CD accompanying Svanobor Pettan (ed.), *Music, Politics and War: Views from Croatia* (Zagreb, 1998).

[4]   Jamal Ahmand, 'Terror pop', *NME*, 12 March 2005, p. 25.

[5]   Ibid.

is a Blair toilet"'.[6] Lest we imagine such practices as confined to exotic cultures, US tank crews in Iraq pump themselves up in the defence of US values with the kinds of songs that would in other circumstances be demonized by the guardians of those values, a particular favourite being Drowning Pool's 'Let the Bodies Hit the Floor' – in the words of a tank crew member, 'The motto for our tank ... fitting for the job we were doing'.[7]

A notorious recent case of musical incitement to violence in the interests of a legitimating political framework was Rwandan musician Simon Bikindi during the genocide in his country in 1994. Bikindi, a Hutu, was accused of using music and radio broadcasts by the RLTM station (in which he was a shareholder) to incite violence against Tutsis.[8] 'RLTM not only expressed and disseminated the message of deep and ideologically sustained ethno-nationalist divisions within Rwandan society, but also focussed the attentions of its listeners on what to do about these divisions.'[9] At the time of writing (2008) Bikindi stands indicted by the International Criminal Tribunal for Rwanda of charges relating to genocide and crimes against humanity. While these are largely based on Bikindi's military activities, they included his collaboration with others to ensure that RLTM contained a mixture of 'popular music and listener participation with news reports and ant-Tutsi propaganda'.[10] Bikindi was also held to have sought to influence Hutu youth through composing songs which fitted the government line and performing them at Government party functions. It was also claimed that his songs 'were a crucial part of the genocidal plan because they incited people to attack and kill Tutsis'.[11] This was allegedly successful since members of Bikindi's Irindiro ballet troupe joined the *Interahamwe* militia and went on to murder Hutus. Bikindi was also further alleged to have planned and taken part in mass killings of Tutsis.

As we move to a consideration of pop music and the outraged reactions its incitements elicit, it is well to recall these state-based validations as a context for moral judgements. Indeed, that transition has been easily negotiated by examples of music which have served both as forms of war-cry or semi-official national anthems, and as popular music in a more general sense. The Touareg group Tinariwen was developed in Gadaffi's training camps in the mid-1980s.

---

[6]   Jeevan Vasagar, 'Mugabe paints MDC as Blairite cronies', *Observer* 27 April 2005, p. 1.

[7]   George Gittoes, *Soundtrack to War*, Film documentary, dir. George Gittoes, prod. Gittoes and Dalton Productions Pty Ltd, with The Australian Film Commission (Australia, 2004).

[8]   Dylan Craig and Mkhize, 'Vocal killers, silent killers: Popular media, genocide and the call for benevolent censorship in Rwanda' in Michael Drewett and Martin Cloonan (eds), *Popular Music Censorship in Africa* (Aldershot, 2006), pp. 36–52.

[9]   Ibid., p. 46.

[10]   International Criminal Tribunal for Rwanada, *The Prosectuor v. Simon Bikindi* (Arusha: 2005), p. 44.

[11]   Ibid., p. 6; see also pp. 12, 13.

Playing what has been described as a rock-based 'desert blues', the group went into battle during the Touareg rebellion against Mali, 'with guns and electric guitars'.[12] Subsequently the band was part of a successful internationally touring World Music package.[13]

Incitement in Popular Music

Individual songs of abuse and malicious intent have appeared in a range of popular music genres. 'Ugly Child', 'Your Feets Too Big', 'Goodie Goodie', 'I'll Be Glad When You're Dead, You Rascal You', 'Cry Me A River', all fall within the spectrum from genial insult to bitter vindictiveness. A high proportion of children's playground songs incorporate vilification and incitement that may be regarded as juvenile forms of the most outrageous pop music lyrics. Apart from ethnic and gendered targets, as in familiar variants of chants such as 'Ching Chong Chinaman' and 'What are little boys made of?', teachers are the subject of a kind of dispassionate brutality that resonates with notorious school killings

> Mr Nelson hit me with a ruler, so I stood behind the door
> With a loaded 24. Aint no teacher any more.
> I went to the funeral, I went to the grave.
> Someone threw in flowers. I threw in a grenade.
> The Coffin went up, the coffin went down.
> The coffin went splat, all over the ground.
>
> Row, row, row your boat
> Gently down the stream.
> Pack your teacher in a port[manteau]
> And listen to her scream.[14]

It is difficult to imagine the repertoire of children's songs without an element of scatological insult and cruelty which seems to be inherent in the genre, and their deployment in play activity throws our attention forward to a possible way of approaching pop music genres that display a high level of violent rhetoric, which we examine in the next chapter.

In any event, in recent decades juvenile playground song, as well as all traditional popular song forms, have been comprehensively overtaken as a vehicle

---

[12]   Mark Espiner, 'Rock the kasbah', *Guardian* 19 January 2005, p. 23.

[13]   Dorian Lynskey, 'Out of Africa', *Guardian G2*, 24 February 2005, pp. 14–15.

[14]   These are just two of many examples in an unpublished collection of Australian playground songs assembled over a number of years by Queensland schoolteacher Michelle Freeman. Bruce Johnson wants to thank her and Emma Freeman for making the collection available to him.

for violent incitement by pop music genres in which it is constitutive rather than incidental. One of these is Rap, and most notoriously, Gangsta Rap, which by 2000 was its dominant subcategory.[15] Already by the early 1990s the music was under attack, including by *Billboard*, the *New York Times* and the National Political Congress for Black Women (NPCBW) for its apparent endorsement of rape and violence.[16] The perception that Gangsta Rap incites violence was sharpened by the 'Cop Killer' controversy of 1992, involving Ice-T's self-titled album with his band Body Count, which included the track 'Cop Killer', released shortly before the Rodney King riots.[17] Warner Brothers withdrew the track worldwide. We shall return to this case below.

Edward G. Armstrong analysed the lyrics of 490 Gangsta Rap songs by 13 artists from 1987–1993.[18] For purposes of the study, he identified four categories of violence against women: 'assault, forcible rape [sic], and murder, and a fourth category combining rape and murder'.[19] In quantitave terms his findings were that

> 22 percent (N=107) of the 490 gangsta rap music songs had violent and misogynist lyrics. Assault was the most frequently occurring criminal offense, portrayed in 50 percent of the violent and misogynist songs. Other rankings: rape only = 11 percent; murder only = 31 percent; rape and murder = 7 percent.[20]

It is noteworthy that this outcome is based only on violence directed at women, and in a sample that ends in 1993. As Armstrong pointed out in 2001, the year in which his study was published, by 2000 his own sample from 1987 to 1993 would look 'tame'.[21] Even by 2001 – setting aside the six more years to the time of our present enquiry – the emergence of subsequent rappers with higher profiles and profits has also been accompanied by increased 'outbidding' competition, with more extreme levels of violence. Eminem, for example, was not included in the original sample, but a subsequent analysis of the rapper's work, in 2000, makes for instructive comparison with the figures quoted for the earlier period: the 22 per cent becomes for Eminen 78 per cent, and the 31 per cent dealing with the murder of women becomes 82 per cent in Eminem's work. In addition, misogyny by no means accounts for all forms of incitement.

---

[15] Armstrong, 'Gangsta Misogyny', pp. 106, 108.

[16] Ibid., p. 103.

[17] See further Martin Cloonan, 'Ice-T: Cop Killer' in Derek Jones (ed.), *Censorship: A World Encyclopedia* (London, 2001), pp. 1139–40.

[18] Armstrong, 'Gangsta Misogyny', p. 98.

[19] Ibid., p. 99.

[20] Ibid., p. 99.

[21] Ibid., p. 105.

Incitement to violence is to be found in racist organizations through Hate Music.[22] These forms of music have been kept under observation by both state agencies and anti-racist campaigners, watchful of its function as a recruiting and fundraising tool, and serving to reinforce group identity.[23] The example of the German National Party is documented later in this chapter. With laws forbidding the inciting of racial hatred, gigs by neo-Nazi bands are often secret and attended in covert circumstances. To some extent anti-racist legislation and activism have muted the impact of such music and it serves as one of our 'usual suspects'. Here we wish to discuss another form of music which has been accused of inciting violence – ragga/raga.[24]

Within the Anglophone world perhaps the most high profile cases of music allegedly inciting violence has been forms of reggae such as ragga within which homophobic lyrics have been present. Artists accused of homophobia and/or inciting the hatred of gays include Buju Banton, Capelton, Elephant Man, TKO, Beenie Man, Vybz Kartel, Bounty Man and Sizzla. In the UK the campaign against the music was spearheaded by the gay rights group OutRage! which, in April 1993, protested to the BBC about Shabba Ranks performing on *Top of The Pops* despite the fact that he had appeared on a Channel 4 programme and said that homosexuals should be crucified.[25] The same year it was reported that gays in London had been taunted by young black men in London who were reciting lyrics by Ranks and Buju Banton, especially the latter's 'Boom Bye Bye' which advocates the shooting of gays.[26] Peter Tatchell of OutRage! claimed that attacks on gays had increased since the rise of ragga,[27] and there were calls for the record to be banned

---

[22]   See www.adl.org/main_Extremism/hate_music_in_the_21st_century.htm and www.aijac.org.au/review/2000/258/sounds.html. For a recent collection of studies of hate music in a range of genres, see Art Jipson (ed.), special issue of *Popular Music and Society* on Hate Rock, 30/4 (October 2007).

[23]   See Nick Lowles and Steve Silver, *White Noise* (London, 1998). Popular music of course has no monopoly on such a stigma. Richard Wagner in the nineteenth century and Richard Adams in the twentieth have both notoriously been boycotted and picketed over charges of anti-Semitism. On Wagner, see for example the controversies regarding performances of his work in Israel, cited Cloonan and Johnson, 'Killing Me Softly', pp. 30–31; on Adams' opera *The Death of Klinghoffer*, see for example Richard Taruskin 'Music's Dangers And The Case For Control', *New York Times*, 9 December 2001, Arts and Leisure section. Our focus, however is on popular music, which has also carried the major burden of such charges.

[24]   Both spellings have been used. We will use 'ragga' to prevent confusion with Indian raga.

[25]   Virek Chauhary, 'Gays to jam BBC lines', *The Guardian*, 14 April 1993.

[26]   According to one account the lyrics of this song were sung by a crowd gathered outside the house of Jamaican gay activist Brian Williamson, to celebrate his murder. See Gary Younge, 'Troubled island', *Guardian*, 27 April 2006, part two, pp. 6–9.

[27]   Ian MacKinnon, 'Ragga music blamed for attacks on homosexuals', *Independent*, 1 October 1993. See also *Independent* letters page, 8 October 1993, p. 25.

in the UK. By 2002 the BBC was more responsive to the campaigns, removing Elephant Man's 'Log On' from its Radio 2 website which hosted its 'History of Reggae' series. The track describes stamping on and setting fire to a gay man and was described by OutRage! as 'a clear incitement to homophobic violence and murder'.[28] Meanwhile the BBC also removed the track 'Bun di Chi Chi' (Burn the Queer) from a top 10 list on the website of its DJ Chris Goldfinger.

OutRage! then protested outside the annual Music of Black Origin (MOBO) awards in London in October 2002 because nominations for various awards had included Capleton, Elephant Man and TKO – all of whom it accused of homophobia. The protesters were physically attacked by fans outside the ceremony.[29] Tatchell later said that while he accepted that his lifestyle was open to criticism, this 'does not include advocating the murder of lesbians and gay men'.[30] In December 2003 two planned gigs by Bounty Killer in Birmingham and London were cancelled at short notice following OutRage!'s campaign. While it was suggested that this was because the singer missed his flight, Tatchell claimed this as a victory against homophobia and said that: 'Our aim is to make Britain a no-go area for singers who incite violence against gay people and other minorities.'[31] The following June a London night club cancelled a planned appearance by Beenie Man (whose song 'Damn' contains the lyrics 'I'm dreaming of a new Jamaica, come execute all the gays'), following intervention by Scotland Yard which had informed the club about OutRage!'s concerns about songs such as 'Bad Man Chi Chi' ('Queer' Man').[32] Beenie Man later issued a statement via his record company apologizing if his previous lyrics had offended anyone and denouncing 'violence towards other human beings'.[33] A month later it was reported that Buju Banton was being sought by Jamaican police for his part in a gang attack on a group of gay men. While Tatchell argued that this arrest 'substantiates our claims of the links between murder music and actual physical attacks on gays',[34] charges against Banton were dropped in January 2006. In the face of continued campaigning by Outrage! industry boycotts were implemented, such as cancelled concerts and tours and

---

[28]   Tania Branigan, 'BBC withdraws "homophobic" reggae tracks', *Guardian*, 30 August 2002, p. 8.

[29]   Fiachara Gibbons, 'Reggae fans attack gay rights protest', *Guardian*, 3 October 2002, p. 7.

[30]   Tania Branigan, 'Anti-gay reggae stars "Should be charged"', *Guardian*, 24 December 2002, p. 6.

[31]   Steven Morris, '"Antigay" singer cancels gigs', *Guardian*, 8 December 2003, p. 11.

[32]   Tania Branigan, 'Beenie Man concert axed over homophobia fears', *Guardian*, 25 June 2004, p. 8.

[33]   Sandra Laville, 'Jamaican star apologises for "hurtful' lyrics"', *Guardian*, 4 August 2004, p. 7.

[34]   Gary Younge, 'Police seek Jamaican singer after attack on gay men', *Guardian*, 17 July 2004, p. 17.

exclusions from industry awards.[35] While these campaigns were most active in the UK, they often targeted Jamaica, home of reggae and also of considerable homophobia.[36] Following lobbying by OutRage! and others in the Stop Murder Music (SMM) campaign, it was reported that 'Jamaica's six biggest sponsors of reggae have announced that they will withdraw sponsorship from artists who incite violence'.[37]

In February SMM had reportedly reached agreement with reggae record companies (VP Records, Greensleeves and Jesstar Records), promoters (including Jammins and Apollo Entertainment) and publishers that there would be no future releases inciting violence against gays and lesbians and that there would be no provocative remarks at concerts. The deal was to cover the UK and other territories. In return SSM agreed to drop its campaign.[38] However, in 2006 Buju Banton and Beenie Man concerts were again targeted by OutRage!. Concerts in Brighton and Bournemouth were cancelled following lobbying by the organization after Banton performed 'Boom Bye Bye' at a Jamaican concert and defended his views on homosexuality. Tatchell agued that even if Banton had promised not to sing 'Boom Bye Bye', he still would have been targeted, since to 'give him a concert platform would be the equivalent of hosting a neo-Nazi singer on the condition that he promised not to sing about gassing Jews'.[39] In June 2007 some re-alignment appeared to have occurred and it was announced that following a deal which had been brokered by SMM activists working with reggae promoters there had been a historic agreement to stop 'murder music'.[40] This was the Reggae Compassionate Act signed by Beenie Man, Capleton and Sizzla. The artists also agreed not to release or re-release homophobic songs. However, OutRage! expressed concern that some artists were only signing the agreement for commercial reasons and, through the editors, urged journalists to test the artists' sincerity.[41] In July Buju Banton also signed the Act.[42]

---

[35]   See further: Lee Glendinning, 'Mobo drops gay hate songs', *Guardian*, 8 September 2004, p. 7; Sandra Laville, 'Anti-gay star's UK tour cancelled', *Guardian*, 4 November 2004, p. 10; Lee Glendinning, 'Anti-gay music banned', *Guardian*, 27 November 2004, p. 7.

[36]   See Gary Younge, 'Chilling call to murder as music attacks gays', *Guardian*, 26 June 2004, p. 14.

[37]   Rob Berkley, 'We won't desert them', *Guardian*, 11 January 2005, p. 21.

[38]   Hugh Muir, 'Ceasefire brokered in reggae lyrics war', *Guardian*, 5 February 2005, p. 4; see further OutRage! press release 4 February 2005.

[39]   OutRage!, 'Buju Banton and Beenie Man concerts axed', 6 July 2006, www.petertatchell.net.

[40]   OutRage! press release 13 June 2007.

[41]   Ibid.

[42]   Alexandra Topping, 'Victory for gay rights campaign as reggae star agrees to ditch homophobic lyrics', *Guardian*, 23 July 2007, p. 7.

At the time of writing (2008) this agreement remains in place, but the issues still smoulder. For OutRage! the issue was clear: the music was inciting anti-gay violence and incitement to murder is against the law in all countries. To those who argued artistic freedom, Tatchell replied that 'free speech does not include the right to commit the criminal offence of incitement to murder'.[43] Moreover, gays were being attacked, especially in Jamaica the home of most of the artists who were promoting homophobia.[44] Proscribing circulation of this music would, argued OutRage!, contribute to stopping the violence. However, Carolyn Cooper, chair of reggae studies at the University of West Indies, argued that rather than being an attack on gays, dancehall/ragga should be seen as a celebration of heterosexuality. She added, 'I don't think that it incites people to violence. I think people understand the metaphor'.[45] The reasons for homophobic attitudes in Jamaica were portrayed variously as being a mixture of strict legislation, colonial legacy, religion and political opportunism.[46]

What is of interest to this book is the role that music played in the debate. The homophobic lyrics appeared to be part of a culture of anti-gay violence, but direct causal links between that violence and the music remain to be demonstrated. Armstrong notes the argument that reading homophobic lyrics as actual incitement or endorsement of rape and homophobia is to miss the point, a failure of reading competencies appropriate to the genre, and of a sense of parody that is well understood by the music's framing culture.[47] It is not clear how that 'framing culture' is demarcated, but NPCBW, who might be expected to be close to it, evidently do not find the argument convincing in relation to songs which graphically present as models of social conduct, acts such as necrophilia and the beating, killing, raping (orally, anally and vaginally) and evisceration of women.[48] If we accept as a freestanding proposition that popular music shapes out imaginary, our sense of the possible, then such songs are part of that shaping force as much as any anthems of emancipation. How such 'imaginaries' might be played out in social practice is another matter, amplified in later chapters.

---

[43] Peter Tatchell, 'It isn't racist to target Beenie Man', *Guardian*, 31 August 2004, p. 14. One interesting aspect of the debate here was those gays who themselves enjoyed the music which Tatchell labelled as Murder Music. For an account of this see Alexis Petridis, '"They're good beat, we don't take the lyrics seriously"', *Guardian*, 6 September 2004, part two, pp. 14–15.

[44] See, for example, http://hrw.org/english/docs/2004/11/23/jamaic9716.htm.

[45] Gary Younge, 'Troubled island', p. 8.

[46] See, for example, Decca Aitkenhead, 'Their homophobia is our fault', *Guardian*, 5 January 2005, www.guardian.co.uk/comment/story.0,1383487,00.html.

[47] Armstrong, 'Gangsta Misogyny', p. 108.

[48] Each category of violence we have listed is exemplified in the sample used by Armstrong, and in terms which emphasize brutality; Armstrong, 'Gangsta Misogyny', pp. 100–103.

Also prominent among genres felt to have a constitutive complicity in violence is Metal, in particular those forms bearing subcategorical discriminators like Heavy, Death, Doom and Gore Metal. As is characteristic of all modern popular music, which bands fit into which categories, how those categories may be defined, and what constitute good and inept examples of each, is the subject of finely discriminated debate among cognoscenti.[49] Apart from musical differences, Robert Walser has also argued that the distinctions between these subcategories in the US correspond to socio-economic differentiations in the performers and fans.[50]

On the basis of his regional ethnographic research on US music scenes, Harris M. Berger concluded that 'a death metal performance is intended as a motivating force, a way of rousing the listener from the tedium of school, a spur to achievement, and a goad to accepting responsibility for one's own destiny'.[51] 'Persuasion to act', the starting point of incitement, is clear in this formulation. But in some forms of Metal, that action is explicitly manifested as violence, including self-harm. This problematizes the status of socially empowering agency, in a way we shall investigate further below. The particular kinds of violence apparently incited and endorsed in Metal overlap with the case of Gangsta Rap,[52] but are not identical, and given the different socio-economic cultures of the two genres, this is worth a comparative study in itself. Various forms of Metal, for example frequently involve the explicit glorification of self-mutilation and suicide, which appears to be entirely absent from the triumphalist survival philosophies of Gangsta Rap. Deicide's 1990 album was entitled 'Sacrificial Suicide'. Leader Glen Benton has an inverted cross branded on his forehead and the band members consistently promulgate Satanism and have reportedly declared a suicide pact for when they reach a certain age.[53] Asked by researcher Keith Kahn-Harris about plans for life and music, the reply of one informant was to play more, to ingest more drugs and 'see how much I can fuck myself up before I die'.[54] Self-harm is one category within a larger project of violent misanthropy, most notoriously exemplified in Norwegian Black Metal of the 1990s. Summarizing his musical mission, Øystein Aarseth (aka Euronymous), leader of Mayhem, declared that he didn't want people to respect each other, but 'to HATE and to FEAR', that he wanted to be

---

[49]   Apart from published discussions, and individual acknowledgements where appropriate, Bruce Johnson would like to thank his students (both connoisseurs and performers) – more than he can personally name here – at Åbo Academy and University of Turku, Finland, and at the Norwegian University of Science and Technology, Trondheim, for esoteric information on these subcategories.

[50]   Robert Walser, *Running with the Devil: Power, Gender and Madness in Heavy Metal* (Hanover US, 1993), pp. 16–17.

[51]   Berger, *Metal, Rock, and Jazz*, p. 67.

[52]   Homophobic vilification is also prominent in some forms of Black Metal – See for example Moynihan and Søderlind, *Lords of Chaos*, pp. 169, 241–88.

[53]   Kahn-Harris, *Extreme Metal*, p. 35.

[54]   Ibid., p. 43.

one of the guardians of immorality, and to kick people in the face.[55] Homophobia, neo-Nazism, Satanism, racism (Gypsies, 'coloured people'[56]), are recurrent themes in public Black Metal statements. As in the case of Gangsta Rap, there are various interpretations of this rhetoric, and we shall explore these further as we investigate questions of motivation and social action.

One site of social action is the moshpit, and this has also infamously been a forum for incitement to violence. Joe Ambrose attended a gig in Brixton Academy in 1994, featuring Hole fronted by Courtney Love, shortly after Kurt Cobain's suicide. Love goaded and cursed the audience, summoning them to the front of the stage – 'C'mon, c'mon' – producing a dangerously densely packed crowd. A week later at a Love performance in Sweden a 19-year-old girl was crushed to death. Love's response: 'I'm really sorry someone died at a festival. Someone, it seems, gets injured or hurt or overdoses or gets squashed at every concert there ever is.'[57] Apart from anything else notable about this comment, it 'naturalizes' concert violence. It detaches incitement from what follows it, displacing responsibility in a way that will become significant as our discussion proceeds. Other musicians are explicit about their responsibility for inciting violence. Atari Teenage Riot leader Alec Empire declared: 'We are doing shows to incite people against the government.'[58] Brian Yap Barry, of One Minute Silence said of one of their gigs at Camden Palace: 'We were trying to incite a riot.'[59] We will return to this statement and in another connection as we explore the ambiguities which frequently inform such comments.

Responses to Incitement: Moral Panic

The foregoing cases exemplify the power and inclination of pop acts to incite violent conduct among audiences, and have brought us to the point where the potential consequences of doing so are recognized. They thus raise the question of causality. How far does such incitement actually arouse audiences to violent action? Before exploring this in more detail in the next chapter, we conclude by reviewing public debate over that question. Suspicion of music has, as we have seen, a long history, with particular opprobrium attached to emergent new musics and their mediations. This has been intensified since the early twentieth century because the pace of such innovations and their increasingly rapid and broad circulation have proliferated the intersecting and conflicting lines of cultural force. The axes along which this suspicion has been articulated may be categorized as aesthetic and moral, sometimes separately, but often in convergence. Jazz,

---

[55] Moynihan and Søderlind, *Lords of Chaos*, p. 76.

[56] Ibid., p. 169.

[57] Ambrose, *Moshpit*, p. 59.

[58] Ibid., p. 142.

[59] Ibid., p. 116.

for example, was demonized both for being unmusical (it was cacophony) and immoral (it unleashed primitive instincts), and part of its offensiveness was also its technologized circulation.[60] Later, rock was offensively noisy and also blamed for antisocial conduct among teenagers. Towards the end of the twentieth century, and particularly from the arrival of punk, a particular kind of anxiety became more pervasive. That is, that new forms of popular music not only released antisocial instincts, but explicitly modelled and incited them.

While objections on the grounds of unmusicality persisted, the moral emphasis has been more amplified, shifting attention more to words (both lyrics and performer media statements) than to actual sonority. Record warning stickers tickers are about words, not music. If early jazz opened the doorway to savage instincts, Rap appeared explicitly to incite its listeners to go through it. Moral panic has over-ridden aesthetic critique, asserting that pop does not merely accompany antisocial conduct; it incites it, and therefore causes it. 'Moral panic' here is a shorthand for arguments based on the hypothesis that music is a direct and primary cause of violent and depraved social conduct. It takes many forms, from measured enquiry to others in which 'panic' has priority. We stress the word 'causes', as opposed for example to 'reflects', let alone something as complex as 'exists in a reflexive, feedback-loop relationship'. They declare in one way or another that pop music is responsible for very specific acts of violence. These include self-harm, the most extreme form of which is suicide, for which Metal and ajacent or sub-categories are prominent scapegoats, as in the case of the allegedly Emo suicides referred to in Chapter 4.

Exemplifying a contrast drawn above, rap is more likely to be blamed for violence inflicted on others. In 2006 UK Conservative Party leader David Cameron accused BBC Radio 1 of playing music that encouraged knife and gun violence, his comments interpreted as a reference to Tim Westwood's Saturday night hiphop programme.[61] In Birmingham England in the early hours of New Year's Day 2003, two teenage girls, Charlene Ellis and Letisha Shakespeare were shot dead outside a party, victims of crossfire between two gangs. The incident occurred in a context of moral panic debate that had been inflamed in June 2002 when a meeting organized by the Black Music Congress – 'a forum for discussing black music issues, networking, and a pathway to music industry education'[62] – had held a conference at which calls were made for black UK musicians to ensure that their music 'does not have a negative impact, particularly on young listeners and that explicit imagery in music videos devalues black music and black people

---

[60]   See further Bruce Johnson, 'The Jazz Diaspora' in Mervyn Cooke and David Horn (eds), *The Cambridge Companion to Jazz* (Cambridge, 2002), pp. 33–54; Bruce Johnson, 'Jazz outside the US', forthcoming in *Encyclopedia of Popular Music of the World*.

[61]   Julia Day, 'Radio 1 glorifies knife crime, says Tory leader', *Guardian* online, 7 June 2006, www.guardian.co.uk/media/2006/jun/07/radio.conservativeparty.

[62]   www.britishblackmusic.com/index.php?module=Pagesetter&func=viewpub&tid=14&pid=3.

by reinforcing racist stereotypes'.[63] Artists said to be causing particular concern included the So Solid Crew, Rodney P and Mel B.

The day after the conference took place the *The Observer* published an opinion piece by Simon Woolley, Director of Operation Black Vote,[64] entitled 'We don't need gangster rap'.[65] Here he argued that in 'recent times, hip-hop and elements of R 'n' B have become increasingly profane with lyrics that are just plain nasty' and approvingly paraphrased an argument that 'lyrics which glorify violence – and gun violence in particular – need to be qualified with a strong health warning that states clearly "it's not for real"'. Woolley laid the blame for the increasing profanity and nastiness purely upon elements within the recording industry arguing that: 'Quite simply, record companies are manipulating black youth into a saleable stereotype to hype up record sales.' In rap, he argued, 'The routine violence that comes with ignorance and poverty is promoted, marketed and cashed in on by record companies who will dump these kids as soon as the fine line between celebrity notoriety and criminal liability is crossed'. He continued that it was 'the continuation of that exploitation through multi-million pound record companies who are selling stereotypical caricatures of ourselves back to us and making millions. Let's return to the tradition of struggle and the project of freedom and equality'.[66]

The New Year's Day killings six months later were given saturation media coverage. Metropolitan Assistant Commissioner Tarique Ghaffur said that record companies and artists who glamorized guns had refused to co-operate with police in tackling teenage attitudes. Guns had become youth fashion accessories, he said, singling out the band So Solid Crew for particular attention.[67] Scotland Yard Commander Alan Brown blamed violent lyrics for 'turning youngsters on to firearms'. Home Secretary David Blunkett attacked 'appalling' rap lyrics and music producer Neil Fraser wrote to the *Telegraph*, 'the producers of BBC Radio 1's ragga and hip-hop shows should share some of the guilt every time a black youth dies from a gun in prison'.[68] The then Minister for Tourism, Film and Broadcasting, Kim Howells declared: 'For years I have been very worried about these hateful lyrics that these boasting macho idiot rappers come out with. It is a big cultural problem. Lyrics don't kill people but they don't half enhance the fare we get from videos and films. It has created a culture where killing is almost

---

[63] Colin Joseph, 'UK hip hop "needs ethics code"', *BBC News* online, 28 June 2002, www.bbc.co.uk/hi/english/entertainment/music/newsid_2073000/2073162.stm.

[64] Operation Black Vote seeks to improve rates of participation in UK politics by its black communities. See www.obv.org.uk.

[65] Simon Woolley, 'We don't need gangsta rap', *Observer Review,* 30 June 2002, p. 14.

[66] All quotes Woolley, 'We don't need gangsta rap'.

[67] Gaby Hinsliff, Martin Bright and Jason Burke, 'Police hit at rappers for making guns glamorous', *Observer*, 5 January 2003, pp. 1–5.

[68] Barham, *Dis/conneced*, p. 1.

a fashion accessory.' On Radio 4 he denied that economics and poverty were connected with crime, and identified rap as a 'key factor in rising gun violence'.[69]

The comments cited here manifest a further pattern in the moral panic profile. The mother of one of the double 'Emo' Melbourne suicides in 2007 simply expressed the wish to understand what had driven her daughter.[70] But the more distant from the particular case and the more authority conferred on the speaker, the more inclination to generalize from single cases to a sweeping jeremiad about the responsibility of pop for the decline of western civilization. For Leonard Pitts, writing in the *Miami Herald*, Gangsta Rap was complicit in causing the decline of urban life, and for Stanley Crouch of the New York *Daily News*, it was destroying American values.[71] From his even loftier intellectual eminence, academic Allan Bloom could see that rock music had one 'barbaric appeal, to sexual desire'.[72] In a breathtakingly undocumented and rather prurient diatribe he concludes that the whole notion of 'progress' had been subverted by a 'pubescent whose body throbs with orgasmic rhythms; whose feelings are made articulate in hymns to the joys of onanism or the killing of parents; whose ambition is to win fame and wealth in imitating the drag-queen who makes the music'.[73] Bloom identifies an exemplary abstract singular in this profile, and it is often the case that one individual becomes the metonym for pop's criminal sabotage of civilized values. Two years before he enjoyed the validation conferred upon him by an Oscar, Eminen was described by US President George Bush as 'the most dangerous threat to American children since polio'.[74]

Perhaps the most 'usual suspect' for arguments that find incitement and then insist it is the cause of violence is Marilyn Manson, who became one of the accessories to the high profile Luke Mitchell case in Dalkeith, just outside Edinburgh. In June 2003, 14-year-old Jodi Jones was brutally murdered, her body tied up, her throat cut and she was repeatedly stabbed. Some hours later her boyfriend Luke Mitchell, also 14, led police to her body. After an interval he was charged with the murder, tried and found guilty in January 2005 and sentenced to 20 years. He disclosed no motive at any time, leaving the question open to media imagination, which seized on two details: the resemblance to the 1947 killing and mutilation of Elizabeth Short in California (the so-called 'Black Dahlia' murder), which was mentioned by the court pathologist, and Marilyn Manson, also noted as being fascinated by

---

[69]   Ibid., p. 2.

[70]   McMahon, 'Bullying on teen's sad road to oblivion'.

[71]   Both cited in Armstrong, 'Gangsta Misogyny', p. 105.

[72]   Allan Bloom, *The Closing of the American Mind; How higher education has failed democracy and impoverished the souls of today's students* (London, 1987), p. 73.

[73]   Ibid., p. 75.

[74]   Barham, *Dis/connected*, p. 3.

the Black Dahlia.[75] It was reported that police had removed from Mitchell's home Marilyn Manson DVDs featuring images of the Black Dahlia case.[76]

Both of these were noted in court and referred to by the judge, Lord Nimmo Smith in his summing up after what he called 'one of the most appalling crimes any of us can remember'.[77] The judge reportedly said that he could not 'ignore that there was a degree of resemblance between the injuries inflicted on Jodi and those shown in the Marilyn Manson paintings of Elizabeth Short we saw. I think you carried an image in your memory when you killed Jodi'.[78] Journalists and Manson himself were moved to respond to these reports.[79] Some substance was given to their responses when, subsequent to the trial, Mitchell's defence team claimed that it was only some time *after* the murder that Mitchell had bought the Manson material.[80] The comments attributed to Lord Nimmo should caution us against underestimating the potential cultural capital of the moral panic reflex. Apart from enjoying the support of the forces of 'moral majority' and right-wing fundamentalisn which became increasingly powerful through the 1990s, many music watchdog groups also have the benefit of extremely well-connected advocates. In 1985 Tipper Gore, wife of US politician Al Gore, founded the Parents' Music Resource Centre, which has lobbied for various forms of music censorship, particularly targeting rap and metal. She also wrote *Raising PG kids in an X-rated society*, 1987, in which she quotes extensively from a pamphlet by a professor of music Joe Stuessy, called 'The Heavy metal user's manual', which, by Robert Walser's assessment, is of dubious validity and based on double standards.[81] Similar lobby groups include MASK, Mothers Against Slipknot, addressing what its members see as a threat posed by one band in particular that has been associated with various forms of violence, and of which more below.[82]

A further stage in the application of moral panic arguments is exemplified in a report in October 2006 that hundreds of Berlin police were assembling in anticipation of an encounter with an expected 1,200 neo-Nazis attending a rally organized by the extremist German National Party (NPD). Its purpose was to

---

[75] See for example: Gerard Seenan, 'Goth fan who craved notoriety and said he was in league with the devil', *Guardian*, 22 January 2005, p. 5; Kirsty Scott, 'Jodi's killer to serve at least 20 years in jail', *Guardian*, 12 February 2005, p. 5; Lorna Martin, 'Jodi murder: teen killer set to appeal', *Observer*, 23 January 2005, p. 4.

[76] Seenan, 'Goth fan'.

[77] Gerard Seenan, '"Truly evil" youth convicted of murdering Jodi', *Guardian*, 22 January 2005, p. 5.

[78] Scott, 'Jodi's killer'.

[79] Helen Pidd, 'Marilyn Manson is innocent', *Guardian*, 25 January 2005 p. 4; Liam McDougall, 'Luke's lawyer: Crown evidence was a surprise ... Manson: don't blame me for Jodi murder', *Herald* (Glasgow), 13 February 2005, p. 4.

[80] MacDougall, 'Luke's lawyer'.

[81] Robert Walser, *Running with the Devil*, pp. 137–41.

[82] Ambrose, *Moshpit*, p. 129.

protest outside the prison in which Michael Regener (aka Lunikoff) was serving a three-year term for racial vilification and membership of a criminal organization. Apart from being a member of NPD, Regener was a former singer, and the 'criminal organization' of which he was a member was the rock group Landser (Foot Soldiers), which had been banned for propagating racial hatred through its music. Previously called The Final Solution, the entire five-member band had been arrested in 2001. The 2006 police deployment was a response to growing numbers of crimes committed by members of neo-Nazi groups – 452 between January and August 2006, resulting in injuries to 325 people.[83] Regener's prosecution, in part for incitement, is conspicuous for its context (including German history in the twentieth century as well as a generalized sense of insecurity in post 9/11 western societies) and for its outcome of incarceration.

These examples of musical incitement and racist conflict occurred in a context of public disorder and criminality. They could not be overlooked by the authorities as just part of the normal community fabric. But as we have seen, incitement is also a feature of pop music as entertainment in everyday life. Ambrose reports that since the mid-1990s moshing has elicited increasing numbers of legal actions for injuries.[84] Many gigs in the UK now have signs prohibiting crowd surfing. In an environment increasingly litigious in matters of responsibility, more tenuous assumptions about a causal relationship between pop and violence have also been tested in courts of law, but with results that generally range from ambiguous to disappointing for the plaintiffs. Kahn-Harris refers to court cases in which Metal has been cited as contributing to suicidal conduct, and on occasion its influence was held to have mitigated responsibility. The film *Paradise Lost* documents the dubious conviction of three youths (the West Memphis Three), partly on grounds of an addiction to heavy metal.[85] On the other hand, in McCollum v. CBS, Inc, the court rejected a claim against CBS which was brought by the parents of a teenager who shot himself while listening to a record by Ozzy Osbourne.[86]

Walser discusses the action brought against Judas Priest for alleged back-masking incitements to suicide. These were thrown out on a number of grounds, including the predominance of other social triggers and the implausibility of a connection between alleged subliminal, backwards messages and suicide. It was also pointed out that that other arguable back-masking messages were on the same album (*Stained Class*); that is, the subjective and inferential nature of these messages. Two other objections to the claim will be considered more

---

[83]   'Police on alert in Berlin for neo-Nazi rally', *SMH* October 22 2006; on the earlier arrest, see Kate Connolly, 'Hate singers rounded up as police swoop in three cities', *SMH*, 9 October 2001, p. 7.

[84]   Ambrose, *Moshpit*, p. 71.

[85]   Kahn-Harris, *Extreme Metal*, p. 27, and see further his citations.

[86]   Rod Smolla, *Deliberate Intent: A Lawyer Tells the True Story of Murder by the Book* (New York, 1999). This account of an action brought against the publishers of a manual for contract killers provides an instructive parallel to the present discussion.

generally later in this study: the fact that no other fans of the album appear to have engaged in suicidal acts, and a precedent which declared lyrics about suicide to be protected under free speech.[87] The bands Deicide (including singer Glen Benton) and Cannibal Corpse (former leader Chris Barnes) were named in a civil lawsuit brought by the relatives of the victim of a murder/robbery in 1994 in Oregon. One of those charged declared during police questioning that 'I did it in essence of Glen Benton and Chris Barnes'. CDs, T-shirts, photos and 'Satanic literature' were found at the homes of the accused. The civil suits were directed against the bands' record labels, Roadrunner and Metal Blade, who paid 'substantial sums' in the out-of-court settlement.[88]

A similar civil suit was brought by the family of Trooper Bill Davidson against Time-Warner, after Ronald Howard, his killer in 1992, claimed he had been driven to the crime by the lyrics of the rapper 2 Pac on a Time Warner release *2 Pacalypse Now*. As a bridge to discussion of the ambiguities of the moral panic response to music as incitement, the Davidson murder takes us back to the debate over Cop Killer. Opponents of the track argued that it constituted incitement. Denis R. Martin, former President of the National Association of Chiefs of Police, claimed that in releasing the record Warner Brothers had misused the First Amendment guaranteeing freedom of speech, to publish a song with 'vile and dangerous lyrics'.[89] He claimed also that the song had been 'implicated in at least two shooting incidents and has inflamed racial tensions across the country ... Those who work closely with the families and friends of slain officers, as I do ... are outraged by the message of Cop Killer'. In the course of his discussion he presents his understanding of the true nature of music, and provides a brief history of the subject, from the perspective of what Cloonan has called a 'golden ager'.[90] This is of particular interest, in drawing his moral objections to Rap into a quasi-aesthetic discourse. In his scheme, a golden age of musical innocence comes to an end with rock and roll: 'For the first time, contemporary music did not reflect the values of society but glamorized rebelliousness and adolescent sexuality' and alleges that 'the trend in American rock music for the last decade has been to promote ever more vile, deviant, and sociopathic behaviors'.

Martin explains that since 'the Rodney King incident and the subsequent riots in Los Angeles, the media has contributed to a climate where police bashing is socially and politically correct'. He argues that those who framed the First Amendment could not 'have imagined a day when music would become a tool to destabilize society by provoking civil unrest, violence and murder' and claim that 'the lyrics of rapper Ice-T's Cop Killer do precisely that by decribing steps to kill a cop'. He links the song directly to the shooting of two LA police officers in July

---

[87]   Walser, *Running with the Devil*, pp. 145–7.

[88]   Moynihan and Søderlind, *Lords of Chaos*, pp. 290, 291.

[89]   Martin, www.axt.org.uk/HateMusic/Rappin.htm, accessed 21 July 2007. All quotations from Martin are from this site.

[90]   Martin Cloonan, *Banned!* (Aldershot, 1996).

1992 'by four juveniles who boasted that Ice-T's Cop Killer gave them a sense of duty and purpose, to get even with "a f-king pig". The juveniles continued to sing its lyrics when apprehended'. He declares that such incidents are predictable in the wake of the song. His comment that 'Freedom of speech ought to end short of advocating violent physical harm to fellow members of society', illustrates a clear understanding on his part that the song does actually advocate violence.

Martin is not only arguing incitement, however, but that the music led to arousal to violence – a causal link. He invokes the case of Trooper Bill Davidson, fatally shot as he approached Ronald Howard's vehicle which he had stopped for a defective headlight. According to Martin, Howard

> ... explained to law enforcement authorities that he felt hypnotized by the lyrics of six songs by the rap group 2 Pac, from their album 2 Pacalypse Now which urge the killing of police officers. Howard claims that the lyrical instructions devoured him like an animal, taking control over his subconscious mind and compelling him to kill Trooper Davidson as he approached Howard's vehicle. The rap's influence, however, apparently continues to affect Howard's judgment. Two psychiatrists found that the music still affects his psychosocial behavior.

Howard was found guilty of murder and executed in October 2005. Martin concludes by arguing for censorship to provide protection for officers from 'abusive speech when that abuse imperils not only their ability to protect citzens, but also their ability to protect their very lives'.

The foregoing examples of moral panic in relation to musical incitement give some sense of the levels at which they are deployed in society and their tactical range. As their erratic progress in the courts suggests, they often combine intense conviction with tenuousness, if not outright speciousness. Martin's online statement is followed by a rebuttal arguing his lack of historical and sociological perspective and a misunderstanding of the politics and aesthetics of Rap. Using Martin's own figures, around 1.5 million would have heard the track, prompting the question as to why only four people responded to it with acts of violence, a proportion of 375,000 to 1, 'a statistical accident rather than a causal equation'.[91] At the same time their own research leads them to conclude that 'contemporary music can in some cases be significantly linked to criminality – but only when particular forms of music take on meaning within the dynamics of specific subcultures like neo-Nazi skinheads (Hamm, 1993) or hip-hop graffiti artists (Ferrell, 1993)'.[92]

Although used here as shorthand, the second word in the term 'moral panic' has a particular aptness to the *ad hoc* sketchiness of many of its examples. As in the Cop Killer and Luke Mitchell cases, arguments tend to be reductively selective,

---

[91]   Mark S. Hamm and Jeff Ferrell, 'Rap, cops and crime: clarifying the "cop killer" controversy', www.axt.org.uk/HateMusic/Rappin.htm, accessed 21 July 2007.

[92]   The sources referred to are Jeff Ferrell, *Crimes and Style* (New York, 1993) and Mark S. Hamm, *American Skinheads* (Westport CT, 1993).

in direct ratio to the magnitude of the violence. Marilyn Manson's name appeared again in the wake of the Columbine High School killings on Tuesday, April 20 1999, near Littleton Colorado. Two students killed 12 colleagues and a teacher and wounded 24 others before committing suicide. In an analysis of charges that Manson was somehow an influence on the event, Gary Burns pointed out other possible suspects and asked: 'What other popular culture did these teenagers consume? Why haven't Marylin Manson's thousands or millions of other fans shot up the local high school? Is "shoot up your school" really a plausible message to draw from Manson's songs?'[93] In the Santana High School killings on 5 March 2000, a 15-year-old killed two and wounded 13 fellow pupils. Regarded as a Columbine copycat killing, Manson was again pilloried, though in fact rumours that the killers were Manson fans were 'urban myth'. But the Santana killer was a fan of Nurap/Metal band Linkin Park, which then enjoyed high media interest in moral panic arguments, in spite of a local sheriff's office spokesman said there was no suggestion of causal connection.[94]

The 'panic' to find explanations as to why apparently ordinary citizens turn out to be monsters, is an eloquent statement about cultural solipsism. The possibility that the 'ordinary citizen' is constituted partly by monstrousness is a proposition too unpalatable to be entertained, since ordinariness should be a guarantee of social acceptability. Mid-April (especially Mondays) is the school-shooting season in the US.[95] At that time in 2006 it was reported that four such plots were foiled. One was in Alaska, where six boys had prepared a hitlist of a score or so of their school-mates, especially the 'cool ones'. The one assigned to provide the weapons failed to come to school, and the boys were overheard discussing their plans. Joe, the father of one of the boys involved, a 13-year-old, was interviewed when his son was arrested for conspiracy to commit mass murder. He had asked his son why the boy did it. The boy couldn't answer, and Joe was mystified.

'He likes to fish,' said Joe. 'He likes to go camping. He likes to make up his own jokes. The counsellor is trying to figure out why they'd do this. These kids don't fit the mould. He doesn't come from a dysfunctional family. I mean, we have our dysfunctions, but he's not abused. I don't use drugs. I don't consider myself an alcoholic. I spend time with him. I coached baseball for him when he was younger.'

Joe paused. 'We have rules. He doesn't dress Goth. He's not allowed to dress Goth. He's not allowed to have baggy pants that hang down. He's not allowed to wear his hat cocked to the side and walk around looking like a little punk. We never let him have violent posters on his walls. He's not allowed to play violent video games. He's never been to the mall by himself. He doesn't have any CDs, like rap CDs, with violent themes. That kind of stuff just doesn't fit in with our lives.'[96]

---

[93] Gary Burns, 'Marilyn Manson and the Apt Pupils of Littleton', *Popular Music and Society*, 23/3 (1999): 3–7; see p. 5.

[94] Ambrose, *Moshpit*, pp. 204–5.

[95] And also the birthday of Adolf Hitler – see Burns, 'Marilyn Manson': 3.

[96] Joe Ronson, 'A timetable for murder', *Guardian* online, 17 April 2007.

Joe is dumbfounded because his son is a normal American boy. If certain kinds of music and conduct proclaim an aberrant sensibility inclined to violence, then conversely the absence of these from an individual's profile must be a predictor of normal behaviour. Joe's incredulity is a microcosm of a failure of imagination which frames much larger international issues. That is, that the regulation of social conduct, appearance and demeanour according to supposedly shared national values is a guarantee of moral rectitude. By contrast, any deviation from those standards must be, or lead to, some form of depravity. The 'darkness' is always somewhere else on the map, never within us. The desperately monitored borderland between Self and Other fails to understand Conrad's message on the eve of the twentieth century about the 'Heart of Darkness'. What Joe cannot accept is that perhaps the US idea of 'normality' is itself the problem. Joe also sees himself as a normal American man and loving father. He doesn't 'think' he is an alcoholic. He disapproved of 'people taking the law into their own hands', but as part of the 'obligation to protect my son and the rest of my family', if people 'push' he will 'push back. And, if that happens, it's not going to be pretty'. He was fighting in Iraq when he heard the news, and was reluctant to leave his peers, hoping to have returned with his unit. His interviewer found Joe's conversation rather like that of a soldier making a report. An ordinary Joe.

The need to separate the ordinary from the monstrous produces a repertoire of brittle inferences incapable of flexible adaptation. Whether or not there is a causal connection between Black Metal *as music* (as opposed to a general culture) and the violence adjacent to it, the attempt to prove (rather than test) this connection as a general principle has to be so selectively applied as to be of little utility. Part of the evidence presented for the connection is the influence of one of the seminal inspirational writers for the Black Metal scene, satanist writer Anton La Vey, who established the Church of Satan in 1966 and formulated the kernel of his ideas in the 'Nine Satanic Statements'.[97] Yet to apply the logic of causality to his own incitements to satanic practices is to come up against an awkward irony. By his own account 'I was listening to Chopin being played in the next room and I was so moved I just wrote them out on a pad of paper lying next to me'.[98] Black Metal was inspired by La Vey's work in acts of homicide and arson. But La Vey was inspired by Chopin. If we are going to line these up in simple terms of cause and effect, this sets up a further step that the demonizers of Black Metal would surely prefer not to take, since it traces backwards a chain of causality from homicide and sacrilegious arson to Chopin.

Careful ethnography also challenges moral panic assumptions. To alterize the supposedly Manson-inspired killer, it is necessary to discursively exile him (and it is most often male) from the spaces in which core social values are articulated and lived out. Hence the emphasis on strange costume and demeanour, secrecy and the image of the Metal or Goth fan as a potentially suicidal/homicidal teenage

---

[97]   Moynihan and Søderlind, *Lords of Chaos*, p. 8.

[98]   Ibid., p. 234.

socio-economic outsider brooding in his locked bedroom to the sound of Marilyn Manson. Yet Kahn-Harris's ethnography discloses the 'generally harmonious relationships' fans and musicians actually enjoy with supportive parents. Many scene members have families of their own.[99] Many are older people, in their late thirties, and notwithstanding general suppositions about class, Kahn-Harris's ethnography finds affluent working class and lower middle class profiles are predominant, with 'no shortage of scene members from relatively wealthy middle-class backgrounds', though there are probably national and regional variations.[100]

The stereotype of metalheads as subhuman berserkers has also been challenged by ethnographic research conducted by Stuart Cadwallader at Warwick University, involving over one thousand members of the university's National Academy for Gifted and Talented Youth, whose members are in the top 5 per cent academically in their age range (11 to 19 years). Six per cent of the group nominated Heavy Metal as their favourite music, and a third of the sample placed it in the top five categories. It appeared that, as gifted youth, they experienced difficulties in social adjustment, and in Cadwallader's reported words, 'turn to heavy metal as a way of relieving that stress'. Many listened to the music 'to "work off" frustration and anger'.[101] This is not to argue that a music is only redeemed by the pleasures it provides for the highly intelligent, but to enlarge and nuance a commonly accepted conception of Metal fandom which validates a facile demonization of the scene. It also foreshadows a later discussion in this study: that while music may promote negative emotions, this may well be socially therapeutic. It also reminds us that there are many ways of feeling out of place in contemporary society. Alienation is not necessarily alienating.

One of the tactics of moral panic is not simply to isolate the perpetrators by demonization, but the offending music as well. This decontextualization makes it much easier to see the music as part of the monstrous Other. However, lyrics about, or even featuring a *persona* contemplating, suicide, are not necessarily incitements when taken in context with the rest of the lyric and the nature of the music itself, any more than a line taken out of Shakespeare can be taken to reflect the intent of the play or the playwright. Nor, as Hamm and Ferrell point out, does this decontextualization tell us much about the vast majority of fan responses to what is regarded as incitement. Walser cites the case of a Metallica fan who thanked the band for a song about suicide that dissuaded him from the option.[102] And Metal is not the only music to propose suicide. We are not aware that anyone has ever blamed Johnny Mandel's *MASH* theme, which begins with the words

---

[99]   Kahn-Harris, *Extreme Metal*, p. 62.

[100]   Ibid., p. 70.

[101]   No byline, 'Metalheads not meatheads but scholars', *Daily Telegraph* (London), 23 March 2007.

[102]   Walser, *Running with the Devil*, p. 150.

'Suicide is painless' for self-harm among *MASH* viewers, or even checked, for the same reason that other pop lyrics are suspect.

The argument that acts of violence are caused by the incitements of pop also simplifies the complex agendas that operate in all social conduct. In the case of the much maligned Norwegian Black Metal, for example the music's overt agenda of principled opposition to various social formations like Christianity and their representatives, is cited as the root of all its associated evils. In light of the murders in which Vikernes was involved (including ultimately as a victim), it is worth noting that at least one grievance expressed by those around him was commercial rather than Satanic: he was alleged to be swindling friends, colleagues and customers at his record shop Helevete.[103] This is a rather unromantic allegation for his defenders and one which is all too familiar to those wishing to single out the genre for condemnation. In this case the 'law enforcement' also appears to be possessed by its own demons, in the words of its chroniclers. One of the police investigators most obsessively dedicated to rooting out the depravity associated with Black Metal was at one point videoed by a neighbour in an act of indecent exposure, one of apparently many, and for which he was under charge at the time he contributed interviews for Moynihan and Søderlind.[104] Indirectly this exemplifies one of the most serious limitations of moral panic arguments. That is, they are not predictive. Not everyone who listens to 'hate music' commits murder. Not everyone who commits murder listens to 'hate music', and the murderer who owns a Marilyn Manson CD may well own others as well which are not violent. Purely in themselves they do not enable us to foresee who will commit crimes and who will not. If Vikernes became violent, it was not simply because he was a Heavy Metaller, but also for other banal reasons. Conversely, as we have seen, those 'ordinary' folk not exposed to musical incitements to violence may nonetheless be monstrous. Apart from abstract 'where will it all end?' generalizations about the inevitable collapse of civilization, the attribution of causality in specific cases of violence associated with music always follows rather than precedes the event. This is partly because such arguments are indeed moral ones; that is, violence, damage, injury occur because listening to Manson has made someone 'evil'. The cases reviewed above, however, indicate that the main problems in the connections with violence are often logistical rather than moral, as recognized by organizers, fans and musicians.

Responses to Incitement: Denial

We cannot leave this topic without considering the denial arguments: that musical incitement has no causal connection with social violence, and should be protected by principles of free expression. Apart from evenhandedness, it is in the murkier

---

[103]   Moynihan and Søderlind, *Lords of Chaos*, p. 121.

[104]   Ibid., p. 232.

spaces where both sides of the debate get bogged down that, ironically, we are most likely to find some illumination. The clumsiness with which moral panic arguments are often deployed provides comfort to their opponents including musicians, industry stakeholders and 'free speech' liberals. This, however is likely to lead to the inference that there is no substance at all in the argument that incitement leads to violence, and that such music is invariably in one way or another positively therapeutic. This reductive position, often taken by fans, can only be defended by disingenuousness. Both Walser and Kahn-Harris encountered a philosophy of independence of mind proclaimed by many metallists. One of Kahn-Harris's female musician informants articulated the connection in the words 'I'm me, I don't need anyone else to tell me what I am'.[105] Her words play straight to the tactic of decontextualization deployed by the opponents of the music, by situating the scene as something separate from the rest of society. Furthermore, rather than socially empowering the individual, declarations such as this write the speaker out of the political processes that do in fact shape us, and thus become an illusory hermeticism and powerlessness – as is explicit in an informant's comment: 'Just be yourself, if you are sick, you are sick, you know, it's nothing you can do about it.'[106] In a similar position are the fans who have withdrawn into the music to the detriment of larger social negotiations, and as a consequence losing jobs, friends and various social opportunities. Kahn-Harris documents examples of some who have so cut their minds off even from the politics of the 'scene' that they don't know how to negotiate their way successfully through it as musicians, as in the case of the musician who wanted to promote his band but had not taken the trouble to work out how to do so.[107]

This compulsion to define membership of a music scene by watertight separation between 'them' and 'us' is apparent in both its opponents and its supporters. For the former it constructs a monstrous other, which by definition they will never understand, and is therefore counterproductive to any morally and socially recuperative objective (though not to that of profitable commodification). But on the other side, it produces a disconnection from the social realities which shape their own lives, and from the discourses through which productive transaction and negotiation may confer agency. It is a residue of a romantic ideology by which the 'artist' accepts social disempowerment as the price of apparent moral and aesthetic liberty, but which also places that artist in the hands of mediations and entrepreneurs. One outcome in contemporary pop is what appears to be a cognitive dissonance, discursive anomalies to which the speaker seems to be entirely oblivious, and this emerges most conspicuously in discussion of the connection between music and social action, and defences against charges of arousing violence.

A sample of illustrations: in January 2000, at Oklahoma City promoters oversold tickets for a Slipknot gig. Helicopters and police were called to deal

---

[105] Kahn-Harris, *Extreme Metal*, p. 40.

[106] Ibid., p. 42.

[107] Ibid., pp. 58–61.

with the ensuing riot and the band expressed anxiety at the possibility of being attacked on stage. 'I used to tell people "come and kill the clown" and now it's actually happening.'[108] If we now continue the quote cited above from One Minute Silence Band member Brian Yap Barry regarding a gig at Camden Palace, we find a similar dissonance: 'We were trying to incite a riot. Come on down, break off the barriers and break your neck, y'know. And some people took offence to it. "You want people to break their necks." Course I don't want them to.'[109] 'I genuinely don't want to see people getting hurt. ... We say "Kill. Kill" but we don't mean that. Just wound each other! And then rub each other.'[110] Barry hates Slayer for an album cover showing the band name carved into someone's arm, because 'Kids are impressionable', yet he has gone on stage with self-inflicted knife wounds. He denies that the band is 'advocating' violence or 'incited' it.[111] 'I may encourage people to come up and bite my face onstage, but I don't want any fucking bites, y'know.'[112]

Yap Barry's bewilderment is disingenuous, but it is also a microcosm of an enveloping hypocrisy in the ideologies underpinning consumerism and music commodification, and the responsibility for music-associated violence. The point is illustrated in the career progress of One Minute Silence, who were 'catapaulted out of the bars and into the halls' by two events in particular. At a gig at the 'industry-friendly' venue The Borderline about 200 young teenagers, 'egged on by the band', ripped out water pipes in the ceiling and 'mashed' the place. Yap Barry: 'We loved it because it's rock'n'roll' (which, he had elsewhere declared was 'dead'[113]). The band was then booked at The Garage, where all tickets were pre-sold, since everybody 'was waiting for a sequel'. The Garage was owned by the influential Mean Fiddler organization, which controls a significant proportion of the London 'small venue circuit' and the Reading Festival. Audience expectations were incandescent, and when Yap Barry exhorted the fans to 'go crazy tonight', the venue 'erupted'. Security staff threw fans out, and 'allegedly' punched them in the street. Hearing of this, Yap stopped playing and 'told the pit to destroy The Garage'. This they duly set out to do.[114] The direct and clear consequence was increased fame. Their label boss Richard Branson, upon being informed, reportedly was only concerned with the question, 'Was there enough media there?' They were banned from all Mean Fiddler venues but 'Within months One Minute Silence were selling out 1,000-seater venues beyond the reach of Mean Fiddler'.[115]

---

[108]   Ambrose, *Moshpit*, p. 130.
[109]   Ibid., p. 116.
[110]   Ibid., p. 117.
[111]   Ibid., p. 118.
[112]   Ibid., p. 118.
[113]   Ibid., p. 113.
[114]   Ibid., p. 120.
[115]   Ibid., p. 120.

The context of such clear double standards was enlarged by Tom Morello from Rage Against The Machine, when he noted Bill Clinton's comment after Columbine that violence should never be used to settle differences: 'Forty eight hours later a US Tomahawk missile blew up a bus of elderly women and children in Yugoslavia, and they also blew up a hospital. That's a war crime. So in America you scapegoat computer games and Marilyn Manson and ignore the rest.'[116] The point has been proposed above in the discussion of Woodstock '99, and argued in a number of studies of metal genres: 'American capitalism impinges on musical performance, not as a cultural style of individualism or a formal structure, but as a concrete context of wealth and poverty, of hard-to-come-by jobs and low wages, of messages of consumerism endlessly repeated in the mainstream media.'[117] Walser's study of Metal is underpinned by a similar argument; the context for his study is

> ... the United States during the 1970s and 1980s, a period that saw a series of damaging economic crises, unprecedented revelations of corrupt political leadership, erosion of public confidence in governmental and corporate benevolence, cruel retrenchment of social programs along with policies that favoured the wealthy, and tempestuous contestation of social institutions and representations, involving formation that had been thought to be stable, such as gender roles and the family. ... Heavy metal is intimately embedded in the social system of values and practices that its critics defend.[118]

The interest shown by sections of the Metal scene in the occult may be seen as responses to that system, including one of therapeutic rejection.[119] At its most simplistic, this model can find refuge in the alibi that Metal is, in the words of Slayer's Tom Araya, just 'a reflection of society'.[120] But the arguments of researchers such as Berger, Kahn-Harris and Walser, suggest that this notion of passive reflection (including despair and helplessness) is inadequate and even a falsification of the Heavy Metal agenda, which, rather, is a sustained attempt at making sense, and constructing community. Walser argues that Metal offers 'fantasies of empowerment'.[121] The two terms are equally important, since 'the logical result of individualism demanded by contemporary capitalism, confounded by widespread disillusionment with the proper channels offered for individual success: corrupt government and a rhetoric of freedom and equality undermined by the obviously systematic maintenance of inequity'.[122]

---

[116] Ambrose, *Moshpit*, p. 125.

[117] Berger, *Metal, Rock, and Jazz*, p. 50.

[118] Walser, *Running with the Devil*, p. xvii.

[119] Ibid., p. 154.

[120] *Metal: A Headbanger's Journey*, DVD, Dir. Sam Dunn, Scot McFadyen, Jessica Joy Wise, Futurefilm 35831, 2005.

[121] Walser, *Running with the Devil*, p. 163.

[122] Walser, *Running with the Devil*, pp. 164–5 ; see further pp. 161–71.

To conclude, the tensions and ambiguities in this dynamic, and the defences advanced by its music participants in relation to violence and the larger cultural context, speak for themselves in the case of an Australian equivalent of Lollapalooza in the US. At the Sydney event for the annual Big Day Out festival in 26 January 2000, during a performance by Limp Bizkit, a 15-year-old girl, Jessica Michalik, died of a heart attack and 12 others were hospitalized after sections of the crowd collapsed.[123] Bizkit frontman/singer Fred Durst (also the 'rich reactionary Vice President of Interscope Records'[124]), has a record of violence including assaulting stage hands and destroying equipment. In addition to his conduct at Woodstock '99 (see above), at another show he said gay men should be 'stomped'. Ozzfest 1998 was a seated show, but Bizkit fans didn't want to sit down so the band encouraged the fans to break the seats.[125] In the 1999 Family Values tour he told the audience: 'I can tell you motherfuckers are out of control, and that's what I like to see.'[126]

At Big Day Out, Sydney 2000, security guards were the first to recognize the danger presented by the crowd and ordered the band to stop. When the band recommenced, the audience energy level increased, especially when the band broke into 'Break Stuff'. As the song climaxed the audience screamed at the band 'Give us something to break'. Around two thirds of the 55,000 crowd began moshing. Following 'My Generation'. Durst stopped the band again because of trouble at the front of the crowd and took a ten minute break.[127] Injured were dragged out of the crowd, which was becoming increasingly hostile. Durst returned to the stage saying 'About fucking time'.[128] Limp Bizkit quit the tour three days before its conclusion (before the death of the young girl in hospital, was announced), and issued a statement claiming they had unsuccessfully requested stronger security measures from the organizers, saying they were: 'Shaken by the injuries that occurred and what the band perceived as a cavalier attitude towards fan safety by festival organisers.'[129] Yet a month after the Big Day Out, Limp Bizkit and their label, Interscope, 'launched a new Internet moshing game for Bizkit fans. The winner in Mosh Master was the one with the least dead bodies when the game was over. One of the main rules of the game was to ignore the rules: 'Avoid the security goons and get on stage, then dive into the crowd to score. If you hit the floor, you lose one life.'[130]

---

[123]   Ambrose, *Moshpit*, p. 211.

[124]   Ibid., p. 215.

[125]   Ibid., pp. 211–15.

[126]   Ibid., p. 214.

[127]   Ibid., p. 217.

[128]   Ibid., p. 218.

[129]   Ibid., p. 219. This places the concert in the same kind of category as car racing or wrestling fixtures, where it is accepted that high levels of risk are associated with the event. The difference is that rather than the audience expectation inciting the performers to take risks, it is the reverse.

[130]   Ibid., p. 222.

Onstage incitement to violence occupies a field that is far more complex than it suits either the extreme moral panic advocates or their deniers to recognize. Apart from the industrial, social and political context of bad faith, the comments from Slipknot, One Minute Silence and Limp Bizkit, reflect some deep disjunctions in the social fabric:

a) A disconnection between act and consequence (incitement and violence);
b) A disconnection between words and actions (words that are no more than an empty rhetoric of resistance);
c) A disconnection between lip-service to an understanding of the inflammatory context, and their actual complicity in that inflammation. As Oliver Wendell Holmes observed the right to freedom of speech does not include falsely shouting 'Fire' in a theatre. Similarly J.S. Mill noted the difference between subversive talk about grain prices between friends, and as a speech outside a Corn Exchange;[131]
d) The idea that someone else will clean up whatever mess is created;
e) The eliding of consequences of violence in its aestheticization in film and TV, the society of simulation. Many of these comments suggest 'theatre', role-play, the playing out of a form of aggressiveness that has become a highly marketable performance accessory. But where does the game end and who is responsible for monitoring its borders? Commenting on the increasing violence in hardcore, Lou Koller, straight edge singer with New York's Sick Of It All blames not the Gangsta-rappers, 'but the kids who listen to it for not being smart enough to understand that those guys are telling stories and not telling people how to live'.[132] This raises the issue of music as a form of role-play conducted within game boundaries (see next chapter).

The question 'Do songs of vilification lead to acts of violence' presupposes a false dichotomy, since a song of vilification is in itself an act of social violence. Among the most radical critiques of what might be called 'symbolic' violence have been those emanating from feminist theorists of pornography, arguing that pornography does not lead to violence against women, but is in itself an act of

---

[131] An opinion that corn-dealers are starvers of the poor, or that private property is robbery, ought to be unmolested when simply circulated through the press, but may justly incur punishment when delivered orally to an excited mob assembled before the house of a corn-dealer, or when handed about among the same mob in the form of a placard. Acts of whatever kind, which, without justifiable cause, do harm to others, may be, and in the more important cases absolutely require to be, controlled by the unfavourable sentiments, and, when needful, by the active interference of mankind. The liberty of the individual must be thus far limited; he must not make himself a nuisance to other people. J.S. Mill (1986/1859), *On Liberty* (Harmondsworth, 1986), p. 119.

[132] Ambrose, *Moshpit*, p. 37.

violence.[133] To dismiss this proposition is to take a narrowly literalist interpretation of violence as something confined to physical assault, while it is a self-evident fact of social life that every human being is susceptible to deep and even lethal trauma by various forms of public vilification. How a culture that also fetishes freedom of speech addresses that fact is of course at the heart of continuing debates about censorship and regulation, and we take this up further in the final section. At this point, however, the question 'Does music that vilifies and incites lead to acts of violence?', is more usefully expressed if the last phrase is rewritten as 'to *further* acts of violence'.

It is asserted that none of the moral panic spokespersons are able to connect heavy metal 'directly with suicide, Satanism or crime'.[134] Yet the word 'connection' may mean many things from causality to adjacency. It is certainly the case, as Walser argues, that perspective and scale are relevant here, that other cultural practices in the US have higher rates of connection with some of the pathologies attributed to metal. However the fact that other areas of social life exhibit higher levels of connectedness does not mean there is *no* connection in the case of metal. What appears to be incontrovertible is that pop and popular music can and do 'incite' violence. In this sense there is no question regarding a 'connection' between certain forms of pop music, and the three pathologies listed by Walser. The question in all these debates is what the nature of that connection is. Apart from clinical studies already referred to, even something as straightforward as dancing suggests that music modifies behaviour, as we shall go on to argue further.

---

[133]   See for example Andrea Dworkin, *Pornography: Men Possessing Women* (London, 1981); Catherine MacKinnon, *Only Words* (London, 1993); Armstrong, 'Gangsta misogyny', p. 105.

[134]   Walser, *Running with the Devil*, p. 143.

Chapter 6
Music and Arousal to Violence

Bruce Johnson and Martin Cloonan

Preamble: Definitions of Arousal

A distinction was made in the previous chapter between incitement and arousal, in that the former is 'in' the music rather than in the audience, while arousal is a potential response by the listener. In contrast to the usual conditions for reading a book or viewing a painting, the audience, especially in popular musics, may well be co-performers by, for example, singing or clapping along with the onstage musicians, and the musician is also normally listening to her/his own performance. This is a further reminder that musical experience challenges the mutual exclusivity of analytical categories, and evokes again the idea of feedback rather than linear causality in the process of arousal in live music situations. Incitement to violence, however, does not necessarily arouse anyone to violence. Incitement need not result in excitement. The point becomes crucial when we investigate the kinds of musical signal that accompany the highest levels of arousal to violence in public life; as we shall argue, it appears in most cases that there is in fact a disjunction between incitement and arousal to violence. Experimental studies in this field give the further authority to the distinction, as in Emery Schubert's differentiation between 'external locus' (EL) and 'internal locus' (IL) of emotion. He addresses a question neglected in the psychology of music as to whether people prefer music that 'expresses emotion ("external locus of emotion") or whether they prefer to feel the emotion ("internal locus of emotion").[1] The two do not necessarily converge, so that for example 'a sad piece (that is enjoyed) may not *induce* sadness in the listener'.[2] Schubert's enquiry suggests that music is enjoyed more for what it arouses than for what it expresses.[3]

The attempt to measure emotional responses to music requires some agreement as to what we mean by 'arousal'. 'Arousal, defined in its most narrow sense [is] stimulation of the autonomic nervous system ... The heart beats faster, the pulse rises, breathing becomes shallower, the skin temperature rises, and the pattern

---

[1]   Emery Schubert, 'The influence of emotion, locus of emotion and familiarity upon preference in music', *Psychology of Music*, 35/3 (2007): 477–93; see 477.

[2]   Ibid., p. 480, italics in original.

[3]   Ibid., p. 488.

of brain waves becomes less regular.'[4] Other markers of musical arousal include 'tears, chills, gooseflesh, overheating, sweating, changed breathing and heart rate, dizziness, pain, dry mouth; dancing, moving, laughing, shouting, or complete motionlessness and silence'.[5] The emphasis here is on measurable physiological symptoms. These are associated with intense positive and negative emotional states, as recorded in, among many other places, the Strong Experiences of Music (SEM) project.[6] But at whatever valence (see below), these emotions cannot be assumed to be unambiguous and homogeneous, and indeed they are often conflicting.[7] The experimental evidence is consistent with other testimony and experience. One apparently straightforward case of arousal referred to in Chapter 5 is of US troops using various forms of pop as 'pump-up' music to energize them, yet even this example of apparent musically generated single-minded belligerence may be compounded by conflicting emotions. For one African-American soldier interviewed for the George Gittoes documentary *Soundtrack to War*, referred to in Chapter 5 in this study, rap was also a link with home: 'I needed to rap to take my mind off the thought that I might be killed the next day.' To complicate the picture even further, even home, in this case Miami, was an ambiguous memory, since 'he was only in the army because it was too dangerous for him in Miami. He said it was safer in Baghdad than back home'.[8]

To attempt to accommodate at least some of the the multi-dimensionalities of emotional responses to music, many studies use a model of two axes, 'valence' and 'arousal', which provide us with a useful distinction underpinning this discussion. Valence 'refers to the affective tone of an emotion', running from negativity (sadness) to positivity (happiness). Arousal refers to 'the amount of activity' of an emotion, from excitement to langour.[9] The two axes intersect to form four quadrants. Negative valence and low arousal cluster in one quadrant with emotions such as depression accompanied by lassitude. Negative valence and high arousal emotions such as anger and terror are located in an adjacent

---

[4]   Judith Becker, 'Anthropological Perspectives on Music and Emotion', in Sloboda and Juslin, *Music and Emotion,* pp. 135–60; see p. 144.

[5]   Alf Gabrielsson, 'Emotions in Strong Experiences with Music', in Sloboda and Juslin, *Music and Emotion*, pp. 431–49; see p. 441.

[6]   Ibid., p. 439.

[7]   Ibid., pp. 440–41.

[8]   Sarfraz Manzoor, 'Baghdad state of mind', *Guardian* online 17 November 2006. The comment seems to have been all too apt. During the making of Gittoes' followup film, *Rampage*, set in Miami, it appears that the informant's brother was shot to death by 'a 16-year-old hitman who already had eight murders to his name' (Clara Iaccarino, '"The way you stay alive is by making people like you real fast"', *Sun-Herald*, 11 June 2006, p. 69).

[9]   Schubert, 'The Influence of Emotion', p. 481; see also for example Patrik Juslin, 'Communicating emotion in music performance' in Sloboda and Juslin, *Music and Emotion*, pp. 309–40; see p. 315.

quadrant, which is the most relevant location for this study. In experimental work it is possible to conduct quantitative analysis of these factors by measurement of the physical symptoms of arousal exemplified above.

Music and Arousal

The precise aetiology of those connections themselves, however, is by no means straightforward. As a society that prioritizes and valorizes the cognitive over the physical, we generally infer emotional state from the physical conduct it supposedly produces (we cry as a consequence of being sad). As long ago as 1884, William James challenged the assumption that the emotion produces the 'bodily expression', suggesting that 'the bodily changes follow directly the PERCEPTION of the exciting fact, and that our feeling of the same changes as they occur IS the emotion'.[10] The proposition has been debated in psychology ever since, but is extended and broadly reinforced in the work of such researchers as Zajonc and LeDoux, referred to in Chapter 1. What matters here relates to the causal arguments and counter-arguments about music and violence. If affective responses are initiated in a set of physiological responses which are inescapable and involuntary, rather than in 'higher' cognitive processes, the usual moral panic arguments about 'hate lyrics' in pop are both right and wrong. Right, in the sense that music does produce involuntary arousal. Wrong, because, first, exactly what it apparently expresses may not correspond to what is aroused, and second because, in turn, that primary 'quick and dirty channel', referred to in Chapter 1, is opened not by something as cognitively mediated as the verbal content of lyrics, but by sound itself. Our interest in this chapter is in the nature and causes of musical arousal to violence, but also how that arousal is managed.

W.H. Auden, in 'In Memory of W.B. Yeats', famously wrote that poetry 'makes nothing happen'. A parallel claim regarding the transcendental detachment of music from mere sublunary affairs has been associated with the history of 'autonomous music' as documented by Tagg and Clarida, who also confirm what every level of musical experience tells us: that the assertion is absurd.[11] Even the great maestro of the repertoire of 'transcendent' high art music, Herbert von Karajan, exhibited higher levels of arousal (heartbeat, respiration) in response to conducting even a slow passage of music than he did to landing his private jet.[12] Work cited in Chapter 1 by, for example Mitchell and Konečni, clearly documents the fact that music is a significant factor in arousal which then affects conduct, and there are numerous studies that explore its complicity in a range of social behaviours, from the highly specific, such as driving competence and various other cognitive and

---

[10] Cited LeDoux, *The Emotional Brain*, p. 43.

[11] Tagg and Clarida, *Ten Little Title Tunes*, pp. 12–14.

[12] Garry Ansdell, *Music for Life: Aspects of Creative Music with Adult Clients* (London, 1995), p. 5.

motor tasks, consumer behaviour, the interpretation of particular visual signals, to more general areas of social life like the management of moods, identity and relationships.[13] Connections with violence are often based on inferences from incitement, as discussed in the previous chapter, and Armstrong cites debates over links between rap and aggression.[14] There is little unanimity in these studies, not least because of other mediating factors contributing to behaviour. It is also because, by the definitions of arousal for experimental conditions as cited above, the appropriate instruments of measurement are rarely to hand in sites of musical violence such as moshpits and festival and concert crowds running amok.

It is helpful, then, to complement such studies conducted in clinical environments, with forms of ethnography and testimony from those who have been caught up in musical arousal. We have observed examples of police and soldiers entering situations of potential conflict. In such abnormal conditions it may be argued that their self-administered doses of musical stimulation have little to do with the ordinary conditions of life. This would falsify what we will argue is the case. Pop music 'arenas' are closer to that life, and provide us with considerable testimony. Musicians are physically well situated to report evidence of arousal among audiences.

When Guns N' Roses played a concert at Castle Donington in 1988 where two teenagers were trampled to death, Axl Rose recalled 'The audience was going crazy, we brought that out in them'.[15] A member of an Akron-based death metal band, responding to a suggestion that moshers were not paying attention to the music, declared the opposite to be true, that a moshing crowd was one 'spurred to near riot by the music'.[16] A Miami hiphop DJ recalled of a 1993 Misfits gig in Los Angeles, 'the music drove the audience, mainly young wiry guys wearing Slayer and Misfits T-shirts, into a sort of mosh pit I'd never seen before. There was a lot of blood and some guys were laying out some serious punches and drop-kicks.[17] Atari Teenage Riot leader Alec Empire declared: 'Digital Hardcore – that is to say guitar samples, distorted breakbeats, magna samples and shouting, very noisy.

---

[13]   See Gianna Cassidy and Raymond MacDonald, 'The Effects of Background Music and Background Noise on the Task Performance of Introverts and Extroverts', *Psychology of Music*, 35/3 (2007) pp. 517–37; Gianna Cassidy, Raymond MacDonald and Jon Sykes, 'The Effects of Aggressive and Relaxing Popular Music on Driving Game Performance and Evaluation', DIGRA (Digital Games Research) Conference, 'Changing Views: Worlds in Play' (Vancouver, 2005); Lana Carlton and Raymond MacDonald, 'An investigation of the effects of music on Thematic Apperception Test (TAT) interpretations', *Musicae Scientiae* (2003): 9–30; on consumer conduct, and a range of other linkages, see the continuing work of David Hargreaves and Adrian North, much of it assembled in their 1997 collection, *Social Psychology of Music* (Oxford, 1997).

[14]   Armstrong, 'Gangsta Misogyny', p. 107.

[15]   Ambrose, *Moshpit*, p. 41.

[16]   Berger, *Metal, Rock, and Jazz*, p. 166.

[17]   Ambrose, *Moshpit*, p. 41.

Riot sounds produce riots.'[18] Dave Chavarri from NY latino band Ill Nino also recognised the mutuality of arousal when he compared looking into the pit from the stage to 'reading a book. But a book written by yourself in part'.[19] Musicians are also audiences, as one reported: 'I think it's just like, an extreme fast death or black metal song yeah just like stirs something inside of you, it's like fucking adrenaline you know what I mean?'[20] Often the most astute judges of the audience dynamic are the organizers, as their sole function is to monitor. It was security personnel who have 'read' and acted upon the first signs of crowd problems, as in Rosskilde, and at Sydney's Big Day Out the organizers considered that the performance of Limp Bizkit was 'of sufficient intensity to provoke unprecedented and ferocious crowd activity in front of the stage'.[21]

While participants might have many reasons to falsify wittingly or unwittingly their recollections, this hardly requires that we ignore their accounts, such as for example that of a Brazilian fan of Sepultura/Soulfly who reported 'I smoked a lot of grass before I came here but the noise has just been making me higher and higher'.[22] A female high school senior and Grateful Dead fan recounted a concert where bongo players performed informally in the intermission. 'They just play and play and they get such ... emotion going. People just dance around them and, during intermission ... nobody can stop, you know, when the feeling starts.'[23] Keith Kahn-Harris reported a comment from a slightly jaded metal fan 'I still get fucking off on good records yeah, for sure, yeah. I thought that band the other night were that good I needed, I literally felt the physical need to go and bounce round like a [inaudible] you know, and go down the pit, fucking fall off the stage and all that sort of shit'.[24] Even more dispassionate, even if only because he appears to have had no prior enthusiasms, is the report of an extreme negative valence response on the part of one of the individuals interviewed for the SEM project, who heard a 'female's band' at an outdoor rock concert:

Malaria was their symptomatic name. They played a hard, heavy, fateful synthetic rock at high volume. We had been sitting quite close, but it became unbearable. The base [sic] was roaring a heavy, deafening monotone sound, that penetrated one's body. The drummer was also beating heavily and tired ... a saxophone screamed in anguish, completely free from melody ... accompanied by a singer who who completely freely sang the most monotonous and howling song I had ever heard. Their makeup was black and pale, they wore black clothes ... This naked and gruesome death music that was

---

[18] Ibid., p. 141.

[19] Ibid., p. 76.

[20] Kahn-Harris, *Extreme Metal*, p. 52.

[21] Ambrose, *Moshpit*, p. 218.

[22] Ibid., p. 178.

[23] Susan D. Crafts, Daniel Cavicchi and Charles Keil and the Music in Daily Life Project, *My Music* (Hanover NE and London, 1993), p. 63.

[24] Kahn-Harris, *Extreme Metal*, p. 66.

flowing from the loudspeakers and drowning us made me feel physically ill. I just wanted to get away from the music, and got on my feet to walk away. At the same time whole groups of black-dressed guys and girls came flowing towards the stage and loudspeakers. Everybody looked so pale and listless without life. I tried to remain but felt that it only provoked a destructive feeling of sickness ... I thought that the Malaria band and the audience, in open anxiety before life and future, allied themselves, horribly and totally, with death and destruction ... It was a deeply negative experience, strong and gruesome.[25]

These experiences emanate from specialized music-dedicated situations, in which, like those of violent encounter before them, it might be argued that contextually generated preparedness of one kind or another could be mediating factors. But as we move closer towards the conditions of ordinary life, there is no diminution of the link between music, arousal and conduct, across a broad profile of audients, as exemplified abundantly in the Music in Everyday Life (MEL) project. The following is a sample from Crafts, Cavicchi and Keil:

Gospel music 'gets me excited' (a sixteen-year-old female Julliard student).[26]

A song by the Pointer Sisters 'makes me excited about doing whatever it is I'm going to do – dancing mainly ... [and] ... "The Vowel Song" just made me want to dance up a storm but there really wasn't any ulterior motive' (a female student, p. 73).

Agreeing that she uses particular songs to 'get charged up', playing people like Aretha Franklin 'gives me the same kind of happiness that being angry gives me. A kind of fierce feeling' (a nineteen-year-old college student, p. 85).

Of Roger Waters: 'It actually hurts me to listen to his music. It just fills up every muscle and vein in my body. You feel so good you don't know what to do with yourself. ... it just intensifies my body' (a college student in her early twenties, p. 91).

Accounts from interviewees ranging from ages sixteen to sixty-five talk of the importance of music in mood modification, inducing tranquility and contentment (pp. 56, 60, 137, 155, 166, 193, 201), happiness (p. 59), excitement and energy stimulation (pp. 58, 118, 158), power (p. 76), sadness (pp. 122, 155, 164), sexuality (p. 122).

Apart from testifying to the power of music to arouse, there is another pattern here which resonates with scientific studies of sonic mediation such as those of Zajonc and LeDoux: the pre-cognitive and corporeal level at which arousal is reportedly

---

[25]   Gabrielsson, 'Emotions in Strong Experiences with Music' p. 439; ellipses in source.

[26]   Crafts, Cavicchi and Keil, *My Music* (Hanover NE and London, 1993, p. 55; all page numbers in the sample in this paragraph are from this source.

experienced. It is striking how often music spontaneously induces movement, and the structure of the MEL study, working from the young to the old, confirms the suggestion that we do not have to be taught to move our bodies to music; on the contrary, as we get older in western society, we are 'taught' not to. A five-year-old boy loves music because he can run and jump up and down when it is loud.[27] Five-year-old Carly likes to sing as she walks around (p. 14), seven-year-old Billy likes to dance to music, eight-year-old Jennie likes jazz because it encourages more moving around than 'ballet' (p. 23). Although reports of spontaneous dance diminish with age, a female college student likes Rickie Lee Jones because 'it makes your feet start bopping all over the room' (p. 70, also pp. 71, 73); a male student from Bolivia likes to dance (p. 101). A 43-year-old female Polish-American dancing teacher's response is equivocal: she won't listen at home to music 'with the big strong beat ... it upsets me ... it makes me feel that I have to keep moving' (p. 143).

In parallel with the corporeality of music arousal is its inaccessibility to cognitively driven discourse, its ineffability. A 21-year-old female student from a highly educated musical family was asked to explain her differentiated responses to various sections of Bach's *Magnificat*. She becomes 'annoyed' at the question 'Why is this part sadder than any other part?'

> Because the fact is that it *is* sad. It evokes certain feelings. ... Why? Well, I don't know why. I could talk about the notes or the voice or the oboe.
> Q[uestion]: Well, go ahead then.
> A[nswer]: But I feel no ... I mean, I feel somewhat of a ... maybe I just want to enjoy it, I don't want to explain it. I don't want to start describing 'what' and 'why.' I just like it and like to hear it ... like to be moved by it. I feel no *need* to explain it ... you can't explain why. I don't know, it makes my epinephrine levels decrease. How's that for a scientific explanation. We should measure my blood ... take a blood sample and analyze it everytime I hear this part of the cantata. And then we'll know what hormonal reason. Maybe it's programmed into my genes so that a G sharp really knocks me out.[28]

The awakening of these reponses is also associated with, not just the projection, but the discovery of identity, even in a disabled man of 65 who may be assumed to have had reflected at length on his identity, but who reported that music 'brings out feelings you didn't even know you had' (p. 193). A 13-year-old African American described how she could express gender through 'ladies' rap', using it to 'punk off the boys' (p. 50); without music a student in her early twenties 'would die. I would not exist. ... I just wouldn't be. I wouldn't have a personality' (p. 90). For a 57-year-old salesman 'music became part of my personality' (p. 183). As suggested elsewhere, however, every musical projection of identity is also a potential violation of some else's. At exactly the same time as music sets someone

---

[27] Ibid., p. 9; all page numbers in the sample in this paragraph are from this source.
[28] Ibid., 97; all page numbers in the sample in this paragraph are from this source.

free, it threatens to arouse a sense of violation in someone else. Interviewed by her husband, a 49-year-old woman took the opportunity to comment on music in her daily life:

> Music is a huge imposition. My son plays the drums whenever he gets the chance. My husband plays the drums, plays the thumb pianos ... and everybody, EVERYBODY, considers it a great affront if I don't particularly feel pleased with the music they play, so on the whole it's an assault.
>
> That's why I love listening to music in the car when I am there because I have to choose from what is there (159).

Such testimony recalls Mitchell's work on imposed music, and in general chimes with experimental evidence of music's capacity to arouse. That arousal is along an axis of both positive and negative valence. Music changes us physiologically, emotionally and in our conduct towards others, and those changes range from a more comfortable adaptation to our environment, to disruptive acts of violence. However, before we get busy with the parental warning record stickers, we must take the discussion to a further question regarding the status and social function of these contracts between music and audiences.

Music, Arousal and Game-Playing

Music is not the only activity which arouses aggressive inclinations in everyday life. Indeed, it is more difficult to think of situations of zero stress in contemporary life, than of those involving various levels of arousal from irritation to violent reaction. Driving, commuting, queuing in shops and service facilities, coping with colleagues, employees, bosses or even recalcitrant computers, attendance at movies and plays and sports events all to a greater or lesser extent entail arousal of potentially violent impulses. These sometimes spill over into anti-social behaviour to the extent that 'road rage' has become the ur-form of a range of urban aggressions from shopping-trolley rage to air-travel rage. In an instructive parallel with what we shall argue about music, these outbursts most commonly accompany banal activities in which violence is not constitutive. Notwithstanding moral panic arguments about violence in entertainment, however, there appear be very few spontaneous outbreaks of violence as audiences attend and emerge from Hannibal Lecter movies or those directed by Martin Scorsese, nor from performances of *Hamlet*, *Titus Andronicus*, Punch and Judy shows or video game parlours. The word 'game' is significant here. Most 'game' activity involves some form of symbolic or actual aggressiveness, from chess to football. In some of these contests violence is in fact the key to success, as in wrestling, boxing and martial arts contests. While there are calls to ban boxing, it is not because it generates the kind of public violence often attributed to music fans. On the other hand, when soccer violence spills into the street, it is rarely if ever proposed that the game itself should be banned, in contrast with forms of pop music.

Indeed, taking into account the totality of competitive 'game' activities in which violence is a major feature, there is a massive disparity between in-game arousal and spillage of violence into its extra-mural public and private spaces. It seems incontrovertible that music can arouse, and that what it arouses includes aggressiveness. A more important question is what happens to that arousal? How is it discharged? The model of 'game playing' is a promising way to open such an investigation. The link should not be so surprising, since there is already prolific crossover between sporting events and music. Apart from the obvious cases of intermission music in sports arenas, the use of rallying music for a range of 'sports' teams has a venerable history, from heraldic music for medieval tourneys to the Oxford boating song.[29] The martial art capoiera is always conducted to the rhythmic chanting and percussion of its participants/onlookers, and contemporary sports teams charge themselves up with contemporary pop, as in the case of the amateur English Sunday football team listening to Guns N' Roses as they kit themselves out in a disused container.[30] The group dynamics of game play and music have a great deal in common. It has been observed that the members of Slipknot 'talk like a football team rather than a rock'n'roll band'.[31] The following discussion would suggest that they talk like a football team *and* a rock'n'roll band.

Some theoretical context for this is indirectly suggested by Kahn-Harris, who relates Bourdieu's fields of production, in which specific forms of cultural capital confirm prestige, to the idea of the 'scene'. We suggest here that these connections can be adapted to the modelling of musical activities as forms of game or role-play. From chess to football, a 'game' is a closed system with its own protocols and rules. Some games are primarily about mastering rules of play which in fact have virtually nothing to do with life outside the game (eg, quoits, blackjack, backgammon, roulette, pokies). Others involve symbolic reference to social practices (chess/warfare), and others move towards role-play and therefore forms of theatricality or performance (playground games like Cowboys and Indians, Mothers and Fathers; wargames, playstation games like Dungeons and Dragons, various car-racing or shooting simulations in playstations). In the full context of such activities it is rare for their protocols to be translated wholesale into social life. The Dice-man was an aberrant experiment. People who play chess do not go out and kill bishops and children do not normally translate playground games of violence into patterns of general social conduct. In a study by the BBC Broadcasting Standards Commission, Director Paul Bolt talked of pre-teen children's responses to on-screen violence: 'They are able to, interpret what they see on screen, to distinguish between reality and fiction and to deploy a moral

---

29   See further Ken McLeod, '"We are the Champions".
30   Peter May, 'Just for kicks', *Guardian Weekend*, 29 January 2005, pp. 24–9.
31   Ambrose, *Moshpit*, p. 130.

imagination in evaluating images.'[32] Nor need it be assumed that people who wear satanist T-shirts or engage in robust behaviour in moshpits are inevitably going to carry that 'habitus' (to draw again on Bourdieu) into their home or professional space. They are different 'fields of production'.

The point emerges in an extended informal ethnographic exercise conducted by journalist Nick Barham.[33] Many of the author's extrapolations are compromised by his determination to configure all youth activity as positively emancipative. However, he does attempt to challenge the moral panic position taken by most media accounts of youth culture, to which his transcriptions of its members' comments on their own activities provide an invaluable counter. They also foreground an understanding of different 'fields of production', and the idea that many forms of popular culture are understood as a form of game-play. At a Download music festival in Donington Park, Barham reports a complete dissociation between the rhetoric and aesthetic of anti-social violence. He refers to 'the split between sign and meaning'[34] of T-shirt slogans, music lyrics, audience rituals and demeanour, and what he calls the politeness of the event. The audience members themselves recognize this dissociation: 'Most people are friendly people', says one of them. 'We're not exactly Bible bashers. But we're not devil worshippers.'[35] Talking to a group of teenaged boys in Gateshead he finds that they unambiguously recognize the separation between the world of playstation violence and 'real' life.

> 'There are consequences in this world.'
> 'It's stupid. ... You've got to be warped in the first place if you play a game and then say, oooh, I'm robbing a shop; you'd rob a shop anyway'.[36]

As in the MEL project, they frequently talk about what music means to them, though *in situ* rather than in quarantined interview situations. A sample of comments indicates a pragmatic assessment of the distinction between the theatricality of a music event and the wider world of social practice. In a rap style, one youth 'cites' Eminem: 'They say music can talk to you, but can it load a gun and cock it too?' and continues: 'It doesn't influence me ... You can tell that Eminem is getting money for it. It's just a laugh. It doesn't offend me. You know when it doesn't mean anything.'[37] Songs about violence 'are not telling you to go

---

[32]   'Children show an informed attitude to images of violence', News release, 22 September 2003; www.ofcom.org.uk/static/archive/itc/latest_news/press_releases/release. asp-release_id=729.html accessed 1 September 2007.

[33]   Barham, *Dis/connected: Why our kids are turning their backs on everything we thought we knew* (London, 2004).

[34]   Ibid., p. 93.

[35]   Ibid., p. 92.

[36]   Ibid., p. 293.

[37]   Ibid., p. 293.

out there, get a gun and shoot people. ... it is up to you'.[38] Members of an informal record production co-operative called Warfare Records treat with contempt the idea that music and lyrics cause social violence, and make an explicit distinction between representations and actualities, with an acute observation that: 'It's like Picasso painting a picture. If he painted a picture of a man stabbing himself in the belly it's art.'[39] Sue Clark, from the British Board of Film Classification, makes the same point: that children, young people, can make the distinction between representations of fictional and real violence, between movie and news.[40]

This suggests that music is generally understood by fans as a specific closed system with boundaries. At an Eminem gig on the edge of Milton Keynes, the rapper shows films of US commentators 'bemoaning his evil grasp on innocent American kids, how his songs are all about rape and murder. Later on, one of the stage animations dramatises his supposed influence. It shows images of school shootings, of drug abuse and revels in his role in making all this happen'. All grist for the moral panic mills. But Barham argues again that there is a disconnection between sign and meaning, that this is all rhetoric and theatricality: 'Angry is the subject. But everyone is loving it. Eminem has turned his very real life into a show for the world. He shares the mess of his personal life and makes it funny, makes it offensive, makes it worth something.'[41] Without being entirely convinced by Eminem's frequent facile disclaimers, we nonetheless suggest that an implied connection between his aggressive tastelessness and stand-up comedy is instructive. Do we accuse Lenny Bruce and his hordes of worse-taste copyists of actually inciting violence, or just of making comedy out of bad taste? Is this the category of Eminem's version of gangsta rap? Eminem's success is based on the appropriation of a rhetoric of violence. But his audiences don't go marauding in the streets; the police presence at the Milton Keynes gig is watchful but benign. On this occasion, even if the music *is* arguably inciting and even arousing the audience, it fails to result in violent action. During Eminem's Australian tour of 2001, a local female fan was quoted as saying 'I listen to Eminem when I'm depressed ... It cheers me up because he has a sense of humour about the bad things in life and you can laugh and dance and then get on with life'.[42]

As in any game involving a shared symbolic system, there is a convergence between the singer and an 'interpretive community'. For Barham, this is a showbiz triumph that frees the human spirit, but he does not test this guess in his usual way, by asking the participants. We can certainly agree that the apparent incitement fails to generate violence, but whether or not the entire audience shares the 'joke' remains to be demonstrated. It is a complex undertaking to 'read' within a specific subcultural interpretive community. Barham implies – and his informants generally

---

[38]   Ibid., p. 17; similarly, p. 43.

[39]   Ibid., p. 47.

[40]   Ibid., pp. 44–6.

[41]   Ibid., p. 279.

[42]   Patrick Donovan, 'Not the Antichrist, just a homeboy', *SMH*, 27 July 2001, p. 3.

confirm this – that these audiences effortlessly traverse different levels of simulation without becoming morally fooled. There is an instructive parallel in the fan base of Australian cabaret satirist Pauline Pantsdown. Pantsdown was a persona developed by gay rights activist Simon Hunt. In response to the homophobic, xenophobic campaign conducted by political aspirant Pauline Hanson in the late 1990s, Hunt created Pauline Pantsdown for cabaret performance. Appearing in Hanson-like drag, he took speeches by Hanson and digitally reconstructed them so that his adversary's own voice could be heard declaring an opposing agenda and outing herself as a homosexual. He then set these speeches to disco music. In effect Hunt stole Hanson's voice and directed it back at her. The recorded songs found their way onto alternative radio programmes and achieved a high level of popularity, to the angry dismay of Hanson and her supporters. The complex game of digitized simulation was understood by Pantsdown's/Hunt's hip, inner city audiences plugged into cyber-realities, amphibiously able to breathe anywhere across the fluid boundaries between the theatre of simulation and of the literal. Pauline Hanson and her constituents were literalists who were completely insensitive to the element of (malicious) play in the Pantsdown persona.[43] Barham's enquiries suggest a similar relationship between youth and their parents: the former are playing an often melodramatic game that the latter simply don't get with their literalist readings.

The idea of role-playing and game-playing as an explanatory model for the relationship between music and violence, is given added authority from, so to speak, the horses' mouths. Subject of virulent moral panic attacks, Alice Cooper, whose act has notoriously included bloody and violent imagery, announced in July 2007 that he had begun work on a concept album about a serial killer, to be called *Along Came a Spider*. Yet in the same press item he declared that in 'real' life he has been for over 20 years a born-again Christian (his 1994 Christian concept album *The Last Temptation*, flopped – perhaps not appropriate to the 'game' he is playing with his fanbase). He likes to relax playing golf with Tiger Woods, and anyone doubting that Cooper has a sense of 'playfulness' has not yet seen the cover of his DVD *Golf Monster: A Rock'n'Roller's 12 Steps to Becoming a Golf Addict*.[44] Cooper's understanding of the difference between real scenarios of violence and play-acting is made explicit in his comment that 'if you're looking for Satanism, firstly you don't look to rock'n'roll. A bunch of kids running around playing loud guitars and going like that [the 'Devil's horns' hand signal] – that's Hallowe'en'.[45]

---

    [43]   Bruce Johnson, 'Two Paulines, Two Nations: An Australian case study in the intersection of popular music and politics', *Popular Music and Society* 26/1 (2003): 53–72.

    [44]   Guy Blackman, 'Fairway to Heaven', *Age* online, 1 July 2007; the cover of *Golf Monster* can be seen at www.alicecooper.com/index2.html, accessed 29 August 2007. Cooper also discusses his Christian devoutness and the importance of role-play in his persona in Bernard Zuel, 'Lock up your chickens', *SMH Metro*, 3–9 June 2005.

    [45]   Dunn, McFadyen and Wise, *Metal: A Headbanger's Journey*, DVD, Chapter 10.

In a region with a particularly dark reputation attaching to its various forms of metal music, the Finnish doom metal band Reverend Bizarre has enjoyed conspicuous success, with fan bases in Europe, the UK and the US, as well as impressive local chart success. Their 15-minute single 'Teutonic Witch' reached number one in the Finnish singles chart, and the subsequent album *So Long Suckers* also sold extremely well, peaking at number six in the official album chart. Their 2005 release 'Slave of Satan' reached number two in the Finnish singles charts, an extraordinary achievement for such a specialized subgenre, and in particular for its length of just under 21 minutes. As transcribed online, the lyrics include such lines as

> I have seen the Prince of Darkness, and he is nothing to be messed with
> He is much stronger than you ever thought
>
> One day you will understand, but I'm afraid that it's too late
> because he has got your soul
> and there is no way to get it back
>
> What do you think, when you lie there at the altar
> waiting for some ugly jerk to rape you
> as a sacrificial fuck?[46]

The music is slow, primarily in low register (the band drop-tunes to C sharp on the bottom string), with hellish groans and cries. The stage presentation is everything one would expect from a heavy metal category group with long hair and strong on leather.[47] The point of this brief description is not to stereotype the band but to situate it in the pop spectrum. All three members use stage names, and guitarist and composer Peter Vicar is actually Kimi Kärki. In his thirtieth year at the time of the release of 'Slave of Satan', he was then an Assistant (Lecturer) in the Department of Cultural History, University of Turku, married to a colleague and with a two-year-old daughter; not exactly the 'moral panic' profile of a lock-up-your-children metalhead. In a recorded interview with Bruce Johnson, 10 May 2005, he talked about the band and its music. The following comments are discrete extracts.

One of the band's missions is to pay 'respect' to the traditions of the genre. Although the levels of engagement with the apocalyptic vision vary from member to member, for Kärki, it's a 'separate space', where he slips 'into another identity altogether ... a kind of double life' that complements but does not equate with his 'studies and research'. With some self-directed humour he says that one way of getting 'into character' is literally to let his hair down by releasing the pony-tail

---

[46] www.lyricsdir.com/reverend-bizarre-slave-of-satan-lyrics.html, accessed 9 February 2008.

[47] See for example, www.youtube.com/watch?v=gyQ4enN58Ykt, accessed 9 February 2008.

which is his everyday hairstyle. He is not a Satanist, he does not see the band as encouraging negative behaviour, although he thinks of the music as reflecting a world in which darkness is a significant presence. His wish for the audience is that they enjoy the music above all, and that it might make them think about ways of changing the world, to see its complexities. 'We are talking very complex, different textures here, simultaneously given to the listener.' One aim is to awaken audiences who have been anaesthetized by mainstream media, and to that extent, the band's mission is indeed subversive, but in a surprisingly lighthearted way. One of the main strategic objectives was a challenge to the local industry itself, by getting a recording of such length into the singles charts, slipping into the category defined by a 21-minute limit at a strategically timed 20 minutes and 59 seconds. There is an element of mischief here which complements a sense of humour.

> It's something that is very common in metal music anyway. It's, um, the humour that most of the mainstream audience doesn't get, because they just think they are very dark and satanist, satanic people that are doing this music. ... It's a play with the mainstream, showing that this is something that you couldn't understand. And also the humour is so well-hidden mostly.

The success of Finnish metal band Lordi in the wholesome Eurovision contest in 2006 is surely some kind of recognition of the element of play that blurs the line between shock and schlock, confirmed as the camera, panning backstage while the judges deliberated, caught the gothic members of the band holding up cards saying hello to their relatives in Finnish. Commenting on the result, the leader declared 'We are not Satanists. We are not devil-worshippers. This is entertainment. Underneath ... there's a boring normal guy, who walks the dogs, goes to the supermarket, watches DVDs, eats candies. You really don't want to see him.'[48] The sense of self-reflexive and playful humour in the metal scene, also documented by Kahn-Harris,[49] is almost wholly missed in mainstream debates over the music, as is the possibility that for the majority of fans the scene is the site of role play, a structured, enclosed game like chess or football, with a repertoire of protocols that are understood as specific to that closed system. The formal pop concert or the framed and bounded rave or party, might be usefully regarded as collective game playing, with rules operating within a closed system, and as such, the least rather than the most socially harmful kind of music experience.

Arousal and Catharsis

Nonetheless, game playing is also associated with high levels of arousal, and we have seen that musical arousal is often accompanied by highly aggressive energies.

---

48   Robert Booth and Helena Smith, *Guardian*, 22 May 2006.
49   Kahn-Harris, *Extreme Metal*, pp. 147–50.

How are those energies discharged? It hardly requires more than reflection on our own behaviour to realize that the functions of play include the exploration of one's identity (it is, literally, 're-creation') by 'playing out' possibilities, including those which are potentially counter-productive in social relationships. Inclinations that are potentially harmful to society but which may also deform the self if rigorously repressed, may be therapeutically discharged. The understanding of 'catharsis' is at least as old as Aristotle. One way in which it is achieved is through individual and group play activity (in all senses of the word 'play'), through which potentially dangerous energies can be worked off harmlessly. Recently, off-duty Australian troops videoed themselves 'at play', dressed and behaving in ways that were reasonably interpreted as offensively racist. The report in *Sydney Morning Herald* 6 August 2007 of the then Prime Minister John Howard's vigorous defence was headlined 'Boys will be boys' – the lads were just harmlessly letting off steam. This is not to endorse Howard's bid for the 'khaki vote', but to suggest that what is good enough for the boys in uniform might also be a constructive approach to popular music. The forms of arousal generated within fields of popular culture, including those associated with music, discharge negative energies in quarantined spaces. Schubert found in his experimental work the paradox of the cathartic 'enjoyment of negative emotions in music'.[50]

In fact, ethnographic evidence suggests that this is a predominant function of aggressive arousal. One of Barham's video game players, 22-year-old Samuel, who plays four to five hours a day, explained that the point of this activity is to build up a 'games knowledge', rather in the way dedicated fans accumulate subcultural capital in the relevant field of production. 'I play violent games but I'm not violent. ... Instead of taking your anger out on other people, you take it out on the video game. You just play a fighting game.'[51] The MEL project yielded similar information. Nineteen-year-old sophomore Abby likes to listen to music that awakens her aggression because she doesn't put that aggression anywhere else.[52] Forty-year-old Wanda, who is a dance teacher, finds that listening to 'depressing' music enables her to 'get over' it, without burdening anyone else with negative feelings.[53] Fifty-year-old Sally likes music that intensifies a 'bitchy mood'. 'I'm going to enjoy my bitch, so just leave me alone, because I earned this here self-pity period, and I'm going to have it, and when it's over with ... why ... then everything will be fine.'[54] One of Kahn-Harris's informants regarding extreme metal declared 'Basically it's like a release of tension [and] emotions basically by listening to the music'.[55] Another, who composed metal songs, spoke of having suffered beatings by young gangs.

---

[50] Schubert, 'The influence of emotion', p. 479.

[51] Barham, *Dis/connected*, p. 285.

[52] Crafts, Cavicchi and Keil, *My Music*, p. 85.

[53] Ibid., p. 144.

[54] Ibid., p. 165.

[55] Kahn-Harris, *Extreme Metal*, p. 53; interpolation in source.

That pisses you off, you get angry and I'm not gonna write that fucking suburb kids beat me up, instead I write lyrics for a song like [name of song]. You know you get pissed off you have to deal with your aggressions. You write lyrics that put into aggressive music … you can live that aggression out, and you can become a much calmer person I think, cos otherwise, otherwise I think if you're not going to be able to put your aggressions out that way, you're going to be, you're going to be drinking in a bar and hitting the first person that say anything wrong about you.[56]

Thus, while there is a demonstrated causal link between music and arousal, including the arousal of aggressive and violent inclinations, this does not necessarily, or even frequently (in relation to overall music consumption), lead to violent social conduct. Violent impulses might be simultaneously intensified *and* dissipated simply by listening to the music, or through violent activity that is contained within the 'field of production', in the same way as in contact sports. If we are looking for models to understand the music/violence nexus, it might be more instructive to look to non-musical recreational activities rather than to adjacent musics.

The suggestion that role-play and performance are significant in the rhetoric of genres such as heavy metal, challenges the assertion of a direct causal link between music and social violence. However it is still not such an easy escape clause. Games sharpen some skills which are also deployed in daily life. Collective games, for example, inevitably foster certain socializing skills, as in the case of group improvisation for pleasurable outcomes (as in jazz), the assessment of possible outcomes, the application of cognitive and physical skills. Social skills cultivated in various games may also be antisocial skills that may be paralleled in daily life: aggressiveness, competitiveness, reification, stereotypification. That is, the boundary of the football pitch, the chessboard, the stage, concert hall and festival space, is a significant one in assessing the limits of the incendiary power of music, but not absolute. The dress and demeanour of Goths, metalheads, jazz musicians etc, are not necessarily cast off at the door of the club. Living 'the jazz life' has been a guarantee of street cred. If 'the street' is part of 'the scene', where is the boundary between 'the game' and social life, especially given the increasing recognition that social identity is itself performance? And what else is carried across the boundary? How is it played out in social practice?

One way in which that connection is sustained is reflected in the fact that even in musical 'game-playing', certain physical and formal characteristics of music are chosen over others to 'play out' violence, and these are not arbitrary in the same way as the rules of billiards. They reflect and refract something of 'real world' expressiveness. There are not many soft ballads in the metal repertoire. That is, they recognize formal musical characteristics which are more appropriate to the representation of violence than others. In seeking to identify these characteristics, public attention is most typically focused on lyrics, as we have seen in moral panic

---

[56]   Ibid., p. 53.

arguments above. When French rapper Monsieur R (aka Richard Makela) was taken to court by a French MP with the support of a large bloc of fellow parliamentarians no mention at all was made of the music; the offence against public decency was wholly in the lyrics which talked about 'pissing' on Napoleon and de Gaulle.[57] It is therefore salutary to remember how rarely, in the larger perspective, it has been demonstrated experimentally, ethnographically or even anecdotally, that a 'musical text' is the originary cause in a sequence of events leading to uncontained social violence. Clearly, it is in some way implicated, as exemplified in numerous cases elsewhere in this enquiry, such as Woodstock '99 and in Rwanda and Iraq. One feature shared by these examples is that they are zones of conflict over other, non-musical issues. The musical text is crucially framed by a context.

Arousal: Lyrics, Sonority and Context

It is useful to keep this in mind as we now turn towards situations in which the connection between music, arousal and violence seems most unequivocal. The nexus between the most frequently scapegoated forms of music and social violence certainly makes for spectacular news copy, yet it is infinitesimal relative to overall music experience. Recall that on that basis Hamm and Ferrell calculated that the 'probability of attacking a police officer with a loaded firearm after listening to "Cop Killer" is ... less than 1 in 375,000'.[58] In the coming chapters we examine specific cases of socially rebarbative outcomes of arousal directly caused by music, and one of the most striking features of these cases is that they rarely involve 'hate music'. We shall find that the forms of musical 'texts' which most frequently actually cause violence, contain no message or intent of incitement to that end.

For moral crusaders against pop (and for some music scholars), the 'text' of a song is equated with its lyrics. 'Hate music' is identified through lyrics, as in the words of neo-Nazi rock or homophobic reggae. It is the lyrics which are cited when Eminem and gangsta rap, or extreme metal groups such as Anal Cunt are pilloried as exemplars of pop tastelessness. When Eminem toured Australia in 2001, issue of his entry visa was delayed 'after concerns were raised about the sexual violence and homophobia in his lyrics'.[59] It is lyrics which are targeted by warning labels on records. Yet only about 1 per cent of CDs in the UK carry such labels.[60] This small percentage is a skewed reflection of an argument to which we now turn. That is, that lyrics, in fact, seem to be the least important component

[57] Angelique Chrisafis, 'Rapper faces jail for song dissing France', *Guardian* online, 29 May 2006, http://arts.guardian.co.uk/news/story/0,,1785103,00.html.

[58] www.axt.org.uk/HateMusic/Rappin.htm, accessed 29 August 2007.

[59] Christine Sams, 'A pointed departure for snubbed Eminem', *Sun-Herald*, 29 July 2001, p. 11.

[60] bpi.co.uk/index.asp?Page=businfo/content_file_146.shtml, accessed 9 February 2008.

in pop music affect and arousal. In order to consolidate the cases covered in the previous chapter as examples of incitement, we concentrated on explicitness: overt encouragement to acts of violence. This inevitably meant a focus exclusively on lyrics, in which exhortations to various forms of mayhem may be unambiguously identified. It is also the primary point of focus of all 'moral panic' exponents, from 'Explicit' stickers, to the jeremiads of police, church and media. Yet it is demonstrated daily that, in terms of overall exposure of audiences to such lyrics, these explicit incitements are rarely followed by violent conduct, and even where apparently so, the argument for a simple causal link is highly debatable. We suggest that the wellsprings of arousal lie in two other sources which can operate singly or in concert: sonority and non-musical context, in particular the relations of power which frame musical experience. In embarking on that discussion we refer back to the arguments in Chapter 1, which underlined the importance of these two factors.

In the case of music, sonority refers primarily to musicality. Certain non-lexical sounds are decisive in the generation of affect. In the discussion of sonority and affect in Chapter 1, several conclusions emerged that are relevant here. The power of certain registers to elicit anxiety is just one example of the way in which sonically mediated affect precedes conscious interpretation. Our first affective response is to the character of a sound, upon which we then construct a culturally articulated interpretation. Our primary emotional reaction to sonority is the foundation upon which a cultural scaffolding is constructed. That scaffolding of course includes aspects of musicality which have become culturally mediated, as the massive directory of music affect compiled by Tagg and Clarida so exhaustively documents.[61] We first register, say, anger, then articulate the anger in terms of the specific cultural memory and context (diachronic and synchronic registers). Particular musical, as opposed to lexical, devices set up specific emotional responses. 'There is now an accumulating body of knowledge that shows that there is a lawful relation between the intensity of emotional qualities experienced in music and the specific structural characteristics of the music at a particular point in time.'[62] In experiments conducted by Sloboda, examples of the connections between musical effects and emotional affects include 'tears or lump in the throat/melodic appoggiaturas, shivers and goose pimples/changes in harmony, heart race/syncopation and acceleration'.[63] Of course lyrics are pivotal in channelling affect into local cultural dynamics, telling us that the specific source of a threat is this or that social agency. Our fear, or anger or yearning, is given precise articulation by lyrics which define specific political dynamics. Research reported from Iowa State University and the Texas Department of Human Services

---

[61]   Tagg and Clarida, *Ten Little Title Tunes*.

[62]   John A. Sloboda and Patrik N. Juslin, 'Psychological Perspectives on Music and Emotion' in Sloboda and Juslin, *Music and Emotion*, pp. 71–104; see p. 91.

[63]   Gabrielsson, 'Emotions in Strong Experiences with Music', p. 433.

finds that 'songs with violent lyrics increase aggressive thoughts'.[64] While we do not deny for a moment that lyrics of, for example, vilification can compound emotional responses, our argument here is that the framing sonority plays a prior role in shaping emotional responses. When Alan Lomax, Theodore Bikel and Pete Seeger were roused to fury (and Seeger's wife Toshi to tears) by Bob Dylan's performance at the Newport Folk festival in 1965, their complaint was to do with sonority. Lomax ordered (in vain) sound technician Joe Boyd 'You've got to turn the sound down. It's far too loud'. The defiant refusal from Stefan Grossman, Peter Yarrow and Paul Rothchild at the sound desk represented a benchmark conflict over sound – no-one commented on what songs and lyrics Dylan was singing.[65] Without the 'affective platform' provided by the music, the most inflammatory lyrics written on a page are likely to produce little more than amusement tinged with irritation.

The importance of musicality in arousing violent emotions can be illustrated from a range of sources, including the Tagg and Clarida index.[66] Succinct, topical and highly relevant exemplifications are to be found in the role of music in nation-building in the former Yugoslavia. Svanobor Pettan's 1998 collection of essays *Music, Politics and War: Views from Croatia* comes with a CD of music written, performed, recorded and broadcast by Croatian radio stations during the 1990s conflicts. Few of these songs deployed in a war fought ostensibly over local cultural and religious issues between two Slavic states, are free of US influence. Several are in US-accented English, and explicitly draw upon very clearly defined genres and musical conventions originating in US pop. This is not just a matter of appropriating a musical style; these styles or genres function as what we have called an affective platform. That is, before we even think about what the song is about, the style sets an agenda – this will probably be a hate song – within which interpretation and affect are circumscribed. Like jazz in the 1920s, the international technologized diaspora of US popular music circulated not just a set of musical practices, but a set of frameworks or matrices within which local political issues could be articulated. To clarify very briefly, a track by the group CLF bears the title 'Hrvatska Mora Biti Slobodna' (Track 5), but the rap lyric is in US-accented English. It exploits the expressive musical tradition of African-American music, yet deployed in the interests of a political position which has nothing at all to do with, and could even be hostile to, US interests. It exemplifies how widely the genre may now be employed internationally as a vehicle for 'hate music'. The lyrics are a violent vilification of Slobodan Milošević, but set within an urban African-American music genre, not simply as a setting for its local political

---

[64] James Meikle, 'Angry music may make listeners aggressive', *Guardian* 5 May 2003.

[65] Joe Boyd, *White Bicycles: making music in the 1960s* (London, 2005), p. 104. For another account see Lee Marshall, 'Bob Dylan: Newport Folk Festival, July 25, 1965' in Ian Inglis (ed.) *Performance and Popular Music* (Aldershot, 2006), pp. 16–27.

[66] Tagg and Clarida, *Ten Little Title Tunes*.

agenda, but exploiting the musicality of the setting to give force and articulation to that violent agenda. It tends to reinforce the proposition that there are specific musical effects that generate transcultural affect.

This is given greater force by a very different track from the same collection. 'Čekam Te ...' features the singing of Anja Šovagović (Track 13). The melody is that of the 1915 composition 'Lili Marlene'. Its interest is increased by the fact that, being sung in Croatian, the only response a non-Croatian speaking listener can make is through its musicality: instrumental and vocal textures, rhythm, tempo, and harmonic development – or as in this case, regression. I (Johnson) have used the song in classes of English, Norwegian, Swedish and Finnish speakers, and have been struck by the near unanimity of the trajectory of affective responses, from an impression of elegiac tenderness to strident martial aggressiveness. It is the rapidity with which this song 'turns nasty' before our ears, and the musical means by which it achieves this that is of interest here. Some of these are obvious, like a harder edge to the vocal and instrumental phrasing and intonation, and the entry of different instruments. There is also of course shared memory of a song that has already served in at least two wars to awaken nostalgia for home and peace. As it opens, although I don't know what the words mean, I know what the song 'means', or more precisely, the affective limits within which I expect that meaning to be defined, because, like every other song on this collection, mass mediations have made it an international possession. Again, a 'but', however: that 'memory' is not such a uniformly shared platform for young students in the Nordic region, so that musicality carries a greater burden than might be the case in a mono-cultural audience.

The question it presents is: what are the musical devices which turn this music from the arousal of tenderness to violence? Among the more obvious changes are volume (it gets louder) and instrumentation. Chorus one is just a caressingly soft female voice over sustained bass notes and delicate high register arpeggios on synth. In two there is increased reverb on the voice over sustained chords and the arpeggios drop out. Percussion enters in chorus three and more staccato bass articulation, and the solitary intimate vocal is joined briefly by a vocal harmony. Chorus four finds the percussion augmented and a longer vocal harmony section, and in chorus five a sharp pizzicato arpeggio layer is added in the back of the mix. Chorus six is a major shift with the arrival of an electric guitar sound, and a hardening of the voice. In chorus seven the percussion is more sharply articulated, with heavier guitar distortion and two or more voices now singing in unison, all of these accentuated in the eighth and final chorus, which ends with a martial drum roll and sustained guitar chord. The volume rises steadily throughout the song. There is nothing particularly surprising in this array of musical devices and their changing affect, and similar links are identified in Tagg and Clarida. More surprising, however, is the regression from harmonic complexity and subtlety. In G major, the changes move basically around G, Am, and D7, but in the first chorus the high-register arpeggios suggest passing chords within that framework, producing a sense of nuanced shifts in the affective contours, like small airpockets in an otherwise stable flight. So, a half tone shift here and there suggests a passing chord that gives a transition from, say G to Am more sinuous plasticity (as in bars 5, 6 and 8 of chorus one, and bar 5 of chorus two). As the militancy increases these harmomic subtleties diappear, banishing the source of that delicately nuanced response. What is this saying about the relationships along the tenderness/toughness spectrum, and harmonic subtlety, ambiguity and complexity? The development of this track in terms of both affect and musical form, is consistent with conclusions arising from more rigorous studies of the relationship between the two. That is, that aspects of musicality or sonority are decisive in mediating affect, to a greater extent than the lyrics. Apart from the more unsurprising dimensions like volume, rhythm and pitch, musical syntax is clearly also significant.[67]

It thus appears that melodic and harmonic complexity are also related to aggression, but in ambiguous ways depending on whether we are its victims or its perpetrators, whether we wish to dissipate or indulge in aggressive impulses. These distinctions themselves challenge schematic generalizations about what is meant by a 'connection' between music and violence. Vladimir Konečni, a pioneer in the study of the relationships between music preference and behaviour, conducted a series of experiments designed to explore various permutations of the connection. His findings relate to several questions central to our discussions: What kinds of music affect our emotional states, and in what way? How does our emotional state affect our choice of music? How does the combination of emotional state and musical choice affect our behaviour towards others? In the course of these he found that melodic complexity, mood and behaviour were mutually complicit. A 'choice between melodies differing in complexity does indeed seem to be affected both by the socially induced emotional states and by the feedback effects on such states from overt actions directed at social targets'.[68] Insulted subjects aroused to anger would be more likely to choose 'the simpler of two types of melodies about 70% of the time'.[69] Konečni also worked in the opposite direction, asking 'Does listening to melodies varying in complexity differentially affect the amount of subsequent aggressive behavior?'[70] The results were ambiguous in detail, as is to be expected in work that explores processes in which so many mediating factors are entangled. But he concluded that the work was a 'tentative demonstration that the exposure to melodies varying in complexity could have a differential effect on an important (anti)social behavior – both directly, insofar as it may combine

---

[67] Apart from Tagg and Clarida, *Ten Little Title Tunes*, see also Philip Tagg, 'Anti-depressants and musical anguish management', Keynote presentation at the conference of the Latin American branch of the International Association for the Study of Popular Music (IASPM), Rio de Janeiro, June 2004, www.tagg.org/articles/iasprio0406.html, accessed 9 February 2008. There is also a brief overview and sources in Schubert, 'The influence of emotion', pp. 477–8.

[68] Vladimir Konečni, 'Social Interaction and Musical Preference', p. 504.

[69] Ibid., p. 503.

[70] Ibid., p. 508.

with the effects of anger, and indirectly, in that it may raise arousal level and create a disposition to aggress'.[71] Notwithstanding the ambiguities of detail in both the experiments and the findings, and to which I have done little justice here, Konečni's work contributes to our understanding of how inadequately a set of lyrics explains connections between music and violence, and of the over-riding importance of sonority itself.

It also reminds us of a second category of factors in musical arousal; that is, the context within which the text is heard. This is hardly news for ethno-musicologists and popular music scholars, and needs little rehearsal here. Context is both diachronic and synchronic. The first raises the question of individual and collective memory. Among the primary sources of emotion in music identified by Sloboda and Juslin are those which they describe as extrinsic, including associations arising from the personal relationship with the music,[72] and in the SEM project associative factors were prominent.[73] The affective power of such personal associations is reflected in the case of a fan at Scotland's T in the Park Festival, reported by the BBC. He had 'run amok' after hearing Keane's 'Somewhere only we know', which had been played at his brother's funeral a few days earlier, and was fined £500 for breach of the peace.[74] Synchronic contextual factors include: who chooses the music, why, and how is it delivered? Expressed most succinctly, what relations of power are enacted in the musical experience? Corroborating Mitchell's work discussed in Chapter 1, Konečni's found that being 'forced to listen' to certain melodies would arouse more negative (in this case aggressive and punitive) impulses.[75] Likewise the studies conducted by Sloboda and O'Neill, which found a high level of resistance to music imposed in public spaces.[76] Sue Hallam's survey produced for the UK Performing Right Society concluded that: 'Music which we have not personally chosen to listen to can have a powerful effect on our emotions and subsequent behaviour. ... It can lead to complaints, legal proceedings and in some cases violence.'[77]

Again, the former Yugoslavia provides exemplification, and over an event so apparently harmless as the Eurovision song contest. The right to appear in the contest, however, is a recognition of an aspirant's statehood. This latent political function of the international contest became inflammatory in the wake of a war about the right of various 'nations' even to exist, as in the case of commmunities seeking political independence like the Kosovans or Montenegrins. In 2006,

---

[71]   Ibid., p. 510.

[72]   John A. Sloboda and Patrik N. Juslin, 'Music and Emotion: Commentary' in Sloboda and Juslin, *Music and Emotion,* pp. 453–62; see p. 459.

[73]   Gabrielsson, 'Emotions in Strong Experiences with Music', p. 440.

[74]   *BBC News* website, 'Keane song "triggered outburst"', 17 February 2006, http://news.bbc.co.uk/1/hi/scotland/4724514.stm.

[75]   Konečni, 'Social Interaction and Musical Preference', p. 509.

[76]   Sloboda and O'Neill, 'Emotions in Everyday Listening to Music', p. 423.

[77]   Sue Hallam, *The Power of Music*, p. 12.

Serbia and Montenegro joined in a loose 'state-union', sharing a flag, an army and some political mechanisms. For Montenegrins wanting independence, the question of who represents Serbia at the contest is not just a question of what is widely regarded as musical fluff, but an issue of statehood. In March 2006 in Belgrade, a Montenegrin band No Name manoeuvred themselves into the position of Serbian/Montenegrin representatives at Eurovision. According to a former Serbian Prime Minister, this aroused 'much more excitement' than the death some hours earlier of Slobodan Milošević. When No Name came onstage at the Sava Centre concert hall to play their winning entry, the audience called them 'thieves' and pelted them with bottles. The band was escorted back to the dressing room with an armed guard, while the runners up, a Serbian band, took the stage in their stead. The Director of Serbian television refused to sign the papers confirming the candidacy of the Montenegrin band, and as a result, Serbia/Montenegro was not represented at the 2006 Eurovision contest, 'a move unprecedented in 51 years of Eurovision and one which pro-independence politicians in Montenegro say *proves why the public needs independence*' (our italics). One of the Montenegrin judges was quoted as saying 'Yugoslavia was divided with guns, Serbia and Montenegro will be divided by songs'.[78]

Conclusions

Whether or not it appears to incorporate incitement, music does produce various forms of arousal, as cases we have referred to exemplify. The crucial importance of sonority and context in arousal emphasizes how tenuous are any conclusions about that link that are based on lyrics, whether conducted in mainstream public discourse or in academic music studies. This is especially so in the case of contemporary moral panic arguments and their reactive tactics. Warning stickers never mention tritones; perhaps the medieval church was more insightful in identifying the source of music's dangerous power. Some form of arousal is almost universal as a direct response to music, yet at the same time lyrics seem to be implicated only erratically. The widespread failure to recognize this in modern media commentary is suggestive of the enormous authority of lexical denotation in a post-Renaissance scientific, scopocentric culture, in which we need only to find and print out the right words to lay hold on reality. To find a widely accepted public understanding of musical sonority as, in itself, inflammatory, we must go to pre- or non-scientific societies or subcultures within our society. In any event, one of the related shifts as we move from incitement to arousal has been from musical narrative inscribed in lyrics, to its inscription in sonority, from denotation to intonation. As we argued in Chapter 1, sound in and of itself arouses emotional responses. Deracinated from musicality, the majority of pop lyrics lose all emotive force except in many cases risibility, thus providing easy subjects for condescension. What can be said of

---

[78]   Tim Judah, 'A warlike song for Europe', *Observer*, 16 April 2006, p. 31.

'A wop bop alu bop a wop bam boom' as letters on a page? In the present context they cannot be described as a form of incitement, but they certainly aroused emotions and animated behaviour. As we turn to examine cases in which causal connections between music and violence become increasingly unambiguous, the most remarkable thing to notice about lyrics involving incitement is their gradual disappearance from the equation. Sonority circumscribes affect, irrespective of lexical content. Relations of power (who chooses the music, and the conditions under which it is experienced), can enable any music to arouse aggressive forces. Indeed, music can itself be the instrument as well as the cause of violence, as we document in the next chapter.

Chapter 7
Music as Violence

Bruce Johnson and Martin Cloonan

One good thing about music, when it hits you, you feel no pain

Bob Marley, 'Trenchtown Rock'

Before exploring the policy issues foreshadowed at the end of the previous chapter we wish to examine one further category of cases in which the connection between music and violence is as close to coalescence as can be imagined. This is music as a sonic weapon. As always, the boundaries of this category are porous, but our main concern here is with the use of music to deliberately inflict pain in ways which are more or less unmasked. In this connection Bob Marley's words, above, are at best ironic, since this chapter will show that music is used to 'hit' people and certainly to cause them pain. The evidence we present here shows how music itself can become both the site and agent of violence. Moreover, music can be delivered by and within a socio-political order in a way that functions to humiliate, disturb, disorient and to torture. We have shown that sound is potentially an instrument of both power and violence, and that this potential has expanded dramatically through technological developments throughout the twentieth century. Indeed, one reason why music may now be used in torture is simply because the advent of modern sound technologies makes it possible to do so in ways which were both impossible and scarcely imaginable prior to the late nineteenth century.

We wish to emphasize that violence is a manifestation of politics, in the sense of relations of power. Having noted in our introduction that 'sound is power, unharnessed', we recall here Mao's dictum that 'political power flows from the barrel of a gun' and Max Weber's famous formulation that the state is that body which has the monopoly of legitimate violence within a given area. Politics (in all senses) is ultimately underpinned by violence. We have already seen that in modern warfare sound has been used to attack both body and mind. Similarly this chapter will demonstrate that musical violence is inherently political and we will tease out the implications of this in the final chapter.

Musical violence is about the attempted exercise of power over someone else and the soundscape. The cases which follow illustrate that that power rests on music's potential to inflict forms of pain in two overlapping ways. The first of these is biologically. As a sonic force, sound may be deployed in a high volume, at particular registers or in other ways which physically hurt and cause organic damage. The second and intertwined way is psychologically. Thus, for example, music may be used to disorient detainees, humiliate them, insult their culture or assert the cultural supremacy of their captors. Here music may become part of psychological warfare and it is unsurprising that a number of our examples come from the deployment of music by the US army's PsyOp (psychological operations) corps. Our broader point with regard to physical and psychological effects is not simply to reproduce a crude dichotomy between body and mind, but to illustrate the different (if often intertwined) ways in which music may be used. Our opening emphasis on the distinctive phenomenology of sound within the sensorium gains further force in the following discussion. It identifies the particular capacity of music to inflict violence, *vis-à-vis* other expressive forms. We know that literature can portray violence. Likewise, painting, ranging from Goya's scarifying portraits of war to Zap! Pow! Comix, can represent violence in myriad ways. But no matter how intense, horrifying, inflaming and arousing these other artistic representations of violence are, a book or a painting can not *become* physical violence (unless we throw it at someone). In contrast, as *sound*, music can become itself the direct agent of violence. Music as aggressive or violent intervention thoroughly pervades contemporary life, ranging from its uses in the regulation of public order, to a means of torture and interrogation under duress. A book may inflame violence by what is read (the content); music can do so simply by being sound, irrespective of a lyric. This distinctive capacity of music again has implications for popular music studies which we will explore in the final chapter.

As we explore this field we shall draw together a number of threads that have coloured the discussion thus far, and supplement this synthesis with further focused cases in such areas as music and choice, sonic trauma and the use of music in warfare and other conflicts. As we saw in Chapters 2 and 3 the connection between sound, music and war has a special intensity. While some, like Laks and Cusick, have found the association aberrant and even shocking, the fact is that both violence and music appear to be ubiquitous in social formations and their paths have perennially crossed. In the preparation of this book it was easier to find cases where music is being deployed as an act of violence in itself than to establish that music unambiguously caused violence. In the latter cases we have seen that there are so many other possible mediating factors that the precise role played is difficult to determine. However, when music is deployed as part of the arsenal of violence, then what is at issue is not whether music *caused* the violence but *how* it is being used; in other words, what sort of weapon music has become. This chapter provides many examples of such uses and teases out the implications. We begin on familiar ground.

Music and War

The connection between music and violence is most vividly illustrated in the deployment of music during wartime, which we discussed in Chapter 2. This association is an ancient one and, as we have argued, the so-called Great War itself provided a major theatre for a transformation of the sonic imaginary and the dramatization of a relationship between technology, sound and violence. Since the early twentieth century and the technologization of sound, the use of music in various forms of warfare has become increasingly notorious. Here we exemplify briefly with two recent cases – Northern Ireland and the wars in the former Balkans.

Northern Ireland is illustrative of a perennial function of music in conflict to which we have already referred. That is, the mobilization of potential perpetrators and/or supporters of violence. Both sides in the conflict had their own 'rebel' songs which served to 'preserve the entrenched sectarian beliefs present in Northern Irish society',[1] and did so in ways that reflected differences in political agenda and the sense of history and identity. While Unionist music is inclined to triumphalism, for example, Republican music tends to be about suffering and vengefulness.[2] Our discussion, however, now moves beyond the role of music in mobilization. Northern Ireland also witnessed the use of sound to disorient prisoners. A Government enquiry found that the security forces had physically mistreated detainees by placing hoods on them, making them stand up against walls, depriving them of food and sleep, and subjecting them to noise.[3] A detainee reported that: 'After a while the noise in the background became more prominent … I couldn't concentrate, this noise was in the centre of my head. I had shit myself and pissed myself a couple of times at this stage.'[4] Although the overall treatment of the detainees was later classified by the European Court of Human Rights as being 'inhuman and degrading' but not torture, the case nonetheless is clearly an example of the use of sonic weaponry by a regime not generally regarded as brutal or totalitarian.

In the previous chapter we discussed the deployment of music in the 1990s wars in the former Yugoslavia. It has been argued that there were three main uses of music in the conflict – encouragement to participants; provoking and humiliating the enemy; and calls for the involvement of those not directly involved.[5] As in Northern Ireland, the music reflected important differences in various antagonists'

---

[1]   University of York, Department of Politics, Topics in British Government, course documentation.

[2]   David Wilson, 'Ulster loyalism and country music, 1969–85', in Wolfe and Akenson, *Country Music Goes To War*, pp. 192–218.

[3]   See Edmund Compton, *Report of the enquiry into allegations against the security forces of physical brutality in Northern Ireland arising out of the events of 9 August, 1971* (London, 1971): HM, Cmnd.4823, p. 16 and Owen Bowcott, 'Army tortured Mau Mau rebels in 1950s', *The Guardian*, 5 May 2005, p. 5.

[4]   Bowcott, 'Army tortured Mau Mau'.

[5]   Pettan, *Music, Politics and War*, p. 13. See also in this collection: Miroslava Hadžihusejnović-Valašek, 'The osijek War-Time Music Scene 1991–1992', pp. 166–73; Zdrayko Blazekovic, 'The Shadow of Politics on North Croatian Music of the Nineteenth Century' esp. p. 66; and see further Petar Lukovic, 'Guns 'n' cassettes', *The Guardian*, 1 April 1993, part two p. 8.

view of themselves.[6] So important was the use of music in the conflict that one radio station, Yellow Submarine (so-called because its listeners were 'submerged' during wartime raids) came into existence purely because of wartime demand in February 1992 and discontinued when the hostilities ceased in June. An apotheosis of the fusion of music and violence was the marriage of folk singer Ceca to Arkan (real name Željko Ražnatović) in Serbia in February 1995. Ceca was the 'Queen of Turbo-folk' a form of music which had become popular during the conflict and was described as being 'the anthem of young Serbian xenophobes.[7] Until his death in January 2000 Arkan was the leader of the so-called 'Serbian Tigers' who were accused of atrocities in Croatia and Bosnia. The marriage of a popular musician to a man of violence made literal the proposition that music and war can make comfortable bedfellows.

The foregoing comments illustrate again the application of music as wartime morale and propaganda. But the role of sound in the interrogation of political prisoners in Ireland points towards a less mediated connection between music and violence; that is, music itself as the direct instrument of violent conflict.

Musical Torture: Disorientation, Humiliation – and Pain

Here we use the term torture in the sense of being the deliberate infliction of physical and/or psychological pain for a sustained period.[8] The following examples suggest that this generally happens in one of two ways – to disorient and to humiliate. Both cases, however, blur the line between the mind and body, and to a greater or lesser extent involve sonically-induced physical pain and damage.

Musical Disorientation[9]

One of the most notorious examples of the use of music to disorient was in December 1989 when US troops played loud music outside the Vatican embassy in Panama City in their attempt to dislodge the fugitive Panamian President, General Noriega who had sought refuge in the embassy.[10] This proved successful

---

6   Naila Ceribašić, 'Defining women and men in the context of war: Images in Croatian popular music in the 1990s' in Pirkko Moisala and Beverley Diamond (eds), *Music and Gender* (Chicago, 2000), p. 225.

7   Yigal Chazan, 'Shotgun wedding thrills Serbia', *Guardian*, 20 February 1995, p. 1.

8   This broadly accords with Amnesty International's formation of torture as 'the systematic infliction of acute pain in any form by one person on another, or on a third person' (Amnesty International, *Report on Torture* (London, 1973), p. 31).

9   See Jon Ronson, *The Men Who Stare at Goats* (London, 2004) 133–5 for a discussion of the origins of the use of music as disorientation.

10   Russell A. Potter, 'Noise, performance and the politics of sound' in Thomas Swiss, John Sloop and Andrew Herman (eds), *Mapping The Beat* (Oxford, 1998), pp. 37–8 and

to the extent that Noriega was driven out of his hiding place.[11] However the actual reasoning behind the use of the music remains opaque. One account says that it had actually been used to muffle the sound of negotiations which were taking place,[12] while another has Noriega complaining about one of the US marines surrounding the compound playing his AC/DC tape too loud and his complaint leading to the deliberate use of loud music to upset him.[13] There was also a cultural dimension as the use of popular music was assumed to be offensive to the opera-loving Noriega.[14]

Whatever the reasoning in the Noriega cases, the use of music here foreshadowed its wider use by the US military as a form of psychological warfare. According to Ben Abel, a spokesman for the US army's PsyOps command, 'Since the Noriega incident, you've been seeing an increased use of loudspeakers. The Army has invested a lot of money into getting speakers that are smaller and more durable, so the men can carry them on their backs'.[15] Apparently inspired by the tactics used in Panama, the FBI then used music and other noise in order to disorient members of the Branch Davidian sect in the Waco siege of March 1993. According to one account this included: 'the sounds of Tibetan Buddhist chants, screeching bagpipes, crying seagulls, helicopter motor blades, dentist drills, sirens, dying rabbits, a train and Nancy Sinatra's (recording of) "These Boots Were Made For Walking"'.[16] It was also said to include Billy Ray Cyrus's 'Achy Breaky Heart'.[17] One of the few survivors noted that the music was distorted,[18] suggesting a further tactic of disorientation. The use of music as a sonic weapon seems to have spread and it was reported that during a siege at Bethlehem's Church of The Nativity in 2002 Israeli soldiers played heavy metal at occupying Palestinians.[19]

Unsurprisingly, music has also been part of the weaponry of the co-called War on Terror. Following the events now referred to as 9/11, music was also used in interrogation, especially in Iraq and Guantánomo Bay. In May 2003 it was revealed that US forces in Iraq were using music to disorient prisoners who were being held in shipping containers. Songs played at the prisoners included Metallica's 'Enter

---

Ronson, *The Men Who Stare at Goats*, p. 203.

[11] 'Now that's what I call music to blast dictators', *Guardian*, 4 July 1998, *Editor*: 21. A list of the songs played was later placed on the US National Security archive website.

[12] Lane DeGregory, 'Iraq and roll', *St Petersubrg Times* online, 21 November 2004, http://s{times/com/2004/11/21/Floridian/Iraq_n_roll.shtml.

[13] Ibid.

[14] Potter, 'Noise, performance and the politics of sound', pp. 37–8.

[15] DeGregory, 'Iraq and roll'.

[16] Ronson, *The Men Who Stare at Goats*, p. 198.

[17] Andrew Mueller, 'Rhyme and punishment', *Guardian*, 21–27 February 2004, *The Guide*, pp. 12–13.

[18] Ronson, *The Men Who Stare at Goats*, p. 199.

[19] Mueller, 'Rhyme and Punishment'.

Sandman' and, most notoriously, Barney The Dinosaur's 'I Love You Song' along with songs from *Sesame Street*.[20] Quoted in many articles was a US Sergeant Mark Hadsell of US PsyOps, whose own favourites were said to include 'Bodies' from the film *xXx* soundtrack as well as 'Enter Sandman'. The BBC quoted Hadsell on the use of Metallica thus: 'These people haven't heard heavy metal. They can't take it. If you play it for 24 hours, your brain and body start to slide, your train of thought slows down and your will is broken. That's when we come in and talk to them.'[21] In reality, of course, it appears that repetition of *any* noise for sustained periods when the prisoner has no power to control it would have had a similar effect. Thus one US operative was quoted as saying, 'In training, they forced me to listen to the Barney "I Love You" song. I never want to go through that again'.[22]

A report in the *Sydney Morning Herald* in May 2004 detailed the arrest of Muwafaq Sami Abbas by US troops while he was visiting Baghdad. In addition to being subjected to other forms of violence: 'Rest was made impossible by loudspeakers blaring, over and over, the Beastie Boys' rap anthem *No Sleep 'Til Brooklyn.*'[23] In March 2006 the *New York Times* ran a story which described 'Camp Nama', a multiple-agency interrogation unit at Baghdad International Airport where 'high-value detainees' were first of all sent to a so-called 'Black Room', a garage-sized, windowless space painted black where 'rap music or rock'n'roll blared at deafening decibels over a loudspeaker'.[24] This account was later verified by soldiers who gave evidence to Human Rights Watch.[25] It thus appears that the use of music to soften up detainees had become an almost routine part of US military operations.

This is further evidenced by the cases which have been documented from the US holding camp at Guantánamo Bay in Cuba. A report from the *New York Times* in October 2004 recounted how detainees were stripped to their underpants, shackled to chairs, placed under strobe lights and forced to listen to rock and rap. According to one observer 'It fried them', 'They were very wobbly ... just

---

[20]   Julian Borger, 'Metallica is latest interrogation tactic', *Guardian*, 20 May 2003, p. 11; Ronson, *The Men Who Stare at Goats*, pp. 130–32.

[21]   No byline, 'Sesame Street breaks Iraqi POWs', *BBC News* online 20 May 2003, http://news.bbc.co.uk/1/hi/world/middle_east/3042907.stm. See also Borger 'Metallica'.

[22]   No byline, 'Sesame Street breaks Iraqi POWs', *BBC News* online 20 May 2003. A young Finn who recently completed his compulsory national service reported to Johnson that the new recruits were woken up on their first morning by having piped into the barracks the Finnish iskelma/schlager song by Johnny Liebkind, 'Ihana aamu' ('Beautiful morning', which begins 'Voiko aamu enää ihanammin alkaa?' ('Could the day begin any happier?').

[23]   Scott Wilson, *SMH* 4 May 2004.

[24]   Eric Schmitt and Carolyn Marshall, 'Task Force 6–26: Inside Camp Nama', *New York Times*, 19 March 2006.

[25]   John Sifton, *'No Blood, No Foul': Soldiers' Accounts of Detainee Abuse in Iraq* (New York, 2006). See also Moustafa Bayoumi, 'Disco inferno', *Nation*, 26 December 2005, http:/www.thenation.com/doc/20051226/bayoumi.

completely out of it'.[26] In the UK *The Guardian* reported in February 2005 that interrogation techniques at Guantánamo included placing detainees on a floor draped in an Israeli flag and immersing them in loud music and strobe music.[27] Two years later *The Guardian* again reported that Guantánamo Bay detainees were 'subjected to strobe lighting, loud music and extremes of hot and cold – all meant to break them psychologically'.[28] This was part of a regime which the Red Cross allegedly believed 'causes psychological suffering that has driven inmates mad, with scores of suicide attempts and three inmates killing themselves last year'.[29] The Australian detainee David Hicks has also documented his mistreatment at Guantánamo and other holding bases which he says included being given electric shocks, simulated drowning, being attacked by dogs and repeatedly beaten. At Guantánamo he was forced to be silent for two weeks and reported hearing 'excruciating loud music from nearby interrogation cells'.[30] According to Suzanne Cusick: 'Documents obtained by the ACLU include an email from an unidentified FBI agent, dated Dec. 5, 2003, that describes at least three incidents involving Guantánamo detainees being chained to the floor and subjected to "extreme heat, extreme cold, or extremely loud rap music".'[31] She also reports that on 12 June 2005 *Time* magazine carried a story based on the log of Mohammed al Qahtani's interrogations in Guantanamo from November 2002 to January 2003. These began at midnight and whenever he dozed off he was awakened either by water poured over his head or the sound of Christina Aguilera's music. In another incident Benyan Mohammed, an Ethiopian who had lived in Britain, had been forced to listen to music by Eminem and Dr Dre for 20 days before the music was replaced by 'horrible ghost laughter and Halloween sounds'.[32]

While any imposed sound is a potential instrument of violence, the choice of the music played here is not incidental. We have referred to Johnson's 'affective platforms': particular forms of sonority and musical genres which can function for specific categories of emotion. The use of heavy rock and rap can be seen as utilizing forms of popular music which have reputations for, and can be heard as being, aggressive. They may also be experienced as culturally aggressive by detainees unfamiliar with such sounds. However, familiar sounds may also be used in a way that disorients detainees. According to the account of one released British detainee, Jamal al-Harith, ordinary CDs with which he was likely to have some acquaintance were played to him. They included 'a girl band doing Fleetwood

---

[26] Neil A. Lewis, 'Frequent prisoner coercion alleged', *New York Times*, 17 October 2004.

[27] James Meek, 'Nobody is talking', *Guardian G2*, 18 February 2005, pp. 2–5.

[28] Vikram Dodd, 'This is a US torture camp', *Guardian* online, 12 January 2007.

[29] Ibid.

[30] Tom Allard, 'Hicks: my life of terror and torture', *SMH* online, 2 March 2007.

[31] Suzanne Cusick, 'Music as torture / Music as weapon', *Transcultural Music Review*, 10 (2006), p. 3, www.sibetrans.com/trans/trans10/cusick_eng.htm.

[32] Ibid.

Mac covers, Kris Kristofferson's Greatest Hits and Matchbox Twenty'.[33] The latter band was also apparently used in Iraq, prompting questions about whether this was used systematically.[34] Jamal al-Harith was one of the so-called Tipton Three British detainees who reported treatment including being 'forced to listen to rap or heavy metal played at deafening volume under the flicker of strobe lights'.[35] Another detainee, Martin Mubanca, said: 'So much went on there that we still don't know about. And even things like being chained to the floor with loud music on, people think that's maybe not so harsh but... Just think if you have to put up with that for years. It's going to affect you, isn't it?'[36] As Hadsell says once disorientation is achieved – or once the detainees have been 'fried' – *then* interrogators come in. The interrogator's job may also be easier if the detainees had been humiliated and deprived of their humanity and music has also played a role in such processes.

Musical Humiliation

Our research has revealed a range of examples of the use of music in humiliation, as in the BBC One News report 2 March 2005 of detainees at an unnamed UK Immigration Centre woken in the mornings by very loud children's music. In February 2000 it was reported that members of the Ivory Coast football team returning from an unsuccessful Africa Cup campaign were detained in a military barracks and forced to sing the national anthem.[37] A follow up story reported that jaywalkers in the Philippines were given the choice of paying a fine or singing the national anthem.[38] While these might be seen as relatively trivial, forced singing can be part of more brutal humiliation. In the wars in the former Yugoslavia, there were documented instances of Serbian forces forcing Croatian prisoners to sing the Yugoslav national anthem at the beginning and the end of the day. The aim was to humiliate the prisoners and make them feel like 'secessionist perpetrators'. According to one account the last verse of the anthem – which includes the line: 'Damned the one who betrays his homeland' – had to be particularly emphasized and those who did not sing loudly enough were beaten.[39] A detainee also recalled that: 'Reservists were walking in front of us checking the singing and they beat anyone who did not sing loud enough... After 49 minutes of singing and being beaten we once again Loudly and Nicely sang the national anthem and consequently were permitted to lie on the cold concrete of the stable.'[40] In Omarska camp Croat

---

[33]   Ronson *The Men Who Stare at Goats*, pp. 175–88.

[34]   Ibid., pp. 179–80.

[35]   David Rose, 'Using terror to fight terror', *Observer Review*, 26 February 2006, p. 5.

[36]   Cusick, 'Music as torture'.

[37]   Bruce Johnson, posting to IASPM email list, 8 February 2000.

[38]   Antti-Ville Karja, posting to IASPM email list 11 February 2000.

[39]   Pettan, *Music, Politics and War*, p. 18.

[40]   Cited ibid.

prisoners were forced 'to sing Chetnik songs and revile (the Croatian leaders) Franjo Tuđman and Alija Izetbegovic.[41] According to Stipe Sosic, a priest detained at the Keraterm detention camp in Bosnia-Herzegovina early one morning a guard 'ordered us to stand up, to raise our hands with three fingers ahead (a Serb gesture) and to sing Chetnik songs ... we had to wait for sunrise in such a position; those who sat or collapsed from exhaustion were taken out and never came back'.[42] According to the report during the war: 'It is no longer enough to finish off the enemy with a sledge-hammer or a stake. He must be forced to revel in his own defeat, listening to "patriotic" songs.'[43] It was also reported that 'it was not unusual for newly composed folk music to accompany incidents of rape, including forced anal and oral sex, and castration'.[44] Such practices were confirmed by Amnesty International and Human Rights Watch, as was the use of music as a background for torture.[45]

In Africa in June 2000 it was reported that a young female member of the Movement for Democratic Change (MDC) in the Midlands province of Zimbabwe was visited by supporters of the ruling ZANU-PF party. The intruders punished her and her husband's support for the MDC by frog-marching them to a tree, tying them to it, beating them for five hours with machetes, batons and axe handles. In addition they were forced to chant ZANU-PF slogans and to sing its liberation songs.[46] A year later staff at a private school outside Harare were forced by militants to 'sing and dance in praise of the regime'.[47] In 2002 a 12-year-old girl was gang raped by 'war veterans' while her mother and younger sisters were forced to sing songs in praise of Robert Mugabe. This was punishment for her father being a member of the MDC and the perpetrators told the victims, 'The game we are about to play needs music'.[48] In May 2005 Heather Bennett, a white MDC member, had been 'abducted while four months pregnant and forced to dance and sing pro-Mugabe songs in the rain while a machete was held to her throat. She had to

---

[41]   Ibid.

[42]   Ibid.

[43]   Peter Lukovic, 'Guns 'n' cassettes'.

[44]   Ceribašić, 'Defining women', p. 223.

[45]   Pettan, *Music, Politics and War*, p. 18.

[46]   Cloonan and Johnson, 'Killing me softly': 35. In 2002 the source we accessed for this was www.mdczimbabwe.com/free/ai000608txt.htm. Given the growing international condemnation of Mugabe and ZANU-PF, it is of interest that the content of this site is now a tourist promotion for Zimbabwe. Of further interest is the website, http://www.zanupfpub. com/ devoted to government atrocities in the country.

[47]   Rory Carroll, 'Zimbabwe slides deeper into chaos', *Guardian*, 7 June 2001, p. 1.

[48]   Christina Lamb, 'Mother forced to sing tyrant's praises as his men raped her daughter', *Sun-Herald*, 1 September 2002, p. 60.

watch two of their workers being murdered, another raped and her children's cat burnt alive. She miscarried hours later'.[49]

Elsewhere in Africa, in July 2004 it was reported that: 'While African women in Darfur were being raped by the Janjaweed militiamen, Arab women stood nearby and sang for joy' and encouraged the atrocities.[50] The singers were also said to have 'stirred up racial hatred against black civilians and celebrated the humiliation of their enemies'. They accompanied the attackers and sang songs praising the government and scorning the black villagers.[51] It was further reported that: 'The songs of the Hakama, or the "Janjaweed women" as the refugees call them, encouraged the atrocities which the militiamen committed.'[52] One victim said: 'They are happy when they rape. They sing when they rape and they tell that we are just slaves and that they can do with us how they wish.'[53] It was also reported that the rapes often took place in front of husbands.

Humiliation can involve forced playing as well as singing. The most chilling accounts of music as part of a regime of violence, are those of the use of music in Nazi concentration camps discussed in Chapter 4. With such a history, many in Israel were shocked in 2004 by images of an Israeli army officer at a checkpoint ordering Arab musician, Wissam Tayem, to 'Play something sad' while soldiers mocked him. After several minutes he was allowed to pass. Critics drew parallels with forced music in camps and argued that this disgraced the holocaust. According to Yoram Kaniuk, author of a book about a Jewish violinist forced to play for a concentration camp commander: 'Our entire existence in this Arab region was justified and is still justified by our suffering, by Jewish violinists in the camps.'[54] Thus the forced playing of music by a detainee was particularly offensive.

The use of forced performing is not restricted to war zones or tyrannies, however, and has been practiced in modern 'democratic' Europe. In Genoa on 21 July 2001, peaceful G8 summit protesters sleeping in a local school were violently attacked by the police, several receiving serious injuries. Some were taken to a holding centre at Bolzento where, it is alleged, they were made to stand spreadeagled (often despite their injuries), threatened with rape and made to shout slogans in support of the fascist dictator Benito Mussolini. They were also made to sing a song with the lyric:

---

[49]   Lorna Martin, 'I won't turn my back on these people', *Observer*, 3 May 2005, p. 7.

[50]   Jeevan Vasager, J. and Ewan MacAskill, 'Arab women singers complicit in rape, says Amnesty report', *Guardian*, 10 July 2004, p. 11.

[51]   Ibid.

[52]   No byline, 'Singing while their men rape', *The Guardian*, Nairobi, 21 July 2004, p. 6 http://www.taipeitimes.com/News/world/archives/2004/07/21/2003179810.

[53]   *BBC News* online 19 July 2004.

[54]   Chris McGreal, 'Israel shocked by image of soldiers forcing violinist to play at roadblock', *Guardian*, 29 November 2004, p. 16.

Un, due, tre. Viva Pinochet.

Quattro, cinque, sei. A morte gli ebrei.

(One, two, three. Long live Pinochet.

Four, five, six. Death to the Jews.)[55]

Victims were beaten if they did not sing.[56]

While humiliation of the detainee is one side of the story, then the other is the exhilaration felt by protagonists when enhanced by music. In Chapter 5 we referred to the George Gittoes' documentary, *Soundtrack to War*, on the use of music by US troops in Iraq. Michael Moore's *Farenheit 9.11* film showed US soldiers playing music, including the Bloodhound Gang's song 'Fire Water Burn' – which includes the line 'Burn motherfucker burn' – to psych themselves up whilst they were in battle. In Saudi Arabia, Ron Jones, a British businessman who was tortured until he falsely confessed to a bombing, reported on his release that on one occasion 'they put me blindfolded in a swivel chair and spun me round singing and then whacked me each time the chair went round'.[57] In the war in Iraq British soldier Donald Payne was jailed for beating a detainee. The court heard that he punched and kicked hooded civilians and 'conducted what he called "the choir", striking the prisoners in sequence, their groans or shrieks making up the "music"'.[58]

Discussion – Musical Pain

All these cases invite questions which go to the heart of music affect and violence: are these acts of violation through music cultural or pre-cultural? What makes music violent? How far can the cultural and the biological be differentiated in mapping music affect? Here we revisit some of the general matters raised in Chapter 1, now more focused in terms of social practice. The ambiguity of the relationship between musical preference and pain is acted out in fans who eagerly expose themselves to music that is physiologically harmful though (sub)culturally agreeable – that is, the music of their choice. On the other hand, people will allow music to be imposed upon them if the context is not overtly hostile (though generally exploitative), as in restaurants. But the intensity of irritation and the

---

[55] Rachel Shabi and John Hooper. 'Now the reckoning', *Guardian Weekend*, 22 January 2005, pp. 22–9. See also Paul Harris et al., '"You can sense the venom and the hatred"', *Observer*, 29 July 2001, p. 16; Paul Kelso, 'Saudi bomb victim's torture ordeal – and Britain's silence', *Guardian*, 31 January 2002, p. 1.

[56] Steven Morris and Rory Carroll, '"I thought my God, this is it, I'm going to die"', *Guardian*, 21 July 2001, p. 3.

[57] Kelso, 'Saudi bomb victim's torture ordeal'.

[58] Steven Morris, 'First British soldier to be convicted of a war crime is jailed for ill-treatment of Iraqi civilians', *Guardian*, 1 May 2007, p. 13.

potential level of violence increase as these two factors converge: culture and biology, sensibility and sense, psychological and physical.

More broadly we can see that the use of music in torture involves a number of inter-related forces. It is obviously a violation of the victims' identity as human beings, and at the same time an assertion of the material and cultural superiority of the aggressor. Being forced to sing the enemy's song denies the victims' right to control the quality of their chosen environment as well as the identity they project acoustically. Being unable to escape the sounds of an economically and culturally hegemonic superpower further diminishes the victim. Being forced to listen to familiar music in appalling circumstances is a violation of cultural identity. Cusick comments that: 'The lyrics of Eminem's *Slim Shady*, played over and over for Guantanamo's "high value detainees", combine rage, misogyny and vivid sexual imagery in ways that seem sure to offend – to confirm detainees' defeat by all that they might find loathsome about the culture of "the infidel".'[59] This resonates with Levi's point about the Nazis revelling in their victory over the Jews through their use of German music. In many ways the use of *American* popular music was an attempt to assert US cultural hegemony at a time when its military was showing its might. The detainee's subjectivity was to be lost in a flood of *American* sounds. Cusick concludes: 'Music, then, is not only a component of "no touch torture" but also a component of the US' symbolic claim to global sovereignty.'[60]

Cusick's work is one of the few attempts to theorize the use of music in torture. She argues that on the battlefield 'the use of music as a weapon is perceived to be incidental to the use of *sound*'s ability to affect a person's spatial orientation, sense of balance, and physical coordination. It is because *music* is incidental that the choice of repertoire is delegated to individual PsyOps soldiers' creativity'.[61] She thus recognizes a distinction between physical and psychological impact: 'What differentiates the uses of sound or music on the battlefield and the uses of sound or music in the interrogation room is the claimed site of the damage. Theorists of battlefield use emphasize sound's bodily effects, while theorists of the interrogation room focus on the capacity of sound and music to destroy subjectivity.'[62]

One variation in the issue of choice in the function of music as violence is not simply choosing *our* music, but being deprived of that choice. This is not to speak of censorship *per se* (which has its own extensive debates), but its mirror image. That is, not preventing others from making the music they like, but forcing them to make that which they do not. The idea that one no longer has ownership of one's own sounds is a profound and painful violation. In addition, as we noted in Chapter 1, any imposed music is always an act of violence. 'Voice theft', by which we mean the various ways in which we find someone else taking over control of our own vocal utterance, is a particularly savage imposition, long recognized

---

[59]   Cusick, 'Music as Torture', pp. 8–9.

[60]   Ibid., p. 10.

[61]   Ibid., emphasis in original.

[62]   Ibid., p. 5.

as an ultimate triumph in the attempt to disintegrate a subjectivity. The separate system in English prisons was so effective as a measure of dehumanization that the Chaplain of Preston Gaol, Rev. John Clay, reported in 1861 that the toughest man becomes 'impressible', and that the Chaplain could then 'fill his mouth with his own phrases and language'.[63] From prisoners of war filmed denouncing their own country, to George Orwell's Winston Smith finally declaring that four is five, and betraying his lover in the novel *1984*, surrendering control of one's own voice is an ultimate recognition of the power of our adversary.[64] And modern sound technologies have made that power increasingly available. In 1897 the poet Ernst von Wildenbruch recorded his voice on to a cylinder and wrote a poem for the occasion, including the lines: 'The fawning face can deceive the eye, the sound of the voice can never lie; / Thus it seems to be the phonograph is the soul's true photograph.'[65]

Andy Bichlbaum and Mike Bonnano are 'artist-activists' who swapped the voice boxes of Barbie and GI Joe dolls, and returned them to the shopping shelves, to the dismay of the purchasers.[66] These agitprop practical jokers dismantled one of the most deeply rooted certainties of all: the correspondence between voice and identity. Their case is amusing, but generally the stakes are higher. In 1936 the Soviet 'film boss' Shumiatsky asked Molotov if he could record Stalin's voice. The chief of the All Union Committee of Radiofication and Radio Sound reported with delight when this had been done, and sought Stalin's permission to make it into a recording. When the officials of the Gramophone Plant Trust factory listened to it in 1937 they were terrified of what his reponse might be, because there was something wrong with Stalin's voice, including '1. Big noises. 2. Big intervals. 3. The absence of whole phrases. 4. Closed grooves. And 5. Jumps and lack of clarity'. It was also found difficult to record his particular sibilance. They reported this to Alexander Poskrebyshev, Stalin's chef de cabinet, thinking they should recall the 1,000 or so copies already pressed. The latter declared that this showed a lack of respect for Comrade Stalin's voice, and it would be more respectful to distribute them as they were. Yet the file on this also includes a report from Komsomlskaya Pravda suggesting that something 'sinister' had happened to Stalin's voice at the factory, which obviously housed 'wreckers' who should be punished.[67]

The Hanson/Pantsdown case, referred to in Chapter 6, the G8 violations, the forced singing in the camps and victims being forced to sing while their families are raped and killed, all to a greater or lesser extent represent the immensely

---

[63] Cyriax, *Encyclopaedia of Crime*, p. 508.

[64] George Orwell, *1984* (Harmondsworth, 1954, first published 1949), pp. 207, 230.

[65] Cited in Friedrich Kittler, *Gramophone, Film, Typewriter*, trans. Geoffrey Winthrop-Young and Michael Wutz (Stanford California, 1999, originally published in German, 1986), p. 79.

[66] Review of film *The Yes Men*, in *Sunday Herald* (Glasgow), *Seven Days* supplement, 6 February 2005, p. 27.

[67] Montefiori, *Stalin*, p. 253 footnote.

disempowering effect of voice theft. The ingenuity with which this particular form of identity violation can be implemented has been increased with the advent of sound technologies. In particular it has enabled the voice to be detached from its owner and redeployed in ways that may be anything from disconcerting to humiliating. If we bring together and amplify the two dimensions involved in both disorientation and humiliation – the physical and the psychic – we have a form of assault so damaging that it has become a major instrument of state violence in the modern world, and a highly resourced subject of military research.[68]

At the same time sonic and musical weapons are now circulated freely throughout civil society. Media commentary almost without exception only takes this 'weaponry' seriously in lyrics of specific music genres in which vilification is conspicuous, and which can be monitored on that basis. By this logic it is assumed that the heavy metal, rap and garage scenes represent the greatest threat to civil order. In the cases we have examined, however, the violence allegedly generated cannot be unproblematically attributed directly to the music, so much as a wide range of mediating factors including dubious business practices or pre-existing backgrounds in criminality. Listening to music or getting involved in certain music scenes does not in itself generate violence, and the worst we might be able to conclude is that the habitus of some scenes makes them fertile sites for violence, but not necessarily outside that habitus. However, consider the following cases. In Cardiff in 1994 one Michael Gilfillan played reggae loudly in his flat all day long. His new neighbour, John Pubrick, complained and was subjected to a brutal attack from Gilfillan which resulted in Purbrick's death 12 hours later.[69] One witness reported hearing Griffin shouting 'If you complain about my music I will kill you'.[70] In 1995 a Billy Clark, from Newlands Park, Sydenham was kept awake at night by the music of Led Zeppelin which was being played by his neighbour David Ravenhall. A row erupted, Clark headbutted Ravenhill who then plunged a knife into Clark's heart.[71] If it is problematic to posit listening to music or involvement in particular music scenes as direct causes of violence, these cases foreshadow a discussion of how music can generate violence in everyday life. It is in anyone's power to mount a sonic assault, through imposed music, voice theft, and sonic violence. States recognize that the issue is a matter of politics. It is also a matter of policy, to which we now turn.

---

[68]   See for example Marshall Sella, 'The sound of things to come', *New York Times*, 23 March 2003, www.nytimes.com/2003/03/23/magazine/23SOUND.html.

[69]   'Loud music lover gets life for killing neighbour', *Guardian*, 16 July 1994, p. 5.

[70]   www.ccrc.gov.uk/canewe/canwe_87.htm.

[71]   Stephen Goodwin, 'Law set to fine noisy neighbours', *Independent*, 17 February 1996, p. 4.

Chapter 8
Policy

Bruce Johnson and Martin Cloonan

Introduction

We began thinking about this study at the IASPM international conference in Sydney in 1999. When the darker side of popular music had hitherto been spoken of it had tended to refer to 'the usual suspects' such as rap or Marilyn Manson, or questionable and exploitative industry practices.[1] However our research relentlessly suggested that the negative side of music was most often to be found in the familiar texture of life. While this was frequently the domain of government or powerful commercial interests, it was also that of the individual music fan. The widespread availability of powerful electronic hardware for playing music has democratized musical violence in everyday life. In an increasingly noisy world the struggle over the control of noise is, as we have suggested, one of the ways we can chart the emergence of modernity. A key site of that struggle is music, and the damage it can cause ranges from minor irritation to severe physical and mental trauma and death.

Sonic Trauma in Modern Life

Discussing the contemporary international soundscape and the damage it produces, Henrik Karlsson's inventory ranges through noisy toys, motor cycles and air traffic.[2] Similar reports include links between noise in offices and heart disease.[3] In a case from Kokomo, Indiana, an unidentified low frequency hum heard by nearly one hundred people caused a vibro-acoustic disease with symptoms including dizziness, headaches and nausea.[4] Researchers in Sheffield, North England, measured noise levels for ten years from 1991 to 2001 and found that 'Average

---

[1]   See for example Butt, 'The grubby face of punk promotion'; Fred Dannen, *Hit Men* (New York, 1991); Johnson, 'The menace of Beatlism'; Sheila Whiteley, *Too Much Too Young* (London, 2005); Woolley, 'We don't need gangsta rap'.

[2]   Henrik Karlsson, 'The Acoustic Environment as a Public Domain', *Soundscape: The Journal of Acoustic Ecology* 1/2 (Winter 2000): 10–13; see 11.

[3]   Gary Evans, 'Low-Level Office Noise Can Increase Health Risks', *Soundscape: The Journal of Acoustic Ecology*, 2/1 (July 2001): 33.

[4]   'Indiana Hum', *Soundscape: The Journal of Acoustic Ecology* 3/1 (July 2002): 31.

noise levels across all the monitored locations have increased by 3 decibels (db), a doubling of acoustic energy. In a few "hotspots" they have increased by as much as 10 times'.[5]

Apart from stress, noise is complicit in deafness, tinnitus, strokes, migraines, peptic ulcers, colitis and hypertension.[6] By the mid 1990s in the UK disputes about noise were held to cause around five deaths a year and a number of suicides.[7] By 2007 it was reported that half a million people a year in the UK move home because of noise.[8] Much of this noise is music. In November 2004 the *Sydney Morning Herald* reported concerns about the popularity of mobile phone ring tones which included 'shotgun blasts, rapid gunfire, horrific screams, bodily functions and even the moans and groans of sexual gratification'.[9] The paper had previously noted the commercial success of ringtones.[10] Unwanted noise during leisure time seems to arouse particular resentment, with complaints about 'irrelevant loud music' at county cricket matches in England,[11] the volume of music in films such as *Armageddon* and *Saving Private Ryan*,[12] high noise levels in Sydney pubs[13] and the intrusiveness of iPods on trains.[14] A dispute over the loud playing of a *Riverdance* CD led to a UK motorist refusing to pay a fine,[15] while in Sydney a lengthy car case ensued after the owner of one car glared at

---

[5]   www.shu.ac.uk/cgi-bin/news_full.pl?id_num=PR137&db=01.

[6]   John Vidal, 'A pain in the ears (anag)', *The Guardian*, 8 September 1993, part 2, p. 2.

[7]   Val Gibson, 'Campaiging against noise: getting into action', *Hearing Rehabilitation Quarterly*, 24/1 (1999); Peter Victor, 'Neighbourhood noise: 17 people have died from it', *Independent on Sunday*, 18 December 1994, p. 19, 1994; David Symons, *Confronting noise in the UK* (Chatham, 2000).

[8]   Andrew Martin, 'Quiet please', *Guardian* 31 October 2007, part 2, pp. 6–11.

[9]   Don Fernandez, 'That's not the start of another war, that's just my mobile phone ringing', *SMH*, pp. 13–14 November 2004, p. 15.

[10]   Anthony Dennis, 'Irritating mobile phone sounds a sweet bonus for tune writers', *SMH*, 18–19/1/03. See further on the problems of ringtones on public transport, Heikki Uimonen, '"Sorry can't hear you! I'm on a train!" Ringing tones, meanings and the Finnish soundscape', *Popular Music,* 23/1 (2004): 51–62.

[11]   David Keen, Letters, *Guardian*, 19 June 2001, p. 17.

[12]   Jacqueline McArthur, 'Lights, camera, earplugs', *Sun-Herald*, 29 November 1998, p. 13; Pat McConnochie, 'Sound advice for victims of cinema's music mafia', *SMH Heckler* online, 10 May 2006.

[13]   Lenny Ann Low, 'Your shout? You'd better make it a loud one at the Angel', *SMH* online, 14 March 2006.

[14]   Kirsty Smith, 'Sour notes drift from those white earphones', *SMH Heckler* online, 1 June 2006.

[15]   Steven Morris, 'Motorist in standoff over Riverdance', *Guardian*, 26 January 2005, p. 5.

another at traffic lights because his music was too loud.[16] Apart from the general problem of noise,[17] there have been protests against plans by the USA's Federal Communication Commission to allow in-flight calls on mobile phones[18] and about partying holiday makers in a Sydney suburb, whose noise intrudes through walls lacking acoustic insulation.[19] In the UK there have been attempts to regulate the loudness of television advertisements,[20] ban mobile phones from some pubs[21] and drafting legislation ensuring acoustic insulation for new apartments, with music a particular problem.[22] Football fans have been investigated and one club fined by the European footballing body, UEFA, for sectarian chanting.[23] The annoying sound of telephone on-hold music has also been researched.[24] We live in a world in which rising noise is the site of contestation.

Of all the elements in the modern soundscape, music is among the most invasive, because over and above basic sonority, it projects finely discriminated markers of social difference such as taste, class, race, age and gender. These may be intermingled in the following scenario. You are in a building which you must occupy at certain times. While there you are randomly assaulted by music over which you have no control. You do not know when it will start – it may be when you are asleep – nor when it will end. It could last seconds or days. It may be a type of music which you actively dislike. Or it may be of a form which you like, but come to detest through repetition. You are powerless. This scenario is not drawn from the experiences of 'detainees' in Iraq or Guatánamo Bay, but from ordinary homes. We are all detainees of the soundscape. In our study, of all the circumstances in which music is the most unambiguous cause or trigger of violence, it is the most banal scenarios, involving the most 'ordinary' (sub)urban participants, that are most often involved – not musicians, not genre-specific fans

---

[16] Dylan Welch, 'Hatchback hate: Lamborghini chased', *SMH* online, 13 March 2006.

[17] Jeffrey Kluger, 'Just Too Loud', *Time*, 5 April, 2004, pp. 48–50.

[18] Ben Hammersley, 'Generation Text', *Guardian*, 13 January 2005, p. 23.

[19] Simone Richards, 'Good time versus full time', *Daily Telegraph* (Sydney), 19 August 2003, p. 17.

[20] Sue Dunlevy, 'Noisy ads face volume control', *Daily Telegraph* (Sydney), 17 June 2001.

[21] Georgina Jerums, Emma-Charlotte Bangay, Natalie Reilly, 'Off your dial', *Sunday Life* (The *Sun-Herald Magazine*, Sydney), 18 June 2006.

[22] Mark Skelsey, 'Home code turns down the volume', *Daily Telegraph*, 30 April, 2001, p. 15.

[23] See, for example, Ewan Murray, 'Rangers facing UEFA inquiry over fan chants', *Guardian*, 20 March 2007, *Sport*, p. 6. England's Football Association has also attempted to ban homophobic chanting at matches. See Press Association, 'Homophobic chanting banned', *Guardian*, 9 February 2007, p. 8.

[24] Neil McMahon, 'Dialing a reply to poor phone form', *SMH*, 17–18 September 2005, p. 4.

in dedicated music spaces, not brutal agents of the state. Not the Other. It is in everyday social intercourse that the connection between music and violence is most pervasively damaging. The most frequently reported association of music and violence is disputes between neighbours.

In the UK a National Society for Clean Air and Environmental Protection undertook a survey which found that 'Amplified music accounted for four-fifths of "neighbour noise" complaints'.[25] In 1994 complaints about noise in the UK had reportedly risen by 20 per cent in one year.[26] The same year 17 people had reportedly died in disputes about noise in the previous six years (including those driven to suicide).[27] At that time only 3 per cent of complaints led to prosecution, with many local authorities reporting that they lacked the staff to tackle the problem.[28] A letter to *The Guardian* in 1996 complaining of noisy neighbours, especially those repeatedly playing Alanis Morrissette, drew dozens more in support.[29] Our examples could have been multiplied several fold; we have selected illustrative cases from a very extensive file.

Beat Your Neighbour[30]

In 1993 residents of Trinidad Crescent, from Poole in Dorset, petitioned their local council to stop their neighbour, Mary Carruthers, from playing Jim Reeves records at full blast for up to 18 hours a day. Following several attempts to make her desist, environmental health officers seized her stereo system. She was ordered not to play music in her flat for two years.[31] Neighbour Linda Moore commented 'they were out to annoy the whole neighbourhood'.[32] In the same year Helen Stephens of Stockton-on-Tees was sentenced to a week's imprisonment for what was described in court as 'psychological torture' by repeatedly playing Whitney Houston's 'I Will Always Love You' at maximum volume.[33] In October 1999 Lisa Wilson of Brighton was sentenced to a year's probation after admitting to four counts of failing to comply with a noise abatement notice, performing step aerobics so loudly that her neighbours complained to the local council, which was eventually forced to confiscate her stereo and tambourine. Brighton magistrates were told that

---

[25]   Megan Lane, 'In search of Peace and Quiet', *BBC News*, 25 April 2002.

[26]   James Erichman, 'Noise epidemic complaints rise', *Guardian*, 5 September 1994, p. 4.

[27]   Victor, 'Neighbourhood noise: 17 people have died from it'.

[28]   Ibid.

[29]   'Noise Annoys', *Guardian*, 5 September 1996, p. 19.

[30]   This subtitle is a none too subtle pun taken from a card game beloved by generations of UK children.

[31]   Alex Renton, '"Distant Drums" goes too far', *Independent*, 21 May 1993.

[32]   Sally Weale, 'Jim Reeves ravers silenced', *Guardian*, 21 May 1993.

[33]   Vidal, 'A pain in the ears (anag)'.

Wilson played Beatles and Rolling Stones records so loudly that a couple living below had to vacate their flat.[34] In May 2005 the *Sydney Morning Herald* reported that in the UK an Anti-Social Behaviour Order (ASBO) had been issued in the UK against 'a man who played the Band Aid single *Do They Know It's Christmas* over and over'.[35] The following April the same paper reported the case of a Japanese woman who had played music so loudly between November 2002 and April 2005 that a neighbour required medical treatment. The defendant was sentenced to a year's imprisonment.[36]

More serious was the report of the suicide of Birmingham resident John Vanderstam in November 1997. The coroner found that Vanderstam died as a result of an assault on his eardrums 'just as much as a man who is hit in the face and falls to the ground'. New neighbours had played loud music and indulged in other anti-social behaviour until late into the night. Ronald Chamberlain of the Coroner's Office said that Vanderstam 'had no psychological problems but had become increasingly depressed because of the noise nuisance'.[37] More frequently the outcome is violence inflicted on others. In January 1999 Plymouth University student Ross Woolaway died from a knife wound to the heart in a stabbing outside his neighbour's flat in Torquay, Devon. Woolaway had gone to the lower ground floor flat of Barry Andrews to complain about the loud music and threatened to smash the stereo. In the ensuing altercation Woolaway was stabbed to death.[38] In February 2007 Tom Pritchard of Western Sydney was stabbed by a gang in Liverpool (outer Sydney) after he intervened following an incident in which his sister had complained to her neighbours about loud music coming from their party.[39] In the UK the notorious 'race riots' in Burnley were apparently precipitated after an Asian family complained to their white neighbours about the loud music they were playing at 4 a.m. on a Saturday.[40] In January 2000 Prince Ernst-August of Hanover, the husband of Princess Caroline of Monaco was among a group who

[34] Jamie Wilson, 'Probation for rock'n'roll noise nuisance', *Guardian*, 6 October 1997, p. 7.

[35] James Button, 'There goes the hood', *SMH News Review*, 18–19 June 2005, p. 27.

[36] No byline, AAP, 'Noisy neighbour gets one year sentence', *SMH* online, 21 April 2006.

[37] 'Noisy Neighbors Helped Drive English Man to Suicide, Coroner Finds', *Daily Telegraph*, 1 April 1998, cited at: http://www.noisepollution.org/news/1998/mar29.htm#Noisy%20Neighbors%20Helped%20Drive%20English%20Man%20to%20Suicide%20Coroner%20Finds.

[38] Press Association Newsfile, 13 December 1999, 'UK Student Stabbed Over Noise Argument', cited at www.noisepollution.org/news/1999/dec12.htm#UK%20Student%20Stabbed%20Over%20Noise%20Argu-ment.

[39] Will Swanton, Laura Parker and John Kidman, 'Rugby league star stabbed', *SMH* online, 18 February 2007.

[40] Angelique Chrisafis, 'Years of harmony wrecked in days', *Guardian*, 26 June 2001, p. 3.

beat up a discotheque owner in Nairobi after the Prince was enraged by noise coming from his premises. The victim planned to sue the Prince.[41]

In 2007 a man was fined £200 by magistrates in Newcastle-Upon-Tyne for playing Wham's 'Last Christmas' repeatedly very loudly after 1 a.m. on 15 May. A neighbour called the music 'a form of torture'.[42] In the same year Diane Duffin of Leeds was given an anti-social behaviour injunction following complaints that she had played music all night. Breaking the injunction meant possible eviction from her home. She was forbidden to play music between 11 p.m. and 7 a.m., in line with UK noise legislation following her breaking a previous noise abatement order. One track, Tammy Wynette's 'D.I.V.O.R.C.E', was allegedly played more than 20 times in a day and press coverage made much of the fact that Dolly Parton's music was also played.[43]

Music can also be deployed purposefully as a weapon in neighbourhood disputes. In June 1998 it was reported that Helen McNeil, owner of the Alexander Hotel in Ballater, Aberdeenshire went round to the house of a local neighbour who had protested against plans to extend the hotel's licensing hours and threatened: 'We'll make trouble for you from now on and have loud music every Friday, Saturday, and Sunday night.'[44] Music also featured at neighbourhood level in the troubles in Northern Ireland in what amounted to forms of ethnic cleansing of areas. The Short Strand area of Belfast is a nationalist enclave surrounded by loyalists who regularly used violence to drive nationalists out. In 2002 one resident, Rosemary Magill, was subject to a campaign to evict her. She reported that one weekend, 'they played loyalist band music for 72 hours; it was psychological torture'.[45] In Antrim Kathleen McCaughey was forced out of her home in Ahoghill following a campaign which included Protestant children being paid £5 each 'to sit on her front lawn banging drums until she caved in'.[46]

Among many extrapolations from these cases is that the problem is not evidently class- or place-specific. Such conflicts seem to be extreme yet not exotic

---

[41]   www.noisepollution.org/news/2000/jan16.htm#Kenyan%20Disco%20Noise%20Le ads%20to%20Violence.

[42]   No byline, 'Wham ban for music fan', *Northern Echo*, 15 August 2007; www. thenorthernecho.co.uk/search/display.var.1619415.0.wham_ban_for_music_fan.php.

[43]   'Music banned for Dolly Parton fan', *BBC News*, 20 August 2007; See further Vicki Robinson, 'Stand by your ban!', *Yorkshire Evening Post*, 8 August 2007, www. yorkshireeveningpost.co.uk/news?articleid=3093701;   Tom Chivers, 'Dolly Parton fan told: keep quiet or lose house', *Daily Telegraph*, 25 October 2007.

[44]   www.noisepollution.org/news/1998/may31.htm#Scottish%20Hotel%20Owner%20Th reatens%20Neighbors%20With%20More%20Noise%20After%20They%20Object%20to%20 Hotels%20Extended%20Hours.

[45]   Rosie Cowan, 'Neighbours caught up in low key war', *Guardian*, 4 November 2002, p. 6.

[46]   Angelique Chrisafis, 'In a corner of Antrim another generation grows up on a diet of sectarian hatred', *Guardian*, 6 September 2005, p. 11.

events in contemporary urbanized life. And, recalling the standard targets of moral panic lobbies, we may ask: where are black metal and gangsta rap? When the specific music is identified, apart from a case of politically aligned band music in an overtly politically partisan site, we have heritage rock, country and western, MOR acts and a couple of sentimental Christmas songs. We further note evidence that such problems are growing. One example is disputes arising during processes of inner city gentrification, the sorts of areas which have been sites of live popular music. In many cases single storey industrial or working class buildings have been replaced by multi-storey yuppie apartments. The change produces different acoustic and cultural dynamics. The result is a convergence of increasingly loud pop music in which bass registers are foregrounded (aggravating problems of sound-source localization, as discussed in Chapter 1), the sonic canyons of high-rise residential development, and an unwilling audience with more pampered expectations of their rights over the sonic environment. The outcome is increased social conflict over music.[47] Australia has seen a number of attempts to address the gentrification versus live music problem.[48] Similar problems have arisen in France where neighbours complained about the noise coming from Paris cabarets, leading to threats of closure for those unable to afford expensive soundproofing.[49]

Material and Economic Damage

For victims of sonic invasion the problem seems intensely personal. But in the aggregate it is an issue that affects the community and the state.

> Present economic estimates of the annual damage in the EU due to environmental noise range from EUR 13 billion to 38 billion. Elements that contribute are a reduction of housing prices, medical costs, reduced possibilities of land use and cost of lost labour days. In spite of some uncertainties it seems certain that the damage concerns tens of billions of euro per year.[50]

---

[47]   See further Bruce Johnson and Shane Homan, *Vanishing Acts: An inquiry into the state of live popular music opportunities in New South Wales* (Sydney, 2003), Johnson, 'Quick and Dirty'.

[48]   See for example Brisbane City Council, *Valley Music Harmony Plan* (Brisbane, 2005); Elizabeth Carbines, *Live Music Taskforce: Report and Recommendations* (Melbourne, 2003); Johnson and Homan, *Vanishing Acts*. For a critique of those complaining and threatening a live music scene see Steve Cannane, 'Tell Sydney's shooshers to shove off', *SMH*, 7 January 2002, p. 10.

[49]   'Paris Cabarets Too Noisy For Public', *Times*, 15 December 1999.

[50]   Robert MacNevin, 'Editorial', *Soundscape: The Journal of Acoustic Ecology* 1/2 (Winter 2000): 4, from: Proposal for a Directive of The European Parliament and of the Council: Relating to the Assessment and Management of Environmental Noise, presented by the Commission of The European Communities. For a list of noise levels see www.e-a-r.com/pdf/hearingcons/T88_34NoiseLevels.xls.

Germany's Federal Environment Agency (UBA) estimated that 13 million Germans are exposed to sound levels that cause health risks and sleep disorders.[51] Such figures do not disclose the full extent of the social problem. The most direct physical impact of sonic violence is deafness. A study found that the incidence of hearing loss, tinnitus, hyperacusis, distortion, diplacusis was higher among rock musicians than classical performers. Several rock and jazz performances 'showed sound levels well exceeding maximum recommended levels'.[52] Fans are no less at risk. In 1979 Dr Maurice H. Miller, Chief of Audiology at New York's Lennox Hill Hospital, found that hearing loss in an 18 to 30 age group was attributable to listening to loud rock music. The US Environmental Protection Agency (EPA) estimates that 16 million Americans suffer from self-induced hearing impairment.[53] A conference in Bologna, May 2002, on 'Urban Music: the Problem of Music Pollution' tabled a conclusion of 'auditory damage present in young people who make constant use of loud music – damage not only to their hearing organ but also to their psychological health and relationship levels, with disorders of the nervous system'.[54] While this is often the result of loud concerts, exposure to damagingly loud music is increasingly pervasive in daily life. A report from Melbourne in 2001 noted that in most of 15 city nightclubs the volume generally exceeded 110 dB (with one as high as 122 dB), while the safe level over an eight-hour period is 85 dB.[55] Effects were said to include tinnitus, depression, anxiety, insomnia. Vince Cousins, an ear, nose and throat specialist from Melbourne's Alfred Hospital, reported that hearing in 18- to 25-year-olds had rapidly declined. A report from the UK's Royal National Institute for Deaf People, which surveyed 1,100 people aged between 18 and 30, found three out of four clubbers at risk of permanent

---

[51]   http://www.umweltbundesamt.de/uba-info-presse-e/2007/pe07-022.htm.

[52]   Kim Kähäri, 'The Influence of Music on Hearing: a Study in Classical and Rock/ Jazz Musicians', *Journal of Acoustic Ecology* 4/2 (Fall/Winter 2003): 11. More detail from this thesis is at http://www.niwl.se/personal/kim.kahari%40niwl.se.htm. See also Janelle McCulloch, 'Silent Revolution', *Sun-Herald* magazine, *Sunday Life*, 3 September 2006, pp. 23–5, which reports that Ipod (100 dB +) and rock concert volume (120dB+) causes hearing damage including on rock musicians known to have suffered irreparable hearing loss. A British study of 23 DJs found that 17 suffered from tinnitus, 16 from temporary hearing loss and three suffered permanent noise induced hearing loss, see 'Turn it down! Too loud to be cool' at   http://www.youth.hear-it.org/page.dsp?page=2978 accessed at 16 February 2008.

[53]   Email circulated from Rebecca Sullivan, 18 July 1996 citing *National Catholic Weekly*, July 22, 1979.

[54]   'Conference Urban Music: the Problem of Music Pollution', *Soundscape: The Journal of Acoustic Ecology*, 3/1, July 2002, p. 28.

[55]   Meg Mundell and Patrick Donovan, 'Nightclub noise threatens hearing of a generation', *Age* online, 2 September 2001. See also Meg Mundell and Patrick Donovan, 'Why the health warnings fall on deaf ears', *Age*, 2 September 2001, which reported serious hearing damage from loud nightclub bands and ambience.

hearing damage, and also expressed concern at use of iPods.[56] In Sydney concern has been expressed about dangerously high levels of noise in pubs caused by piped music and poker machines.[57] Another Sydney report cited noise in restaurants as a problem; in a paradox articulated in Chapter 1, however, the noisier places are often the most popular.[58]

Personal stereos also represent a danger to hearing acuity. A 2006 study found that: 'Listening to loud music on a digital music player should be limited to 90 minutes a day to avoid damage to hearing, and listening at top volume for more than five minutes risks permanent damage.' This cited a US study of a hundred students, concluding that people should not listen at 80 per cent volume or above for more than 90 minutes a day or they would risk hearing impairment. Dr Brian Fligor, an audiologist at the Children's Hospital of Boston and Harvard Medical School, said that problems may take years to show up; 'I worry about the teenager who's going to be 23, 24, 25 years old and has a measurable noise-induced hearing loss, and now has another 60-something years to live with his hearing, which is only going to get worse'.[59] As ye hear, so shall ye speak: apart from confirming the deleterious effects on hearing of iPod and MP3, Professor Christian Huggenot reported findings in France that compressed sound in media 'in which weak signals are boosted to the level of stronger ones', is affecting speech patterns. 'Once the ear has got accustomed to this kind of sound, it finds it very hard to return to sounds of weak intensity', producing speech that is a 'loud monotone'.[60] Much is made of the emancipative power of iPods and the creation of one's own musical space. In his study of personal stereos Michael Bull notes the positives, 'technologically empowering the subject',[61] providing users with a 'private experiential world', 'enhancing their sense of control' and enabling them to 'successfully confront whatever the day holds'.[62] The technology alleviates the 'acute alienation' one user feels towards his 'daily routine'.[63] Yet Bull also notes that the way his informants often talk suggests a technology that enables users

---

[56]   Ruth Pollard, 'Your mum was right – it will send you deaf', *SMH*, 29 September 2005, p. 1.

[57]   Ephraem Chifley, 'A word in your ear … a night in the pub could be deafening', *SMH*, 19 November 2004, p. 15; see also Angela Cuming, 'Why pub drinkers must shout', *Sun-Herald*, 29 May 2005, p. 33.

[58]   Terry Durack, 'I'll *shout* you dinner', *SMH Good Living*, 23 April 1996, pp. 1–2.

[59]   Kenneth Nguyen and Reuters, 'Turning up volume on risks to hearing', *SMH* online, October 19, 2006.

[60]   Dewl Cooke, 'Tuned in may mean young ears tune out', *SMH*, 9 September 2008, p. 3.

[61]   Michael Bull, *Sounding Out the City: Personal Stereos and the Management of Everyday Life* (Oxford and New York, 2000), p. 119.

[62]   Ibid., p. 24.

[63]   Ibid., p. 64.

to avoid 'interactional possibilities'[64] and to 'block out reality'.[65] Bull himself writes of 'enhancing' users' 'powers of disengagement'.[66] It is not evident how disengagement from the social reality that shapes us is a form of empowerment.

Notwithstanding Bull's overall idealization of the empowering potential of the technology, various cases also point in the opposite direction. A Sydney bus driver complained about the growing risk of users being run over as they were lost in their 'own bloody music world'.[67] Bull cites a woman who felt that wearing an iPod can arm against sexual harassment.[68] Perhaps, but it can also make her more vulnerable. In Sydney a woman was subjected to an attempted daytime sexual assault in the Central Business District, unaware of her assailant's approach because of her iPod. A police spokesman commented that: 'We're encouraging people to look after their safety and be aware of their surroundings and what is happening.'[69] Apart from deafness, music can thus be complicit in diminished competence in navigating social life. Research on the effects of telephone hold music found that certain kinds of music were more likely to lead to hanging up, even in the case of help lines. The music had a potential to calm listeners, but also to irritate them beyond endurance.[70] Thus there was an indirect connection between aversive imposed music and failure to gain help. Although listening to music is often thought to enhance cognitive and motor performance, it can also compromise it, as reported in Gianna Cassidy's work on the effects of music listening on cognitive tasks and video driving game performance.[71]

Noise doesn't have to cause certifiable deafness to produce organic damage. The World Health Organization suggests that thousands of people are dying prematurely from long-term exposure to noise. Deepak Prasher, Professor of Audiology at

---

[64]   Ibid., p. 26; see similarly p. 50.

[65]   Ibid., p. 63.

[66]   Ibid., p. 100.

[67]   Angela Cuming, 'Must-have music box takes over the street', *Sun-Herald*, 19 December 2004.

[68]   Bull, *Sounding Out the City*, p. 105.

[69]   'Fear iPod deafened woman to sexual predator', *SMH* online, 1 March 2007.

[70]   Liesi-Vivoni Ramos, 'The Effects of On-Hold Telephone Music on the Number of Premature Disconnections to a Statewide Protective Services Abuse Hot Line', *Journal of Music Therapy*, 30/2 (1993): 119–29.

[71]   See for example Gianna Cassidy and Raymond MacDonald, 'The Effects of Background Music and Background Noise on the Task Performance of Introverts and Extraverts', *Psychology of Music*, 35/3 (2007); Gianna Cassidy, Raymond MacDonald, Jon Sykes, 'The Effects of Aggressive and Relaxing Popular Music on Driving Game Performance and Evaluation', DIGRA (Digital Games Research) Conference, 'Changing Views: Worlds in Play', Vancouver, Canada (June 2005). The possible dangers are likely to be more fully disclosed through her current research into real driving conditions. Bruce Johnson would like to thank Dr Cassidy for her generous discussion of these topics with him.

University College, argued that new data showed earlier deaths because of noise. 'Until now, noise has been the Cinderella form of pollution and people haven't been aware that it has an impact on their health.' He noted that adverse reactions to noise, such as stress, high blood pressure and immune deficiency, could be afflicting victims without them being aware of it.[72] The deployment of music in social spaces thus has unforeseen implications which have long-term effects on 'quality of life'. This is not a conservative jeremiad against contemporary pop or 'the youth of today' because, as we have seen, it is not solely youth music that is the problem, but the way music in general can be circulated. Lapses in task-performance can be serious and even fatal, but a more fundamental problem is the growing desensitization to the diversity, content and nuances of sonic information that is generated by continuous exposure, aggravated by organic deterioration of hearing acuity. Similarly, conflict over control of the sonic environment has longer-term social effects than discrete (albeit alarmingly frequent) outbursts of neighbourhood violence. There is individual and collective welfare impact, from which theatrical media anecdotes and economic statistics tend to be a distraction. These include the normalization of stress, friction and depression as features of contemporary urban life. They produce dismaying complications in hitherto relatively coherent parameters of collective and individual life and its tempo and rhythm, and demolish the boundaries between public and private space.[73]

The circulation of sound and music in contemporary urban society disturbs the sense of where Self ends and Other begins, both at an individual and a collective level, and in doing so it problematizes social formations. This raises the question of globalization. The wholesale suppression of western music in such regions as Iran and Nepal is not simply anti-western boycott for its own sake, but an attempt

---

[72]   Alok Jha, 'Says WHO … All that noise is the death of us', *Age* online, 24 August 2007. For more on the health problems caused by noise see William Hal Martin, Robert L. Folmer, Y-B. Shi Baker, 'Tinnitus and Sound', *Soundscape: The Journal of Acoustic Ecology* 6/1 (Spring/Summer 2005): 15–17; Hearing Industries Association, 'A White Paper Addressing the Societal Costs of Hearing Loss and Issue in Third Party Reimbursement' (2004) at www.audiologyonline.com/articles/pf_arc_disp.asp?article_id=1204; R. Hetu, L. Getty and H.T. Quoc, 'Impact of occupational hearing loss on the lives of workers', *Occupational Medicine: State of the Art Reviews*, 10/3 (1995), pp. 495–512; Sergei Kochkin, 'HEARING SOLUTIONS – The impact of treated hearing loss on quality of life' (Alexandria Va: Better Hearing Institute, 2005), www.betterhearing.org/hearing_solutions/qualityOfLifeDetail.cfm.

[73]   For further examples of noise damage, see the following sample: Arline L. Bronzaft, 'The effect of a noise abatement program on reading ability', *Journal of Environmental Psychology*, 1 (1981): 215–22; Arline L. Bronzaft and D. McCarthy, 'The effect of elevated train noise on reading ability', *Environment and Behaviour*, 7 (1975): 517–52; Gary. W. Evans and Stephen J. Lepore, 'Nonauditory effects of noise on children: a critical review', *Children's Environments*, 10 (1993): 31–51; Thomas Fay, *Noise and Health* (New York); Willy Passchier-Vermeer and Wim Passchier, 'Noise exposure and public health', *Environmental Health Perspectives* 108 (2000): 123–31.

to reconstruct cultural boundaries that create a sense of Self, a macrocosm of the individual who objects to the neighbour's music or the fellow-passenger's ring-tones. Music is implicated centrally in the often violent encounters between local identity and the tide of globalization. We have spoken of the international appropriation of rap to articulate local political conflicts and of the importance of local music literacies. But these local rhetorics are now circulated globally, taken up in their international destinations, assimilated into regional cultures, becoming accretions to the interpretive community. The distinction between the culture of origin (where it is claimed specific music literacies render it innocuous) and the rest of the world, has collapsed because of the infinitely reproducibility and circulabilty of visual and acoustic images. Would the same defences of gangsta rap be made of an equivalent discourse exported from, say Afghanistan or Pakistan, in validations of women being stoned for being victims of rape? Would the arguments that justified this be accorded the same cultural relativistic tolerance as the homicidal and misogynistic arguments embedded in gangsta rap?

Intervention, Regulation

Musicality is a material presence that can constitute and generate the most extreme forms of violence. This becomes particularly so in the specific conditions of contemporary everyday urban life, both because of the nature of pop music and the material conditions of existence. The distinctiveness of this convergence is proclaimed in recent complaints from apartment dwellers in Sydney, reported, interestingly, by a journalist who covers 'urban affairs', rather than 'music'. In July 2007 Sydney Lord Mayor Clover Moore called upon the State Government to consider controlling the use of sub-woofer speakers in flats. She told a panel reviewing NSW noise regulations that one of her constituents had suffered illness from a neighbour's sub-woofer speakers. The mayor reported that the constituent said that 'the low frequency noise caused vibrations and sensations within her body beyond the noise levels themselves, and that she suffered a series of associated health concerns including heart palpitations, nausea and vomiting, and inflammation of skin and other organs'.[74] For Mayor Moore, the problem was that existing legislation did not recognize that sub-woofers emit low frequency noise which can travel much further than high or mid-range frequencies, and could penetrate many layers of building material. One proposal was to make tenants reponsible for sound emissions in the same way that the Australian Consumer Trade and Tenancy Tribunal had ruled that smokers must ensure that their smoke did not affect neighbouring apartment dwellers.

The Mayor of Sydney's concerns are representative of a growing realization that some kind of regulation of noise and music is necessary. The unprecedented

---

[74]   Sunanda Creagh, 'Mayor blasts super speakers that give out bad vibes', *SMH Urban Affairs* online, 24 July 2007, www.smh.com.au.

proliferation of measures to achieve this is a further reminder that the distinctive modern condition includes a radical change in the sonic order. Given that music is ubiquitous in defining identity and territory, and exercising violence, and given the radical changes in the 'range' of that weaponry, there are implications for the freedoms and responsibilities associated with the use of music. Much is made by the US gun lobby of the constitutionally enshrined right to bear arms, and, in a disturbing generalization of the American citizen, attempts to regulate gun ownership are therefore interpreted as an assault on basic human rights. But the right for the individual to bear arms in a frontier wilderness and where the 'arms' are a knife, sword and single shot firearms, is simply not the same as in a massive modern conurbation dense with personal frictions, and where 'arms' that may be carried include Uzi machine guns, anti-tank weapons and lightweight missiles capable of downing an aircraft. Where those personal frictions may be increased by a casual adjustment of volume to produce music which is literally deafening, which may be deployed as psychological and physical weaponry, perhaps state 'regulation' is needed in the documented absence of self-regulation. So we come to the deeply contentious questions which throw up terms such as 'censorship', 'nanny state' and 'human rights violations'. But we live at a time when the slightest personal gesture has a radius of potential damage infinitely greater than at the time of the Enlightenment which gave birth to what continue to be contemporary notions of 'rights' of free expression. This potential for damage arises both from the 'weaponry' available, and the density of the populations in which it is deployed. We now examine this context.

Academic Interventions

In academia there has been increasing research into the acoustic environment, particularly under the inspiration of the founding work of Murray Schafer since the 1960s on soundscape studies. His original investigation of the soundscapes of five villages is now being updated in a project led by Helmi Järviluoma of Finland's University of Joensuu. Other influential longstanding contributors to the field include Steven Feld, CRESSON and Barry Truax and the World Forum for Acoustic Ecology (WFAE), whose activities are published in the journal *Soundscape: The Journal of Acoustic Ecology*.[75] The Bologna conference referred

---

[75]   See for example: R. Murray Schafer (ed.), *Five Village Soundscapes* (Vancouver, 1977); R. Murray Schafer and Helmi Järviluoma (eds), *Yearbook of Soundscape Studies: 'Northern Soundscapes'*, vol. 1 (Tampere, 1998); Barry Truax, *Acoustic Communication* (Norwood, NJ, 2001); Helmi Järviluoma, and Gregg Wagstaff, *Soundscape Studies and Methods* (Helsinki, 2002); Helmi Järviluoma, 'Memory and 'Acoustic Environments: Five European Villages Revisited', in EllenWaterman (ed.), *Sonic Geography Remembered and Imagined* (Toronto, 2002), pp. 21–37. A list of some CRESSON reports dealing with sound is published in *Soundscape* 5/1 (Spring/Summer 2004): 12. In introduction to Steven Feld's

to above on 'Urban Music: the Problem of Music Pollution', was in conjunction with the inauguration of a Master's degree in noise pollution, to produce graduates with government advisory skills.[76]

Together with scholars in the International Association for the Study of Popular Music (see Chapter 1), studies of the ecology of the sonic environment have produced some of the most important socially interventionist work in the field of acoustic ecologies and the social impact of sound and music, particularly on the way sound affects the sense of space, time, and collective identity. On occasions, however, one gets the impression that for both research communities there is felt to be a disjunction between a soundscape and music.[77] Our argument is precisely the opposite: music is part of the soundscape and as such is potentially one of its most ubiquitous and damaging components. It is specifically identified as a potential social problem as well as social asset in various one-off Government funded research projects into the sonic environment, especially within Australia which appears to be at the forefront of such issues.[78] It is to government initiatives that we now turn.

Government Intervention

As evidenced in several cases referred to above, government agencies themselves have been responsive and even pro-active in addressing problems of objectionable music. The most basic form of regulation has simply been the imposition of penalties for offensively loud music. In the UK, for example, music has been prominent in a significant number of ASBO breaches. Proscriptions on unwanted music are supplemented by legislation relating to places and situations where, although apparently incidental to the primary function of the venue, it reaches nuisance level. These include the issue of entertainment licenses to pubs.[79] The

---

prolific work may be found at Steve Feld, 'From ethnomusicology to Echo-Muse-Ecology', http://www.acousticecology.org/feld/index.html accessed at 12 February 2008.

[76]   'Conference Urban Music', *Soundscape.*

[77]   See for example Noora Vikman's initial feeling as a soundscape ethnographer that she was 'changing the subject' when beginning to study men's choirs in Combra (Noora Vikman, (2005), 'Vuorilla vuorilta vuorille – Moniäänisiä laulamisen tiloja, paikkoja ja menneisyyksiä pohjoisitalialaisessa Cembrassa' in Antti-Ville Kärjä and Markus Mantere Markus (eds), *Etnomusikologian vuosikirja 17*, Yearbook of Ethnomusicology. The Finnish Society for Ethnomusicology (Helsinki, 2005), pp. 48–70); see also Bronzaft's suggestion that music is an antidote to noise pollution, in Arline Bronzaft, 'An International Voice Against the Perilous Noise Pollutant', presented at Hör upp! Stockholm Hey Listen!! WFAE Conference, Stockholm (June 1998) p. 16.

[78]   The opinion is expressed by Cloonan, who cites for example, Brisbane City Council, *Valley Music Harmony Plan*; Carbines, *Live Music Taskforce*; Johnson and Homan, *Vanishing Acts.*

[79]   See Johnson and Homan, *Vanishing Acts.*

unpredictable ramifications of the deployment of portable and amplified music in everyday life require continuous revisiting of legislating regarding the control of music and the potential violation of rights. The difficulties encountered by copyright legislation in coping with new music production technologies has been the subject of both applause (especially from opponents of the multi-nationals) and complaint (from the multinationals themselves, but also from performers). Both sides, however, are in contention over music, and the encounter becomes increasingly loaded with potential for personal violation. New software 'Natural Voices' can clone the voice from recordings. How does copyright deal with the theft of one of the prime guarantees of personal identity, the voice? Will new voice-licensing clauses be inserted in recording contracts?[80] The question illustrates the unforeseeable complexities in the relationship between developing sound/music technologies and the law. In a speech to the UK Noise Association in 2003 Professor Francis McManus of Napier University argued that the

> fundamental problem which the government has had to confront in formulating noise legislation is that it is uncertain about the public's values about noise pollution.... the problem confronting legislators as far as noise is concerned is that reaction to noise is so subjective that it is fiendishly difficult to set appropriate standards.[81]

This has been echoed at governmental level in the UK where the Department for Environment, Food and Rural Affairs (DeFRA) has recognized that while 'more needs to be done to minimize the nuisance (noise) causes, the factors influencing human reactions to noise and the options for dealing with the problems however, are many and complex'.[82] Nevertheless governments have intervened in matters of noise regulation and we can illustrate this at three levels: local, national and international.

Exemplifying local initiatives, in Madrid in September 2002 the City Council initiated a scheme called SSSHH, encouraging citizens to control their noise.[83] In other instances music has been used to discipline potential and actual miscreants. Thus Glasgow City Council reported that: 'Following complaints about youths playing loud techno music, Knowsley council visited schools and played Dolly Parton to teenagers until they begged for it to be turned off. Then asked them to consider how their granny would feel listening to their music! The message was well received.'[84] In Sydney the New South Wales government introduced measures in June 2007 to ban the use of 'noisy musical instruments and sound systems'

---

[80] Syndicated from NY Times, 'Speech cloning tunes into distant voices', *SMH* 2 August 2001, p. 25. For a related case see Johnson, 'Two Paulines'.

[81] Francis McManus, 'Noise Law – Where do we go from here?' (2003).

[82] DefRA, *Noise and Nuisance Research Newsletter* 1 (2006), p. 6.

[83] *Soundscape: The Journal of Acoustic Ecology* 3/2 (Winter 2002) with 4/1 (Spring 2003), p. 56.

[84] Glasgow City Council, *Noise Action Week* (Glasgow, 2005).

after 10 p.m., instead of the current midnight deadline. Labor MP Verity Firth, the Minister Assisting the Minister for Environment, said that the Government wanted 'people to be able to live in peace and not put up with constantly loud neighbours'.[85] In New York Arline L. Bronzaft has been drafted on to the Mayor's Council on the Environment of New York, serving under four successive mayors. Her research in the 1970s found that noise could compromise children's learning and she has since become a committed campaigner against noise. Her research has suggested that 'citizens are very much disturbed by neighbor noises as well as street noises which include car alarms, honking horns, and boom cars'.[86] The latter now has a website devoted to countering its influence (http://www.noboomers. com/). New York introduced a Noise Code in the 1970s, but 30 years on the most frequent complaint to the City's Quality of life hotline remains noise.[87] In October 2002 Mayor Bloomberg launched *Operation Silent Night* to combat excessive noise in 24 high-noise neighborhoods. Police were issued with sound meters, with authority to seize audio equipment and issue fines and summonses to violators. The campaign led to over 200,000 summonses being issued, 200 cars being seized and over 15,000 arrests being made.[88] The city's attempts have attracted international media interest and appear to offer some solace to noise victims.[89]

Local problems generate local solutions. In 2004 a Florida judge sentenced a driver whose car stereo breached noise nuisance legislation, to listen to hours of opera. The driver, Michael Carreras, had been playing 50 Cent with windows and sunroof open at 5 a.m. The judge told Carreras, 'You impose your music on me, I'm going to impose my music on you' and gave him the choice of a $500 fine or listening to two and a half hours of *La Traviata*.[90] Local authorities in Scotland reported that around 50 per cent of their neighbour mediation cases were about noise.[91] Discos were cited as a potential problem and one of the case studies cited involves dealing with a neighbour's noisy stereo and the procedures which should be followed. It is noted that the problem may not be one of inconsiderate behaviour as 'even homes with good sound insulation may not cope with noise from powerful modern equipment'.[92] In 2005 in Glasgow the city council introduced a scheme whereby residents could be fined up to £1,000 if found guilty of breaching noise

---

[85]   'Noise laws "won't mean cranky neighbours"', *SMH* online, 7 June 2007.

[86]   Arline L Bronzaft (nd), 'Researching Noise Effects' http://noisefutures.org/ documents/ARLINE%20BRONZAFT.pdf.

[87]   Arline L. Bronzaft (nd), 'Reflecting On the Lack of Acoustical Consideration at Ground Zero', www.noiseoff.org/groundzero.shtml.

[88]   Ibid.

[89]   Christine Kearney, 'Keep quiet out there; this is New York', *SMH*, 9 June 2004, p. 14.

[90]   Mueller, 'Rhyme and punishment'.

[91]   See www.scotland.gov.uk/Topics/Environment/Pollution/Noise-Nuisance/16871/ 8360.

[92]   All quotes from Scottish Executive, *Sound Advice on Noise* (Edinburgh, 2006).

regulations and failing to pay a fixed-penalty fine within a month. The Council reported 2,000 noise complaints a year. In order to provide 24-hour service it recruited ten new staff funded by the Scottish government's initiatives to counter noise related to anti-social behaviour. It was also reported that: 'The most common complaints received by the council's Noise Pollution Unit relate to *music*, shouting, footsteps, barking dogs and DIY.'[93] The city hosts a Noise Action Week which included issuing advice that the first thing victims should do was to approach the neighbour concerned and ask them to be reasonable. However it also cautioned that 'some neighbours may react angrily and an approach to them might not be successful'.[94]

At a national level the UK has witnessed a plethora of legislation designed to combat noise problems, including the Control of Pollution Act 1974, Environmental Protection Act 1990, Noise and Statutory Nuisance Act 1993, Noise Act 1996 and the Clean Neighbourhoods and Environment Act 2005. Under the 1990 and 1993 Acts local authorities are given a duty to investigate noise and other nuisance complaints. If their Environmental Health Officers are satisfied that problem complained about is a nuisance the local authority is obliged to serve an abatement order on the person responsible. In March 2004 local authorities gained the power to issue Fixed Term Penalty Notices to people found responsible for domestic night time, with powers given them under the Anti-social Behaviour Act 2003. If notices are ignored local authorities may seize equipment making the noise. The guidelines note that 'noisemaking equipment will typically comprise electronic items such as a HiFi, mixer desk, loud speakers, TV, DIY equipment, and musical instruments such as drum-kits, keyboards or guitars and their amplification. It may potentially also include a collection of CDs, records, minidiscs or tapes'.[95]

Even so, UK Ministers have sought further powers. In November 2006 the government was to introduce new powers allowing police to evict 'neighbours from hell', including immediate closure of 'premises being used for drunken parties, raves, brothels' for three to six months. A British Crime Survey published at the same time showed that one in seven people report incidents involving noisy neighbours and more than one in four of them have considered moving to get away from the problem.[96] The UK government enlisted the help of Encams, the organizers of the Keep Britain Tidy campaign, to get their message across. Encams' Chief Executive, Alan Woods, argued that: 'It must be seen as socially unacceptable as vandalism and other petty crime. People who play loud music, do DIY or gardening at unsociable hours or fight like cats and dogs can make life a

---

[93] Mona McAlinden, 'Nuisance noise fines to the tune of £1000', *Herald*, 22 May 2005, p. 16, emphasis ours.

[94] Glasgow City Council, *Noise Action Week*.

[95] DeFRA, *Noise Act 1996* (London, 2007).

[96] Alan Travis, 'Reid wants police to evict noisy neighbours', *Guardian*, 15 November 2006.

real misery for their neighbours.'[97] In 2003 it was proposed that councils be given the power to issue a ten-minute warning against noise with a £100 fine following.[98] DeFRA has developed its policy as part of a strategy to protect the environment and improve health.[99] At the time of writing it was conducting research in an attempt to develop an Ambient Noise Strategy and a Neighbourhood Noise Strategy. Previous research included two reports in 2005 and 2006 on the noise problems of music in pubs and clubs undertaken by a team from Salford University.[100]

There have also been international efforts to address the problem of noise. In October 1969 the General Assembly of the International Music Council of UNESCO, passed the following declaration:

> We denounce unanimously the intolerable infringement of individual freedom and of the right of everyone to silence, because of the abusive use, in private and public places, or recorded or broadcast music. We ask the Executive Committee of the International Music Council to initiate a study from all angles – medical, scientific and juridical – without overlooking its artistic and educational aspects, and with a view to proposing to UNESCO, and to the proper authorities everywhere, measures calculated to put an end to this abuse.[101]

At a European level International Noise Awareness Days have been organized.[102] In 2005 the European Agency for Safety and Health at Work used the Day to launch the 'Stop that Noise' campaign. Aimed at tackling noise at work, it received the backing of the European Parliament and the Commission.[103] A new European Directive on occupational noise came into force on 15 February 2006 and set a limit of 87 decibels for workers' daily exposure to noise.

Campaigning against Noise: The Pressure Groups

Recognition of noise damage has generated consciousness-raising lobbies against the unrestricted circulation of music. Many are grass-roots driven by the victims themselves, citizen groups that include Sane Aviation for Everyone (New York); Noise Network (London); The League for the Hard of Hearing (New York), Noise

---

[97]   John Vidal, 'Government turns up the mood music in battle for quieter cities', *Guardian*, 13 December 2002, p. 3.

[98]   Home Office, *Respect and Responsibility* (London, 2003), p. 39.

[99]   www.defra.gov.uk/environment/noise/research/index.htm.

[100]   www.defra.org.uk/environment/noise/research/index.htm.

[101]   Cited Schafer, *The Tuning of the World*.

[102]   www.personneltoday.com/articles/2005/04/21/29386/be-quiet-for-international-noise-awareness-day.html.

[103]   http://osha.europa.eu/press_room/050420_EW2005_Launch_Int.

Free America (founded in Southern California).[104] The website of Noise Pollution Clearinghouse (Montpelier Vermont) lists groups from across the globe.[105] Others have more specific targets. In the wake of the noise complaints in Adelaide (Australia), demands for more acoustic insulation led to the formation of The People's Environmental Protection Alliance, which initiated a new noise policy.[106] The group Public Transport in Sydney have lobbied against audio-advertising on trains and buses, while Perth (Australia) commuters successfully protested against commercial radio broadcast over buses.[107] In the UK the Thurrock Rail Users' Group supported protests against the use of televisions on trains, as this violated the cherished silence on the way to work.[108]

Also in the UK a major music-centred anti-noise campaign has been the anti-Muzak group Pipedown whose celebrity supporters include Simon Rattle and Julian Lloyd Webber. The organization has claimed success in removing piped music from Gatwick airport and persuading Tescos and Sainsburys supermarket chains not to introduce it. It also reports a MORI survey from January 1997 in which 17 per cent of people cited piped music as *the* one thing which they detested about modern life. Pipedown initiated measures including providing lists of Muzak-free hotels and stories and campaigning against the use of piped music in hospitals and loud, irrelevant, music in television programmes. The organization argues that piped music is a misuse of public space.[109] The Noise Network seeks to restrain advertisements for music players which urge buyers to 'turn up the music' and which boast of their product's ability to 'annoy the neighbours'.[110] The Campaign for Real Ale has also complained of piped music in pubs being remorselessly on the increase.[111] The UK Noise Association (www.ukna.org.uk) is a coalition of groups campaigning against traffic and aircraft noise, neighbourhood noise, piped music, low frequency and firework noise. Its charitable arm carries out research into noise and provides education programmes, and its work includes providing briefing documents and organizing conferences.

A prominent campaigner in the UK has been Val Weedon, co-ordinator of the National Noise Association, who became involved in anti-noise campaigns following a dispute with a neighbour who repeatedly played loud music, especially

---

[104] See further www.wired.com/news/medtech/0,1286,57564,00.html and www.nonoise.org/resource/related/uk.htm.

[105] www.noisepollution.org/.

[106] Chris Pippos, 'Why we're copping an earful', *Sunday Mail*, 26 October 2003, p. 21.

[107] McCulloch, 'Silent Revolution'.

[108] Alan Hamilton, 'Sit-down protest over TVs for trains foiled by broken toilets', *Times*, 9 February 2005, p. 15.

[109] For all this see www.pipedown.info. See also Martin, 'Quiet please'.

[110] http://www.bbc.co.uk/dna/actionnetwork/A8252552.

[111] John Ezard, 'Brewers accused as prices come to head', *Guardian*, 22 October 2002, p. 13.

Lisa Stansfield's 'All Around The World'.[112] Of her experience as a victim of noise, Weedon wrote that: 'Enduring the thump thump thump of the bass beat was like torture and eventually wore me down.'[113] She launched the Right to Peace and Quiet Campaign which disbanded in 1997 with its work being picked up by the Noise Network. As this book was being completed Weedon was undertaking research into the growing problem of the impact of piped music on shop workers.

Initially concern in retail focused upon customers. In 1993 the journalist Andrew Mueller complained that while shopping: 'Even if you like music, the chances of walking into a shoe shop and them playing something you like is about the same as dialing a phone number at random and getting Saddam Hussein's valet.'[114] He contacted DMX who supply music for retailers and was told 'music is part of brand identity'. But why, wondered Mueller, do we tolerate 'noise pollution' in various outlets? His concern was picked up nearly ten years later by Alexis Petridis, *The Guardian*'s music critic. He wanted to spend a day listening to the music played in UK shops, restaurants and bars and found himself 'plunged … into a strange and complex netherworld of secretly encoded CDs, shadowy music programmers, involuntary behavioural modification and ruthless record company promotion'.[115] He called eminent popular musicologist Philip Tagg who told him that one reason for loud music in clothes shops is that: 'Silence gives you time to reflect, and you might start to worry.'[116] Petridis reported that despite the fact that some customers didn't like the music, staff in many of the pubs cannot do anything about the music as they are told what to play by head office. Concern has now shifted to employees exposed to workplace music. In 2005 a report on 1,400 British retail workers by the recruitment website retailchoice.com found that Britney Spears and Kylie Minogue were among the artists whose music most irked shop workers. Around half of those interviewed said that customers had complained about piped music.[117] A third of staff reported having to listen to the same album for up to 20 times a week.[118] Unsurprisingly Christmas was found to be the worst time, with songs including 'Jingle Bells', Slade's 'Merry Christmas' and Bing Crosby's 'White Christmas' causing respondents particular stress.[119]

---

[112]   Martin, 'Quiet please'.

[113]   Val Gibson, 'Campaigning Against Noise: Getting Into Action', *Hearing Rehabilitation Quarterly*, 24/1 (1999): 1–3.

[114]   Andrew Mueller, 'Can't stop the muzak', *Independent on Sunday*, May 2003, www.andrewmueller.net/print.lasso?ID=178, accessed 2 March 2004.

[115]   Alexis Petridis, 'Soundtrack of our lives', *Guardian*, 9 August 2002, *Friday review*, p. 2.

[116]   Ibid.

[117]   'Spike', 'Workplace hazards', *SMH*, 23 September 2005, p. 20.

[118]   Ibid.

[119]   See also www2b.abc.net.au/science/k2/stn/archives/archive70/newposts/839/topic839634.shtm.

In April 2007 in the USA another pressure group, the House Ear Institute, noted that in the USA some 5.2 million six- to 19-year-olds show a hearing loss directly related to noise exposure. In response they launched a noise awareness campaign aimed at young people, via 'Ear Bud', an ear-shaped cartoon character whose MySpace site featured celebrity friends including The Rolling Stones, Beyoncé and John Mayer. Its message was that 'it's cool to have smart listening habits and protect hearing'.[120] In the US The League for the Hard of Hearing sponsors International Noise Awareness Day, with the thirteenth scheduled for 16 April 2008.[121] The League advises on noise problems.[122] Its website argues that: 'Numerous studies can be found to document that noise, like other stressors, is related to negative physical and psychological changes in humans ... Individuals and communities no longer accept that noise is a natural by-product of an industrial society.'[123]

Moral and Ethical Problems

With the constant opening of new channels through which music can be directed to produce social friction, attempts to regulate its use come into increasing conflict with arguments regarding freedom of expression and censorship (ranging from licensing of political activities such as marches and demonstrations, to outright censorship). The more spectacular outcomes of this encounter mask a darker side to the connection between music and regulation. The two terms most often open a discussion about the regulation *of* music. But there is also regulation *by* music. The more spectacular examples – military parades, brutal interrogation chambers – dominate public consciousness through media reports. If we think of such control as part of our own soundscape, the first examples likely to spring to mind are rallying music at sports events either for teams or, as in the case of British tennis player Barry Cowan, the heroic individual representing his nation, who listened to music associated with his favourite football team, Liverpool, to boost his performance.[124] The rhetoric of such reports reinforces the perception of music's capacity to inspire 'us' to heroic conduct. But there is a more disturbing side to the regulation of conduct by music in our own lives. A similar account of the connection between music and sports performance has more sinister overtones, not simply because of its association with illegal practices, but because of the role of the state in the use of music as a way of regulating behaviour. In September 2007 it was reported that East German authorities used western popular music

---

[120] www.hei.org/news/releases/070423noiseday.htm.

[121] www.lhh.org/noise/index.html.

[122] www.lhh.org/noise/communities.html.

[123] www.lhh.org/noise/getting_started.htm.

[124] Vivek Chaudhary, 'Music lifts Britain's Wimbledon hopes', *Guardian*, 26 June 2001, p. 4 and Stephen Bierley, 'Cowan pushes champion to limit', *Guardian*, 28 June 2001, p. 34.

(which was often unavailable to the general populace) as a soundtrack to athletes' training to improve motivation.[125]

This relates to what appear to be special conditions unconnected with the mundane circumstances of music in everyday life. The music we hear around us is often that of a passing iPod, spilling out of a car radio or a pub. Except in static situations, as in neighbouring apartments, these are momentary, even if irritating transitory encounters in the city street. But much, and probably most, of this unsought music is both sustained and purposeful, and its purpose is to regulate our mood and therefore our behaviour. What makes it so insidious is how rarely we are conscious of it. Unlike noisy neighbours who keeps us awake, or the club where we have come specifically to hear music, this is almost subliminal in the sense that it is fully taken for granted. Yet its purpose is control. We hear it in supermarkets and department stores, and if we reflect on it, we recall that its function is to make us less critically reflective as spenders. Or we hear it in workplaces, where it functions to make us more productive workers, as in the use of AC/DC to increase workrate as deadlines drew close.[126] It is also heard in restaurants, where its function seems to be to provide the most appealing atmosphere for dining pleasure. Again, however, in cases of marketing sophistication, there is a further purpose as it has been noted that the use of jazz, classical and easy listening were likely to lead to increased spending.[127] Adrian North summarizes research showing that 'fast music leads to faster shopping than either slow music or no music', slower music in restaurants led to slower eating (and thus greater consumption of drink) and that overall 'the evidence ... provides a strong indication that under certain circumstances at least, the arousal-evoking qualities of music can influence the speed of customer activity'.[128] One industry recognition of this has been the production of CDs especially for dining.[129]

These uses of music may seem a long way from violence. They are intended to decrease stress, to induce less critical reflection, and to turn us into more biddable citizens as consumers and workers. However this Huxleyan scenario also represents the use of music to manipulate relations of power, and it is a small step from producing those who are biddable, to expelling those who are not. To make that transition, consider the so-called 'Mozart effect' to enhance pupils' performance and overcome bad behaviour. Additionally Tchaikovsky's *1812 Overture* and the

---

[125]   Bojan Pancevski, 'Bonn in the USA: hit tunes fired up East German athletes', *SMH*, 24 September 2007.

[126]   McCulloch, 'Silent Revolution'.

[127]   Patricia Karvelas, 'If music be the food for mood, play on', *Australian*, 19 February 2003, p. 23. In the UK a great deal of research into the impact of music upon customer preference has been conducted by Adrian North; see for example www.psychology.hw.ac.uk/staffDetails.php?staff_id=55.

[128]   Adrian North, *The Commercial Uses of Music* (London, 2003), pp. 14, 16, 18.

[129]   Dugald Jellie, 'Tuning forks', *SMH Good Living*, 5–11 June 2001, pp. 12–13.

'Mission Impossible' theme were useful in energizing students.[130] If music may be used in such an ordinary situation to encourage good conduct, how long before it is also used to punish and expel? This is not fanciful. Perhaps the most widespread example is the use of music to deny certain people public space. On a daily basis across the globe, music is used to disperse gangs of youths and others held to be potential trouble-makers. The following is just a sample of an increasingly widespread practice.

In 1998 Newcastle-Upon-Tyne Metro reported a drop in vandalism at its Shiremoor station following the playing of Delius. Nexus, the company running the network explained that: 'The psychology is that people who are not familiar with this type of music will go elsewhere. Delius was chosen at random, but we don't play very popular pieces in case the vandals might like them.'[131] The scheme was later extended to other stations with different forms of classical music and in 2005 it was reported that it has solved the problem of youngsters hanging round the stations and indulging in anti-social behaviour. A spokesman commented: 'The young people seem to loathe it. It's pretty uncool to be somewhere where Mozart is playing.'[132] London Underground also began playing classical music on parts of its East London line which had been plagued by petty vandalism, verbal and physical abuse. The result of installing CD players in the public announcement system was that incidents fell by 33 per cent.[133] According to Metronet, which was responsible for the Underground system: 'The music has reduced the number of youngsters hanging around the stations – probably because it is "uncool" for them to be around this kind of music.'[134] The accompanying press release was headlined 'music to deter yobs by' – perhaps a compilation album in the making. The following year it was reported that foyers in a number of stations would play 40 hours a week of classical music, primarily in order to reduce passenger stress.[135] In 2002 a MacDonalds branch in Southampton, England started using classical music in response to 'yobs who plague its customers. Instead of Eminem, they will hear artists such as Nigel Kennedy playing Vivaldi and Mozart'.[136] Stoke-On-Trent Council played Beethoven's Ninth Symphony continuously in car parks to deter

---

[130]   Press Association, '"Play Mozart to tackle poor behaviour", teachers urged', *Guardian* online, 29 September 2006.

[131]   Dan Glaister, 'Harmony on the line as Metro tunes in to Delius to turn off vandals', *Guardian*, 30 January 1998, p. 3.

[132]   Melissa Jackson, 'Music to deter yobs by', *BBC News*, 10 January 2005, http://news.bbc.co.uk/1/hi/magazine/4154711.stm.

[133]   Metronet, 'Metronet installs "music to deter yobs by"', Press Release January 2005.

[134]   Ibid.

[135]   Helen Pidd, 'Mozart for muggers', *Guardian*, 13 February 2006, www.guardian.co.uk/arts/features/story/0,,1708364,00.html. See also Andrew Clark, 'Music to drive away tube louts', *Guardian*, 13 January 2005, p. 6.

[136]   'Brandenberger with fries?', *Observer*, 16 June, 2002, p. 6.

rough sleepers.[137] St. James Church in Carlisle used music by Bach and Handel to deter drinkers who had been gathering on its steps and vandalizing church property. These composers, said the local vicar, were 'particularly effective'.[138] In Worcester, Bristol and across North Wales – where their local stores may be the only shop in an area – branches of the Co-Op found themselves attracting teenagers who hung around outside them. The stores dispersed them by fitting loudspeakers outside and piping music by composers including Rachmaninov and Rimsky-Korsakoff.[139] Authorities in Copenhagen used Bach to drive drug addicts away from the city's main railway station.[140]

It doesn't have to be classical music, just music that is 'uncool' with its unwilling target. Since that target is most often loitering youth, 'golden oldie' and MOR popular musics are equally effective. In the Sydney suburb of Rockdale the local council played Barry Manilow over loudspeakers on Saturday nights in a car park which had been a hotspot for youths gathering to show off their cars, revving engines, playing 'doof doof' music and allegedly acting in anti-social ways. It was reported that the council hoped that the music would move the youths on as it was associated with being 'daggy' (uncool).[141] In 1998 in Wollongong, New South Wales, Bing Crosby's music had been used to drive teenagers away from shopping malls. One 15-year-old was reported as saying that he used to hang round the malls with friends until Crosby's music drove them all away. The song 'My Heart Is Taking Lessons' was said to be particularly effective.[142] Press and televison later reported that Sydney's City Rail and the Rundle Mall in Adelaide were using piped classical music to deter criminal activity following success in Wollongong and also shopping malls in Kogarah, a Sydney suburb.[143]

Carters Steam Fair, a travelling funfair, found that Cliff Richard's 'The Young Ones' dispersed a gang of youths who had gathered near its rides during a stay at Hayes, Middlesex. The local police said they could do nothing to disperse the youths unless a crime had been committed. However, Seth Carter, of the fair, who felt that the youths were putting people off taking rides, recalled that on a previous occasion playing Richard's records had lessened numbers on the dodgems. So he put the record on and the gang dispersed. Carter commented: 'They don't

---

[137]   'Don't roll over Beethoven', *Guardian*, 30 July 2003, p. 5.

[138]   Gerard Seenan, 'Bach for church "dogged by youth"', *Guardian*, 24 March 2005, p. 6.

[139]   Jackson, 'Music to deter yobs by'.

[140]   Mueller, 'Rhyme and punishment'.

[141]   Jacqueline Mabey, 'Forget Asbos. Australia uses Barry Manilow', *Guardian*, 6 June 2006, p. 19.

[142]   'Crosby's hits drive teens out of stores', *South China Post*, 9 July 1999.

[143]   Kelvin Bissett, 'Crimefighters of note' *Daily Telegraph*, 17 August 1999; Johnson holds video footage of the television reports.

like that kind of music; it's not cool enough.'[144] One report of the incident also reported that: 'Last year the Local Government Association urged councils to use the "Manilow method" to break up gangs.' The recommendation came after the authorities in Sydney, Australia drove away gangs in car parks by playing them 'Copacabana' and 'Mandy'. The LGA produced a list of 20 songs that would deter teenagers. Top of the list was 'Release Me', by Englebert Humperdinck. Cliff Richard's 'Mistletoe and Wine' appeared at number 19.[145]

On the face of it these are relatively innocuous ways of keeping the streets safe and orderly. But for whom? It is noteworthy that the same anxiolytic music that welcomes the big spenders into supermarkets and restaurants, is the music that drives out those who will not or cannot spend, who do not fit the ideology of citizen as paying consumer. Residents of the luxury apartments in Salamanca Square in Hobart (Australia) requested the piping of Bing Crosby into the Square to deter youthful loiterers, a clear example of a class-based musically controlled differentiation of occupancy of public space.[146] This is not simply the regulation of conduct. However much we may prefer to see public spaces cleared of drug addicts, beggars, vandals or just young people hanging out, nonetheless we must also recognize that the issue here is a question of citizenship and of who has the right to occupy public – note: public – space. These cases remind us again of how important sound has been in defining community identity. All those born within the sound of Bow Bells are cockneys. But in these cases, music is used to drive a wedge into society and to declare in effect: if you don't like this music (and all the ideological baggage it carries), you do not belong. You are banished by virtue of your musical tastes. When Samuel Johnson chose to exclude from his lexicon of English all words that had not appeared in print, he made literacy (and therefore class) a criterion of membership of a linguistic community.[147] In part our argument here relates to notions of citizenship. In order to be responsible citizens, people require certain skill sets which might be thought of as a type of literacy. Recently notions of literacy have moved from a set of assessable reading and writing skills to a more complex understanding of various types of competency. Here the key notion is 'literacies' – plural – encompassing areas like computer literacy, numeracy, foreign language skills, media literacy as well as reading and writing.[148] We are arguing here that to be literate in the modern world – and thus to be an active citizen – a level of musical literacy is required as part of a broader notion of literacies. Genuine musical literacy would involve not only appreciation of music, but also a considered approach to one's own use of music. In the cases

---

[144]   Matt Weaver, 'Problems with young ones? Get wired for sound', *Guardian*, 7 June 2007, http://society.guardian.co.uk/youthjustice/story/0,,2097595,00.html.

[145]   Ibid.

[146]   Andrew Darby, 'Not old Bing again: let's go!', *Age*, 31 May 2001, p. 2.

[147]   See Johnson, 'Divided Loyalties'.

[148]   Jim Crowther, Mary Hamilton and Lynn Tett (eds), *Powerful Literacies* (Leicester, 2001).

we have cited, a very specific form of musical literacy becomes a condition of community membership.

A further point: if public and private corporations are entitled to quarantine public spaces in this way, why may not others? Barbra Streisand reportedly kept photographers away from her wedding to James Brolin by means of a van parked near the media encampment, playing White Zombie's 'Thunder Kiss '64' on a loop for four hours.[149] If Streisand may legally impose this form of torment on particular sections of the community, why in principle may not others, including those who were served with ASBOs precisely for doing so? In spite of the flippant tone of the great majority of these reports (see further below), they raise crucial moral and ethical questions relating to human rights and social responsibilities, to the definition of cultural formations, autonomy, diversity and relativism. As this study has shown, forms of music ranging from Mozart to Riverdance are deployed (legally and illegally) by all sectors, all generations, ethnic groups, gendered positions, classes, by public and private corporate interests, in ways that create conflict or attempt to control behaviour. In an era of portable and amplifiable music, these activities have destabilized the relationship between public and private space, upon which all conduct relies for the parameters of civilization. From the local to the global, they therefore raise urgent questions regarding cultural policy and regulation, including citizens' rights, urban planning and cultural policy. How is it possible to reconcile the need for regulation with the fertilization of musical diversity and richness? More generally, where in this debate do we place the mantra of 'human rights', with its implications of universality, yet in a global music market characterized by profoundly unbalanced power relations?

In the contemporary world the deployment and functions of music constantly interrogate the interface of individual rights and responsibilities, the local and the global and definitions of citizenship and community. Because of the distinctive physiology and phenomenology of sound, exercising our 'right' to choose our own music and when, where and how it is delivered, inevitably comes into sometimes lethal tension with the right of others to choose their own acoustic environment. Music preferences become sites of conflict within and between communities, between state and citizenry, between hegemonic and subordinate blocs. These tensions are exacerbated in the case of what is broadly understood as 'popular' music for a range of historical reasons. So-called classical or art music has a tradition of being quarantined from everyday life, while popular music saturates it. The democratization and proliferation of music technologies have exponentially increased this saturation, in turn driven by the fetishization of individual rights. The specific profile of much contemporary pop, its tempos, textures, volume and prominent bass registers, confer upon it intimidating sonic authority.

This is further amplified in congested urban spaces with their reverberant sonic canyons. In November 2004 the music of Metallica and AC/DC was reportedly used to prepare the battleground during the siege of the Iraqi town

---

[149]   No byline, 'Shutterbugs v Stars' *Sun-Herald*, 3 October 2004, p. S 12.

of Fallujah, often projected by Long Range Acoustic Devices (LRADs).[150] Ben Abel, a spokesman for the US arm's PsysOps unit, commented: 'These harassment missions work especially well in urban settings like Fallujah. The sounds just keep reverberating off the walls … it's not the music so much as the sound. It's like throwing a smoke bomb. The aim is to disorient and confuse the enemy to gain a tactical advantage.'[151] While commanding offices decided whether or not to employ music, soldiers on the ground made the choice about *which* music: 'our guys have been getting really creative in finding sounds they think would make the enemy upset … These guys have their own mini-disc players, with their own music, plus hundreds of downloaded sounds. It's kind of personal preference how they choose the songs. We've got very young guys making these decisions'.[152] This comfortably distant 'special case', however, is in fact no more than a state-sponsored version of everyday urban civilian scenarios.[153] While they don't occur in formally designated military conflict zones, it is clear from our research that they can generate the most extreme conflict. As western societies become ever more sonic, responsible citizenship, policy and legislation will require musical literacy and civility, an appropriate awareness of the power of music.

Implications for PMS

We feel that this enquiry also holds implications for Popular Music Studies. Many of these have emerged during the discussions, and may be expressed as general principles of scholarship. This particular project has heavily underlined the basic objective of research, which is not to prove assumptions but to test them, to be asking, 'Where are we wrong?' Also specific to this investigation was the importance of avoiding knee-jerk reactions to those apparently positioned in ideological opposition to popular musics. The starkness of the moral panic arguments in the public domain tempts an equally schematic dismissal, and popular music scholarship has often been built on that platform. Scorn, however, is a poor research tool. Because of the reactive agenda of much popular music studies, it is instructive to review the public discourses against which it often reacts. We have exemplified the moral panic position. But there is another equally obdurate theme, which may be illustrated by revisiting some of the cases we have referred to and the way they are reported.

---

[150] DeGregory, 'Iraq and roll'.
[151] Ibid.
[152] Ibid.
[153] See further Johnson 'Sites of Sound'.

Media Reactions

The horror involved in many of the cases cited above means that humour is the last thing one might want to associate with them. However, it is precisely humour which is frequently deployed in media analyses of such cases. Moreover when loud music is used to cause pain to neighbours, it is often seen as humorous by perpetrators themselves. In 1993 when Jane Carruthers was fined for constantly blaring Jim Reeves songs she posed for photographers with tapes of the musician.[154] *The Independent* reported flippantly that Jim Reeves was not available for comment as he had died in 1964. Noting that Carruthers' boyfriend, Bill Kirkwood, said that he planned to carry on playing Reeves, but on headphones, the reporter joked that perhaps suitable tracks would be his hit 'Guilty' or 'Distant Drums'.[155] *The Guardian* joked that the latter had not been distant enough. All this, despite the fact that one neighbour had described the noise as 'unbearable'.[156]

The same year Diane Welfar, fined £12,500 at Leicester magistrates for playing records very loudly despite a noise abatement order and ten visits from the local authorities, said after being found guilty of breaking the order: 'This seems like a joke to me.'[157] Reflecting on the case cited earlier of the Florida music offender sentenced to listen to opera, journalist Andrew Mueller commented: 'Speaking for myself, about 15 minutes of Dido's dishwater wittering, even at a mild volume, would induce a confession to just about anything.'[158] Mueller also quipped that the fact that playing Billy Ray Cyrus's 'Achy Breaky Heart' during the Waco siege 'takes this sort of punishment well and truly into the realm of the cruel and unusual'.[159] In the sorry tale of a man who ran amok on hearing Keane's 'Somewhere Only We Know', a report ended with: 'Fiscal Deputy Hannah Kennedy said the accused had tried to bite one of the officers, but added: "He has no teeth so he wasn't really a threat".'[160] Reporting the appalling Beasts of Satan case, music journalist James Jam concluded: 'And that's the kind of aftershow that even the most party hungry of *NME* lig hounds would pass on, thanks.'[161] When the *Death Metal Murders* programme about the case was aired, *The Guardian*'s reviewer said that bands such as Deicide and Cannibal Corpse were 'bands you'll never see on Parkinson'

---

[154]   Alex Renton, '"Distant Drums" goes too far', *Independent*, 21 May 1993; see also Sally Weale, 'Jim Reeves ravers silenced', *Guardian*, 21 May 1993.

[155]   Renton, 'Distant Drums'.

[156]   Weale, 'Jim Reeves'.

[157]   *Independent*, 3 July 1993. See further examples of the joke-and-quip response to noise and music conflicts, Vidal, 'A pain in the ears (anag)'; Wilson, 'Probation'.

[158]   Mueller, 'Rhyme and Punishment'.

[159]   Ibid.

[160]   'Keane song "triggered outburst"', http://news.bbc.co.uk/go/pr/fr/-/1/hi/scotland/4724514.stm.

[161]   James Jam, 'Italian goth metal murder', *NME*, 12 March 2004, p. 25. Similar jollity from Jam can be enjoyed throughout this article.

and that when Count Grishnackh of Norwegian metal band Mayhem murdered guitarist Euronymous, this was 'more exciting than Westlife'.[162] The Dolly Parton case alluded to above was headlined 'Stand by your ban!' in the *Yorkshire Evening Post* of 8 August 2007, while *Sky News* headlined with the snappy 'Too Loud! Music Ban for Doll Fan' and spoke of the music being 'outside the hours of nine to five', a winking reference to the title of another Parton hit.[163]

The war in Iraq has been an especially rich source of humour. The *St Petersburg Times* in Tampa Bay asked its readers which songs they would use to 'drive the insurgents out of Fallujah, break down Iraqi prisoners or just drive their neighbors nuts'.[164] Metallica's James Hatfield also saw the funny side when he discovered that the US military was using his music to torture detainees: 'We've been punishing our parents, our wives, our loved ones with this music forever …. Why should Iraqis be any different?'[165] When he first broke the Metallica story in *Newsweek*, journalist Adam Poire was told to get a full play list and write it up in a humorous way.[166] The disclosure that the 'I Love You' song by Barney The Purple Dinosaur was being used to torture prisoners in Iraq was quite a hoot, in Jon Ronson's words 'the funniest joke of the war'.[167] Media outlets ran it as a funster story and the internet was swamped with people saying what their own idea of musical torture was.[168] *The Guardian* – the UK's leading *liberal* newspaper – headlined an article with the title 'Not the Barney song' and suggested that 'if Barney had been walking the earth when the Geneva conventions were drawn up, there would be laws against this sort of thing'.[169] It concluded:

So pity the poor prisoners, but we parents are made of sterner stuff. I suspect that that coalition of forces have not yet made full use of their potential psy-ops armoury. You had better believe that no one will be able to keep Saddam Hussein's whereabouts secret once the British interrogators employ their secret weapon: a battered audi tape of the theme to Merlin the Magic Puppy.[170]

---

[162]   Rupert Smith, 'I used to think that heavy metal rock was harmless vaudeville for friendless teenagers. Then I watched Death Metal Murders', *Guardian*, 25 November 2005, part two, p. 28. *Parkinson* is a middle of the road UK chat show.

[163]   http://news.sky.com/skynews/article/0,,30000-1289886,00.html.

[164]   Lane DeGregory, 'Anything but "MacArthur"', *St Petersburg Times*, 21 November 2004, http://sptimes.com/2004/11/21/Floridian/Anything_but__MacArth.shtml.

[165]   DeGregory, 'Iraq and roll'.

[166]   Ronson *The Men Who Stare at Goats*, p. 131.

[167]   Jon Ronson, 'The Road to Abu Ghraib', *Guardian Weekend*, 30 October 2004, p. 18.

[168]   Ronson, *The Men Who Stare at Goats*, p. 153. See further Cusick, 'Music as Torture', pp. 7–8.

[169]   Michael Hann, 'No, not the Barney song!', *Guardian*, 21 May 2003, part two, p. 7.

[170]   Ibid.

When the story was reported on the NBC's 'Stars and Stripes' the reporter, Ann Curry, played a clip of Barney and assumed a tone of voice which drew laughter from the studio audience. Weatherman Al Roker joined in the joke: 'And if Barney doesn't get 'em, switch to the Teletubbies, and that crushes 'em like a bug.' When *Newsweek* broke the story the editor added a last line to the article – 'It broke us too!'[171]

Let us remember that the subject of all this hilarity is the studied destruction of a human being. Would anyone end a report on the stoning of a rape victim with a waggish, 'I guess she could start a nice rockery'? At Human Rights Watch Kenneth Roth could not tell whether the Barney song had been deliberately chosen so that when the story broke humour would dominate public responses.[172] The organization expressed concern that the Barney story was turning stories about interrogations into a joke and that those expressing concern would be dismissed as lacking a sense of humour.[173]

The use of music from *Sesame Street* was also something of a thigh-slapper.[174] On a Channel Four (UK) documentary *Crazy Rulers of the World*, Christopher Cerf, composer of *Sesame Street* songs, was contacted by his publishers about what royalties he might be owed. Cerf joked with Danny Epstein, music supervisor on *Sesame Street*, about the morality of accepting money for the use of his music in torture: 'Why not? It's an American thing to do. If I have the knack of writing songs that can drive people crazy sooner and more effectively than other, why shouldn't I profit from that?'[175] Even UK human rights activist Clive Stafford Smith was unable to restrain a smile, suggesting that if Toby Keith's music was used on him: 'This kind of torture would be on-message and much more effective: I, for one, would confess after enduring the first verse.'[176]

Apart from the empirical interest offered by these cases, there is a curious mindset at work here, to which it is instructive for popular music scholars to attend. The general refusal of the media to take these issues seriously is symptomatic of its trivialization of pop. It also refracts a much more deeply embedded ideology that shadows popular music studies by placing it on the defensive. The media attitude to pop music reflects a form of cognitive dissonance or double standard. In Chapter 5 we reviewed moral panic responses to incitement to violence in popular music. Paradoxically these responses attached the greatest seriousness to forms of pop in which a general direct causal connection with public violence was most tenuous. These responses even went to the point of bringing legal action to bear

---

[171]   Ibid.

[172]   Cusick, 'Music as Torture', p. 155.

[173]   Ronson, *The Men Who Stare at Goats,* p. 154.

[174]   'Sesame Street breaks Iraqi POWs', *BBC news* online 20 May 2003, http://news.bbc.co.uk/1/hi/world/middle_east/3042907.stm.

[175]   Ronson, *The Men Who Stare at Goats*, p. 137.

[176]   Clive Stafford Smith, 'Torture by music', *New Statesman*, 6 November 2006, www.newstatesman.com/200611060029.

against specific bands or producers. That such actions were invariably unsuccessful underscores a basic wrong-headedness driving them. In a corresponding paradox, the media and other watchdogs of pop music morality relentlessly trivialize musics which are not only most clearly causally implicated in violence, but which come to media notice for precisely that reason.

It would be well for popular music scholars to beware of mirroring (constructing a reverse image of) this perversity in its own enthusiasms and emphases. There is a tradition of rebel chic in pop associated with noise, from Public Enemy's call to 'Bring The Noise' through Ted Nugent's proclamation that 'If it's too loud you're too old' and including the *Addicted To Noise* fanzine. There is also the Noise Rock scene around artists such as Mark Patton with important precursors such as Big Black and Sonic Youth.[177] A review of pop music studies literature suggest a tendency to foreground and glorify 'outlaw' genres such as rap and to neglect or trivialize those musics which, as we have seen, are most demonstrably the major sites of conflict in the westernized urban societies in which most of us pursue our research. And conflict is at the heart of any politically engaged scholarship, which takes us back to the wellsprings of popular music studies.

If, as the Introduction argues (from Dai Griffiths), PMS is a 'certain literature of the left', the one question is how leftist/PMS scholars should respond to the problems we have identified. For us this means not simply celebrating 'resistance', but recognizing the rights of the victims of musical assault. Above all it seems that PMS must reassert its political credentials. The academic Society for Ethnomusicology was so concerned about the use of music in torture by the US that they published a statement in 2007 condemning the practice and urging the US government to cease using music in this way.[178] The use of musical violence involves disenfranchizing and/or dehumanizing the victims. At the very least it is about marginalization – something in which, as a marginal field of study, PMS might expect to be interested. Likewise, issues of power and ideology. The flippant media reactions noted above can be seen as occluding the power relations involved. They are part of a rhetoric of euphemism that hides the politics and thus helps sustain the prevailing hegemony.

Bill O'Reilly, host of Fox News in the USA, has claimed that if blaring music at someone is torture, the phrase has become meaningless and that to take such a view was 'just nuts'.[179] This was in response to claims that Abu Zubaydah, one of the first Al-Qaeda leaders captured after 9/11, was subjected to the notorious practice of water boarding and then having the music of the Red Hot Chilli Peppers blasted at him. O'Reilly stated categorically that 'the Red Hot Chill Peppers isn't

---

[177] http://uk.real.com/music/genre/Noise_Rock/.

[178] http://webdb.iu.edu/sem/scripts/aboutus/aboutsem/positionstatements/position_statement_torture.cfm.

[179] *Media Matters for America*, 15 September 2006, http:mediamatters.org.items/200609160003.

torture'.[180] Meanwhile a syndicated jock, Laura Ingram, decared that such cases showed that 'the word "torture" has become meaningless'.[181] O'Reilly penned an article on the Zubaydha case lampooning the idea that music could be torture.[182] Contrast this with Amnesty International's view: 'Forcibly exposing a prisoner to loud, discordant or relentlessly repeated music is meant to inflict suffering. It amounts to torture or cruel, inhuman and degrading treatment.'[183] It seems to us that PMS has some obligation to express a stand on this.

The political tradition of PMS also means constantly rethinking its own relationship to the economic system within which popular music operates. We noted earlier that a history of music and violence would do much to illustrate a broader history of capitalism and much of what we are critiquing here involves business practices of one sort or another, from seeking to secure oil supplies in the middle east, to keeping shopping malls cleared of disenchanted youth, or using music to generate greater spending. Popular music is used in business practices well beyond its own economic bases. Its association with violence is more understandable if we recall the Marxist characterization of capitalist society as *necessarily* based upon class conflict. In such conflicts popular music can be used for oppression as well as for liberation. Indeed, given present economic structures, the former is the more likely than the latter. Popular music is a site of competing ideas about how the world is and how it should be. Thus after the destruction of New York's twin towers popular music was enlisted to rebuild the USA as an idea as well as physically.[184]

With its roots in leftist discourse regarding mass society and the culture industries, PMS has always been interested in the economic underpinning of pop. Early PMS pioneers such as Simon Frith, Dave Harker and Dave Laing fruitfully drew upon various Marxist forms of analysis to produce illuminating accounts of popular music. In more recent times there have also been analyses which bring together business practice and musical violence.[185]

Conclusion

In view of the research underpinning this book, why is there such neglect of the banal and unglamorous musics which, after all, seem most to provoke and constitute acts of violence? This takes us to two other lessons to be drawn from

---

[180]   Ibid.

[181]   Ibid.

[182]   Bill O'Reilly, 'Red Hot Torture', www.billoreilly.com/column?pid=20369.

[183]   Dorian Lynskey, 'Torturer's jukebox', *Guardian*, 24 April 2007, http://arts.guardian.co.uk/art/visualart/story/0,,2064090,00.htm.

[184]   Martin Cloonan, 'Music responses to September 11th", *Beiträge Zur Popularmusikforschung*, 32 (2004): 11–32.

[185]   See for example Coates, 'If Anything'.

this study. The first is to do with how we distribute our attentions in the study of popular music. Very clearly, what has mattered in the music/violence nexus is not primarily what the music is, but how and under what circumstances it is used. Metal presents itself as inherently violent, but seems most often to be used cathartically. There is not a trace of violence that can be reasonably located in 'White Christmas' or Whitney Houston's 'I Will Always Love You', yet they became 'torture' for unwilling listeners, and other music innocuous in itself has provoked murder. It is not the music, it's the user, not the musician but the fan. This, incidentally, is why ethnography can play such a valuable role in the study of music as social practice. Most of the accounts we have sourced here are media ones which inevitably do not follow up cases or go into great detail. There is a need for more documentation and for accounts from perpetrators and victims.

The second point foreshadowed is that, if a focus on specific genres can be misleading in the study of music and conflict, so to an even greater degree is an excessive reliance on lyrics by advocates of both regulation and free expression. It is assumed that violence is generated primarily by what words mean, by the verbal component of a song. This is a profound misunderstanding of both music and the contemporary world. Sonority is central to both, and never more so than since its technologized forms became widespread from the early twentieth century. Sound itself is an instrument of enormous social power and of violence. The failure to recognize this is a residue of the scopic model of knowledge and power that conspicuously accompanied the period of the ascendancy of print, roughly from the seventeenth to the late nineteenth centuries. The less amenable to 'reading' (as opposed to 'hearing') a message is, the less authority it is felt to carry, especially by those whose cultural capital is sustained by print.[186] Lyrics can be written down. They make great moral panic press copy. But as the authority and usage of sonic information networks increase, this assumption will simply wither on the vine, and it is arguable that we are witnessing this in the rapid rise of acoustic internet circuits, creating an alternative information network which is increasingly the first choice of a younger generation. In the meantime a pop song might incorporate, but is not, poetry, though of course musicality informs both. Similarly, we may, and often must, analyse music as an artform, but before it is that, it is sound. It is as such that the foundations of affective responses are defined. We suggest that popular music studies might profitably pay closer attention therefore to the phenomenology and physiology of hearing and the acoustic profiles of listening spaces, since these are absolutely crucial in the way we respond to music.

Finally, the most fundamental lesson to be derived from the subject of this research goes to the heart of the rhetoric popular music studies. Most if not all of us are fans as well as scholars and often practitioners. We are also advocates of a research field which is often trivialized in public as well as academic discourse. We generally position ourselves in indignant defence against poorly informed public, media and government prejudices. The result can all too easily be a shrill

---

[186] See further Johnson, 'Divided Loyalties'.

and strident one-dimensional idealization of the music that matters so much to us. Scholarship is easily compromised by the implicit frame of an uncritical celebration of popular music. To validate our work in academic and wider social terms, it behoves us to be more, rather than less, rigorous than adjacent established fields of research. Facile romanticization does us no good as a scholarly community, and is a mark of an ill-formed and immature discipline. One of the field's strengths is its potential for reflexive critique. In light of our earlier work in this field, Simon Frith recently acknowledged that: 'If music empowers people, if it is a means of articulating physical and cultural and ideological identity by occupying sonic territory, then it can only do so at the expense of other people's sense of identity.'[187] As noted in the Introduction, Frith also observed that the uncritical celebration of popular music has tended to mandate all public music usage.[188]

We come to the end of this enquiry, but its reverberation and amplitude increase, its case studies proliferate. On the day we finish this draft, the *Sydney Morning Herald* carries two news items on music, newsworthy because they are both centred on conflict and regulation in everyday life. A Florida teenager is arrested for singing a commercially released rap song containing 'expletive-laden lyrics' while walking down the street.[189] The other item is about 'silent parties', which, among other benefits, address the problem of noise nuisance. They are increasingly adopted by public and private dance party venues, allowing organizers to to 'do away with booming speakers and instead pump music directly into party-goers ears over an FM radio broadcast from the DJ booth'.[190] Popular music is one of the most important of all cultural practices, but one of the key reasons lies in its ambiguity. It is not a one-dimensional site of Disneyesque benevolence. It is at the same time dark and ugly. In London in 2007 a performance called Clamor took place in London's Serpentine Gallery. It presented the work of Jennifer Allora and Guillermo Calzadilla and featured a bunker and a forty minute soundtrack of music used in various war-zones. Allora noted that 'Any pop song could potentially be a weapon'.[191] Weapons are morally neutral. We need to recognize and respect the dialectic of every musical transaction, the dark side of the tune.

---

[187]   Simon Frith, 'Why does music make people so cross?'.

[188]   Ibid.

[189]   Ninemsn Staff, 'Teen arrested for rapping in public', *SMH* online, 6 February 2008.

[190]   Asher Moses, 'Head banging to the sounds of silence', *SMH* online, 6 February 2008.

[191]   Lynskey, 'Torturer's jukebox'.

Select Bibliography

Note: the Finnish 'ä' comes at the end of the alphabet; thus, for example, work by Järviluoma will follow work by Juslin.

Adorno, Theodor, 'On popular music', in Simon Frith and Andrew Goodwin (eds), *On Record* (London: Routledge, 1990): 301–14.

Ahmand, Jamal, 'Terror pop', *NME*, 12 March 2005: 25.

Aitkenhead, Decca, 'Their homophobia is our fault', *Guardian* online, 5 January 2005.

Alexander, Harriet and Braithwaite, David, 'Annabel drug alert as woman charged', *Sydney Morning Herald* online, 22 February 2007.

Allard, Tom, 'Hicks: my life of terror and torture', *Sydney Morning Herald* online, 2 March 2007.

Alvin, Juliette, *Music Therapy* (London: John Clare Books, 1975).

Ambrose, Joe, *Moshpit: The Violent World of Mosh Pit Culture* (London: Omnibus, 2001).

Amnesty International, *Report on Torture* (London: Duckworth, 1973).

Anon (former police officer), 'All Pumped Up', *Sydney Morning Herald News Review* 13–14 November 2004: 34.

Ansdell, Garry, *Music for Life*: *Aspects of Creative Music with Adult Clients* (London: Jessica Kingsley, 1995).

Ansdell, Garry, 'Response to Simon Frith's Essay', *Nordic Journal of Music Therapy*, 13/1 (2004): 70–72.

Appleson, Gail, 'Rapper "lied over gun battle"', *Guardian*, 2 March 2005: 17.

Armstrong, Edward G., 'Gangsta Misogyny: a Content Analysis of the Portrayals of Violence Against Women in Rap Music, 1987–1993', *Journal of Criminal Justice and Popular Culture*, 8/2 (2001): 96–126.

Arnett, Jeffery, *Metalhead: Heavy Metal Music and Adolescent Alienation* (Boulder Colorado: Westview Press, 1995).

Associated Press 'Bodyguard of Busta Rhymes shot dead', *Guardian*, 7 February 2006: 23.

Atkins, E. Taylor, 'Toward a Global History of Jazz', in E. Taylor Atkins (ed.), *Jazz Planet* (Jackson Miss: University of Mississippi Press, 2003): xi–xxvii.

Augoyard, Jean-François and Torgue, Henry (eds), *Sonic Experience*: *A Guide to Everyday Sounds*, trans. Andra McCartney and David Paquette (Montreal: McGill-Queen's University Press, 2005).

Babington, Anthony, *The English Bastille*: *A History of Newgate Gaol and Prison Conditions in Britain 1188–1902* (London: Macdonald, 1971).

Barbero, Alessandro, *The Battle: A History of the Battle of Waterloo*, trans. John Cullen (London: Atlantic Books, 2005).

Barham, Nick, *Dis/connected: Why our kids are turning their backs on everything we thought we knew* (London: Random House, 2005).

Barker, Juliet, *Agincourt: The King, The Campaign, The Battle* (London: Little Brown, 2005).

Barkham, Patrick, 'Doherty expresses pain of fame in blood and Goethe', *Guardian*, 1 February 2005: 7.

Bayoumi, Moustafa. 'Disco inferno', *The Nation*, 26 December 2005, www. thenation.com/doc/20051226/bayoumi.

Becker, Judith, 'Anthropological Perspectives on Music and Emotion', in John A. Sloboda and Patrik N. Juslin (ed.), *Music and Emotion: Theory and Research* (Oxford: OUP, 2001): 135–60.

Benjamin, Walter, 'Theses on the Philosophy of History', *Illuminations*, trans. Harry Zohn, ed. Hannah Arendt (London: Pimlico, 1970).

Bennett, Andy, *Cultures of Popular Music* (Buckingham: Open University Press, 2001).

Berger, Harris M., *Metal, Rock, and Jazz: Perception and the Phenomenology of Musical Experience* (Middletown CT: Wesleyan University Press, 1999).

Bergmeier, Horst and Lotz, Rainer, *Hitler's Airwaves: The Inside Story of Nazi Radio Broadcasting and Propaganda Swing* (New Haven and London: Yale University Press, 1997).

Berkley, Rob, 'We won't desert them', *Guardian*, 11 January 2005: 21.

Bethell, Tom, *George Lewis: A Jazzman from New Orleans* (Berkeley, Los Angeles, London: University of California Press, 1977).

Bijsterveld, Karen, 'The Diabolical Symphony of the Mechanical Age: Technology and Symbolism of Sound in European and North American Noise Abatement Campaigns, 1900–1940, in Michael Bull and Les Back (eds), *The Auditory Culture Reader* (Oxford: Berg): 165–89.

Birdsall, Carolyn, '"Affirmative resonances" in the City? Sound, Imagination and Urban Space in early 1930s Germany', in Mieszkowski, Sylvia, Smith, Joy and de Valck, Marijke (eds), *Sonic Interventions in Race, Gender and Place* (Amsterdam and New York: Rodopi, 2007): 57–86.

Bierley, Stephen, 'Cowan pushes champion to limit', *Guardian*, 28 June 2001: 34.

Bissett, Kelvin, 'Crimefighters of note', *Daily Telegraph*, 1 August 1999.

Blackman, Guy, 'Fairway to Heaven', *Age*, 1 July 2007.

Blazekovic, Zdravko, 'The Shadow of Politics on North Croatian Music of the Nineteenth Century' in Svanibor Pettan (ed.), *Music, Politics and War: Views From Croatia* (Zagreb: Institute of Ethnology and Folklore Research, 1998): 65–78.

Bloom, Allan, *The Closing of the American Mind* (New York: Simon and Schuster, 1987).

Bodanis, David, *Electric Universe: How Electricity Switched On the Modern World* (London: Abacus, 2006).

Booth, Robert and Smith, Helena, *Guardian*, 22 May 2006 (Article on Lordi).

Borger, Julian, 'Metallica is latest interrogation tactic', *Guardian*, 20 May 2003: 11.

Bosma, Hanna, 'Different Noises in Electroacoustic Music', *ASCA Conference Sonic Interventions: Pushing the Boundaries of Cultural Analysis, Reader for Panel 2: The Sonic in the 'Silent' Arts and Bring in the Noise*, 2005, Coordinator: Sylvia Mieszkowski: 18–23.

Boureau, Alain, 'Franciscan Piety and Voracity: Uses and Stratagems in the Hagiographic Pamphlet' in Chartier, Roger (ed.), *The Culture of Print: power and the uses of print in early modern Europe* (trans Lydia G. Cochrane) (Cambridge: Polity Press, 1989): 15–58.

Bourke, Angela, *The Burning of Bridget Cleary: A True Story* (London: Pimlico, 1999).

Bowcott, Owen, 'Army tortured Mau Mau rebels in the 1950s', *Guardian*, 5 May 2005: 5.

Bowden, Betsy, *Performed Literature: Words and Music by Bob Dylan* (Bloomington: University of Indiana Press, 1982).

Boyd, Joe, *White Bicycles: making music in the 1960s* (London: Serpent's Tail, 2005).

Branigan, Tania 'BBC withdraws "homophobic" reggae tracks', *Guardian*, 30 August 2002: 8.

Branigan, Tania, 'Anti-gay reggae stars "Should be charged"', *Guardian*, 24 December 2002: 6.

Branigan, Tania, 'Beenie Man concert axed over homophobia fears', *Guardian*, 25 June 2004: 8.

Brisbane City Council, *Valley Music Harmony Plan* (Brisbane: Brisbane City Council, 2005).

Bronzaft, Arline and McCarthy, Dennis, 'The effect of elevated train noise on reading ability', *Environment and Behaviour*, 7 (1975): 517–28.

Bronzaft, Arline, 'The effect of a noise abatement program on reading ability', *Journal of Environmental Psychology*, 1 (1981): 215–22.

Bronzaft, Arline, 'An International Voice Against the Perilous Noise Pollutant', presented at Hör upp! Stockholm Hey Listen!! WFAE Conference (Stockholm, 1998): 16.

Bronzaft, Arline, 'Researching Noise Effects', http://noisefutures.org/documents/ARLINE%20BRONZAFT.pdf.

Bronzaft, Arline, 'Reflecting On the Lack of Acoustical Consideration at Ground Zero', http://www.noiseoff.org/groundzero.shtml.

Bugliosi, Vincent with Gentry, Curt, *Helter Skelter: The Shocking Story of the Manson Murders* (the word '*Shocking*' becomes '*True*' on the title page) (London: Random House/Arrow, 1992; first published 1974).

Bull, Michael, *Sounding Out the City: Personal Stereos and the Management of Everyday Life* (Berg: Oxford, 2000).

Burke, Peter, *Popular Culture in Early Modern Europe* (London: Temple Smith, 1978).

Burns, Gary, 'Marilyn Manson and the Apt Pupils of Littleton, 1999', *Popular Music and Society*, 23/3 (1999): 3–7.

Bush, Douglas, *English Literature in the Early Seventeenth Century* (Oxford: OUP, 1945).

Butt, Ronald, 'The grubby face of punk promotion', *Times*, 9 December 1976: 14.

Button, James, 'There goes the hood', *Sydney Morning Herald News Review*, 18–19 June 2005: 27.

Buxton, John, *Elizabethan Taste* (New York, St Martin's Press, 1964).

Campbell, Sean and Smyth, Gerry, *Beautiful Day: Forty Years of Irish Rock* (Cork: Atrium, 2005).

Cannane, Steve, 'Tell Sydney's shooshers to shove off', *Sydney Morning Herald*, 7 January 2002: 10.

Carbines, Elaine, *Live Music Taskforce: Report and Recommendations* (Melbourne: Government of Victoria, 2003).

Carlton, Lana and MacDonald, Raymond, 'An investigation of the effects of music on Thematic Apperception Test (TAT) interpretations', *Musicae Scientiae*, Special Issue (2004): 9–30.

Carney, Shaun, 'Transparent Tactic', *Sydney Morning Herald* online, 29 September 2007.

Carroll, Rory, 'Zimbabwe slides deeper into chaos', *Guardian*, 7 June 2001: 1.

Carroll, Rory, 'The Alsace vote for Le Pen was just a protest. Wasn't it?', *Guardian*, 27 April 2002: 11.

Cashman, Sean Dennis, *America in the Twenties and Thirties: The Olympian Age of Franklin Delano Roosevelt* (New York and London: New York University Press, 1989).

Cassidy, Gianna and MacDonald, Raymond, 'The Effects of Background Music and Background Noise on the Task Performance of Introverts and Extraverts', *Psychology of Music*, 35/3 (2007): 517–37.

Cassidy, Gianna, MacDonald, Raymond and Sykes, Jon, 'The Effects of Aggressive and Relaxing Popular Music on Driving Game Performance and Evaluation'. DIGRA (Digital Games Research) Conference, 'Changing Views: Worlds in Play' (Vancouver, 2005) Cellini, Benvenuto *Autobiography*, trans. George Bull (Harmondsworth: Penguin, 1979).

Ceribašić, Naila, 'Defining women and men in the context of war: Images in Croatian popular music in the 1990s' in Pirkko Moisala and Beverley Diamond (eds), *Music and Gender* (Chicago: University of Illinois Press, 2000).

Chad, Sheldon and Farley, Maggie, 'Montreal killer wanted to die in a hail of bullets', *Sydney Morning Herald* online, 16 September 2006.

Chaudhary, Vivek, 'Gays to jam BBC lines, *Guardian*, 14 April 1993.

Chaudhary, Vivek, 'Music lifts Britain's Wimbledon hopes', *Guardian* 26 June 2001: 4.

Chazan, Yigal, 'Shotgun wedding thrills Serbia', *Guardian*, 20 February 1995: 1.

Chifley, Ephraem, 'A word in your ear ... a night in the pub could be deafening', *Sydney Morning Herald*, 19 November 2004: 15.

Chivers, Tom, 'Dolly Parton fan told: keep quiet or lose house', *Daily Telegraph* 25 October 2007.

Chrisafis Angelique, 'Years of harmony wrecked in days', *Guardian*, 26 June 2001: 3.

Chrisafis, Angelique, 'In a corner of Antrim another generation grows up on a diet of sectarian hatred', *Guardian*, 6 September 2005: 11.

Chrisafis, Angelique, 'Rapper faces jail for song dissing France', *Guardian* online, 29 May 2006.

Clark, Andrew, 'Music to drive away tube louts', *Guardian*, 13 January 2005: 6.

Cloonan, Martin, *Banned!* (Aldershot: Ashgate, 1996).

Cloonan, Martin, 'Ice-T: Cop Killer' in Derek Jones (ed.), *Censorship: A World Encyclopaedia* (London, 2001): 1139–40.

Cloonan, Martin, 'Music responses to September 11th', *Beiträge Zur Popularmusikforschung*, 32 (2004): 11–32.

Cloonan, Martin, 'What is popular music studies? Some observations', *British Journal of Music Education*, 22/1 (2005): 77–93.

Cloonan, Martin and Garofalo, Reebee (eds), *Policing Pop* (Philadelphia: Temple University Press, 2003).

Cloonan, Martin and Johnson, Bruce, 'Killing me softly with his song: An initial investigation into the use of Popular Music as a tool of repression', *Popular Music*, 21/1 (2002): 27–39.

Coates, Norma, 'If anything, blame Woodstock. The Rolling Stones, Altamont, December 6, 1969', in Ian Inglis (ed.), *Performance and Popular Music* (Aldershot: Ashgate, 2006): 58–69.

Cohen, Sara, *Rock Culture in Liverpool* (Oxford: Oxford University Press, 1991).

Cohn, Nik, *WopBopaLooBopLopBamBoom* (St Albans: Paladin, 1970).

Compton, Edmund, *Report of the enquiry into allegations against the security forces of physical brutality in Northern Ireland arising out of the events of 9 August, 1971* (London: HMSO, Cmnd.4823, 1971).

Congreve, William, *The Mourning Bride,* in *The Complete Plays* (ed. Herbert Davis), Chicago and London, 1967).

Connolly, Kate, 'Hate singers rounded up as police swoop in three cities', *Sydney Morning Herald*, 9 October 2001: 7.

Conrad, Peter, *Modern Times, Modern Places: Life & Art in the 20th Century* (printed in Hong Kong: Thames and Hudson, 1998).

Cooke, Deryck, 'The Lennon-McCartney songs', *Listener*, 1 February 1968.

Cooke, Dewl, 'Tuned in may mean young ears tune out', *Sydney Morning Herald*, 9 January, 2008: 3.

Cowan, Rosie, 'Neighbours caught up in low key war', *Guardian*, 4 November 2002: 6.

Crafts, Susan, Cavicchi, Daniel and Kiel, Charles, and the Music in Daily Life Project, *My Music* (Hanover, NE: Wesleyan University Press, 1993).

Craig, Dylan and Mkhize, Nomalanga, 'Vocal killers, silent killers: Popular media, genocide and the call for benevolent censorship in Rwanda', in Michael Drewett and Martin Cloonan (eds), *Popular Music Censorship in Africa* (Aldershot: Ashgate, 2006): 36–52.

Creagh, Sunanda, 'Mayor blasts super speakers that give out bad vibes', Urban Affairs Reporter, *Sydney Morning Herald* online, July 24, 2007.

Crowther, Jim, Hamilton, Mary and Tett, Lynn (eds), *Powerful Literacies* (Leicester: NIACE, 2001).

Cuming, Angela, 'Must-have music box takes over the street', *Sun-Herald*, 19 December 2004.

Cuming, Angela, 'Why pub drinkers must shout', *Sydney Morning Herald*, 19 November 2004: 15.

Cyriax, Oliver, *The Penguin Encyclopedia of Crime* (Harmondsworth: Penguin, 1996).

Dannen, Fred, *Hit Men* (New York: Vintage Books, 1991).

Darby, Andrew, 'Not old Bing again: let's go!' *Age*, 31 May 2001: 2.

Day, Gary, *Class* (London and New York: Routledge, 2001).

Day, Julia, 'Radio 1 glorifies knife crime, says Tory leader', *Guardian* online, 7 June 2006.

DeGregory, Lane, 'Anything but "MacArthur Park"', *St Petersburg Times*, 21 November 2004, http://sptimes.com/2004/11/21/Floridian/Anything_but__ MacArth.shtml.

DeGregory, Lane, 'Iraq and roll', *St Petersburg Times* online, 21 November 2004, http://s{times/com/2004/11/21/Floridian/Iraq_n_roll.shtml.

De Kloet, Jeroen, *Red Sonic Trajectories* (Amsterdam: University of Amsterdam, 2003).

Department for Environment, Food and Rural Affairs (DeFRA), *Noise and Nuisance Research Newsletter* 1 (London: DeFRA, 2006).

Department for Environment, Food and Rural Affairs (DeFRA), *Noise Act 1996* (London, DeFRA, 2007).

Denney, Peter, 'Scythes, Swords and the Bitter-Sweet Melody of Merry England', in *Plebeian Prospects: Landscape, Liberty and Labouring-Class Culture in Britain, 1700–1830* (doctoral diss., University of York).

Dennis, Anthony, 'Irritating mobile phone sounds a sweet bonus for tune writers', *Sydney Morning Herald*, 18–19 January 2003.

De Nora, Tia, and Belcher, Sophie, '"When you're trying something on you picture yourself in a place where they are playing this kind of music" – musically sponsored agency in the British clothing retail sector', *Sociological Review*, 48/1 (2000): 80–101.

Dodd, Vikram, 'This is a US torture camp', *Guardian* online, 12 January 2007.

Donovan, Patrick, 'Not the Antichrist, just a homeboy', *Sydney Morning Herald*, 27 July 2001: 3.

Duncan, Michelle, 'Hydromancy: Of Sirens, Songs, and Soma', *ASCA Conference Sonic Interventions*: *Pushing the Boundaries of Cultural Analysis*, Reader for Panel 2: *The Sonic in the 'Silent' Arts and Bring in the Noise*, Coordinator: Sylvia Mieszkowski (2005): 59–64.

Dunlevy, Sue, 'Noisy ads face volume control', *Daily Telegraph*, 17 June 2001.

Durack, Terry, 'I'll *shout* you dinner', *Sydney Morning Herald, Good Living*, 23 April 1996: 1–2.

Durschmied, Erik, *The Hinges of Battle*: *How Chance and Incompetence Have Changed the Face of History* (London: Hodder and Stoughton, 2002).

Dworkin, Andrea, *Pornography*: *Men Possessing Women* (London: The Women's Press, 1981).

Easton, Carol, *Straight Ahead*: *The Story of Stan Kenton* (New York: Da Capo, 1973).

Editorial, *Guardian*, 4 July 1998: 21.

Erichman, James, 'Noise epidemic complaints rise', *Guardian*, 5 September 1994: 4.

Espiner, Mark, 'Rock the kasbah', *Guardian*, 19 January 2005: 23.

Evans, Gary W. and Lepore, Stephen J., 'Nonauditory effects of noise on children: a critical review', *Children's Environments*, 10 (1993): 31–51.

Evans, Gary, 'Low-Level Office Noise Can Increase Health Risks', *Soundscape: The Journal of Acoustic Ecology*, 2/1 (July 2001): 33.

Ezard, John, 'Brewers accused as prices come to head, *Guardian*, 22 October 2002: 13.

Ezard, John, 'Bob Dylan fan wins Oxford poetry post', *Guardian*, 17 May 2004: 8.

Fackler, Guido, '"This music is infernal": Music in Auschwitz', http://lastexpression.northwestern.edu/essays/Fackler2.pdf.

Fay, Thomas, *Noise and Health* (New York: New York Academy of Medicine, 1991).

Feld, Steve[n], 'From ethnomusicology to Echo-Muse-Ecology', http://www.acousticecology.org/feld/index.html.

Fernandez, Don, 'That's not the start of another war, that's just my mobile phone ringing', *Sydney Morning Herald*, 13–14 November 2004: 15.

Ferrell, Jeff, *Crimes and Style* (New York: Garland, 1993).

Fleischer, Tzvi, 'Sounds of Hate: The Neo-Nazi music scene in Australia and Beyond', Australia/Israel & Jewish Affairs Council (AIJAC) (August 2000), http://www.shu.ac.uk/cgi–bin/news_full.pl?id_num=PR137&db=01.

Foley, Robert and McCartney, Helen, *The Somme*: *an eyewitness history* (London: Foley, 2006).

Frith, Simon, *The Sociology of Rock* (London: Constable, 1978).

Frith, Simon, '"The magic that can set you free": the ideology of folk and the myth of the rock community', *Popular Music* 1 (1981): 159–68.

Frith, Simon, *Sound Effects* (London: Constable, 1983).

Frith, Simon, 'Why does music make people so cross?', *Nordic Journal of Music Therapy*, 13/1 (2004): 64–9.

Gabrielsson, Alf, 'Emotions in Strong Experiences with Music', in John A. Sloboda and Patrik N. Juslin (eds), *Music and Emotion: Theory and Research* (Oxford: OUP, 2001): 431–49.

Garrett, David, *Programme Notes* to Monteverdi's Books: Motets and Madrigals of Claudio Monteverdi, presented by Sydney Philharmonia Choirs, 30 April and 1 May 2004.

Gibbons, Fiachara, 'Reggae fans attack gay rights protest', *Guardian*, 3 October 2002: 7.

Gibson, Jano, 'PM blasts "sickening" gang videos', *Sydney Morning Herald* online, 24 January 2006.

Gibson, Val, 'Campaigning Against Noise: Getting Into Action', *Hearing Rehabilitation Quarterly*, 24/1 (1999): 1–3.

Gillespie, Dizzy with Al Fraser, *Dizzy: The Autobiography of Dizzy Gillespie* (London: D.H. Allen, 1980).

Gillett, Charlie, *Sound of The City* (London: Souvenir, 1983).

Ginzburg, Carlo, *The Cheese and the Worms: The Cosmos of a Sixteenth-Century Miller*, trans. John and Anne Tedeschi. (Baltimore: Johns Hopkins, 1992).

Glaister Dan, 'Harmony on the line as Metro tunes in to Delius to turn off vandals', *Guardian*, 30 January 1998: 3.

Glasgow City Council, *Noise Action Week* (Glasgow, 2005).

Glendinning, Lee, 'Mobo drops gay hate songs', *Guardian*, 8 September 2004: 7.

Glendinning, Lee, 'Anti-gay music banned', *Guardian*, 27 November 2004: 7.

Goddard, Chris, *Jazz Away from Home* (New York and London, 1979).

Goldstein, E. Bruce, *Sensation and Perception* (Pacific Grove CA: Brooks/Cole, Fourth ed., 1996).

Griffiths, Dai, 'The high analysis of low culture', *Music Analysis*, 18/ iii (1999): 389–434.

Gronow, Pekka, *The Recording Industry: An Ethnomusicological Approach* (Tampere: University of Tampere, 1996).

Grossberg, Lawrence, 'Reflections of a disappointed popular music scholar, in Roger Beebee, Denise Fulbrook and Ben Saunders (eds), *Rock Over The Edge* (London: Duke University Press): 25–59.

Hadžihusejnović-Valašek, Miroslava, 'The osijek War-Time Music Scene 1991–1992' in Svanibor Pettan (ed.), *Music, Politics and War: Views From Croatia* (Zagreb: Institute of Ethnology and Folklore Research, 1998), pp. 163–84.

Hallam, Susan, *The Power of Music* (London: PRS, 2001).

Hamilton, Alan, 'Sit-down protest over TVs for trains foiled by broken toilets', *Times*, 9 February 2005: 15.

Hamm, Mark S., *American Skinheads* (Westport, CT: Praeger, 1993).

Hamm, Mark S., and Ferrell, Jeff, 'Rap, cops, and crime: clarifying the "cop killer" controversy', at *Rapping about cop killing*, http://www.axt.org.uk/HateMusic/Rappin.htm at 29 August 2007.

Hammersley, Ben, 'Generation Text', *Guardian* 13 January 2005: 23.

Hann, Michael, 'No, not the Barney song!', *Guardian*, 21 May 2003, part two: 7.

Hargreaves, David and North, Adrian (eds), *Social Psychology of Music* (Oxford: OUP, 1997).

Harker, Dave, *One For The Money* (London: Hutchinson, 1980).

Harker, Dave, *Fakesong* (Milton Keynes: Open University Press, 1985).

Harker, Dave, 'The Wonderful World of IFPI: Music Industry Rhetoric, the Critics, and the Classical Marxist Critique', *Popular Music*, 16/1 (1997): 45–79.

Harris, Paul, 'Eight miles of murder', *Observer*, 16 April 2006: 26.

Harrison, Grahame, *Night Train to Granada – From Sydney's Bohemia to Franco's Spain: an offbeat memoir* (Annandale NSW: Pluto Press, 2002).

Hastings, Max, *Armageddon:The Battle for Germany 1944–45* (London: Pan/Macmillan, 2004).

Hawkins, Stan, *Settling The Pop Score* (Aldershot: Ashgate, 2002).

Hetu, R., Getty, L. and Quoc, H.T. 'Impact of occupational hearing loss on the lives of workers', *Occupational Medicine: State of the Art Reviews*, 10/3 (1995): 495–512.

Henley, Joe, 'Teenagers jump to death in front of boyfriends', *Sydney Morning Herald*, 28 September 2005: 8.

Hesmondhalgh, David, 'Digital sampling and cultural inequality', *Social and Legal Studies*, 15/1 (2006): 53–75.

Hesmondhalgh, David and Negus, Keith (eds), *Popular Music Studies* (London: Arnold, 2002).

Hinsliff, Gaby, Bright, Martin and Burke, Jason, 'Police hit at rappers for making guns glamorous', *Observer*, 5 January 2003: 1–5.

Holmes, Richard, *Tommy: The British Soldier on the Western Front 1914–1918* (London: Harper Perennial, 2005).

Homan, Shane, *The Mayor's a Square: Live music and law and order in Sydney* (Newtown NSW: Local Consumption Publications, 2003).

Home Office, *Respect and Responsibility* (London: Home Office, 2003).

Hooper, John, 'Beast of Satan band members jailed for killings', *Guardian*, 23 February 2005.

Horner, Bruce and Swiss, Thomas (eds), *Key Terms in Popular Music and Culture* (Oxford: Blackwell, 1999).

Hughes, Robert, *The Fatal Shore: A History of the transportation of Convicts to Australia 1987–1868* (London: Collins Harvill, 1987).

Iaccarino, Clara, '"The way you stay alive is by making people like you real fast"', *Sun-Herald*, 11 June 2006: 69.

Independent, Letters page, 8 October 1993: 25.

Index on Censorship, *Smashed Hits*, *Index on Censorship* 6: 1 (1998).

Ingold, Tim, *The Perception of the Environment* (London: Routledge, 2000).

International Criminal Tribunal for Rwanda, *The Prosectuor v. Simon Bikindi* (Arusha: United Nations, ICTR–2001072–1, 2005).

Jackson, Melissa, (2005) 'Music to deter yobs by', BBC News, 10 January, 2005, http://news.bbc.co.uk/1/hi/magazine/4154711.stm. CUT URL?

Jam, James, 'Italian goth metal murder', *NME*, 12 March 2004: 25.

Jellie, Dugald, 'Tuning forks', *Sydney Morning Herald, Good Living*, 5–11 June 2001: 12–13.

Jenkins, Roy, *Churchill* (London: Pan, 2001).

Jerums, Georgina, Banguay, Emma-Charlotte, and Reilly, Natalie, 'Off your dial', *Sunday Life* (The *Sun-Herald Magazine*, Sydney), 18 June 2006.

Jervis, John, *Exploring the Modern* (Oxford: Blackwell, 1998).

Jha, Alok, 'Says WHO ... All that noise is the death of us', *Age*, 24, 2007.

Jinman, Richard, 'Fans keep hopes alive for missing', *Guardian*, 1 January 2005: 7.

Johnson, Bruce, *The Oxford Companion to Australian Jazz* (Melbourne: OUP, 1987).

Johnson, Bruce, 'From Gallipoli to Gundagai', in Richard Nile (ed.), *War and Other Catastrophes*, Special Issue of *Journal of Australian Studies* 60 (1999): 66–72.

Johnson, Bruce, *The Inaudible Music: Jazz, Gender and Australian Modernity* (Sydney: Currency Press, 2000).

Johnson, Bruce, 'The Beatles in Australia', in Yrö Heinonen, Markus Heuger, Sheila Whiteley, Terhi, Nurmesjärvi and Jouni Koskimäki (eds), *Beatlestudies 3: Proceedings of the Beatles 2000 Conference* (University of Jyväskylä, Department of Music, 2001), pp. 69–78.

Johnson, Bruce, 'Unsound Insights', in Kimi Kärki, Rebecca Leydon and Henri Terho (eds), *Looking Back, Looking Ahead: Popular Music Studies 20 Years Later* (Turku, University of Turku, 2002): 704–12.

Johnson, Bruce, 'Jazz as Cultural Practice', in Mervyn Cooke and David Horn (eds), *The Cambridge Companion to Jazz* (Cambridge, Cambridge University Press, 2002): 96–113.

Johnson, Bruce, 'The Jazz Diaspora', in Mervyn Cooke and David Horn (eds), *The Cambridge Companion to Jazz* (Cambridge: Cambridge University Press, 2002): 33–54.

Johnson, Bruce and Shane Homan, *Vanishing Acts: An inquiry into the state of live popular music opportunities in New South Wales* (Sydney: Australia Council and the NSW Ministry for the Arts, 2003), at www.ozco.gov.au and www.arts.nsw.gov.au.

Johnson, Bruce, 'Two Paulines, Two Nations: An Australian case study in the intersection of popular music and politics', *Popular Music and Society*, 26/1 (2003): 53–72.

Johnson, Bruce, '*Hamlet*: voice, music, sound', *Popular Music* 24/2 (2005): 257–67.

Johnson, Bruce, 'Voice, Power and Modernity', in Joy Damousi and Desley Deacon (ed.), *Talking and Listening in the Age of Modernity* (Canberra: ANU E Press, 2007): 114–22.

Johnson, Bruce, 'Divided Loyalties: Literary Responses to the Rise of Oral Authority in the Modern Era', *Textus*, XIX (2006): 285–304.

Johnson, Bruce, '"Quick and Dirty": Sonic Mediations and Affect', forthcoming in Carolyn Birdsall and Anthony Enns (ed.), *Sonic Mediations: Body, Sound, Technology* (Cambridge: Cambridge University Press, forthcoming).

Johnson, Bruce, 'Sites of Sound' in *Sound Effects* (forthcoming).

Johnson, Bruce, 'Applause, Admiration and Envy: crime and the prehistory of stardom' (forthcoming).

Johnson, Paul, 'The menace of Beatlism', *New Statesman*, 28 February 1964: 326–7. Johnstone, Doug, 'We don't need no education', *NME*, 29 March 2003: 61.

Joseph, Colin, 'UK hip hop "needs ethics code"', *BBC News* online, 28 June 2002, www.bbc.co.uk/hi/english/entertainment/music/newsid_2073000/2073162. stm.

Judah, Tim, 'A warlike song for Europe', *Observer*, 16 April 2006: 31.

Juslin, Patrik N, 'Communicating emotion in music performance' in John A. and Patrik N. Juslin (ed.), *Music and Emotion: Theory and Research* (Oxford: OUP, 2001): 309–40.

Järviluoma, Helmi and Wagstaff, Gregg (ed.), *Soundscape Studies and Methods* (Helsinki: Finnish Society for Ethnomusicology, 2002).

Järviluoma, Helmi, 'Acoustic Environments: Five European Villages Revisited' in Ellen Waterman (ed.), *Sonic Geography Remembered and Imagined* (Toronto: Penumbra Press; 2002): 21–37.

Kahn-Harris, Keith, *Extreme Metal: Music and Culture on the Edge* (Oxford: Berg, 2007).

Karlsson, Henrik, 'The acoustic environment as a public domain', *Soundscape: The Journal of Acoustic Ecology*, 1/2 (2000): 10–13.

Karvelas, Patricia, 'If music be the food for mood, play on', *Australian*, 19 February 2003: 23.

Kater, Michael, *Different Drummers: Jazz in the Culture of Nazi Germany* (New York: Replica Boos, 1992).

Kearney, Christine, 'Keep quiet out there; this is New York', *Sydney Morning Herald*, 9 June 2004: 14.

Keegan, John, *The Face of Battle: A Study of Agincourt, Waterloo and the Somme.* (London: Pimlico, 2004).

Keen, David, Letters, *Guardian*, 19 June 2001: 17.

Kelso, Paul, 'Saudi bomb victim's torture ordeal – and Britain's silence', *Guardian*, 31 January 2002: 1.

Kennedy, Les, 'Party girl's dance with death', *Sydney Morning Herald* online, 11 August 2007.

Kent, Nick, *The Dark Stuff* (London: Penguin, 1994).

Kernan, Alvin, *Samuel Johnson and the Impact of Print* (Princeton: Princeton University Press, 1989).

Kernfeld, Barry (ed.), *The New Grove Dictionary of Jazz* (London: Macmillan, 1988).

Kershaw, Ian, *Hitler*, two vols (London: Penguin, 2001).

Kettle, Martin, 'Ode to Mauthausen', *Guardian*, 28 April 2000, part two: 2–3.

Kittler, Friedrich, *Gramophone, Film, Typewriter*, trans. Geoffrey Winthrop-Young and Michael Wutz (Stanford CA: Stanford University Press, 1999).

Kluger, Jeffrey, 'Just Too Loud', *Time*, 5 April 2004, pp. 48–50.

Kochkin, Sergei. 'HEARING SOLUTIONS – The impact of treated hearing loss on quality of life' (Alexandria Va: Better Hearing Institute, 2005), www.betterhearing.org/hearing_solutions/qualityOfLifeDetail.cfm.

Konečni, Vladimir, 'Social Interaction and Musical Preference', in David Deutsch (ed.), *The Psychology of Music* (New York: Academic Press, 1982), pp. 497–516.

Kontominas, Belinda, 'Rock and Poll: Talking 'bout my degeneration', *Sydney Morning Herald* online, 4 September 2007.

Kähäri, Kimi, 'The Influence of Music of Hearing: a Study in Classical and Rock/Jazz Musicians', *Journal of Acoustic Ecology* 4/2 (2003): 11. More detail from this thesis is at http://www.niwl.se/personal/kim.kahari%40niwl.se.htm.

Laing, Dave, *The Sound of Our Time* (London, Sheed and Ward, 1969).

Laing, Dave, *Buddy Holly* (London: Studio Vista, 1971).

Laing, Dave, *One Chord Wonders* (Milton Keynes: Open University Press, 1985).

Laks, Szymon, *Music of Another World* (Evanston: Northwestern University Press, 1989).

Lamb, Charles, *The Essays of Elia and the Last Essays of Elia* (London: Oxford University Press, 1959).

Lamb, Christina, 'Mother forced to sing tyrant's praises as his men raped her daughter', *Sun-Herald*, 1 September 2002: 60.

Lamont, Leonie, 'Ozzy Osbourne fanatic's bid to rape girl', *Sydney Morning Herald* online, 31 August 2006.

Lane, Megan, 'In search of Peace and Quiet', *BBC News*, 25 April 2002, http://news.bbc.co.uk/1/hi/uk/1944202.stm.

Lanza, Joseph, *Elevator Music: A Surreal History of Muzak, Easy Listening, and other Moodsong* (New York: St Martin's Press, 1994).

Laville, Sandra, 'Jamaican star apologises for "hurtful" lyrics', *Guardian*, 4 August 2004, p. 7.

Laville, Sandra, 'Anti-gay star's UK tour cancelled', *Guardian*, 4 November 2004: 10.

Laville, Susan and Muir, Hugh, 'So Solid Crew killer gets life sentence', *Guardian*, 29 October 2005: 13.

LeDoux, Joseph *The Emotional Brain* (London: Phoenix, 1998).

Lewis, Neil A, 'Frequent prisoner coercion alleged', *New York Times*, 17 October 2004.

Levi, Primo, *Is This A Man* (London: Abacus, 1979).

Linebaugh, Peter, *The London Hanged: Crime and civil society in the eighteenth century*, second ed. (London: Verso, 2006).

Link, Stan, 'Sympathy with the devil? Music of the psycho post-Psycho', *Screen*, 45/1 (2004): 1–20.

Linnane, Fergus, *London's Underworld: Three Centuries of Vice and Crime* (London: Robson Books, 2004).

Livy, *The War With Hannibal* (trans. Aubrey de Selincourt) (Harmondsworth: Penguin, 1965).

Low, Lenny Ann, 'Your shout? You'd better make it a loud one at the Angel', *Sydney Morning Herald* online, 14 March 2006.

Lowles, Nick, and Silver, Steve, *White Noise* (London: Searchlight, 1998).

Lukovic, Petar, 'Guns 'n' cassettes', *Guardian*, 1 April 1993, part two: 8.

Luckyj, Christina, A *moving rhetoricke: gender and silence in early modern England* (Manchester: Manchester University Press, 2002).

Lynskey, Dorian, 'Out of Africa', *Guardian*, 24 February 2005, part two: 14–15.

Lynskey, Dorian, 'Torturer's jukebox', *Guardian*, 24 April 2007.

Macdonald, Lynn, *They Called it Passchendaele: The Story of the Third Battle of Ypres and of the men who fought in it* (Harmondsworth: Penguin, 1993).

MacInnes, Colin, *England, Half English* (Harmondsworth: Penguin, 1966).

MacKinnon, Catherine, *Only Words* (London: Harper Collins, 1993).

MacKinnon, Ian, 'Ragga music blamed for attacks on homosexuals', *Independent*, 1 October 1993.

MacNevin, Robert, 'Editorial', Soundscape: *The Journal of Acoustic Ecology* 1/2 (2000): 4.

McAlinden, Mona, 'Nuisance noise fines to the tune of £1000', *Herald*, 22 May 2005: 16.

McArthur, Jacqueline, 'Lights, camera, earplugs', *Sun-Herald*, 29 November, 1998: 13.

McClary, Susan and Walser, Robert, 'Start making sense! Musicology wrestles with rock' in Simon Frith and Andrew Goodwin (eds), *On Record* (London: Routledge, 1990), pp. 277–93.

McCulloch, Janelle, 'Silent Revolution'. *Sun-Herald Magazine*, 3 September 2006: 23–5.

McConnochie, Pat, 'Sound advice for victims of cinema's music mafia', *Sydney Morning Herald*, 10 May 2006.

McDougall, Liam, 'Luke's lawyer: Crown evidence was a surprise ... Manson: don't blame me for Jodi murder', *Herald*, 13 February 2005: 4.

McGarry, Andrew, 'Live song soundtrack to Snowtown murders, court told', *Weekend Australian*, 1–2 March 2003.

McGreal, Chris, 'Israel shocked by image of soldiers forcing violinist to play at roadblock', *Guardian*, 29 November 2004: 16.

McGuigan, Jim, *Rethinking Cultural Policy* (Buckingham: Open University Press, 2004).

McKay, George, *Circular Breathing: The cultural politics of jazz in Britain* (Durham NC: Duke University Press, 2005).

McLeod, Ken, '"We are the Champions": Masculinities, Sports and Popular Culture', *Popular Music and Society*, 29/5 (December 2006): 531–47.

McLuhan, Marshall, *The Gutenberg Galaxy: The Making of Typographic Man* (Toronto: University of Toronto Press, 1962).

McMahon, Neil, 'Dialling a reply to poor phone form', *Sydney Morning Herald*, 17–18 September 2005: 4.

McMahon, Neil, 'Bullying on teen's sad road to oblivion', *Sydney Morning Herald* online, April 28, 2007.

McManus, Francis, 'Noise Law – Where do we go from here?' (2003), www.ukna. org.uk/index_files/page0006.htm.

Maley, Jacqueline, 'Forget Asbos. Australia uses Barry Manilow', *Guardian*, 6 June 2006: 19.

Maley, Jacqueline, 'Snoop Doggy Dogg held by police after Heathrow brawl', *Guardian*, 28 April 2006: 7.

Man, John, *Attila the Hun: A Barbarian King and the Fall of Rome* (London: Bantam Books, 2005).

Mann, Wilfred, 'What songs The Beatles sang', *Times*, 27 December 1963.

Manzoor, Sarfraz, 'Baghdad state of mind', *Guardian* online, 17 November 2006, http://arts.guardian.co.uk/filmandmusic/story/0,,1949249,00.html.

Marotti, Arthur, and Bristol, Michael (ed.), *Print, Manuscript and Performance: The changing relations of the media in early modern England* (Columbus: Ohio State University Press, 2000).

Marshall, Lee, 'Bob Dylan: Newport Folk Festival, July 25, 1965' in Ian Inglis (ed.), *Performance and Popular Music* (Aldershot: Ashgate, 2006) pp. 16–27.

Martin, Dennis R., 'The music of murder', at *Rapping about cop killing*, http://www.axt.org.uk/HateMusic/Rappin.htm at 29 August 2007.

Martin, Andrew, 'Quiet please', *Guardian*, 31 October 2007, part two: 6–11.

Martin, Lorna, 'Jodi murder: teen killer set to appeal', *Observer*, 23 January 23, 2005: 4.

Martin, Lorna, 'I won't turn my back on these people', *Observer*, 3 May 2005: 7.

Martin, William Hal, Folmer, Robert and Baker, Y-B. Shi, 'Tinnitus and Sound', *Soundscape: The Journal of Acoustic Ecology*, 6/1 (2005): 15–17.

May, Peter, Just for kicks', *Guardian Weekend*, 29 January 2005: 24–9.

Meek, James, '"Nobody is talking"', *Guardian G2*, 18 February 2005: 2–5.

Meikle, James, 'Angry music may make listeners aggressive', *Guardian*, 5 May 2003: 5.

Mellers, Wilfrid, *Twilight of The Gods* (London: Faber, 1973).

Mellers, Wilfrid, *A Darker Shade of Pale* (Oxford: Oxford University Press, 1985).

Metronet, 'Metronet installs "music to deter yobs by"', press release, 12 January 2005.

Middleton, Richard, *Studying Popular Music* (Milton Keynes: Open University Press, 1990).

Middleton, Richard, 'Popular music analysis and musicology: Bridging the gap' in Richard Middleton (ed.), *Reading Pop* (Oxford: OUP, 2002): 104–21.

Mill, John Stuart, *On Liberty* (Harmondsworth: Penguin, 1986).

Mitchell, Laura, *An Experimental Investigation of the Effects of Music Listening on Pain* (unpub. doctoral diss., Department of Psychology, School of Life Sciences, Glasgow Caledonian University, 2004).

Mitchell, Laura, MacDonald, Raymond and Brodie, Eric, 'Temperature and the Cold Pressor Test', *The Journal of Pain*, 5/4 (2004): 233–8.

Mitchell, Laura and MacDonald, Raymond, 'An Experimental Investigation of the Effects of Preferred and Relaxing Music on Pain Perception, *Journal of Music Therapy*, XLIII/4 (2006): 295–316.

Mitchell, Laura., MacDonald, Raymond, Knussen, Christina. and Serpell, Michael, 'A survey investigation of the effects of music listening on chronic pain', *Psychology of Music*, 35/1 (2007): 37–57.

Mitchell, Susan, *All Things Bright and Beautiful*: *Murder in the City of Light* (Sydney: Macmillan, 2004).

Montefiore, Simon Sebag, *Stalin*: *The Court of the Red Tsar* (London: Phoenix, 2003).

Moodie, David and Callahan, Maureen with Schone, Mark and Schreiber, Michael, 'Don't Drink The Brown Water', *Spin* 15/10 (1999): 100–114.

Moore, Allan, *Rock: The Primary Text*, second ed. (Aldershot, Ashgate 2001).

Morris, Alan, *Bloody April* (London: Jarrolds, 1967).

Morris, Steven and Carroll, Rory, '"I thought my God, this is it, I'm going to die"', *Guardian*, 21 July 2001: 3.

Morris, Steven, '"Antigay" singer cancels gigs', *Guardian*, 8 December 2003: 11.

Morris, Steven, 'Motorist in standoff over Riverdance', *Guardian*, 26 January 2005: 5.

Morris, Steven, 'First British soldier to be convicted of a war crime is jailed for ill-treatment of Iraqi civilians', *Guardian*, 1 May 2007: 13.

Moses, Asher, 'Head banging to the sounds of silence', *SMH* online, 6 February 2008.

Moynihan, Michael and Søderlind, Didrik, *Lords of Chaos*: *The Bloody Rise of the Satanic Metal Underground* (Los Angeles: Feral House, 1998).

Mueller, Andrew, 'Can't stop the muzak', *Independent on Sunday*, May 2003, www.andrewmueller.net/print.lasso?ID=178, accessed 2 March 2004.

Mueller, Andrew, 'Rhyme and Punishment', *Guardian Guide*, 21 February 2004: 12–13.

Muir, Hugh, 'Ceasefire brokered in reggae lyrics war', *Guardian*, 5 Feburary 2005: 4.

Muir, Hugh, 'Gun crime squad face questions over Megaman trials', *Guardian*, 30 September 2006: 11.

Muir, Hugh, 'So Solid Crew leader cleared of ordering street murder', *Guardian*, 29 September 2006: 5.

Mundell, Meg and Donovan, Patrick, 'Nightclub noise threatens hearing of a generation', *Age* online, 2 September 2001.

Mundell, Meg and Donovan, Patrick, 'Why the health warnings fall on deaf ears', *Age* online, 2 September 2001, http://news.bbc.co.uk/1/hi/uk/1944202.stm.

Munro, Catherine, 'Vandalism and violence', *Sydney Morning Herald*, 15 October 2006.

Murray, Charles Shaar, *Shots from the Hip* (London: Penguin, 1991).

Murray, Ewan, 'Rangers facing UEFA inquiry over fan chants', *Guardian Sport*, 20 March 2007: 6.

National Catholic Weekly, 22 July 1979; cited in email circulated by Rebecca Sullivan, 18 July 1996.

Negus, Keith, *Producing Pop* (London: Arnold, 1992).

Negus, Keith, *Popular Music in Theory* (Cambridge: Polity, 1996).

Negus, Keith, *Music Genres and Corporate Cultures* (London: Routledge, 1999).

Nehring, Neils, 'The Situationist International in American Hardcore Punk, 1982–2002', *Popular Music and Society* 29/5 (2006): 519–30.

Nguyen, Kenneth and Reuters, 'Turning up volume on risks to hearing', *Sydney Morning Herald* online, 19 October 2006.

North, Adrian, *The Commercial Uses of Music* (London: PRS, 2003).

North, Adrian and Hargreaves, David, 'Problem Music and Self-Harming', *Suicide and Life-Threatening Behaviour*, 36/5 (2006): 582–90.

Oe, Kenzaburo, *A Healing Family*, trans. Stephen Snyder (Tokyo: Kodansha International, 1996).

Oliver, Paul, *The Story of The Blues* (London: Barrie and Jones, 1970).

Ong, Walter, *Orality and Literacy: The Technologizing of the Word* (London: Routledge 1982).

O'Reilly, Bill, 'Red Hot Torture', www.billoreilly.com/column?pid=20369.

Orwell, George, *1984* (Harmondsworth: Penguin, 1954).

OutRage! press release 4 February 2005, www.petertatchell.net.

OutRage! 'Buju Banton and Beenie Man concerts axed', 6 July 2006, www.petertatchell.net.

OutRage! press release 13 June 2007, www.petertatchell.net.

Palmer, Tony, *All You Need Is Love* (London: Futura, 1976).

Pancevski, Bojan, 'Bonn in the USA: hit tunes fired up East German athletes, *Sydney Morning Herald*, 24 September 2007.

Parvulescu, Anca, 'The Sound of Laughter', *ASCA Conference Sonic* Interventions: Pushing *the Boundaries of Cultural Analysis*, Reader for Panel 2: *The Sonic in the 'Silent' Arts and Bring in the Noise*, Coordinator: Sylvia Mieszkowski (2005): 117–19.

Passchier-Vermeer, Willy and Passchier, Wim, 'Noise exposure and public health', *Environmental Health Perspectives* 108 (supplement) (2000): 123–31.

Pepper, Art and Pepper, Laurie, *Straight Life: The Story of Art Pepper* (New York and London: Schirmer/Macmillan, 1979).

Peretz, Isabelle, 'Listen to the Brain: a Biological Perspective on Musical Emotions', in Sloboda, John A. and Patrik N. Juslin (ed.), *Music and Emotion: Theory and Research* (Oxford: OUP, 2001), pp. 105–34.

Petridis, Alexis, '"They're good beat, we don't take the lyrics seriously"', *Guardian*, 6 September 2004, part two: 14–15.

Petridis, Alexis, 'On the edge', *Guardian Arts*, 16 February 2005: 12.

Pettan, Svanobor (ed.), *Music, Politics and War: Views from Croatia* (Zagreb: Institute of Ethnology and Folklore Research, 1998).

Philips, Graham, 'Voices from the deep', *Sunday Telegraph*, 28 July 2002: 32.

Philpott, Trevor, 'The Bermondsey Miracle' (1957), reprinted in *The Faber Book of Pop*, Jon Savage and Hanif Kureshi (eds) (London: Faber and Faber, 1995): 63–6.

Picker, John, *Victorian Soundscapes* (Oxford and New York: OUP, 2003).

Pidd, Helen, 'Marilyn Manson is innocent', *Guardian*, January 25, 2005: 4.

Pidd, Helen, 'Mozart for muggers', *Guardian* online, 13 February 2006, www.guardian.co.uk/arts/features/story/0,,1708364,00.html.

Pilger, John, *Heroes* (London: Pan, 1986).

Pilger, John, 'Year Zero 1979' in John Pilger (ed.), *Tell Me No Lies: Investigative Journalism and its Triumphs* (London: Vintage, 2005): 120–57.

Pippos, Chris, 'Why we're copping an earful', *Sunday Mail*, 26 October 2003: 21.

Pocock, Tom (ed.), *Trafalgar: An Eyewitness History* (London: Penguin, 2005).

Pollard, Ruth, 'Your mum was right – it will send you deaf', *Sydney Morning Herald*, 29 September 2005: 1.

Popular Music, 'Can we get rid of the "popular" in popular music? A virtual symposium with contributions from the International Advisory Editiors of *Popular Music*', *Popular Music* 24/1, 2005: 133–45.

Popular Music and Society, Special Issue on Hate Rock, ed. Art Jipson, 30/4 (2007).

Potter, Russell, 'Noise, performance and the politics of sound' in Swiss, Thomas, Sloop, John and Herman, Andrew (eds), *Mapping The Beat* (Oxford: Blackwell): 37–46.

Porter, Roy, *Flesh in the Age of Reason: How the Enlightenment Transformed the Way We See Our Bodies and Souls* (London: Penguin, 2003).

Press Association, 'Homophobic chanting banned', *Guardian*, 9 February 2007: 8.

Proctor, David, *Music of the Sea* (London: National Maritime Museum, 1992).

Ramos, Liesi-Vivoni, 'The Effects of On-Hold Telephone Music on the Number of Premature Disconnections to a Statewide Protective Services Abuse Hot Line', *Journal of Music Therapy*, 30/2 (1993): 119–29.

Reese, Hans, 'Relation of music to diseases of the brain', in Edward Podolsky (ed.), *Music Therapy* (New York: Philosophical Library, 1954): 43–54.

Renton, Alex, '"Distant Drums" goes too far', *Independent*, 21 May 1993.

Richards, Simone, 'Good time versus full time', *Daily Telegraph*, 19 August, 2003: 17.

Ricks, Christopher, *Dylan's Visions of Sin* (London: Viking, 2004).

Rifkin, Benjamin and Ackerman, Michael, *Human Anatomy: From the Renaissance to the Digital Age* (New York: Harry N. Abrams Inc, 2006).

Robinson, Vicki, 'Stand by your ban!', *Yorkshire Evening Post*, 8 August 2007.

Ronson, Jon, *The Men Who Stare at Goats* (London: Picador, 2004).

Ronson, Jon, 'The Road to Abu Ghraib', *Guardian Weekend*, 30 October 2004: 18.

Ronson, Joe, 'A timetable for murder', *Guardian* online, April 17, 2007.

Rose, David, 'Using terror to fight terror', *Observer Review*, 26 February 2006: 5.

Saenger, Paul, 'Silent reading: its impact on late medieval script and society', *Viator: Medieval and Renaissance Studies* 13 (1982): 367–414.

Saenger, Paul, 'Books of Hours and the Reading Habits of the Later Middle Ages' in Roger Chartier (ed.), *The Culture of Print: power and the uses of print in early modern Europe*, trans. Lydia G. Cochrane (Cambridge: Polity Press, 1989): 141–73.

Sams, Christine, 'A pointed departure for snubbed Eminem', *Sun-Herald*, 29 July 2001: 11.

Sawday, Johnathan, *The Body Emblasoned: Dissection and the human body in Renaissance Culture* (London and New York: Routledge, 1995).

Schafer, R. Murray, *The Tuning of the World* (Toronto: McClelland and Stewart, 1977).

Schafer, R. Murray (ed.), *Five Village Soundscapes* (Vancouver: A.R.C. Publications, 1977).

Schafer, R. Murray and Järviluoma, Helmi, (eds) *Yearbook of Soundscape Studies: 'Northern Soundscapes'*, vol. 1 (Tampere: University of Tampere, 1998).

Scherzinger, Martin and Smith, Stephen, 'From blatant to latent protest (and back again): on the politics of theatrical spectacle in Madonna's "American Life"', *Popular Music* 26/2 (2007): 211–29.

Schmidt, Leigh Eric, 'Hearing Loss', in Michael Bull and Les Back (eds), *The Auditory Culture Reader* (Oxford and New York: Berg, 2003): 41–59.

Schmitt, Eric and Marshall, Carolyn, 'Task Force 6–26: Inside Camp Nama', *New York Times*, 19 March 2006.

Schubert, Emery, 'The influence of emotion, locus of emotion and familiarity upon preference in music', *Psychology of Music* 35/3 (2007): 477–93.

Scott, Kirsty, 'Jodi's killer to serve at least 20 years in jail', *Guardian*, 12 February 2005: 5.

Scott, Ronald McNair, *Robert the Bruce: King of Scots* (New York: Peter Bendrick Books, 1989; first published 1982).

Scottish Executive, *Sound Advice on Noise* (Edinburgh: Scottish Executive, 2006).

Seal, Graham, *Inventing Anzac: The Digger and National Mythology* (St Lucia Qld: University of Queensland Press, 2004).

Seale, Patrick and McConville, Maureen, *French Revolution 1968* (Harmondsworth: Penguin, 1968).

Sella, Marshall, 'The sound of things to come', *New York Times*, 23 March 2003, www.nytimes.com/2003/03/23/magazine/23SOUND.html.

Seenan, Gerard, 'Goth fan who craved notoriety and said he was in league with the devil', *Guardian*, 22 January 2005: 5.

Seenan, Gerard, 'Bach for church "dogged by youth"', *Guardian*, 24 March 2005: 6.

Seenan, Gerard, '"Truly evil" youth convicted of murdering Jodi', *Guardian*, 22 January 2005: 5.

Shabi, Rachel and Hooper, John, 'Now the reckoning', *Guardian Weekend*, 22 January 2005: 22–9.

Shakespeare, William, *Twelfth Night, or, What You Will*, in *William Shakespeare: The Complete Works*, ed. Alfred Harbage (Baltimore: Pelican, 1969).

Shakespeare, William, *The Second Part of King Henry The Fourth*, I, in *William Shakespeare: The Complete Works*, ed. Alfred Harbage (Baltimore: Pelican, 1969).

Shuker, Roy, *Understanding Popular Music*, second edn (London: Routledge, 2001).

Sifton, John, *"No Blood, No Foul": Soldiers' Accounts of Detainee Abuse in Iraq* (New York: Human Rights Watch, 2006).

Skelsey, Mark, 'Home code turns down the volume', *Daily Telegraph*, 30 April 2001: 15.

Sloboda, John A. and Juslin, Patrik N., 'Psychological Perspectives on Music and Emotion' in John A. Sloboda and Patrik N. Juslin (eds), *Music and Emotion: Theory and Research* (Oxford: OUP, 2001): 71–104.

Sloboda, John A. and Juslin, Patrik N, 'Music and Emotion: Commentary' in John A. Sloboda and Patrik N. Juslin (eds), *Music and Emotion: Theory and Research*, (Oxford: OUP, 2001): 453–62.

Sloboda, John A. and O'Neill, Susan A, 'Emotions in Everyday Listening to Music' in John A. Sloboda and Patrik N. Juslin (ed.), *Music and Emotion: Theory and Research* (Oxford: OUP, 2001): 415–29.

Smith, Bruce, *The Acoustic World of Early Modern England* (Chicago and London: Chicago University Press, 1999).

Smith, Kirsty, 'Sour notes drift from those white earphones', *Sydney Morning Herald*, 1 June 2006.

Smith, Mark M., 'Listening to the Heard Worlds of Antebellum America' in Michael Bull and Les Back (eds), *The Auditory Culture Reader* (Oxford and New York: Berg, 2003): 137–63.

Smith, Rupert, 'I used to think that heavy metal rock was harmless vaudeville for friendless teenagers. Then I watched Death Metal Murders', *Guardian*, 25 November 2005, part two: 28.

Smolla, Rod, *Deliberate Intent: A Lawyer Tells the True Story of Murder by the Book.* (New York: Crown Publishers, 1999).

Smyth, Gerry, *Noisy Island: A Short History of Irish Popular Music* (Cork: University of Cork Press, 2005).

Soundscape: The Journal of Acoustic Ecology, 2/1 (2001), 3/1 (2002), 3/2 (2002) with 4/1 (Spring 2005), 5/1 (2004).

'Spike', 'Workplace hazards', *Sydney Morning Herald*, 23 September 2005, p. 20.

Stack, Steve and Gundlach, Jim, 'The effect of country music on suicide', *Social Forces* 71/1 (1992): 211–18.

Stack, Steve and Gundlach, Jim, 'Country music and suicide: Individual, indirect and interaction effects. A reply to Snipes and Maguire', *Social Forces* 74/1 (1995): 331–5.

Straw, Will, 'Systems of articulation, logics of change: Scenes and communities in popular music', *Cultural* Studies, 5/3 (1999): 361–75.

Stafford Smith, Clive, 'Torture by music', *New Statesman*, 6 November 2006, www.newstatesman.com/200611060029.

Stone, Irving, *Clarence Darrow for the Defense* (New York: Doubleday, 1961).

Street, John, *Rebel Rock* (Oxford: Blackwell, 1986).

Street, John, *Politics and Popular Culture* (Cambridge: Polity, 1997).

Swanton, Will, Parker, Laura and Kidman, John, 'Rugby league star stabbed', *SMH* online, 18 February 2007.

Sweetman, John, *Bomber Crew: Taking On the Reich* (London: Abacus, 2004).

Symons, David, *Confronting Noise in the UK* (Chatham: UK Noise Network, 2000).

Tagg, Philip and Clarida, Bob, *Ten Little Title Tunes* (New York: Mass Media Music Scholars' Press, 2003).

Tagg, Philip, 'Anti-depressants and musical anguish management', Keynote presentation at the conference of the Latin America Branch of the International Association for the Study of Popular Music (IASPM), Rio de Janeiro, June 2004, http://www.tagg.org/articles/iasprio0406.html, accessed 1 September 2007.

Tait, Robert, 'Almost impossible to play rock in this hard place', *Sydney Morning Herald*, 29 August 2005: 15.

Taruskin, Richard, 'Music's Dangers And The Case For Control', *New York Times*, 9 December 2001, Arts and Leisure.

Tatchell, Peter, 'It isn't racist to target Beenie Man', *Guardian*, 31 August 2004: 14.

Topping, Alexandra, 'Victory for gay rights campaign as reggae star agrees to ditch homophobic lyrics', *Guardian*, 23 July 2007: 7.

Toynbee, Jason, *Making Popular Music: Musicians, Creativity and Institutions* (London: Arnold, 2000).

Truax, Barry, *Acoustic Communication* (Norwood, NJ: Ablex Publishing Corporation, 2001).

Travis, Alan, 'Reid wants police to evict noisy neighbours', *Guardian*, 15 November 2006.

Trynka, Paul, *Iggy Pop: Open Up and Bleed* (London: Sphere Books, 2007).

Tysome, Tony, 'Do they deserve degrees?', *Times Higher Educational Supplement*, 23 January 2004: 8–9.

Uimonen, Heikki, '"Sorry can't hear you! I'm on a train!' Ringing tones, meanings and the Finnish soundscape', *Popular Music*, 23/1 (2004): 51–62.

Vasagar, Jeevan, 'Mugabe paints MDC as Blairite cronies', *Observer*, 27 April 2005: 1.

Vasagar, Jeevan and MacAskill, Ewan, 'Arab women singers complicit in rape, says Amnesty report', *Guardian*, 10 July 2004: 11.

Victor, Peter, 'Neighbourhood noise: 17 people have died from it', *Independent on Sunday*, 18 December 1994: 19.

Vidal, John, 'A pain in the ears (anag)', *Guardian*, 8 September 1993, part two: 2.

Vidal, John, 'Government turns up the mood music in battle for quieter cities', *Guardian*, 13 December 2002: 3.

Vider, Stephen, 'Rethinking Crowd Violence: Self-Categorization Theory and the Woodstock 1999 Riot', *Journal for the Theory of Social Behaviour*, 34/2 (2004): 141–66.

Vikman, Noora, 'Vuorilla vuorilta vuorille – Moniäänisiä laulamisen tiloja, paikkoja ja menneisyyksiä pohjoisitalialaisessa Cembrassa' in Antti-Ville Kärjä and Markus Mantere Markus (ed), *Etnomusikologian vuosikirja* 17 (Helsinki: Finnish Society for Ethnomusicology, 2005): 48–70.

Wainwright, Martin, 'Mob's antics may force festival move', *Guardian*, 27 August 2002: 5.

Wallace, Lewis, 'Can You Turn That Down, Please?', *Wired* online, 15 February 2003, www.wired.com/news/medtech/0,1286,57564,00.html.

Walser, Robert, *Running with the Devil: Power, Gender and Madness in Heavy Metal Music* (Hanover: Wesleyan University Press, 1993).

Ward, David, 'A nice line in cheap hats' www.publications.bham.ac.uk/ birmingham_magazine/b_magazine1996-99/pg14_98.htm.

Ward, Lucy, '3,300 sales and still rising – ultrasonic answer to teenage gangs sets alarm bells ringing', *Guardian*, 17 March 2007: 13.

Weale, Sally, 'Jim Reeves ravers silenced', *Guardian*, 21 May 1993.

Wearing, Deborah, *Forever Today: A Memoir of Love and Amnesia* (London: Doubleday, 2004).

Weaver, Matt, 'Problems with young ones? Get wired for sound', *Guardian*, 7 June 2007.

Welch, Dylan, 'Hatchback hate: Lamborghini chased', *Sydney Morning Herald* online, 13 March 2006.

Wheale, Nigel, *Writing and Society: Literacy, print and politics in Britain 1590–1660*, (London and New York, 1999).

White, Glenn and Louie, Gary, *The Audio Dictionary* (third edition) (London: University of Washington Press, 2005).

Whiteley, Sheila, *The Space Between The Notes* (London: Routledge, 1992).

Whiteley, Sheila, *Too Much Too Young* (London: Routledge, 2005).

Williams, John, *Anzacs, the Media and the Great War* (Sydney: UNSW Press, 1999).

Wilson, David, 'Ulster loyalism and country music, 1969–85', in Charles K. Wolfe and James E. Akenson (eds), *Country Music Goes To War* (Lexington: University of Kentucky Press, 2005): 192–218.

Wilson, Elizabeth, 'Gut Feminism', *Differences: A Journal of Feminist Cultural Studies*. 15/3 (2004): 66–94.

Wilson, Hugh, 'Cosmetic enhancement, so to speak', *Sydney Morning Herald*, 21 July 2004.

Wilson, Jamie, 'Probation for rock'n'roll noise nuisance', *Guardian*, 6 October 1997: 7.

Wilson, Scot, *Sydney Morning Herald*, 4 May 2004.

Wolfe, Charles T. and Akenson, James E. (eds), *Country Music Goes To War* (Lexington: University of Kentucky Press, 2005).

Wooldridge, Harry Ellis, *Old English Popular Music* (New York: Jack Brussel, 1961).

Woolley, Simon, 'We don't need gangsta rap', *Observer Review*, 30 June 2002: 14.

Wordsworth, William, *Poetical Works*, ed. Thomas Hutchinson (London, Oxford, New York: Oxford University Press, 1969).

Yang, Mina, 'Für Elise, circa 2000: Postmodern Readings of Beethoven in Popular Contexts', *Popular Music and Society*, 29/1 (2006): 1–15.

Young, Robert, Sweeting, Helen and West, Patrick, 'Prevalence of deliberate self harm and attempted suicide within contemporary Goth and youth subculture: longtitidunal cohort study", *British Medical Journal*, 332 (2006): 1058–61.

Younge, Gary, 'US police put hip-hop under surveillance', *Guardian* online, 11 March 2004, http://arts.guardian.co.uk/news/story/0,,1166792,00.html.

Younge, Gary, 'Chilling call to murder as music attacks gays', *Guardian*, 26 June 2004; 14.

Younge, Gary, 'Police seek Jamaican singer after attack on gay men', *Guardian*, 17 July 2004: 17.

Younge, Gary, 'Troubled island', *Guardian*, 27 April 2006, part two: 6–9.

Zajonc, Robert B., *The Selected Works of R.B. Zajonc* (USA: Wiley, 2004).

Zamoyski, Adam, *1812: Napoleon's Fatal March on Moscow* (London: Harper Perennial, 2004).

Zuel, Bernard, 'Lock up your chickens', *Sydney Morning Herald, Metro*, 3–9 June 2005.

Press and Online Items without Bylines

'Books hip-hop off the shelves' (Reuters), *SMH* online, 10 January 2007.
'Brandenberger with fries?', *Observer*, 16 June 02: 6.
'Conference Urban Music: the Problem of Music Pollution', *Soundscape: The Journal of Acoustic Ecology*, 3/1, July 2002, p. 28.
'Crosby's hits drive teens out of stores', *South China Post*, 9 July 1999.
'Cruise ship captain gave pirates a sound thrashing' (AAP Reuters), *SMH*, 9/11/05, p. 12.
'Don't roll over Beethoven', *Guardian*, 30 July 2003: 5.
'Dozens of arrests, three overdoses at dance party', *SMH* online, 26 February, 2006.
'Eight in hospital after dance party', *SMH* online, 2 July 2006.
'Fear iPod deafened woman to sexual predator', *SMH* online, 1 March 2007.
'Federline attacked by wrestler', *SMH* online, 19 October 2006.
FenceDefence™ construction site intruder detection systems, Compound Security Systems, http://www.compoundsecurity.co.uk/.
Hearing Industries Association, 2004, 'A White Paper Addressing the Societal Costs of Hearing Loss and Issue in Third Party Reimbursement' at www.audiologyonline.com/articles/pf_arc_disp.asp?article_id=1204.
'Indiana Hum', *Soundscape: The Journal of Acoustic Ecology*, 3/1 (July 2002): 31.
'Japanese man cooks mother on hotplate', *SMH* online, 26 April 2006.
'Karaoke bar brawl: five taken to hospital', *SMH* online 14 April 2007.
'Keane song "triggered outburst"', *BBC News* online, 17 February 2006, http://news.bbc.co.uk/1/hi/scotland/4724514.stm at 14 September 2007.
'Korean tycoon indicted for karaoke brawl', *Age* online, 5 June 2007.
'Leeds festival violence: eight sentenced', *NME*, 1 March 2003: 4.
'Leeds looks to future after more scenes of violence', *NME*, 10 September 2005: 10.
'Loud music lover gets life for killing neighbour', *Guardian*, 16 July 1994: 5.
'Loud music lung collapse warning', *BBC News* online, 31 August 2004, http://news.bbc.co.uk/1/hi/health/3614180.stm.
'Man shot dead for bad singing in Philippine Karaoke bar', *Yahoo* news online, 31 May 2007.
Media Matters for America, 15 September 2006, http:mediamatters.org.items/200609160003.
'Metalheads not meatheads but scholars', *SMH* online, syndicated from *Telegraph* (London), 23 April 2007.

'Music banned for Dolly Parton fan', *BBC News*, 20 August 2007, http://news. bbc.co.uk/go/pr/fr/–/1/hi/england/west_yorkshire/6955250.stm.

'Noise annoys', *Guardian*, 5 September 1996, part two: 19.

'Noise laws won't mean cranky neighbours', *SMH* online, 7 June 2007.

'Noisy neighbours helped drive English man to suicide, coroner finds', *Daily Telegraph,* 1 April 1998, http://www.noisepollution.org/news/1998/mar29. htm#Noisy%20Neighbours%20Helped%20Drive%English%Man%20to%20Sui cide%20Coroner%20Finds.

'Noisy neighbour gets one year sentence' (AAP), *SMH* online, 21 April 2006.

'Now that's what I call music to blast dictators', *Guardian*, 4 July 1998, *Editor*: 21.

'Paris Cabarets Too Noisy For Public', *Times*, 15 December 1999, http://www. noisepollution.org/news/1999/dec12.htm#Paris%20Cabarets%20Too%20Noi sy%20For%20Public.

'Plan to ban muzak goes to the Lords', *BBC News* online, 16 June 2002, http:// news.bbc.co.uk/1/hi/uk_politics/5086054.stm.

'"Play Mozart to tackle poor behaviour"', teachers urged', *Guardian* online (Press Association) 29 September 2006.

'Police on alert in Berlin for neo-Nazi rally', *SMH*, 22 October 2006.

'Rapper Snoop Dogg arrested in the US', *SMH* online, 28 October 2006.

'Rapper sues over fatal basketball stampede' (Associated Press), *SMH* online, 31 October 2006.

'Rapper to face four trials', *Age* online, 11 July 2007.

Review of film *The Yes Men*, in *Sunday Herald* (Glasgow), *Seven Days* supplement, 6 February 2005, p. 27.

'Shutterbugs v Stars', *Sun-Herald*, 3 October 2004, p. S 12.

'Speech cloning tunes into distant voices', *SMH* (syndicated from *New York Times*), 2 August 2001: 25.

'Sesame Street breaks Iraqi POWs', *BBC news* online, 20 May 2003, http://news. bbc.co.uk/1/hi/world/middle_east/3042907.stm.

Singing while their men rape', *The Guardian*, Nairobi, 21 July 2004, p. 6, http:// www.taipeitimes.com/News/world/archives/2004/07/21/2003179810.

'Teen arrested for rapping in public', *SMH* online (Ninemsn Staff), 6 February 2008.

'Ten killed in Java rock concert stampede' (Reuters), *SMH* online, 20 December 2006.

'Turn it down! Too loud to be cool', http://www.youth.hear-it.org/page. dsp?page=2978 accessed at 16 February 2008.

'UK Student Stabbed Over Noise Argument', Press Association Newsfile http:// www.noisepollution.org/news/1999/dec12.htm#UK%20Student%20Stabbed %20Over%20Noise%20Argument, 13 December 1999.

'Wham ban for music fan', *Northern Echo*, 15 August 2007, http://www. thenorthernecho.co.uk/search/display.var.1619415.0.wham_ban_for_music_ fan.php.

'Woman dies after Brighton party fall', *BBC News* online, 16 July 2002, http://news.bbc.co.uk/1/hi/entertainment/music/2132185.stm.

General and Other Websites

Subject or title, whichever provides better trace, is given in italics.

Alice Cooper's 'Golf Monster', http://www.alicecooper.com/index2.html

BBC News online, http://www.bbc.co.uk/

Black Music Congress, www.britishblackmusic.com/index.php?module=Pagesetter &func=viewpub&tid=14&pid=3

Cardiff noise related death, www.ccrc.gov.uk/canewe/canwe_87.htm

City centres noise headache, http://www.shu.ac.uk/cgi–bin/news_full.pl?id_num=PR137&db=01

ConvictAustralia: PardonandPunishment, http://www.pilotguides.com/destination _guide/pacific/australia/convict_australia/pardon_and_punishment.php

Department for Environment, Food and Rural Affairs (DeFRA), www.defra.gov. uk/environment/noise/research/index.htm.

European Agency for Safety and Health at Work, 'Stop that Noise' campaign. http://osha.europa.eu/press_room/050420_EW2005_Launch_Int

Fred Durst violence, http://www.spin.com/features/magazine/2003/12/soap_opera_ year_fred_durst_acts_up/

Freemuse, www.freemuse.org

Germany's Federal Environment Agency (UBA) on health risks from noise, http:// www.umweltbundesamt.de/uba-info-presse-e/2007/pe07-022.htm

Hate music, http://www.adl.org/main_Extremism/hate_music_in_the_21st_ century.htm

Homophobic reggae, http://hrw.org/english/docs/2004/11/23/jamaic9716.htm

House Ear Institute noise awareness campaign, www.hei.org/news/releases/ 070423noiseday.htm

House of Commons Hansard debates for 16 February 1996, Pt 6, www.publications. parliament.uk/pa/cm199596/cmhansrd/vo960216/debtext/60216-06.htm

International Association for the Study of Popular Music, www.iaspm.net

International Noise Awareness Day, www.personneltoday.com/articles/2005/04/ 21/29386/be-quiet-for-international-noise-awareness-day.html

League for the Hard of Hearing sponsors International Noise Awareness Day, www.lhh.org/noise/index.html

League for the Hard of Hearing advisories, www.lhh.org/noise/communities.html www.lhh.org/noise/getting_started.htm.

Led Zeppelin noise related death in Sydenham, www.publications.parliament.uk/ pa/cm199596/cmhansrd/vo960216/debtext/60216–06.htm

Love Not Riots, www.lovenotriots.com/about.php

Mosquito sonic youth deterrent, http://www.compoundsecurity.co.uk/

Nairobi disco violence, www.noisepollution.org/news/2000/jan16.htm#Kenyan%
20Disco%20Noise%20Leads%20to%20Violence

Niggaz With Attitude, NWA World, http://www.nwaworld.com/bio.shtml

Noise Association, UK, www.ukna.org.uk

Noise Awareness Day: Stress levels in Germany too high; Press Release 022/2007,
http://www.umweltbundesamt.de/uba–info–presse–e/2007/pe07–022.htm

Noise levels in contemporary life, www.e-a-r.com/pdf/hearingcons/T88_34Noise
Levels.xls

Noise Network advice, http://www.bbc.co.uk/dna/actionnetwork/A8252552

Noise nuisance in Scotland, www.scotland.gov.uk/Topics/Environment/Pollution/
Noise–Nuisance/16871/8360

Noise Pollution Clearinghouse, www.noisepollution.org/

Noise organizations outside the US and Canada, http://www.nonoise.org/resource/
related/uk.htm

Noise rock scene, http://uk.real.com/music/genre/Noise_Rock/

Operation Black Vote, www.obv.org.uk

Pipedown, www.pipedown.info

Potentially offensive content at BPI, http://www.bpi.co.uk/index.asp?Page=
businfo/content_file_146.shtml

*Proposal for a Directive of The European Parliament and of the Council: Relating
to the Assessment and Management of Environmental Noise, presented by
the Commission of The European Communities*, http://europa.eu.int/comm/
environment/docum/00468_en.htm

ReverendBizarre,http://www.lyricsdir.com/reverend-bizarre-slave-of-satan-lyrics.
html and http://www.youtube.com/watch?v=gyQ4enN58Yk

Scottish hotelier threatens neighbours with noise, http://www.noisepollution.org/
news/1998/may31.htm#Scottish%20Hotel%20Owner%20Threatens%20Neig
hbors%20With%20More%20Noise%20After%20They%20Object%20to%20
Hotels%20Extended%20Hours.

'Selling the drama' lyrics from the album Throwing Copper, by the group Live,
http://www.azlyrics.com/lyrics/live/sellingthedrama.html

Shop staff exposure to piped music, www2b.abc.net.au/science/k2/stn/archives/
archive70/newposts/839/topic839634.shtm

Snoop Dogg refused entry to Australia, http://news.bbc.co.uk/1/hi/
entertainment/6594557.stm

'Testimonies of rape in Sudan', BBC News online, 19 July 2004, http://news.bbc.
co.uk/2/hi/africa/3900777.stm

'Too Loud! Music Ban for Doll Fan', Sky News, http://news.sky.com/skynews/
article/0,,30000–1289886,00.html

Society for Ethnomusicology condemns use of music for torture, http://webdb.iu.
edu/sem/scripts/aboutus/aboutsem/positionstatements/position_statement_
torture.cfm

Wall of Death, http://www.youtube.com/results?search_query=wall+of+death&s
earch=Search

Warning stickers on CDs in the UK, http://www.bpi.co.uk/index.asp?Page=businfo/content_file_146.shtml

Documentary Film

Metal: A Headbanger's Journey, DVD, dir. Sam Dunn, Scot McFadyen, Jessica Joy Wise, Futurefilm 35831 (2005).
Soundtrack to War, Film documentary, dir. George Gittoes, prod. Gittoes and Dalton Productions Pty Ltd, with The Australian Film Commission (2004).

Index